F People

Black Socialists in the United States, Africa and the Caribbean

Asante Publications/San Diego

Cataloging in Publication Data

Grigsby, Daryl Russell (1955-)
 For The People

 Bibliography: p.
 1. Afro-American Communists—Biography. 2. Communists—Caribbean Area—Biography. 3. Communists—Africa—Biography. 4. Communism—United States—History. 5. Communism—Caribbean Area—History. 6. Communism—Africa—History.

I. Title
HX84.A2G75 1987   335.43'08996073   87-70544
ISBN 0-9614210-2-9 (pbk.)

For Book Ordering Information, please turn to last page.

Copyright © 1987 by Daryl Russell Grigsby

   The information in this book has been copyrighted in order to protect the author from someone abusing his labor by using large amounts of material without proper credits and for personal gain. If however, you wish to share with others some of the information herein because you believe it will benefit the cause of social justice, please feel free to copy some material and pass it on. In order to protect yourself, however, if you quote liberally (what that means depends on which attorney you ask) from this book, please write us for permission. Any questions about the book or more information on the author or Asante Publications should be directed to:

Asante Publications
Box 1085
San Diego, CA 92112

First Edition
1   2   3   4   5   6   7   8   9   10

Dedication

Dedicated to the memories and sacrifices of Grenadian Prime Minister Maurice Bishop (slain October 19, 1983) and Mozambican President Samora Machel (slain October 19, 1986); two of the most recent in a long line of murdered black radicals. Though one was from the Caribbean and the other from Africa, they were bound together in an undying commitment to both socialism and black liberation. Their selfless labors for self-determination in the midst of foreign intervention, economic sabotage, and subsidized mercenaries will never be forgotten.

Forward Ever!

Maurice Bishop　　　　Samora Machel
1944-1983　　　　　　1933-1986

The launching of the struggle and the victories we have won reveal concretely there is no such thing as fateful destiny; we are capable of transforming society and creating a new life.

—Samora Machel, 1974; during the tenth year of FRELIMO's armed struggle against Portuguese colonialism. Mozambique won its independence in 1975.

People of Grenada, this revolution is for work, for food, for decent housing and health services, and for a bright future for our children and great-grandchildren.

—Maurice Bishop, March 13, 1979 in a radio address on the day the New Jewel Movement seized power from Eric Gairy's dictatorship.

"Daryl Grigsby has recorded the socialist radical movement of Afro-Americans, Africans and Afro-Caribbeans. We hear again the struggles of the giants; Paul Robeson, Angela Davis, and Walter Rodney, and the rising tide of black workers engaged in their struggle for liberation. And their voices are on time for us, still working in this disturbing present."

Sonia Sanchez
Professor of Literature at Temple University
Author of *Homegirls and Handgrenades* and *Under A Soprano Sky*

To order copies of *For The People*, please write to:

Asante Publications
Box 1085
San Diego, California 92112

Asante Publications is an Afro-American press committed to promoting the legacy of and potential for struggle by Third World peoples. Although we are very small and very young, our aim is to inspire people's movements in their quest to create a better society for us and for our children. We welcome your correspondence and feedback.

Acknowledgements

The writer is often viewed as a solitary performer, an eccentric artist divorced from the cares of the world as he or she pounds away at a typewriter. Writers, however, are like the rest of us in that they are products and creations of a community of people.

For The People was not an idea that spontaneously flashed in my mind. It was the result of thousands of hours of discussions with family, friends, activists, and writers. Through these talks the idea of a book on the amazing legacy of black Socialists was born and nurtured.

Transforming the idea into a book would have been utterly impossible it it were not for the following people: Jihmye Collins for the many hours he spent drawing the eleven powerful pencil sketches you see in this book. Charles Elster for his invaluable editing skills, his advice on format, and for talking me into using footnotes.

Michael Grigsby for his astute comments, his advice for material in the Epilogue, and for encouraging me to include a Glossary. Dennis Kobata for his editing the first draft and for his advice on cover design, marketing and pulling all the loose ends together. Joe Wainio and Dan Epperly for their many hours of hard work and suggestions. Anson Pang for his helpful suggestions and work on the cover design and layout.

Glenn Horiuchi for encouraging me to include A.M. Babu and for allowing me to use his printer. Marge at Midnight Special Books for her advice to include Ngugi wa Thiong'o and for sharing titles of books I did not have access to. Sekou Nkrumah for sharing his hard-to-find books on George Padmore, Sekou Toure, and Kwame Nkrumah. Mike Richards for his advice on printing and binding.

Jean Cornwell for drawing the maps of Africa and the Caribbean. Robyn Broughton, Peter Brown, the Black Writers and Artists, and all the family, friends and co-workers who encouraged me to continue writing. Lauren Alyssa Grigsby who at eight weeks old began sleeping through the night so I could stay up late and type uninterrupted. The seventeen attendees at my

Proofreading Party who proofed the final draft in exchange for pizza and beer.

Brother James Curtis who stayed up all night helping number pages. Sonia Sanchez for her cooperation and assistance to a total stranger (me). And finally, my dear wife Leslie whose patience, love and encouragement sustained me through this project and enabled me to complete this book in the midst of full-time work and full-time parenting.

In a real sense, I would be remiss if I did not also thank the Afro-American, Afro-Caribbean, and African Socialists and workers whose tremendous sacrifices made this book possible. Often when I was tired and frustrated my energy was renewed as I recalled the bitter sacrifices of black Socialists at war with racism, capitalism and imperialism. The murder of Patrice Lumumba, the imprisonment of Angelo Herndon, and the exile of Frances Baard definitely reminded me that I indeed had the easy part.

Of course, nothing can be done in America (or anywhere else, perhaps) without money. Therefore, I gratefully note,

THIS PROJECT WAS PARTIALLY FUNDED BY THE NATIONAL ENDOWMENT FOR THE ARTS, THE CITY OF SAN DIEGO, AND COMBO.

Permission

I gratefully acknowledge the following publishers for permission to reprint copyrighted selections from their publications.

The Citadel Press, *A Documentary History of the Negro People in the United States: 1933 - 1945.* Edited by Herbert Aptheker.
Heinemann Educational Books Ltd., *Writers In Politics* by Ngugi wa Thiong'o. *Detained: A Writer's Prison Diary* by Ngugi wa Thiong'o.
Monthly Review Press, *A Difficult Road: The Transition To Socialism In Mozambique.* Edited by John Saul.
Lawrence Hill & Co., and Faith Berry, *Good Morning Revolution: Uncollected Social Protest Writings.* Edited by Faith Berry.
Pathfinder Press, *Maurice Bishop Speaks: The Grenada Revolution 1979-83.* Edited by Bruce Marcus and Michael Taber.
Lawrence Hill & Co., *The Future In The Present* by C.L.R. James.
International Publishers, *Paul Robeson: The Great Forerunner.* Edited by *Freedomways. Organize or Starve: The History of the South African Congress of Trade Unions* by Ken Luckhardt and Brenda Wall. *The Autobiography of W.E.B. Du Bois* by W.E.B. Du Bois.
Random House, *Angela Davis: An Autobiography*, by Angela Davis.
Verso Press, *Black American Politics: From the Marches on Washington to Jesse Jackson* by Manning Marable.

Preface

My purpose in writing this book is to in some small way impress upon the reader the incredible sacrifices and struggles made by black Socialists in the United States, the Caribbean, and Africa. If we can understand the exploits and achievements of Hoji Ya Henda of Angola's MPLA, Elijah Mampuru of South Africa's Farm, Plantation and Allied Workers' Union, Miranda Smith of Local 22 in North Carolina, Jacques Romain of the Haitian Communist Party, and hundreds of other revolutionary blacks, we can defuse what Kenyan Marxist writer Ngugi wa Thiong'o called the "cultural bomb."

For Ngugi, the cultural bomb is imperialism's use of culture to rob from the oppressed the memory of their radical past. In *Decolonizing the Mind*, Ngugi writes,

> But the biggest weapon wielded...by imperialism against...collective defiance is the cultural bomb. The effect of a cultural bomb is to annihilate a people's belief in...their heritage of struggle, in their unity, in their capacities and ultimately in themselves. It makes them see their past as one wasteland of nonachievement and it makes them want to distance themselves from that wasteland....It makes them want to identify with that which is decadent and reactionary....It even plants serious doubts about the moral rightness of struggle. Possibilities of triumph or victory are seen as remote, ridiculous dreams. The intended results are despair, despondency and a collective death-wish.

It appears as though the cultural bomb has exploded with force among Afro-Americans. While 20% of blacks are jobless, 35% don't graduate from high school and 45% are born in poverty (often in single parent homes), self-righteous pontiffs drone on about "the need for a work ethic" and bemoan the fact that Afro-Americans lack the unity and discipline of the Vietnamese and the Jews. (I really become irate when I hear people talk about our lack of a work ethic. From my vantage point no one has worked harder to build America than blacks. Also, what the hell do they think my father was doing all those days I didn't see him until midnight?)

In this context the purpose of *For The People* is simple. To break the silence America has imposed on the achievements of black Socialists and to convince the reader that struggle for change is both necessary and possible. When I researched Hosea Hudson's leadership of Birmingham's Local 2815, Amilcar Cabral's tremendous lectures for PAIGC cadre, Walter Rodney's work among Guyanese laborers, and the sacrifices of Bobby Hutton, Claudia Jones, Nelson Mandela and others, I was filled with the sense that individuals conscious of history and committed to human welfare could change society for the better.

Through struggle (revolutionary struggle), we can build a nation in which our children and their children will not go uneducated while space missiles circle the earth, a country where our grandparents will not starve to finance CIA skulduggery, and a society in which human beings are not warped by a culture which relegates human rights and dignity beneath private property and individual wealth.

Glossary

Out of necessity, *For The People* relies heavily on the "isms", communism, imperialism, etc. Since these words often elicit emotional responses rather than clarify reality, I have included this glossary as an aid to the reader. Bear in mind that volumes have been written on the terms and my brevity obviously limits the scope of the definition. Bear also in mind that even the individuals and organizations in *For The People* may disagree somewhat with my definitions.

Capitalism: The economic system in which private individuals are allowed to own and control the means of production (i.e. mines, mills, banks, factories, forests). This allows them to accumulate wealth from the labor of a working class which receives less than the value of their labor. (This concept is known as "surplus value" and is explained in Karl Marx's *Wages, Price and Profit*) Since capitalism allows private individuals to accumulate wealth regardless of the social implications or the conditions of the workers, the land and wealth of the few contrasts with the poverty of the laborers. Consequently, the main contradiction under capitalism is that the workers, who produce all the wealth of the society, do not reap the benefits.

Colonialism: Total domination of one country by another. The status of much of the Third World prior to the last twenty to thirty years. Under colonialism, all aspects of the oppressed country or region are controlled by another country, including the government of the oppressed country. Examples include Puerto Rico and the U.S. Virgin Islands, both of which are colonies of the United States. Under colonialism, the oppressed country does not control any significant aspect of its economy, military, or government. While colonialism is disappearing because of Third World revolutions and the increased usage of neo-colonialism (see glossary: Neo-colonialism), this type of relationship is still used by capitalist countries to secure their investments and profits in the Third World.

Communism: The higher stage of socialism in which there are no classes and therefore no basis for one group to exploit another. Communism does not exist as a social economic system at this time. Marxists believe communism would only come about with the end of the state, the formal apparatus for imposing the rule of one class over another class (see glossary: state). This can only happen after socialism exists in all or most of the countries and nations of the world. With communism there would be no more classes, no more exploitation, no more states, and no more borders.

Fascism: A particular form of the capitalist/imperialist state. Fascism may occur in periods when the ruling class is relatively weak and the working class is relatively strong. Generally, fascism is characterized by the creation of a military state, intense nationalistic fervor and the oppression (even genocide) of other peoples.

Imperialism: The highest stage of development of capitalism. It is the stage where some of the most basic features of capitalism start to turn into their opposites. (Free competition capitalism turning into monopoly capitalism, etc.,) Imperialism also means world wide exploitation and oppression of the non-imperialist countries, especially the Third World. Under imperialism, each major power has carved out a niche of the world to exploit and yet still maintains an irrepressible need to expand. The only way for this to be resolved among the imperialists powers is through war; e.g., World War I and World War II. The clearest explanation of imperialism is Lenin's *Imperialism, The Highest Stage of Capitalism.*

Nationalism: Strictly speaking, nationalism evolves from and supports capitalist society. Nations came about under rising capitalism. Prior to then, there was no need for nations. As the early capitalists sought to protect their markets (the regions where their products would be sold exclusively) they needed defined areas where other capitalists could not sell without paying a tariff. Along with the formation of nations came about a whole body of thinking to justify their existence. Nationalism is the belief that your nation/nationality is superior to others. It promotes division between workers of the same country (if there is a multi-racial population) and is used to justify conflict and wars between workers in different nations. The most vicious, divisive nationalism we see in the U.S. is the white chauvinism that promotes racism towards African Americans, Chicanos, and other minority groups. It also promotes hatred toward Japanese workers and others for "taking away American jobs." The nationalism that is cited in this volume is black nationalism, primarily. Nationalism is sometimes confused with national pride or national identity. Among people of color in the U.S., these are positive traits and speak to their resistance to the dominant culture which demeans them. This is not nationalism. The national pride of Third World people in the U.S. propels their struggles for equality and democracy.

Neo-colonialism: The more "sophisticated" form of colonialism practiced by the imperialist powers after colonialism was exposed. From the viewpoint of the imperialists, there are no basic changes in how and to what extent they exploit the resources of the Third World. What does change are the faces of the immediate oppressors. Under colonialism, the rulers of the country are imported from the mother country—while under neo-colonialism, the rulers are representatives of the traitor class of the oppressed nation.

Party: As is relevant to this text, a party is an organization dedicated to making fundamental change in society. What this change will be and how it will come about varies widely among the different parties described here.

Revolution: The culmination of class struggle. Insurrection where workers and oppressed peoples seize power and begin the task of rebuilding society in the interests of working people. Revolution, then, is not merely the seizure of power but is also the construction of a socialist and just society. Under colonialism or imperialism, revolution is against a foreign power (Mozambique), while under neocolonialism and capitalism revolution is a civil war (Grenada, South Africa).

Ruling Class/ Bourgeoisie: In capitalism, the class which owns the means of production (factories, land, forests, energy sources) and benefits from this ownership in exploiting the workers. In the U.S., 420,000 families own or control 45% of the wealth of the ocuntry. This class does not work, but through its ownership of the means of production is able to appropriate the wealth created by the labor of the working class.

Socialism: The economic/ political system where all the major means of production are owned and controlled by the workers. Under socialism the wealth created by the workers is not consumed by private owners but is returned to the workers. Socialist societies, to the extent possible, guarantee to the workers the employment, educational opportunity, cultural development and political power denied them under capitalism. Socialism removes the basis for exploitation that exists under capitalism/imperialism, because private competition for survival is replaced with production for the benefit of the entire society. Consequently, racism, sexism, nationalism, and chauvinism become obsolete.

State: The governing institutions of a society (i.e. government, schools, universities, courts, law enforcement agencies, etc.). These institutions are the vehicle through which one class maintains dominance over other classes. Under capitalism, the state reflects the values and protects the interests of the bourgeoisie, while under socialism the state mirrors the concerns of the working class. The claim by "democratic" captalist nations that the state serves all people equally is untrue. In America, for example, the highly-touted "democracy" and equality is contradicted when the National Guard is called out against strikers, courts protect private property, and schools educate the children of the elite and neglect the children of poverty and color. Under capitalism, democracy means the freedom to elect one of several white capitalist candidates, freedom to choose one of two white capitalist parties and freedom to express your opinion through white capitalist media. Any activity beyond this is tolerated only to the extent that such activity does not alter the private ownerhip of wealth and does not empower workers, Afro-Americans, Chicanos, or other people of color.

Working Class/Proletariat: The class which produces all the wealth of society. This is true under capitalism or socialism. The difference is that under socialism, workers would have a much greater say in determining the direction of the society and would have a greatly elevated positon in society. The working class is composed of the people in society who work in the factories, provide the services, transport the goods and raw materials that are needed to make the things we need to live, and who provide the supportive services (clerical workers) to make things go. The working class does not own or control the means of production in capitalist society. They have only their ability to work, which they sell to the capitalist for wages that they use to buy the things they need to live.

Table of Contents

List of Illustrations xvii
Introduction 1
Maps of the Caribbean and Africa 7

1. Under the Hammer: Black Workers in the United States and South Africa 11
    The Afro-American Worker: Three Centuries of Struggle 14
    A. Philip Randolph and Black Trade Union Power 29
    Hosea Hudson: From Sharecropper to Communist 35
    League of Revolutionary Black Workers 42
    Worker Profiles: Charles Denby and James Boggs 48
    Black Workers Under Apartheid: South African Congress of Trade Unions 51
    Carrying the Torch: The Congress of South African Trade Unions 60

2. Sisters in Struggle: Black Women Socialists 63
    Angela Yvonne Davis 66
    Lucy Parsons: The Forerunner 74
    Capitola Tasker, Lulia Jackson & Mabel Byrd ... 75
    Lousie Thompson: Communist in Harlem 76
    Claudia Jones: To Die Fighting 77
    Ericka Huggins: Poems and Revolution 79
    Sandy Smith: The Price of Freedom 82
    Joanne Chesimard: Assata Shakur 83
    Women in Zimbabwe: Teurai Ropa Nhongo 84

3. In The Vanguard: Black Revolutionary Parties in the United States and the Caribbean 86
    African Blood Brotherhood 89
    Congress of Afrikan Peoples and the Revolutionary Communist League 94
    Maurice Bishop and Grenada's New Jewel Movement: Forward Ever! 98
    The Black Panther Party: Revolutionary Suicide 109

4. The Party of the Negro People: Communist Party United States of America 1919-1944 126
    Party of the Negro People 129
    Harry Haywood: Black Bolshevik 145
    Angelo Herndon: Convert to Communism 157
    Henry Winston: My Vision Endures 164

5. Incarcerated Revolutionaries 167
    George Lester Jackson: Soledad Brother 170
    San Rafael Courthouse Rebellion:
Jon Jackson and Ruchell Magee 180

6. Revolutionary Giants 183
    Paul Robeson: Artist of the Revolution 186
    W.E.B. DuBois: The Soul of Black Folk 198

7. Beyond Rhetoric: Armed Revolutions in Africa . 210
    Amilcar Cabral and the PAIGC 213
    Frelimo and the Mozambican Revolution 224
    Angola: The Grieved Land of Africa 237
    Zimbabwe: Chimurenga! 247

8. Writers and Revolution 253
    Langston Hughes: Good Morning
Revolution 256
    Richard Wright: Black Boy................... 267
    Amiri Baraka: Voice of the Black Nation 274
    Writers from the Caribbean 279
    Ngugi wa Thiong'o: Decolonizing the Mind 283

9. Scholars in Service to the Masses 291
    Walter Rodney: Revolutionary Scholar 294
    C.L.R. James: Marxism and Black
Liberation 305

10. The Kingdom is at Hand: Black Socialist Preachers 314
    Rev. George Washington Woodbey............ 317
    Rev. George W. Slater, Jr. 322
    Other Black Socialist Preachers 324

11. African Socialism 326
    Kwame Nkrumah and Ghana 329
    Patrice Lumumba: The Star of Africa 333
    Sekou Toure and Guinea 338
    Julius Nyerere and Tanzania 343
    Frantz Fanon 346
    George Padmore: Zealot for Black Liberation 347
    Stokely Carmichael: Kwame Toure 351
    Abdul Rahman Mohamed Babu 353
    Nelson Mandela and the African National Congress 356

Epilogue: *A Luta Continua (The Struggle Continues)* 361
Notes (Bibliography and Footnotes) 375

Illustrations and Photographs
Illustrations
by Jihmye Collins

Title	Page
"Work Ethic and the Fallacy"	Cover
(South African miners, Angolan women, Georgian cotton pickers)	13
"A Connection: Women in Struggle"	65
(Teurai Ropa, Elizabeth Mafekeng, Angela Davis, Ericka Huggins over Africa, the United States, chains, and the books *Roots* and *With My Mind On Freedom*)	
"Self-Determination"	88
(Huey Newton and Maurice Bishop; Black Panther raised fist, banner of Grenada workers' union)	
"And Justice for All?"	128
(Al Murphy, Angelo Herndon, Harry Haywood in front of the scales of justice)	
"For the Love of Dignity and Freedom"	169
(George Jackson in chains and behind bars)	
"Limited Liberty"	185
(W.E.B. Du Bois and Paul Robeson; in front of the Liberty Bell, American flag and hammer and sickle)	
"Beyond Rhetoric: Revolution"	212
(Samora Machel, Amilcar Cabral and the weapons of war)	
"Expressions Denied/Unexposed Truths"	255
(Langston Hughes, Amiri Baraka and a scroll with "Dream Deferred" and "Culture and Revolution")	
"Scholars of Modern Politics and Social Change"	293
(Walter Rodney and C.L.R. James)	

"Religion/ Man Is One" 316
   (Rev. George Washington Woodbey and religious symbols of unity)

"The Rock/ African Socialism" 328
   (Patrice Lumumba, Kwame Nkrumah, Julius Nyerere and the rock of African socialism)

The Artist

Jihmye Collins is a member of the Black Writers and Artists, the San Diego Black Arts Project, and the Multi-Cultural Art Coalition. As a freelance artist, Jihmye has displayed his work in cultural festivals, political events and art gallerys. His works depict the Afro-American struggle for dignity and humanity's development toward a better world. For more information on Jihmye's work, contact Asante Publications.

Photographs

"Workers of the World Unite," 34
   Messenger Magazine, 1919 (copyright, *Messenger*)

Hosea Hudson 41
   (Photo by Nell Irvin Painter)

Geronimo Pratt 125
   (Photo from *Unity* newspaper)

"The Angolan Struggle: Produce and Resist" 242
   (From *Black Scholar* magazine)

Samora Machel's Funeral A Luta Continua 374
   (From *Africa Report* magazine)

Back cover photo of author by Byron Tucker

Introduction

Where is the road to liberation? Who is the enemy? What are the strategies by which we achieve self-determination? These questions and other questions are asked by American, African and Caribbean blacks in search of justice and human dignity. From the banana farmer in Grenada to the janitor in Newark to the cotton planter in Angola, blacks seek to resolve these critical issues. The questions are not taken lightly, for black survival hinges on the correct answers.

In the United States, Afro-Americans who see white racism as the primary enemy turn to black nationalism and racial separatism. Other black Americans, attributing our poverty to exclusion from America's economy, call for black capitalism and the revival of the work ethic. A third force, the black Socialist, views our condition not as an aberration of American "democracy," but as the inevitable consequence of U.S. capitalism.

Whether in the United States, Africa, or the Caribbean, black Socialists do not believe capitalism or nationalism will liberate their people. To the black Socialist, inclusion in the capitalist economy will benefit a few while the masses remain in poverty. Nationalism, likewise, is to the Socialist a doctrine that promotes illogical racial supremacy and creates divisiveness between races. Grenada's New Jewel Movement, Detroit's League of Revolutionary Black Workers, Angola's Popular Movement for the Liberation of Angola (MPLA), and other black Communists see socialism as the only path to self-determination, not for a few, but for all.

Black Socialists do not play at socialism. It is not a part-time hobby, a passing fad, or an academic exercise. Socialism for black radicals is an analytical tool and guide to action that enables them to study the precise conditions of oppression, participate in the struggles of the working class, and lead the fight for a just and classless society.

Black Socialists understand the cost of their calling. George Jackson in Soledad Prison, Samora Machel of

FRELIMO and Walter Rodney of the Working People's Alliance had no illusions about capitalism's response to their demands. Black Socialist scholar Manning Marable wrote, "If really pressed, the liberal bourgeoise will shed its ideals, its great liberal expressions of humanism and will crush Black and proletarian social movements with every means at its disposal." No one knows this better than blacks who have chosen the arduous path of socialism. The brutal murder of Patrice Lumumba, the mass repression of the Black Panther Party and the Congress of South African Trade Unions, and the banning of Paul Robeson expose the treachery of capital toward black revolutionaries.

Uninvolved bystanders err when they attribute violence to black Socialists. Violence already exists in the horrible living conditions blacks are subjected to. When Huey Newton, Bobby Hutton and Bobby Seale carried guns in Oakland, they did not create confrontation, they were simply addressing the atrocities of the Oakland police department. When Amilcar Cabral and his six comrades formed the PAIGC, their revolution did not initiate violence, it was to end massacres like Pidiguiti where fifty unarmed strikers were murdered by Portuguese colonialists. Black Socialists seek not violence, but the creation of a humane society. The violence arises when the ruling elite protects its privilege and maintains inequality through the barrel of a gun.

Black Socialists seek to build a society where the authority of the state, the machinery of the economy and institutions like schools, courts, hospitals, and jails are controlled by working people. They want a society where the ownership of land, minerals, and resources lies with the people for the benefit of the people. Rather than allow 420,000 American families to own 45% of all private wealth in the United States, the black Socialist would spread that wealth among those who created it. Vacation homes, ocean yachts and Lehr jets for the few would give way to adequate employment, cultural development, health care and educational opportunity for all.

To the black Socialists the touted freedom of capitalism is merely the freedom to starve; in the words of

Manning Marable, where "people may not eat or shelter themselves unless in the production of food and shelter some individual makes a profit." It is the aim of black Socialists to redefine freedom to mean freedom for all people to participate in, work for, and benefit from a society whose primary aim is to benefit the masses and not enrich the few.

To the black Socialist, racism is no accident. It is the inevitable consequence of an economy based on competition and exploitation, divide and rule. It did not take long to understand this dynamic. In 1877, Peter H. Clark (perhaps the first Afro-American Socialist), prinicpal of Cincinnati's Colored High School, applauded the black and white railroad workers who stood up to the rail barons. He understood then, over one hundred years ago, that racism was merely a device which undermined labor unity and accelerated ruling class profits. In South Africa, black miners work the most back-breaking jobs, are paid less, and are denied medical benefits because capitalism demands that the few be enriched from the sufferings of the many.

Black Socialists are not heroes who lead the ignorant masses. They are, rather, reflections of the militancy of the black worker. The illiterate peasant from Angola, the rural Georgia sharecropper, the Guyanese domestic worker; those whose labor created the wealth of the world, these are the people who create and inspire the Walter Rodneys, Harry Haywoods and Louise Thompsons in the struggle for socialism.

If one were to read American, African or Caribbean history, you would think that blacks have shunned socialism. Accounts abound of black integrationists, black capitalists, black preachers, and black nationalists. Seldom, however, do we ever read the lives and struggles of those hundreds of blacks whose search for justice led to socialism. Absent from history is the energy of the Harlem women who in the 1930s led Tenant Leagues and Councils of the Unemployed. Seldom do schools teach the Communist influences of Langston Hughes and Richard Wright. And in Africa, where U.S. imperialism paints black revolutionaries as mindless "terrorists" duped by Russian propaganda, we know nothing of how Agostinho Neto in Angola and Eduardo Mondlane in Mozambique planned their homeland's liberation with a Socialist analysis rooted in Africa's soil.

Despite America's claim to freedom of expression and freedom of the press, most people know nothing of the struggles and sacrifices of black Socialists, in and outside the United States. Given the absence of black Socialist history, we must ask ourselves, Why? What is so frightening about black men and women who want and fight for decent housing, adequate compensation, and an end to racism. It is because in the United States, Africa, and the Caribbean, the black Socialist is the greatest threat to the continued exploitation of the working class. The state knows that black Socialists are not impressed with gala Fourth of July parades and glowing reports of the unemployment rate. Media hype of black progress and the alleged decline of racism does not hide the misery of Newark, West Kingston, and Nairobi.

Black Socialists know and will never forget that their people in the United States, Africa, and the Caribbean still rank at the top of misery indices and at the bottom of prosperity measures. In America, one-third of all blacks live in poverty, roughly 15% of adults and 45% of teenagers are unemployed, and Afro-Americans own ten times less wealth than white Americans. Afro-American Socialists know this misery requires more than a Democratic Congress and a smattering of liberal reforms.

In the Caribbean, black suffering is masked by tourist ads of glittering beaches and elegant sunsets. Yet, hidden in the shadows, Haitian sugar cane-cutters remain semi-slaves to the multinational corporations, squalor abounds in Jamaica, and unemployment, drugs, and economic dependence flourishes on vanquished Grenada.

Africa, the home of the black race, is not the home of black wretchedness. Since the 1884 Berlin Conference where European parasites divided African resources and people into artificial "spheres of influence," the African people have struggled and died for self-determination. Famine, political instability, and economic underdevelopment move Africans in a desperate search for revolutionary change.

Black Socialists are intensely aware of their people's suffering, and it is this consciousness and anger that frightens the ruling elite. The state knows the black Socialist is serious and has therefore reserved its greatest treacheries for them. Brilliant scholar Walter Rodney was blown up by a car bomb in Guyana. Labor organizer Vuyisile Mini was hanged in South Africa. Black Panther Party leader Fred Hampton was murdered in his sleep by Illinois law officers. These comrades are but three of hundreds murdered because they wanted too much freedom, too much democracy, and too much wealth.

Yet the black Socialist is not stopped. Despite the wreckage of Walter Rodney's car, the funeral wreath of Vuyisile Mini, or the blood-stained mattress of Fred Hampton, there are still those whose vision of a just society is stronger than their fear of violent repression. It is to their courage this book is dedicated.

At the center of this book is the black worker. Despite the awesome intellect of W.E.B. Du Bois, the powerful novels of Richard Wright, or the military genius of Samora Machel, the focal point of change and struggle is the black worker. The sweat of South African miners, North Carolina tobacco stemmers, and Grenadian banana farmers creates the wealth of the capitalist world. For their labor, families are divided, health and education are ignored, and movements for change are viciously repressed. Their awareness of this contradiction fuels black worker militancy and unsettles the ruling elite. The blood black workers have shed at Cabo Delgado in Mozambique, Luanda in Angola, Gastonia in North Carolina, Elaine in Arkansas, and Port-au-Prince in Haiti will someday be vindicated by the creation of just and democratic societies in the United States, Africa, and Caribbean.

For many decades communists were the only political

group in South Africa who were prepared to treat Africans as human beings and their equals; who were prepared to eat with us; talk with us, live with us, and work with us. They were the only political group which was prepared to work with the Africans for the attainment of political rights and a stake in society. Because of this, there are many Africans who, today, tend to equate freedom with communism.

—*Nelson Mandela, jailed leader of the African National Congress, from his 1964 court speech, "I am Prepared to Die." Mandela has been imprisoned since 1963 by the racist South African government. (From his book,* The Struggle Is My Life.*)*

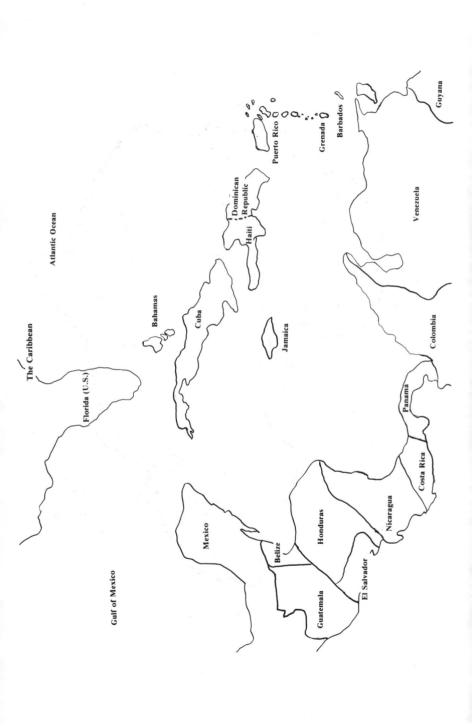

The European Conquest of Africa 1885

Africa Today

Under The Hammer

- **Black Workers in the United States**
- **A. Philip Randolph**
- **Hosea Hudson**
- **League of Revolutionary Black Workers**
- **Worker Profiles**
- **Black Workers in South Africa**

Under The Hammer: Black Workers In The United States and South Africa

Any study of socialism or communism must begin with the workers. The men and women who pick strawberries, haul cotton bales, rivet automobile frames, cut timber, wash dishes, pick up trash, stem tobacco and produce the wealth of society are the focus and power of socialism. The basic tenet of socialism is that those who produce the wealth of a given society must share its benefits.

The contradiction between private wealth and worker demands is the driving force of Socialist movements. Exploited as workers and abused as blacks, black workers have no time for theory and rhetoric; the struggle is here and now. Their struggle is for more than higher wages and civil rights. Black workers' struggles in South Africa, Grenada, and Mississippi have advanced the cause of socialism and put the black working class on the vanguard of revolutionary change.

> Hitherto the whole creative genius of the human intellect has labored only to give the advantage... to the few, and to deprive the rest of the most elementary necessities... But now all the marvels of technique... are the property of the whole people, and henceforth human intellect and genius will never be twisted into a means of oppression. We know this: surely it is worth striving with all our might to fulfill this stupendous historic task? The workers will carry out this titanic historic labor, for there are vast revolutionary powers slumbering in them, vast powers of renovation and regeneration.[1]
>
> —*Vladimir Ilyich Lenin, 1918*

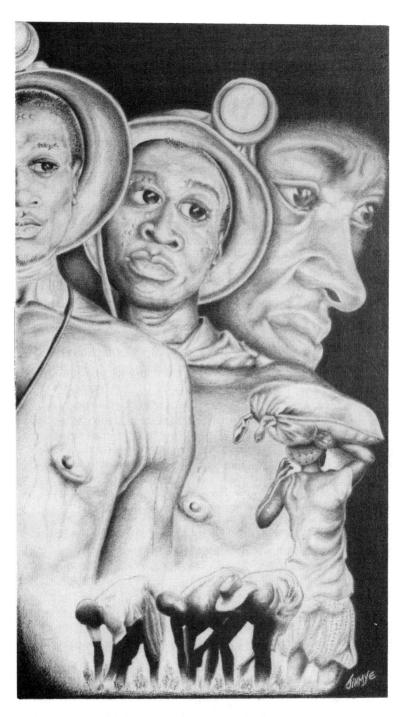

Work Ethic and the Fallacy

The Afro-American Worker: Three Centuries of Struggle

Afro-American workers are descendants of slaves. While European immigrants streamed through Ellis Island in search of wealth and opportunity, the ancestors of the black working class were expendable commodities in the transatlantic slave trade. As Guyanese scholar Walter Rodney noted, "If an African slave was thrown overboard, the only legal problem was whether or not the ship could claim compensation from the insurers."[2]

The African encounter with capitalism was murderous. Black men, women, and children were kidnapped from their villages and homes, packed like cattle in the putrid holds of slave ships, hauled across the Atlantic, auctioned to the highest bidder, and worked to death by Jamaican planters and Mississippi farmers, their lives sacrificed for dollars, rum and cotton.

African pain from the slave trade boggles the mind. It is estimated that ten million died from "trade wars," disease, and imprisonment in Africa; another thirty million perished during the torturous Middle Passage to the Americas; ten million more died during the "seasoning" period in the West Indies. The African men and women who survived the wars, forced marches, beatings and sexual assaults were auctioned, branded, and enslaved for life.

With slavery, American capitalism gave new meaning to Karl Marx's theory of "surplus value" as the formation to exploitation. According to Marx, surplus value is the difference between what a worker earns and the value of what that worker produces. If a worker produces a bale of cotton worth one dollar and is paid fifty cents, then the fifty cents difference is the surplus value or profit. Under slavery, surplus value is accelerated. The planter keeps the whole dollar and provides the slaves with only enough food and shelter required to keep them alive and productive.

For the Afro-American worker slavery is not a historical relic. The same banks, landowners, and corporations that benefited from slavery still function to relegate Afro-American workers to the bottom of society. Although the lynch mobs, cotton fields, and whipping posts have been replaced by the FBI, steel mills, and prisons, the end result remains. Black workers, like their slave ancestors, sweat and toil to enrich a few parasites while the black masses go without adequate schooling, health care, and employment opportunities.

The African slaves, however, did not submit passively to their exploitation. Harriet Tubman built the Underground Railroad, Dangerfield Newby and Shields Green followed John Brown to Harper's Ferry, and Gabriel Prosser, Jemmy the African, Denmark Vesey, Nat Turner, and David Walker answered slavery's violence with armed revolution. This brilliant legacy of resistance foreshadowed the courageous black worker struggles that followed.

Soon after the fall of slavery, Afro-American workers asserted themselves as a progressive force in U.S. society. Despite being thrust into the labor market without land or cash, Afro-Americans took control of their destiny. Four years removed from a system that classified them as property, black workers formed the Colored National Labor Union. Although the union did not last beyond Reconstruction's end in 1877, the Colored National Labor Union demonstrated the revolutionary potential of black workers. In an amazing display of internationalism, these landless illiterate workers supported Cuban independence, welcomed Chinese workers into the union, and admitted women members without dispute. The democratic principles of the ex-slaves contrasted sharply with America's sexism, racism and international bullying.

After the decline of the Colored National Labor Union, black workers joined the Knights of Labor. Formed in 1869, the Knights of Labor took the revolutionary position that black and white farmers could survive oppression only through worker unity. Black workers in the South were attracted by the militancy of the Knights of Labor, and by 1887 ninety thousand black farmers and workers were registered members. Thousands of black farmers, struggling against racist landlords and mob violence, were members of the four hundred all-black locals in the South. The mere existence of an all-black local was a powerful statement of black resistance to the racist violence of the South. Organized black workers and farmers threatened white economic dominance, which was resurrected after the overthrow of Reconstruction.

Life for black workers after Reconstruction was little different from slavery. Black Communist Party member Otto Huiswood wrote of the post-Reconstruction era:

> ...the Southern Negro was practically completely reenslaved on the plantations. The courts enacted innumerable laws which served to keep the Negro under the complete domination of the landowners. Every instrument at its disposal was used by the ruling class to shackle the Negro workers and bind them to the plantations...The poor farmer and sharecropper can never hope to own the land he tills, due to a credit and mortgage system which makes him a serf of the merchants, landowners, and bankers. Not only the land, but even the implements, crops—everything is mortgaged, placing them under the complete domination of the white ruling class.[3]

Imbued with a spirit of resistance inherited from the African slaves, black farmers fought back. In 1887, black Knights of Labor leaders George and Henry Cox led ten thousand black and white sugar workers on strike in Louisiana. The response was brutal: the Sugar Planters' Association formed its own army with the local residents, and the governor called out the militia. After three weeks of evictions and mob violence, the black and white workers stood by their demands.

With the first night of frost and the workers still on the picket line, the plantocracy panicked. White mobs attacked the black town of Thibodaux and massacred thirty Afro-Americans. The strike leaders, including George and Henry Cox, were arrested and jailed by the sheriff. The planters' revenge was still not satisfied. A few days later frenzied mobs dragged George and Henry from the prison and brutally beat and lynched them. The sugar strike of 1887 was broken and the workers returned with no more protection or wages than before. Nationally, the Knights of Labor succumbed to racism and compromised its earlier militancy. Not only did it abandon the ten thousand sugar workers of the Louisiana locals, but by 1894 it was advocating that blacks emigrate back to Africa.

While the Knights of Labor capitulated to America's reactionary climate, black workers continued their struggle. In 1888, one year after the massacres and lynch mobs in Louisiana, black farmers in Texas created the Colored Farmers' National Alliance. By 1891, 1.2 million black members worked in co-ops, published newspapers, and raised funds for black school children. Like the all-black locals in the Knights of Labor, their most powerful weapon was their labor. As demonstrated in Louisiana, whenever black workers stood up to white exploitation, white rage erupted in calculated violence and treachery. When Alliance farmers organized a strike in Lee County, Arkansas, twenty-five black cotton strikers were murdered by white planters.

Worker resistance was not the private domain of black men. By 1870, forty-nine percent of all black women worked, approximately four times the percentage of white working women. The dirtiest and most difficult jobs were reserved for black women, who fought bitterly for their dignity against both white racism and male chauvinism. In 1881, the black washerwomen of Atlanta refused to be spectators to their own exploitation and went on strike. Three thousand militant black women eventually joined the strike, demanding one dollar per twelve pounds of wash. The ruling elite went into a frenzy at the sight of these defiant black women. Landlords evicted them into the streets, the companies refused to negotiate, and the city council regulated them out of the work force. Despite their defeat, the black washerwomen of Atlanta left a fighting legacy later embodied in Miranda Smith and Mary Ann Moultrie.

*   *   *

The link between racist violence and economic exploitation is clearly visible in the 1919 massacre in Elaine, Arkansas. White landlords routinely cheated black sharecroppers by moving decimal points, changing interest rates, and "losing" records. In southeastern Arkansas black farmers combatted this fraud by organizing into a union to demand fair accounting and written contracts. When some black farmers challenged a white landowner's records, the innate violence of capitalism erupted. White mobs rampaged through black communities, hunted down union leaders like dogs, and massacred fifty black farmers in the bloody weeks that followed.

While black farmers contested racism on the land, black miners did so under the dark earth. Sweating in dismal shafts, listening intently for creaking earth, black coal miners in Birmingham and West Virginia suffered under constant abuse and degradation. In 1890, the United Mine Workers' Union (UMW) was founded by Richard Davis, a black mine worker and organizer. In spite of racist unions and avaricious mineowners, Davis dedicated himself to improving the lives of those whose misery was hidden in the mines.

Overcoming arrests, threats and blacklisting, Richard Davis built a union which by 1900 had twenty thousand black members. The all-black UMW locals in Alabama and West Virginia were particularly harassed by the mining companies. In 1903, West Virginia sheriffs shot three black union organizers asleep in their tents. (Murder during sleep is a common tactic of the agents of American capitalism; Fred Hampton of the Black Panther Party was murdered in similar fashion sixty-four years later.)

Despite this and other sadistic attacks, black miners in the UMW fought for years against mining company exploitation. Union leader Richard Davis was isolated and overwhelmed by the forces of reaction. For his selfless work among black miners, Davis was blacklisted by the owners and abandoned by the white union leadership. At age thirty-four, a penniless and embittered Davis died of lung fever contracted from years of hard toil in the mines.

*   *   *

Black workers stood with unions that were serious about confronting racism. While the AFL unions wallowed in racism, the Industrial Workers of the World (IWW) proclaimed, "There is no color line in the furnace hells of the steel trust and there will be none in the one Big Union."[4] Black workers, now increasingly northern and urban as families fled the landlords and hanging trees of the South, joined the IWW in large numbers. Radical workers R.T. Sims and Ben Fletcher exemplified the militancy of Afro-Americans in the IWW.

In the early 1900s lumber mill operators had perfected the exploitation of workers. For twelve hours of hard labor, black and white workers were paid in "scrip," paper money for use only at the company store. Not only were workers forced to buy at the company store, but the goods there were twenty-five to fifty percent more expensive than at other stores. The workers were herded into dismal camps run by the company and forced to pay exorbitant rents for damp corrugated shacks. The company withheld insurance premiums more than the cost of insurance, and the workers paid for medical care they never received.

For the IWW—or Wobblies, as they were often called—the lumber mills became a key battleground for the rights of working people. Organizing by cover of darkness and disguised as insurance agents and evangelists, IWW workers carried the message of strength through unions to mills all over the South.

In 1912, the Brotherhood of Timber Workers (BTW) arose from the oppression of the southern lumber mills. Of the twenty-five thousand registered members, one-half were black. Lumber barons appealed to racism, but most of the white lumber workers stood with their fellow black workers. In turn, when the companies locked out BTW members but sought to divide the union by offering blacks jobs at higher wages, not one black member of the brotherhood betrayed the union. In another tactic, the capitalists offered locked-out BTW members a chance to return to work by signing an oath of loyalty to the company. One black timber worker called the oath a "yellow dog contract" and said, "Only a low-life lickskillet would do such a thing... I would live on wild plants that grow in the hills before I would sign."[5]

This solidarity with the BTW was a direct result of the union's policy that "Although there are two colors in the South, we are organizing only one class." With black and white lumberjacks raising the cry, "Don't be a peon, be a man!" the BTW successfully fought off evictions, trials, blacklists, race-baiting, and other anti-union harassment by the owners. The sight of black lumberjacks struggling with their white co-workers led the owners to charge, "The BTW is a revolutionary organization seeking to undermine the fabric of Southern society."[6] Black worker militancy in the Brotherhood of Timber Workers is a stirring chapter in the history of Afro-Americans in the IWW and in organized labor.

The Wobblies finally succumbed to America's post-World War I union-busting tactics. The police, the FBI, and corporate America joined forces to rid the country of this menace to free-flowing profits. In an instance typical of the repression of this period, Marine Transport Workers' Union organizer Ben Fletcher was convicted of "seditious activity" for his speeches against what he called "the imperialist war," and sentenced to a ten-year term.

*   *   *

When Lenin and the Bolsheviks seized power under the slogan "Bread, Peace and Land" in Russia in 1917, Afro-American workers were imbued with new hope. With the formation in 1919 of the Communist Party U.S.A., black and white Party organizers brought a revolutionary theory to the black workers' legacy of struggle. Since 1919, most major militant union actions were influenced by the Communist Party's members.

By 1930, Richard Davis's United Mine Workers had capitulated to racism, leaving black coal miners subject to the greedy whims of the owners. Led by the aggressive black miner Isaiah Hawkins, the Communist Party helped build the militant National Miners' Union (NMU). Like Richard Davis thirty years earlier, Hawkins risked his life by organizing in mining camps among gun-toting goon squads. In the Thirties black miners in the NMU participated with white workers in Kentucky's bloody strikes in Harlan and Bell counties. These historic strikes pitted black and white workers against mine owners who would even starve the strikers' families to force them back to work. During the workers' historic resistance, black miners Essley Philips and Gaines Eubanks exemplified the irrepressible spirit of the Afro-American worker by leading strikers past machine guns, batons and bricks.

*   *   *

The National Negro Congress (NNC), a united front organization influenced by Afro-American Communists, participated in black worker struggles in the 1930s and 1940s. NNC organizers founded and led radical union movements in Pittsburgh, St. Louis, Chicago, and other major cities. Black organizers Benjamin Carethers and Henry Johnson enrolled thousands of black steel workers into the aggressive Steel Workers' Organizing Committee (SWOC), an NNC affiliate.

The Southern Negro Youth Congress, another Communist Party organization, assisted four hundred black female tobacco workers in protesting their terrible working conditions and starvation salaries in Virginia. The black women left their tobacco leaves and rollers for the picket line, and within forty-eight hours the bewildered owners reached into their profits to meet the workers' demands.

The Communist Party was not alone in organizing the oppressed sectors of the Afro-American working class. In the 1930s the Socialist Party organized the Southern Tenant Farmers' Union (STFU) in Georgia, Alabama, Arkansas, and other southern states. Black farmers joined in massive numbers, and within a few years five hundred thousand black farmers were organized with thousands of whites into STFU locals.

In 1934, thirteen hundred black and white sharecroppers, led by black union leader Rev. Owen Whitfield, camped by the highways of Missouri to demonstrate their plight to the government. The squatters were eventually dispersed by the National Guard. Despite the setbacks, many blacks who in the past had to shuffle and buck dance for a few crumbs from the planter now boldly demanded a fair share of the wealth they had created.

Afro-American workers took their struggle to the very oceans on which their ancestors sailed as black cargo years earlier. Black maritime workers were excluded from the benefits and protection of the maritime unions. Veteran black seaman and militant organizer Ferdinand Smith worked tirelessly to improve working conditions for his Afro-American co-workers. Smith and black and white members of the Communist Party helped form the powerful National Maritime Union (NMU). The shipping companies used racism to perfection, dividing workers, segregating ships, and keeping down wages. With the rise of the NMU, black union executive board members and ship delegates worked with progressive whites in gaining substantial concessions from the owners.

Afro-American Communists also influenced the Congress of Industrial Organizations (CIO). CIO organizers worked with migrant workers in Florida, domestic workers in New York, and with other severely oppressed sectors of the black working class. The CIO provided a vehicle through which black labor leaders Ferdinand Smith, Dora Jones of the Domestic Workers'

Union, and Floretta Andres of the Teachers' Union could agitate for justice and social change on behalf of the Afro-American workers. The practical gains made by Afro-American workers through union struggle are summed up by Joe Cook, black president of an Illinois SWOC chapter: "Has the CIO played fair with Negro Workers? Well, look at the clothes our children wear...since the SWOC showed us how to wage a fight for decent living wages."[7]

During World War II many radical unions backpedaled from workers' struggles and succumbed to the cry, "Everything for the war effort!" A few black tobacco workers, however, thought otherwise. At the R.J. Reynolds factory in Winston-Salem, Afro-Americans sweltered in unsanitary conditions for forty cents an hour. These factories were run like old plantations, with white armed guards pacing the floor to ensure black worker productivity.

In 1943, a veteran black tobacco worker asked his white supervisor to be excused to see the doctor about stomach pains. The supervisor angrily hurried him back to work. The pain worsened, but profits were more important than the health of Afro-American laborers. Later that day, next to his work station, the black worker died.

This flagrant act of corporate murder met the resistance of the black workers of R.J. Reynolds. Under the leadership of Velma Hopkins and Miranda Smith, Local 22 of the Food, Tobacco, Agricultural and Allied Workers' Union (FTA) led a bitter strike against the tobacco giant of the South. Local 22 was too militant for the CIO, which by then was shedding its radical image in exchange for inclusion in the American system. Abandoned by the CIO, Miranda Smith and Local 22 used a grass roots campaign involving hundreds of black tobacco workers to win significant concessions from the company.

Velma Hopkins, Miranda Smith, and the other black women of Local 22 were the offspring of the African women who resisted rape and exploitation aboard slave ships and on southern plantations. Their heroic struggle is a testament to the enduring spirit of resistance among Afro-American workers. Smith, a member of the Communist Party, was a dynamic organizer who later achieved the highest position of any black woman in the labor movement when she was appointed the FTA's Southern Regional Director. Miranda Smith was just as militant in the union office as she was on the floor, standing firm in the face of both threats and bribes.

* * *

When the guns of World War II fell silent, the United States fired the opening volleys of the Cold War against its own citizens. Militant black workers were among the first to fall. Using laws and tactics borrowed from the Nazis, the United States government and corporations scuttled militant unions, blacklisted organizers, and created an anti-Communist hysteria reminiscent of the Salem witch-hunts. Hugh Bryson, the aggressive black president of the National Union of Maritime Cooks and Stewards (MCS) was arrested. Ferdinand Smith of the NMU was branded an "undesirable alien" by President Truman and deported to his native Jamaica. Upon leaving, Smith said, "I helped build a union which enabled sailors to marry and have children and a house like other workers instead of being kicked around like bums. For this I earned the enmity of the shipowners and their agents."[8] Loyalty oaths, where workers signed anti-Communist pledges, screened hundreds of other black workers from the maritime industry.

The unions most susceptible to attack from the government and the capitalist were those where black and white worked together. In fact, many black workers were considered Communists if they answered "yes" to the question, "Have you ever had dinner with white people?" The AFL and CIO joined government and capital in this vicious assault on militant workers, bouncing out radical union leaders and dropping support of unions like Local 22 in North Carolina. The Cold War put black worker gains in a deep freeze, robbing the Afro-American working class of its most dynamic union leaders and allowing corporations to roll back gains that black people had died for.

Just as ex-slaves did after Reconstruction, the Afro-American worker arose from the wreckage of Cold War anti-unionism to create another labor organization. In 1951 black labor leaders formed the National Negro Labor Council (NNLC) to fight racism in both industry and the unions. One of the organizers, Jostlin' Joe Johnson, linked Afro-American worker demands with the rising Third World liberation movements. He said, "The darker peoples of the world want to chose their own leaders. It makes me mad as hell for our administration to give millions to maintain rulers in colonial countries and then don't want to give me my unemployment insurance."[9]

Paul Robeson, the great Afro-American artist and activist, captured the spirit of the NNLC with his brilliant 1952 speech, "The Battleground is Here." Ridiculing the idea that black workers should go fight "communism" in Korea and Guatemala, Robeson urged the NNLC to remember the struggles against racism on the home front. Never one to turn his back on the laboring masses, Robeson thundered,

> I will never forget that the ultimate freedom and immediate progress of my people rests on the sturdy backs and unquenchable spirits of the coal miners, clerks, domestics, bricklayers, stewards, cooks, sharecroppers, steel and auto workers, longshoremen, tenant farmers, and tobacco stemmers—the vast mass of Negro-Americans from whom all talent and achievement arise in the first place.[10]

With this stirring introduction, the NNLC adopted a "Program of Action" to break the pattern of job discrimination against blacks in American industry and to promote worker unity by smashing union racism. Militant black workers from all sectors of the economy were active in the NNLC. Estelle Holloway from Local 22 in Winston-Salem, Joe Johnson fron the Marine Cooks and Stewards, William Hood from the Amalgamated Clothing Workers, and labor activists like Coleman Young, Cleveland Robinson, and Ernest "Big Train" Thompson symbolized the diversity and strength of the NNLC.

In the midst of the Cold War witch-hunts and union-busting, the NNLC defied reactionary repression by fighting for hotel jobs in New York, tobacco work in North Carolina, and electrical jobs in St. Louis. One-third of the membership was black women, and they soon distinguished themselves by courageously standing up to the helmeted police and sadistic company owners. Black women members of the NNLC could be found organizing and agitating for worker rights in mills, shops, and farms all over the nation.

NNLC organizers ventured onto the sugar cane fields of Louisiana, the same blood-soaked fields where blacks and whites in the Knights of Labor fought for human dignity in 1887. In 1953, the NNLC led sixteen thousand sugar workers to the picket line, and the sons of the thugs and vigilantes came out to enforce the brutal rule of the landowners. After a long and costly struggle, the sugar workers and the NNLC forced the owners to meet the strikers' demands.

By 1954, the successes of the NNLC had come to the attention of the fascists on the House Committee on Un-American Activities. These brave Afro-American workers were hauled in front of the committee, red-baited by congressmen and the AFL, and forced to dissolve the NNLC after draining its treasury for legal defense costs. Nevertheless, the gains of the NNLC could not be undone, and historian Philip Foner says that one of the most significant events of the pre-Civil Rights era is "That between 1950 and 1955 an organization manned and led predominantly by black workers was engaged in a struggle not only for the civil rights of the black people and an end to segregation but also for jobs for blacks and an end to racism in industry and organized labor."[11]

The Civil Rights Movement began when black seamstress Rosa Parks defied an angered white bus driver and southern custom by ignoring demands that she relinquish her seat to a white man. Millions followed her lead and challenged segregation and violence throughout America. At the cutting edge of this challenge was a group of low-paid black southern orderlies and aides in Charleston, South Carolina.

Tired of degrading treatment, low wages, few benefits, and arbitrary punishments, Local 1199B of the Hospital Workers' Union went on strike in 1969. The South demonstrated again why it was considered America's showcase of worker oppression. The strikers were attacked by vigilantes, evicted by landlords and ordered by the courts to return to work. Led by twenty-seven year-old hospital worker Mary Ann Moultrie, the members of Local 1199B refused to surrender. The governor called out the National Guard and the state miltia, but whenever strikers were arrested, more workers appeared to replace them on the picket line.

The black community in Charleston lined up solidly behind the strikers; nearly thirty percent of the entire Afro-American population marched and rallied for 1199B. The hospital workers' strike in Charleston was a fight for job benefits as well as an indictment of America's confusing priorities. As Mary Ann Moultrie noted while in jail, "I was thinking of the astronauts we are sending to the moon while children in Charleston go hungry."[12] With dedication similar to the black Knights of Labor and the lumberjacks of the Brotherhood of Timber Workers, the men and women of 1199B stood firm in the face of racist attacks and won gains from which later generations will benefit.

*   *   *

Black workers' resistance to exploitation has been the cornerstone of Afro-American survival. Lynchings, disenfranchisement, miseducation, lack of health care, and cultural oppression all revolve around the subjugation of the black working class. When militant black workers in the Colored Farmers' National Alliance, Southern Tenant Farmers' Union, and the National Negro Labor Council won job security, wage increases, and employment opportunities for the black masses, this security provided Afro-Americans with the foundation from which to launch other struggles in the schools, courts, and political arena.

It is the black worker, then, who has borne the brunt of capitalist oppression and in a real sense serves as a bridge over which later generations of Afro-Americans continue the struggle in other areas. Without miner Richard Davis, maritime worker Ferdinand Smith, and tobacco stemmer Velma Hopkins, the gains Afro-Americans have made in politics, education and social welfare would not exist.

The harsh conditions of the black workers created radicals at war with capitalist oppression. Even for those black labor leaders who did not embrace socialism, their demands often resembled the principles of socialism. By insisting that the parasites who ran the farms, mines and mills of America end racism and provide decent wages, housing, education, and child care, Afro-American workers called for a radical redistribution of wealth.

While white workers, mainstream unions, and middle-class blacks compromised their struggles against capitalism in hopes of personal aggrandizement, black workers stood firm, with hammer and shovel in hand, demanding that the wealth they created be used for the welfare of the entire society. Black workers sweated, grunted, pushed, hammered, planted, picked, lifted, carried, chauffered, waited, and served and for that labor simply demanded that the profits be divided so that none would suffer as they had suffered.

> The union is my mother and my father and I am the son who will give my life for it. The union has put bread in the mouth of my chidren. It has given me a home, it straightened my back so I do not bend to any man.[13]
> —*An Afro-American cook who was a member of the militant Union of Marine Cooks and Stewards (MCS)*

A. Philip Randolph and Black Trade Union Power

For six decades Asa Philip Randolph was the most important figure in Afro-American trade union organizing. By the 1960s Randolph had compromised his militancy and aligned himself with reactionary labor leaders. His later moderation, however, did not invalidate his many contributions to black workers or erase the fact that, from 1916 to the 1950s, A. Philip Randolph was America's foremost black union leader.

In 1911, Randolph left Crescent City, Florida for the vibrancy of Harlem. He encountered socialism and the teachings of Karl Marx in a city college philosophy course. Captivated by the possibility of social change, Randolph later said, "I studied Marx like a child read *Alice in Wonderland*." Randolph was not interested in socialism as an academic study; he sought immediately to use it as a means to liberate his people from white economic bondage. By 1914, Randolph and his fellow student and comrade Chandler Owens were the most popular street corner agitators in Harlem, calling for a radical redistribution of wealth and demanding full employment.

It was, however, the appearance of the radical newspaper *The Messenger* that catapulted Randolph and Owen into prominence as uncompromising black leftists. Booker T. Washington told blacks to accept second-class lives by performing menial labor. Marcus Garvey told blacks to separate completely from white society. Randolph and Owens, however, told black workers through the *Messenger* that they not only built America but also had the ability to transform it.

Within months *The Messenger* established itself as a powerful proponent of black worker radicalism. In 1919, America was herding Native Americans onto reservations, exploiting and disenfranchising women, and allowing corporations to abuse Afro-American, Chinese, and Mexican workers at home and Cubans and Hawaiians abroad. *The Messenger* meanwhile demanded that the government provide free food for the elderly;

that workers form consumer and farm cooperatives; and that employers provide equal pay and maternity leave for women.

In one editorial Randolph wrote, "Most Negro families are on the brink of poverty, they are not striving to live but they are struggling to keep from dying...private ownership of the tools of production...is the mother of poverty, ignorance, crime, prostitution, and race prejudice."[14] Fearing the power of class conscious organized black workers, the Justice Department wrote, "By long odds *The Messenger* is the most dangerous of all Negro publications."[15]

During World War I, Randolph, Owen, and *The Messenger* became increasingly critical of capitalism, declaring, "wars of contending groups of capitalists are not the concern of workers." Fearing a black worker revolt in the midst of a war, President Woodrow Wilson charged, "A. Philip Randolph is the most dangerous Negro in America."[16] By 1918, Wilson had imprisoned both Randolph and Owen for their opposition to the war. Government repression only enhanced Randolph and Owens's reputations among the black working class, and the two soon were known in Harlem as "Lenin and Trotsky."

Prison did not dampen Randolph's zeal for Afro-American workers. He was soon to make history with a group of persecuted black railroad car porters. In the early Twenties, black sleeping car porters began to question the oppressive working conditions of the Pullman Company. The porters worked for hundreds of hours a month, often riding thousands of miles without sleep and without pay. Their meager salary was docked for uniforms, meals, sleeping quarters, and anything else the Pullman Company accountants decided. "Yes sir, boss," "I'm sorry, ma'am"—these black men in caps and gloves were personal slaves to the railroad patrons who could "reward" them with tips or have them fired with a complaint.

The perpetuator and beneficiary of this traveling plantation was the Pullman Company, a giant among

U.S. corporations. Company president E.F. Carey, one of the nation's mightiest industrial monarchs, was praised by the black press and black middle class for providing jobs to Afro-Americans. These spokespersons for blacks believed a job without dignity was better than no job at all.

The sleeping car porters, however, had other ideas. Despite the terrorists the company hired to "keep the workers in line" and the automatic firing of union organizers, several of the fifteen thousand railroad workers held a secret meeting to discuss the need for organization. Milton Webster, Ashley Totten, C.L. Dellums, Rory Lancaster, Morris Moore, T.T. Patterson, and William Des Verney emerged from darkened locker rooms with a plan to build the Brotherhood of Sleeping Car Porters. Ashley Totten heard one of Randolph's fiery street corner orations and enlisted Randolph's help. Randolph accepted the challenge and the presidency, and 1925 marked the beginning of the Brotherhood of Sleeping Car Porters.

In the tradition of the old southern mob attacks on organized black workers, E.F. Carey struck hard at the brotherhood. Union leaders, some with a decade of service at Pullman, were fired without warning and denied medical or retirement benefits. Other brotherhood activists were beaten by hired thugs in broad daylight, often in sight of other sleeping car porters. With a few exceptions, the black press sided with Pullman, taking the attitude, "Y'all be grateful for what Pullman has done for us, they give us jobs when no one else would." Some black papers called Randolph and the brotherhood leadership "reds" and ran full-page advertisements for Carey and the Pullman Company. The U.S. government joined the attack by harassing union activists and spying on the black porters.

The black men whose jobs hinged on servile acceptance of tips, courageously fought back against Carey and his agents in the black press and the government. Despite the threat of violence and the specter of unemployment, the porters planned to strike unless granted pay raises and union recognition. When Carey threatened to import Mexicans and Filipinos should the black workers strike, the brotherhood was unmoved. When the ballots were counted on the strike vote, 6,053 of 6,070 brotherhood members voted to walk out. It was here that Randolph made a compromise which many historians feel robbed the porters of their bargaining power. In exchange for a shadow of what the rank and file of the brotherhood demanded, A. Philip Randolph called off the strike.

When their leadership backpedaled, many brotherhood members felt betrayed and left the union. Although members and morale sank after the aborted strike, Randolph continued to lead the brotherhood in several bitter battles with Pullman and in other causes of black survival. Under Randolph's leadership, the union supported the Scottsboro Boys, assisted the Communist Party in forming Unemployment Councils during the Depression, and in 1935 finally won major concessions (including recognition and a contract) from the Pullman Company. Throughout their struggle with the Pullman Company, the Brotherhood of Sleeping Car Porters became an inspiration to black workers everywhere. On tenant farms, in factories, and in mine shafts, black workers spoke proudly of the struggle and victories of the Brotherhood of Sleeping Car Porters.

Frank Crosswaith, a fiery black Socialist from Harlem, took over as executive secretary of the porters' union, and Randolph expanded his struggle for black trade union power. In 1936, he and other black labor leaders founded the National Negro Congress (NNC) at a Chicago convention attended by five thousand delegates representing two hundred and fifty-six trade unions, and eighty community, youth, women's, and cultural organizations. The NNC was the most progressive collection of black activists ever assembled, with representatives from the most militant black trade unions, Communist Pary organizations like the Southern Negro Youth Congress, and other Afro-American organizations. Under the leadership of A. Philip Randolph, the NNC represented the first time black unionists, intellectuals, civic reformers, Communists and Socialists had organized a united front against racist exploitation. The revolutionary nature of the NNC was evidenced by greetings sent from Mao Zedong, then provisional chair of the Chinese Soviet Republic: "I greet... the First National Congress of the fighting Negro people, 12,000,000 strong in America struggling against every form of national and racial oppression."[17]

For several years before World War II the NNC and their affiliates struggled against white racism and class exploitation in factories, mills and farms all over the nation. A national black workers' organization was the capitalist's worst nightmare, and big business, the AFL, and the FBI took every opportunity to subvert NNC activity. They charged that the NNC was dominated by "reds," and many moderate affiliates of the congress were pressured out. Increasingly critical of the Communist Party's deference to Moscow, Randolph echoed the reactionary charge that Part members controlled the congress and he eventually resigned as president. Although the NNC continued to function after Randolph's departure, during World War II the organization ceased to exist.

In 1941, A. Philip Randolph turned his attention to other struggles of black workers. Although thousands of defense industry jobs were created during the war, discrimination effectively barred black workers from employment. Continuing his tireless struggle for black workers, Randolph initiated the March on Washington Movement. With defiant boldness, Randolph proposed to lead one hundred thousand angry black workers to the nation's capital to demand an immediate end to job discrimination.

The Brotherhood of Sleeping Car Porters was the core of the Movement and spread the message of black labor power among Afro-American janitors, mail carriers, auto workers, sharecroppers, domestics, and other black workers. Randolph insisted that the marchers be restricted to Afro-Americans to fully dramatize the anger of black working people.

Never before had any Afro-American proposed such a radical challenge to the economics of racism. Brotherhood leaders like C.L. Dellums, Ashley Totten and others spent countless hours in union halls, on street corners, and at church services prompting enthusiam for the march, and soon one hundred thousand black workers had pledged to march on Washington in 1941.

Roosevelt panicked when he realized that Randolph and the Movement organizers were serious. The specter of one hundred thousand black workers marching on Washington during a war sent shock waves through the president and his cabinet. Liberals, reformers, and even white Communists believed that black workers should relax their demands while the nation rallied to defeat Nazi Germany. Roosevelt pleaded with Randolph to call off the march in exchange for Executive Order 8802 "prohibiting discrimination in the employment of workers in defense industries because of race, creed, or national origin."[18] After much deliberation, and to the relief of Roosevelt, Randolph called off the march.

From Messenger Magazine *2 (Aug. 1919). Copyright © 1919 Messenger Magazine.*

Although the 1941 march never occurred, the Movement prefigured the Civil Rights struggle in the Fifties and Sixties, as well as the famous 1963 March On Washington. Even more significantly, A. Philip Randolph and the Brotherhood of Sleeping Car Porters' leadership in the Movement marked the first time in Afro-American history that a black labor organization was the vanguard of a mass movement for democracy.

With *The Messenger*, the brotherhood, and the march movement behind him, by the late Fifties and into the Sixties Randolph was coopted by the very system he sought to change. He supported U.S. involvement in Vietnam and condemned radical trade union actions in Third World countries. Nevertheless, from 1916 to 1946, a full thirty years, A. Philip Randolph was the single most significant figure in the black worker trade union movement.

Hosea Hudson: From Sharecropper to Communist

Born in 1898 in a dreary Georgia shack, Hosea Hudson symbolized the torment of the black worker in the Deep South. Hudson's life as a sharecropper and steelworker is a mirror in which we see a reflection of the misery Afro-Americans suffered in both the city and on the farm. The most significant aspect of his life, however, is his membership in the Communist Party USA. As an exploited black worker and a member of a revolutionary party, Hosea Hudson threatened the foundations of monopoly capitalism, class oppression and white racism.

Hudson learned early that racism had economic consequences. By age ten, he had witnessed white mobs hunt down his uncle (for being successful in business) and watched his family work like slaves to enrich a white landowner. In his book, *Black Worker in the Deep South*, Hudson writes of the crushing poverty and perpetual debt of sharecropping.

Every year he and his wife Sophie purchased the seed,

tools and fertilizer required to plant and harvest cotton. Since the Hudsons had no cash, the landowner extended credit at his overpriced plantation store. At the end of the year, after sixteen hours a day, seven days a week of backbreaking work, Hudson and the landowners would "square up." No matter how many bales of cotton the Hudsons produced, they always owed something at the end of the year.

If by chance a black family earned enough to pay off their loans, many white farmers simply rigged the books. For several years Hudson worked like a slave only to owe Mr. Jackson money at the end of the year. Since they could not leave the farm until the debt was paid off, Hosea and Sophie were tied to the white man's land like their slave forebears. What the gun and the whip had done under slavery, perpetual debt did under sharecropping.

In 1923, Hudson planted and sold peanuts along with his cotton. Saving enough through peanut sales to pay off Mr. Jackson, Hosea and Sophie packed up their meager possesions and moved to Birmingham. The economic exploitation of the rural South followed Hudson to the Stockham Pipe and Fittings steel plant in Birmingham. Hudson and his black co-workers were paid less than the whites, relegated to the dirtiest jobs, and customarily cheated on payday. The white armed guards who passed out checks on Friday told the black workers to come back Monday, and on Monday invariably the pay window would be closed all day. Hudson and his co-workers had no recourse. Those who complained would be fired or paid a night visit by the local chapter of the Ku Klux Klan.

White southern terror reserved its worst for militant black workers: it was not uncommon to find the mutilated body of a recalcitrant Afro-American worker hanging from a lynching tree. Southern black sharecroppers and steelworkers fought alone against racist violence. Of the NAACP, the black church, the Democratic Party and the Republican Party, not one was willing to openly challenge the rule of the white southern capitalist and his army of racist white working class and peasant buffers. This changed, however, with the arrival of the Communist Party USA in 1930.

One winter evening in 1931, black Communist Party member Al Murphy invited Hudson to a meeting with other steelworkers to discuss improving black living conditions. That night Hudson and seven of his coworkers listened to Murphy present the Party's program for the Deep South. Hudson later wrote,

> We was sitting there, and Murphy got to outlining about the role of the Party and the program of the Party—the Scottsboro case and the unemployed and the Depression and the imperialist war... He was explaining how the Scottsboro case is a part of the whole frame-up of the Negro people in the South—jim crow, frame-up, lynching, all that was part of the system. He went through all that kind of stuff, and I understood it.[19]

Murphy also explained the Communist Party's view of blacks in the South: that slavery, Reconstruction, and the disenfranchisement and economic exploitation that followed Reconstruction molded blacks into a separate and distinct nation. The Party's Black Belt thesis held that the Black Nation had the right to self-determination with the option of building a socialist society to benefit the impoverished mass of southern workers.

To the black steelworkers in that room, the white man in the South was in total control, cheating, terrorizing, and overworking blacks at will. Nevertheless, Hudson, Will Cal, Fred Walker, and the other workers sensed an unprecedented commitment from Murphy and the Party. Instead of prayers, promises, and betrayals, the Party offered these hardened men the possibility of liberation. Hudson later wrote, "We all eight signed up, each paying 50 cents to join and the 10 cents a month... It looked like the thing I had been looking for."[20] In signing the membership roster of the Communist Party, Hosea Hudson and his seven comrades declared war on capitalism and the racism, poverty, and misery it created.

Hudson's commitment to the Party was tested when

Stockham Foundry fired him for asking questions about the harsh treatment of blacks in the mill. Hosea, however, was undaunted. Unemployed, cold and hungry, he and comrade Henry Mayfield selflessly organized a Party unit composed of other black workers in Birmingham. Under the leadership of Hudson and Mayfield, this radical black collective sold newspapers, passed out leaflets, and worked to get coal, groceries, rent moratoriums, and other relief for unemployed families.

The Party leaflets that Hudson distributed in Alabama clearly demonstrated the revolutionary boldness of black Party members in the South. At a time when the Democratic and Republican Parties openly courted racists, the Communist Party demanded:

1. full equality to the Negro people and the right of self-determination to the Negro people in the Black Belt of the South.
2. freedom for the Scottsboro boys.
3. no discrimination against the Negro people and women in all public jobs.
4. cash relief for all unemployed workers.
5. free government housing.
6. death to the lyncher.
7. the right of Negro sharecroppers to sell their crops.[21]

In 1930, the Alabama legislature declared membership in the Communist Party a criminal act. State repression only increased Hudson's resolve to build the Party and advance the rights of black workers. In 1932, he was elected to the leadership of the Alabama branch of the Communist Party. What Hudson lacked in formal education he made up for in his intimate knowledge of southern white oppression and in his dedication to those who reeled under the hammer of capitalist exploitation. As a leader in the Party he organized black steelworker strikes, led anti-lynching campaigns, and worked to free the Scottsboro Boys. Hudson helped Al Murphy and Mack Coad build the militant Sharecroppers' Union in Alabama's rural counties, and in 1938 he joined the Right to Vote Club to demand an end to disenfranchisement and build black political power.

In 1941, Hudson organized five hundred black and white steel workers into Local 2815 at the Jackson Foundry. In six years as its president, Hudson negotiated three contracts for the workers in a plant that had once vowed never to bargain with any union, especially an intergrated one. By 1947, however, the manufacturers and local authorities had tired of Hudson's meddling with "their nigras." After World War II, with red-baiting in full swing, the Alabama authorities manipulated anti-Communist hysteria to get Hudson removed from the leadership of Local 2815.

Newspaper headlines blared, "Hosie Hudson, President of Local 2815, is suspected of being a Communist." While most of the white workers voted to expel Hudson, a black member of Local 2815 expressed the sentiment of Afro-American workers: "Hell, I don't care what Hosie is. Damn, he's my man, cause he gets things done here, better conditions, better wages, we wouldn't have had if it hadn't been for him."[22] Abandoned by white union leaders, Hudson was expelled from Local 2815, fired from Jackson Foundry, and blacklisted by other steel plants.

Accustomed to adversity and struggle, Hudson worked as an underground organizer for the Party in Atlanta for several years before moving to Atlantic City, where he agitated for the rights of the low-income elderly. Financial help from black Party leaders Henry Winston and William Patterson allowed Hudson to write his autobiography, *Black Worker in the Deep South*. Unbroken by fifty-four years of revolutionary struggle, in 1985, at age eighty-seven, Hudson was still a member of the Communist Party USA.

*   *   *

Although Hudson symbolized black resistance, he was not alone in his struggle. Frank Williams, Addie Adkins, and Henry Mayfield helped him organize black steelworkers. Ralph Gray and Mack Coad suffered beatings, arrests and death threats in organizing the Sharecroppers' Union with Hudson. Hazel Stanley and Jimmy Hooper led the Right to Vote Club, which Hudson later joined.

In building the aggressive CIO unions in Alabama, Hudson worked with the courageous William Norman. Irrepressible in his commitment to Afro-American workers, Norman constantly warned his comrades, "I ain't got no time to throw away, let's talk about how we goin' to build this union."[23] In tribute to his comrades in struggle, Hudson wrote, "It wont none of these little people that got they hand in the pie, thinkin' they goin' to get a dollar from their good white friends. It was the people out there who knowed they didn't have nothin' but they chains of slavery to lose."[24]

Because of its demonstrated commitment to the complete liberation of the southern black working class, the Communist Party attracted a dedicated cadre of Afro-American workers. In Hudson's words:

> What the Party was doing was taking this lower class like myself and making people out of them, took the time and didn't laugh at you if you made a mistake. In other words, it made the lower class feel at home when they sit down in a meeting. If he got up and tried to talk and couldn't express himself, nobody liable to laugh at him. They tried to help them and tell them 'You'll learn.' There was always something to bring forward, to give you courage...The Party made me to know that I was somebody...I found this Party, a party of the working class, gave me rights equal with all others regardless of color, sex, age, or educational standards. I with my uneducation could express myself, without being made fun of by others who could read well and fast, using big words. I was treated with high respect. I had a right to make policy.[25]

As the Party developed black working class leaders, so did these same leaders build the Party.

We Negroes who was members of the Party was far in advance in understanding of how to organize people more than the rest of the Negroes or whites. We was able to meet among ourselves in the Party and discuss problems and place out our tactical approach, utilizing our Marxist-Leninist understanding on how to go about to try to bring the people together. We was always busybodys.[26]

The Party in the South was overwhelmingly black and working class. When white members quit the CPUSA over revelations about Stalin's repression or philosophical differences with Party ideology, their black comrades remained loyal. The unity between militant black workers and the Communist Party was forged in brutal struggle against white landowners in the Sharecroppers' Union and against mill owners in unions like Local 2815, and could not be diminished by what Stalin did in the Kremlin or by esoteric squabbling over the fine points of Marxist doctrine. Locked in a contest for the very survival of Afro-Americans, black Communists were serious about revolution. As Hudson wrote, "The '30s were the rough days that created a tough communist... men and women that went to their graves as communists."[27]

Hosea Hudson, Communist Party USA

Hudson was one of those "tough Communists." He was threatened by the Klan, beaten by sheriffs, and fired from jobs. Alabama rednecks were not the only ones interested in neutralizing Hosea Hudson. In 1941, the Birmingham branch of the FBI said, "Hosea Hudson is the #1 Negro communist in this locality,"[28] and kept a dossier on him that by 1978 had grown to three thousand pages.

Despite lynch mobs and the FBI, Hudson's life stands as a tribute to the revolutionary power of oppressed black workers. His courageous struggle is proof that racism and exploitation cannot stop the march of black folk toward liberation. In 1968, Hudson told a college audience: "To sum up the meaning of my 70 years of living, I will say four words are sufficient, learn, struggle, organize, unite!"[29]

League of Revolutionary Black Workers

Detroit, 1967. A city afire. Afro-American workers, tired of unemployment, segregation, disenfranchisement, and police violence, stormed the streets in six days of protest. The power structure reels, then reacts brutally. Armored cars, jeeps, and military vehicles roll through ghetto streets and alleys. Young white troops, poisoned by racism and ordained by the rulers to crush this "slave" rebellion, shoot to kill. The Sunday sun rises, and thirty-four blacks—three executed at the Algiers motel, others shot in the back for "looting"—lie motionless in Detroit morgues.

On the outskirts of the city, young black auto workers suffered from grueling, backbreaking work on the assembly lines. The United Auto Workers (UAW) assisted white workers to the total exclusion of their exploited black colleagues. Charles Denby, a long-time black auto worker, wrote that blacks were overworked, given the dirtiest, most difficult jobs, and subjected to merciless speedups which increased production and profits but did nothing for the worker. Denby and his co-workers were often too tired to shower at the end of their shift.

At Detroit's Dodge Main plant, young black workers began studying a black leftist newspaper called *Inner City Voice*, distributed by John Watson, Ken Cockrel, General Baker, Mike Hamlin, and John Williams. The publishers of the *Inner City Voice* followed the teachings of Mao Zedong, Che Guevara, Frantz Fanon, and Malcom X, and in their newspaper these Afro-American Marxists called on black workers to develop the class consciousness required to lead a socialist revolution in the United States.

Energized by the possibility of change, the readers of the *Inner City Voice* joined white co-workers in a wildcat strike for better wages and improved conditions. After the strike ended, the white males were allowed to return to work, while General Baker and four other black organizers were immediately terminated. The selective punishment of Afro-American auto workers in the 1967 strike was ignored by the racists in the UAW, and black auto workers were again left alone in their struggle for human dignity.

Determined never to be caught unorganized and unprotected against racist auto companies and indifferent unions, the Afro-Americans at Dodge Main created an organization which would reflect their interests as blacks and as workers. Chuck Wooten and eight other auto workers went to a Detroit bar to discuss ways of "putting a stop to this bullshit." Shouting over jazz and blues, these angry nine black auto workers created the Dodge Revolutionary Union Movement, or DRUM.

Talk of DRUM swept through the auto plant. White foremen were unnerved by the prospect of organized black workers. The founders of DRUM invited the editors of *Inner City Voice* to help build the union and infuse the organization with the vigorous analysis of Marxism-Leninism. DRUM was not to be a "Union for shuffling and buck-dancin' Negroes, we are serious about revolution." The Movement's first newspaper was dedicated to Afro-American martyr Malcolm X, and, like Malcolm, urged black workers to join DRUM and do for themselves what the racists at Dodge and the UAW would never do. Many young black workers, some participants in the 1967 Detroit insurrection and several just off the unemployment lines, eagerly joined DRUM. A poem in an early issue of the newsletter dramatized the rebellious spirit of these young militant workers:

> ...For hours and years
> with sweated tears
> Trying to break our chain...
> But we broke our backs and
> died in packs
> To find our manhood slain...
> But now we stand for DRUM's
> at hand
> to lead our freedom fight,
> And now till then we'll fight
> like men
> For now we know our might...
> And damn the plantations
> and the whole Dodge nation
> ...For DRUM has dried our tears
> For now as we die
> we have a different cry
> For now we hold our spears!
> UAW is scum,
> OUR THING IS DRUM![30]

In 1968, DRUM led a rousing wildcat strike in which Chrysler's production dropped by nineteen hundred cars and the Movement gained the respect of black workers in auto plants all over Detroit. Within weeks black workers created Revolutionary Union Movements at Ford (FRUM), General Motors (GRUM), and other auto manufacturing plants. In a bold attempt to link the struggles of black workers with other issues affecting black survival, the DRUM leadership utilized Afro-American students, the unemployed, and community activists on the picket line. For DRUM the struggle was for more than higher wages for a few workers, it was about health care for black babies, good schools for children, and self-respect for the black people of Detroit.

Later that year the various 'RUMS combined to form the League of Revolutionary Black Workers. If the thought of isolated radical black labor groups was frightening to the owners, the idea of a united league was a nightmare. Like the manufacturers, the UAW was haunted by the specter of organized black workers. The white reactionary leaders of the UAW were often a bigger obstacle to the League than the auto giants. UAW officials feared an independent black union outside of their control would upset the cozy relationship they had with the corporate giants. Eager to sabotage the League, the UAW called the leadership "black commies," and "black fascists."

At union election time, the UAW, local police, and white workers rigged the ballot boxes to prevent dedicated DRUM organizer Ron March from winning a union seat in 1968. Instead of retreating from these attacks, the League struck back with a fury. In 1969, they demanded that the UAW have a black president, a black vice-president, and that fifty percent of the staffers be black. Baker, Mike Hamlin, and the other League leaders also demanded that the UAW recognize the League, financially support the League's community work, and invest strike funds in black banks.

The black auto workers of the League believed U.S. imperialism in Vietnam and Dodge and UAW exploitation in Detroit were flip sides of the same capitalist coin. Joining the anti-war movement, the League of Revolutionary Black Workers called for an end to the Vietnam War and demanded the government impose increased taxes on corporate profits for use in black and poor communities. In the article "Here's Where We Are Coming From," League leaders wrote,

> The League of Revolutionary Black Workers is dedicated to waging a relentless struggle against racism, capitalism, and imperialism. We are struggling for the liberation of black people in the confines of the United States as well as to play a major role in the liberation of all oppressed people in the world.[31]

The League did more than talk. By 1969, hundreds of young blacks had joined chapters in auto plants all over Detroit, New Jersey, and California, and thousands more supported them. As black worker radicalism increased, the League evolved from a black worker organization into a left vanguard party with extensive ties in the black community. Students, the unemployed, and intellectuals joined the League in establishing the Black Star Publishing Company, Black Star Book Store, Parents and Students for Community Control, and several black student unions.

In Detroit particulary, the League was involved wherever black survival was at stake. The executive committee—composed of General Baker, Chuck Wooten, John Watson, Ken Cockrel, Mike Hamlin, Luke Tripp, and Jim Williams—was respected in black working-class homes for its single minded determination to improve the living conditions of Afro-American workers. When the National Black Economic Development Conference was held in Detroit in 1969, all seven members of the League's executive committee were included on the twenty-four member board. From this vantage point, League members were able to radicalize the conference and shift the initial call of "black capitalism" to an urgent call for socialism. The famous *Black Manifesto*, which called for reparations from white churches and synagogues, was prepared with input from the leadership of the League.

League members kept police "red squads" and FBI informers busy following their radical activities. Mike Hamlin advised black student unions. Ken Cockrel defended blacks arrested in a police shoot out. John Williams organized street youth and the unemployed. John Watson helped form the Parents and Students For Community Control. Luke Tripp and John Williams walked the streets and alleys of Detroit's black community to form the Detroit Chapter of the Black Panther Party. Where there was struggle in Detroit's black community, there was the League, organizing, educating, and empowering blacks, not for reform but for revolution. The factory floor, school boards, colleges and the streets were all arenas of the black liberation struggle.

*   *   *

This flurry of activity revolved around a Marxist ideology which saw black workers not as a part of the vanguard, but THE vanguard. The League felt pure class struggle was immobilized by white racism. In the words of Mike Hamlin, "Whites in America don't act like workers, they act like racists. And that is why I think blacks have to have organizations independent of whites."[32] This view was verified by the racism of the UAW and other white workers. The League, therefore, admitted only black members, while maintaining alliances with progressive whites and revolutionary white organizations.

By 1971, the League suffered external persecution and internal dissent. The UAW, police, and the Big Three auto makers continued to harass and sabotage League activities in the plants and in the streets. Internally, divisions arose between those who leaned toward building a revolutionary union concerned only with black workers (General Baker and Chuck Wooten represented this nationalist trend) and those who favored increased ties with the black community and the development of a multinational workers' party (John Watson, Ken Cockrel, and Mike Hamlin were leaders of the Marxist trend in the League).

In 1971, the latter three resigned from the League to form the Black Workers' Congress (BWC), a multinational, anti-imperialist vanguard party led by black workers. For several years BWC chapters were at the forefront of black, labor, and anti-war campaigns. The Congress also influenced other black leftist organizations, including the Congress of Afrikan Peoples and the Revolutionary Communist League.

With the departure of Watson, Cockrel, and Hamlin, the League focused primarily on black workers' struggles. Unfortunately, the economic recession of 1973 decimated the League. Many of the most active members were young blacks with little seniority (many had been hired since the Detroit rebellion of 1967) who were fired when the auto companies laid off hundreds of workers in 1973. The League finally disbanded in 1973 with many of its cadre continuing their black liberation work in the Black Workers' Congress, the Revolutionary Communist League, and other Socialist organizations.

Despite its dissolution, the League made concrete improvements for black workers on the shop floor, in the union hall, and in the streets of Detroit. Moreover, the League's activities and struggle are evidence of the revolutionary potential of black workers. Like the black sharecropper strikes of the 1880s, the Afro-American auto workers of Detroit showed that history is written not by a gifted few, but by the masses of exploited toilers.

> But while we talk of revolution...we must also talk of the type of world we want to live in. We must commit ourselves to a society where the total means of production are...placed into the hands...of the people. We HAVE an ideology...we are dedicated to building a socialist society...led by revolutionary blacks who are concerned about the total humanity of this world...whether it happens in a thousand years is of no consequence. It cannot happen unless we start.[33]
> —*James Forman, Black Workers' Congress*

Worker Profiles: Charles Denby and James Boggs
Charles Denby

The life of Afro-American worker Charles Denby is typical of the millions of black men and women whose journey from the southern plantation to the northern factory resembled not escape from exploitation but merely a change in its setting. His book, *Indignant Heart: A Black Worker's Journal*, is a window into the harsh world of racist oppression.

Born in Leavitt County, Tennessee, Denby was the son of a "halfer," a folk term for a tenant farmer forced to give the landlord half of all he earned. In 1943, Denby left the riding bosses, cheating landlords and Klan rallies, and moved north to Detroit.

In Detroit, Denby found work in auto factories he described as being little different from the Berger plantation in Tennessee. Racist supervisors acted like plantation overseers, and the United Auto Workers (UAW) shop foremen abused black workers. As one of the plant's few blacks, Denby fought against discrimination and demanded that more Afro-Americans be hired and promoted.

Although worn and tired from the assembly line, Denby still found time for his people. In Local 212 and in Detroit's black and Communist organizations, Denby became known as a fearless leader and militant organizer. In *Indignant Heart* he describes his work in the NAACP, his association with the Communist Party, and his membership in the Trotskyist Socialist Workers' Party (SWP). Denby was one of the SWP's most active black members, but he eventually left the Party in protest over their lack of a program designed specifically for Afro-Americans. His biggest complaint against the SWP was, "Negro Marxists were seen not as Negroes, but as Marxists."

Despite his active participation in the rallies, demonstrations and protests of the Sixties, Denby's main struggle was on the shop floor. He fought against time-studies, speedups, and other oppressive conditions instituted by the auto companies. Denby published the newspaper *News and Letters* to link his Afro-American co-workers with other labor struggles and to organize them for survival in a brutally racist environment.

Black auto workers, Denby noted, were not so consumed in their own problems to miss the connection between racism at home and imperialism overseas. He wrote, "Where the middle-class black was very quiet, working-class blacks began to speak their minds during the assassination of Patrice Lumumba, lining up solidly behind him and the nationalist movements. The workers in my shop eagerly followed all developments...in the Congo."[34]

Denby concludes *Indignant Heart* with this manifesto:

> I consider my life story as part of the worldwide struggle for freedom. As a Black from the South U.S.A. and a Black auto production worker in Detroit, my experience has proved to me that history is the record of the fight of all oppressed people...to get human freedom in this world. I'm looking forward to that new world, and I firmly believe it is within reach, because so many others all over the world are reaching so hard with me.[35]

James Boggs

Like Charles Denby, James Boggs was born in the South and moved north where he worked twenty-seven years in Detroit's auto factories. Through his association with Trinidadian Marxist C.L.R. James, Boggs combined a sharp Socialist ideology with bitter experiences from twelve-hour days on the factory floor. Working class revolution was not something he learned in the abstract; it was an urgent remedy to the sufferings of his black co-workers.

In a 1970 article entitled, "Black Revolutionary Power," he wrote, "the role assigned to blacks in the U.S. is as scavengers; to take the leavings in every sphere, whether it be jobs, homes, schools, or neighborhoods that whites had run down and now considered beneath them."[36] In the same article Boggs criticizes nationalism, noting, "we must move beyond black nationalism before it breeds cultism...neither black capitalism, black culture, or stargazing constitutes revolution."[37]

Boggs believed that black workers were the most advanced force in the United States and were therefore obligated to lead the revolution. Embittered by their experience of suffering in America, blacks were best able to reject the fundamental values of the U.S.

Written during the Vietnam War, "Black

Revolutionary Power" condemns the United States for its technological advances and political backwardness. Boggs says a society that diverts millions to an imperialist war while people go without food, shelter, and health care must face a radical change. For this militant Afro-American auto worker, the solution was to "reverse the whole process of dehumanization by which the United States achieved its present state of material eminence, giving priority instead to the development of man as a politically conscious, socially responsible individual."[38] For Boggs, the only way to change America was for a black revolutionary party to lead a socialist revolution. Black power was not enough, for black power without revolution would duplicate the same misery as capitalism and merely change the color of the ruling class exploiters.

Black Workers Under Apartheid: The South African Congress of Trade Unions

Basebenzi Manyanani! (Workers Unite!)

Without question the most valiant warriors for workers' rights have been the black miners, laundry workers, railway workers, nurses, farmers, and domestics of South Africa. While this section deals primarily with the South African Congress of Trade Unons (SACTU), they are but one example of the courageous battle for human dignity waged by black South Africans. The struggles today of the Congress of South African Trade Unions (COSATU) are possible because of SACTU's legacy of courage and sacrifice.

South Africa combines racism, militarism and capitalism in a manner exceeded only by Adolf Hitler's Nazi Germany. The apartheid policy of the Nationalist Party relocates, miseducates, bans, arrests, fires, starves, shoots, tortures, and murders blacks at will. In no other country is it as clear that the laboring majority is producing wealth for the well-armed minority. Class oppression in South Africa is so aligned with racism that the two are indistinguishable.

Despite white military power, black South Africans have resisted white domination since the first arrival of Europeans in 1648. Although Cecil Rhodes and other ravenous capitalists won their wars with the Africans, the black struggle for self-determination continued.

When the South African Congress of Trade Unions was founded in 1955, it was not the first time black workers had arisen to battle the beast. In 1919, black workers formed the Industrial and Commercial Union of Africa (ICU). Later that year, black labor leader Clements Kadalie led two thousand African dock workers on a militant strike in Cape Town. The leaders of the strike were whisked away by the Security Police and the ICU staged several street rallies demanding their release. In a pattern that repeats itself continually in South African history, the police and army protected the interests of the dock owners by murdering twenty of the striking workers. Despite Kadalie's arrest and the police massacre, the ICU persisted with strikes, rallies, and boycotts until the dock owners relented and granted some of the union's demands.

Black members of the Communist Party South Africa (CPSA) joined the African workers to build the ICU into one of the first black working class organizations to openly defy the dehumanization of apartheid. Party members Moses Kotane, James LaGuma, Edward Khaile, Gana Makabeni, John Gomas, and Thomas Mbeko organized laundry workers, domestic servants, and factory workers into unions that challenged racist working conditions. It is no accident that the CPSA and ICU were in their heyday around the same time. In 1928, sixteen hundred of the Party's seventeen hundred and fifty members were black South Africans.

During the Twenties the ICU dominated the black South African political scene, extending their workers' rights struggle to the issues of landlessness and police repression. Black South African workers responded to the militancy and strength of the ICU, and in 1923 the union had thirty thousand members. Four years later, stunning ICU victories over racist employers had attracted one hundred thousand workers into the organization.

The South African police state panicked over the large crowds of women, students, workers, and unemployed the ICU attracted to rallies in the townships and villages. The state struck hard at the ICU, and government harassment, arrests, and sabotage wore it down. In the late Twenties, mine owners, manufacturers, and landowners refused to deal with the ICU unless they expelled their Communist Party members. Many unions in the ICU were affected by this anti-Communist hysteria and dropped some of their most radical black members. Weakened by this expulsion of a committed cadre, the ICU in the early Thirties was only a shadow of its former radicalism. A few years later the ICU was disbanded, a victim of the harsh measures taken by the police and army in concert with the capitalist vultures of South Africa.

Black South African mine workers were among the most oppressed workers in the industrialized world. Cut off from fresh air, sunlight, and firm ground, black miners were forced into the most dangerous jobs and paid as little as one-tenth of what white miners earned. Almost every day in South Africa the lifeless body of a black miner was hauled up and pulled from the mine shaft. Dozens more were buried alive, their cries muzzled under the cold earth and their outstretched hands stilled from their search for the white man's gold. So dangerous was the life of the black miner that white mine owners relied exclusively on migrant workers. White South Africans imposed "hut taxes" on black farmers in order to make farming unprofitable and to force African men into the labor market as underpaid miners.

In 1941, black Communist Party member J.B. Marks founded the African Mine Workers' Union (AMWU). The AMWU did not simply arise from nowhere; it was the result of Marks, his Communist comrades, and oppressed miners defying death as they met by the moonlight in the dilapidated quarters of the migrant workers. Black women food vendors helped recruit members and announce meetings by hiding union flyers and pamphlets inside food wrappings. Active in the CPSA, the ANC, and the African Mine Workers' Union, Marks was one of the most influential black Communists in South Africa. He was respected by black workers for his tireless commitment to their cause and his dedication to the liberation of South Africa. In 1944, the AMWU had twenty-five thousand members, hundreds of them recruited and trained by the indomitable J.B. Marks.

In 1946, the AMWU tested its labor power. One hundred thousand Africans defied company threats and walked out for better wages, vacations, and safety inspections. Twenty-six mines were shut down, silent monuments to the strength of the African workers. The owners had no intention of sharing their wealth with black migrant workers, and with the help of the government, viciously attacked the unarmed strikers. For two weeks South African police and company vigilantes terrorized the miners with machine guns, hand grenades, and batons. With twelve strikers murdered and another twelve hundred injured, Marks and the leadership of the AMWU called off the strike.

After the 1946 miners' strike, the government sought to ensure the mine owners would never again be troubled by complaining workers. The Nationalist Party passed the Suppression of Communism Act, a law that made communism illegal and defined as a Communist as anyone who fought for the rights of black workers. It was evident that the law especially targeted black radicals when Security Police arrested and imprisoned J.B. Marks under the act.

Repression only intensified the militancy of black African workers. In 1955, black miners, textile workers, laundry workers, farmers and railway workers formed the South African Congress of Trade Unions (SACTU). The first multi-racial trade union to struggle both for workers' rights and political power, SACTU noted in its "Declaration of Principles": "The future of the South

African people is in the hands of its workers. Only the working class, in alliance with progressive minded sections of the community, can build a happy life for all South Africans, a life free from unemployment, insecurity and poverty, free from all racial hatred and oppression, a life of vast opportunities for all people."[39]

Black workers responded to SACTU as they had to ICU forty years earlier. Thousands of black workers belonged to SACTU affiliates in Natal, Cape Town, Port Elizabeth, and Johannesburg. By 1956, twenty thousand workers, overwhelmingly African, belonged to SACTU. Six years later, one hundred thousand workers were members of SACTU unions. The black workers, leaders, and organizers in SACTU were among the most courageous and dedicated people in the history of the working class struggle. Leslie Massina, Harry Gwala, Elijah Mampuru, Elizabeth Mafekeng and others rocked the racist South African state with their dedication to their people, the black workers.

SACTU's first major campaign was the "Pound-A-Day" struggle in 1950. Under apartheid black workers earned starvation wages. Families where parents and children worked long hours often did not even have enough money for food or adequate shelter. The "Pound-A-Day" campaign demanded minimum earnings of a pound a day and an end to apartheid.

The campaign began with a bus boycott in the Transvaal led by SACTU organizer Leslie Massina. Marching and shouting "*Asinamali!*" (We have no money!), seventy thousand African workers boycotted the buses and walked to work. The boycott gained momentum, first in the Transvaal and later all over South Africa. Talk of the boycott and the "Pound-A-Day" project was everywhere as black townships were alive with activity and the promise of change. Women defied the pass laws, children marched with their parents in the streets, and SACTU emerged as a powerful voice of the African working class. South Africa again answered black defiance with military might. Mass arrests and violence negated the workers' power and few of their demands were recognized.

In 1960, a mining tragedy vividly depicted the heartlessness of South African capitalism. In the book *Organize or Starve*, Ken Luckhardt and Brenda Wall describe the incident:

> On 28 December 1959 African mine workers complained of rumblings in the Clydesdale Colliery. One day in early January 1960 at 4:20 p.m. miners on the day shift smelled gas and rushed to the pithead, only to be ordered back to work below. Twenty African miners going to work on the late shift smelled gas as they went underground. When they refused to go to the coalface, mine officials gave them the choice of returning to work, or being arrested by mine police. Two were arrested and eighteen went down under. At 7:20 p.m., three hours after the warning by the workers, the Clydesdale cave-in occurred, killing 429 Africans and 6 whites.[40]

Such is the murderous callousness of capitalism. SACTU charged the company with murder and gross neglect, but the white judge ruled, "The company has suffered enough with the loss of a valuable mine," and fined them a mere 260 pounds. The Clydesdale owners then humiliated black widows by giving them a meager lump sum payment as opposed to the lifetime pension granted to white widows and their children.

Hunted, banned, and often murdered by the South African gestapo-like secret police, the SACTU leaders struggled against a murderous machine built on black labor and sustained by white force. Discussed below are but a few of the leaders and their activities, each one of whom deserves to be the subject of an entire book.

* * *

Lawrence Ndzanga organized the South African Railway & Harbor Workers' Union into a powerful advocate for African workers in those industries. In 1963, Ndzanga was forced to resign from all trade union activity under the threat of death. During the Soweto rebellion of 1976, he was detained by the secret police and brutally murdered while in their custody. South Africa demonstrated its viciousness when on the same day they murdered Ndzanga they arrested without charge his wife Rita Ndzanga and their children.

In the Eastern Cape, Gladstone Tshume and Govan Mbeki led the Allied Food and Canning Workers' Union in a militant strike, which by 1959 forced the companies to provide paid holidays and other benefits. Tshume and Mbeki also led political education classes where they trained Vuysile Mini, Wilson Khayinga, and Zinakile Mkaba. These three men went on to Port Elizabeth where they organized African dock workers. They so infuriated the shipyard owners that all three were arrested on trumped-up charges and hanged in 1964 for a murder someone else had confessed to committing!

Harry Gwala organized African trade unions in the brick and tile industries of South Africa. Despite arrests, beatings, and harassment, Gwala was nevertheless active in both SACTU and the ANC whenever he was not in a South African prison. Eight years on Robben Island did not squelch his revolutionary spirit, for upon his release he once again joined the struggles of the black working class. In 1977, during the post-Soweto crackdown on black activists, Gwala was arrested again and imprisoned for life by the racist South African state.

In the 1930s, black CPSA member Dan Tloome worked with African trade unions until SACTU was created in 1955. Tloome worked both with SACTU and the ANC. In the mid-1950s, he published *Liberation*, a theoretical journal for radical African trade unions.

African agricultural workers were easily the "ultimate exploited." Hidden on white farms in the South African countryside, black farmers were abused unmercifully. Often forced to work fourteen-hour days without health care or adequate food, their plight resembled the Afro-American slaves'. White farmers instituted the treacherous "tot" system, which paid black children in wine and created young alcoholics.

SACTU leader Gert Sibande organized the Farms, Plantations, and Allied Workers' Union (FPAWU) to fight for the rights of black workers isolated on white farms. Elijah Mampuru, one of the best organizers in SACTU history, would leave his home in the morning for his daily rural trek and return in the evening with long lists of new members and a pocket full of dues. In one three-week period Elijah recruited four hundred African farmers into FPAWU. While the farmers' union did not revolutionize life for blacks on the farm, it did build a buffer between the tyranny and greed of white farmers and the individual black worker.

Laboring under the weight of male chauvinism, class oppression, and white racism, women in SACTU nevertheless created a brilliant legacy of struggle and courage. In 1961, black nurses led by Mate Mfusi participated in a historic strike that dramatically improved working conditions for black nurses. Before the strike, black nurses were customarily beaten with canes for alleged "offenses," and pregnant nurses were fired immediately (so the hospital would not have to pay maternity leave or hold a position open). Rather than face starvation, many pregnant nurses submitted to dangerous backyard abortions.

Conditions for the black nurses were so harsh that when the strike began, three hundred janitors, cooks, and clerks picketed in solidarity with them. After a long strike, the nurses' demands for better pay, an end to abuse, and maternity leave were granted. Mate Mfusi became a hero to African nurses everywhere as she traveled to other hospitals to organize nurses' strikes and unions.

Elizabeth Mafekeng is one of those remarkable black women activists ignored by the history books. As a girl of fourteen, Mafekeng worked in the canning industry, where workers were given no protective clothing, injuries and sickness were common, no sick leave was provided, and employees were forced to put in unpaid overtime.

After several years sweating and suffering to profit the canning owners, Mafekeng organized a local of the Allied

Food and Canning Workers' Union in her plant. A president of the local, Mafekeng fearlessly defied company threats and challenged every layoff, wage freeze, and firing in her plant. Mafekeng later joined the African National Congress and the Federation of South African Women to demonstrate her commitment to the liberation of her nation and her sisters.

In 1959, Mafekeng went to Port Elizabeth to organize the workers (sixty percent of whom were African women) against upcoming wage cuts. The government and company management could not have any rabble-rousers spoiling their plans to accelerate profits at the expense of the workers. In concert with the factory owners, the fascist Security Police banned Elizabeth Mafekeng from South Africa. The government even restricted her family from accompanying her; only one of Mafekeng's eleven children was allowed to follow her into exile in Lesotho. Separated from her family and her struggle, Mafekeng continued to urge foward her comrades through letters and the memory of her example.

Like Elizabeth Mafekeng, Frances Baard was a member of the ANC and the AFCWU. As a canning worker she fought white economic exploitation by organizing her co-workers into a local of SACTU's canning workers' union. In the Fifties and Sixties Baard could be seen in the forefront of every demonstration, strike, speech, boycott, and picket in Port Elizabeth. The South African police called her *"'n'groot agitator"* (the great agitator), a backhanded tribute to her tireless work on behalf of the oppressed.

In a 1955 rally, Baard inspired black workers with a stirring speech: "No matter where you work, unite against low wages... unite in an unbreakable solidarity and organization which is the only protection we can possess against low wages, injustice, and oppression."[41] The government hated Baard's popularity among the workers of Port Elizabeth and finally decided she had to be eliminated. Banned, jailed, and finally exiled, Baard was forcibly moved to a corrugated iron shack one thousand miles from her home and family. Now over 60, Frances Baard, the trade union activist, freedom fighter, and women's activist, will probably die in exile, hundreds of miles from the struggle to which she committed her life.

The arrest of J.B. Marks, the murders of Lawrence Ndzanga and Vuysile Mini, and the exiles of Frances Baard and Elizabeth Mafekeng are clear proof that the economic exploitation of apartheid will never change except by armed revolution. Any hopes of peaceful change are but wishful thinking and fleeting illusions. The stand of South African miners, railroad workers, nurses, farmers and canning workers against the hideous monster of apartheid is a leading force in the struggle for self-determination.

Carrying The Torch:
The Congress of South African Trade Unions

Despite the bloodshed and sacrifice of dedicated SACTU members from 1955 to 1976, their struggles were not wasted. These courageous African miners, railway workers, nurses, and farmers paved the way for the powerful Congress of South African Trade Unions (COSATU) presently challenging the apartheid regime.

Although formed in 1985, within two years the predominantly black union federation had six hundred thousand members. COSATU's growth is due primarily to its strategy of building strength on the shop floor, and from that base addressing the injustices both in the workplace and throughout South African society.

During the peoples' movements in South Africa in the 1980s, COSATU directly challenged the foundation of aparthied. On May 1 and June 16 of 1986, COSATU leaders Elijah Barayi, Jay Naidoo, Amon Msane, Maxwell Xulu, Geoffery Vilane, and others led massive general strikes where two million black workers walked out. The strikes were held on the anniversaries of May Day and the Soweto rebellion of 1976, vividly portraying the political consciousness of South Africa's working class.

While Bishop Desmond Tutu brought apartheid to the attention of the world, the ANC organized in the townships, and the United Democratic Front agitated through protests and demonstrations, COSATU members struck apartheid at its most critical area: the point of production. Strikes in chemical companies, mines, and food processing plants paralyzed South Africa's industry. Although the western press minimized the significance of two million South African workers on strike, the 1986 actions inspired black folk all over the world, from Newark to Haiti to Brixton.

Realizing their vulnerability to militant black worker actions, South Africa struck back like a savage hound. During the 1986 state of emergency (South Africa's fascist ruling which allows detention without charge or trial), hundreds of COSATU leaders and shop stewards were arrested. Militant black workers, in fact, were suppressed as hard as any other anti-apartheid organization. Several of those arrested were tortured and beaten.

COSATU moved forward despite the repression. Maxwell Xulu, national treasurer for the union federation, explains their strategy for survival:

> COSATU is formed around four principles. We aim to have one union in each industry...Unless there is an organized working class movement, we will not be able to dismantle apartheid. Secondly, our policy is of non-racialism. The question of 'divide and rule' has always been very helpful to the employers...The third point is our policy of relations with other organizations. We must have links with other unions around the world. The fourth point is on disinvestment. In South Africa, it is a treasonable crime to call for economic sanctions. But nevertheless, we at COSATU adopted a resolution where we support all kinds of pressures against the South African regime.[42]

If Clements Kadalie of the ICU and J.B. Marks of the African Mine Workers' Union ignited the torch of resistance, then the workers of COSATU continue to carry it. The South African regime's repeal of the hated pass laws in 1986 was not due to any sentimental change of heart. Their decision came days after COSATU threatened a massive boycott unless P.W. Botha and his racist Nationalist Party repealed this symbol of degradation. Botha's concession demonstrated how organized black workers can transform a racist and exploitative society.

In 1987, a COSATU affiliate, the National Union of Mineworkers (NUM), defiantly challenged a cornerstone of apartheid—migrant labor. Members of the largest black trade union in South Africa, NUM coal miners boldly brought their wives and children to live with them in South Africa's notorious single-sex hostels. This audacious act crumbled the foundation of apartheid's attempt to squelch resistance by destroying black families. Johnson Mpukumpa was typical of the exploited migrant worker. For eighteen years Mpukumpa shared a "kitchen room" with another mineworker, visiting his family in a Transkei village twice a year at Christmas and Easter.

Through NUM, Mpukumpa and thousands of his comrades defied the mineowners by moving their wives and children into the hostels of seven coal mines. Cyril Ramaphosa, general secretary of NUM, reflected the sentiments of the rank and file when he noted, "The time has come for miners and their families to start living naturally."

Like those before them in the ICU and SACTU, the hardened workers and organizers of COSATU are engaged in a life and death struggle with contemporary Nazism. It is only a matter of time before South Africa's black worker prevails over the beast, and the shame and horror of apartheid becomes a historical artifact. The indescribable pain, sweat and suffering of black workers is matched only by their tenacious resistance and determination in South Africa, their victory could ignite anti-imperialist struggles among Third World peoples in Africa, Central America and the United States.

Black Women Socialists Sisters in Struggle:

- Angela Davis
- Lucy Parsons
- Capitola Tasker
- Louise Thompson
- Claudia Jones
- Ericka Huggins
- Sandy Smith
- Joanne Chesimard
- Women in Zimbabwe

Sisters In Struggle: Black Women Socialists

Every historical phase of human civilization has been marred by the subjugation of women. Capitalism, with its worship of private property and the individual's right to exploit, continues this sorry tradition. In a 1919 *Pravda* article, V.I. Lenin wrote,

> In words bourgeois democracy promises equality and freedom, but in practice not a single bourgeois republic...has granted women and men complete equality...or delivered women from the dependence on and the oppression of the male...Education, culture, civilization, freedom—all these high-sounding words are accompanied in all the capitalist, bourgeois republics of the world by incredibly foul, disgustingly vile, bestially crude laws that make women unequal in marriage and divorce.[1]

For black people living in capitalist societies, whites have superimposed racism over a system that already exploits the working masses. Under capitalism, therefore, whether in African neo-colonialism or U.S. "free enterprise," black women suffer as workers, as blacks, and as women.

Fighting against odds that stagger the imagination, pressed up against the wall by forces that seek to destroy her and her children, the black woman resists with indescribable courage. The women discussed in this chapter, Angela Davis, Ericka Huggins, Capitola Tasker, Claudia Jones, Teurai Nhongo and others, merely reflect the black woman's will to resist. No radical black movement, whether it be the Black Panther Party, Angola's MPLA or the African National Congress, has moved forward without contributions from black women.

A Connection: Women in Struggle

Angela Yvonne Davis

Angela Davis is unquestionably the most celebrated of the remarkable Afro—American, African, and Caribbean women who participated in Socialist struggles for black liberation. No memoir of the Sixties and Seventies is complete without an account of her struggle against Governor Ronald Reagan and the University of California Regents, and her solidarity with the imprisoned Soledad Brothers.

Angela's radicalism, however, did not begin on the UCLA campus. The seeds of her revolutionary activity were planted in the racism, exploitation, segregation, and poverty in her hometown of Birmingham, Alabama. Angela's early years, like other southern-born blacks, were stained with burning crosses, racist mobs, and terrorist bombings. Her neighborhood was such a frequent target for racist bomb attacks that it was nicknamed "Dynamite Hill." Dilapidated black schools, carloads of drunken cursing white men, and the agony of being black in the racist South created in Davis both a gnawing bitterness and a desire to improve society.

As a teenager, Angela spent hours in Birmingham libraries (in the "colored" section, of course) searching in books for an answer to the misery of her people. Birmingham was too small and stifling for Angela's inquiring mind, and she escaped the mediocrity of the South's "education for servitude" to attend high school in New York City.

Despite McCarthyism, some New York public schools continued to deal objectively with socialism in history classes. Angela notes in her autobiography, *With My Mind On Freedom*:

> When I learned about socialism in my history classes a whole new world opened up before my eyes. For the first time, I became acquainted with the notion that there could be an ideal socioeconomic arrangement... The *Communist Manifesto* hit me like a bolt of lightning. I read it avidly, finding in it answers to many of the seeming unanswerable dilemmas which had plagued me.

> I read it over and over again...enthralled by the possibility of a communist revolution here...I began to see the problems of black people in the context of a large working class movement.[2]

Marx explained the force behind white racism. Klan rallies, school segregation, and poll taxes were the means by which Afro-Americans were maintained as an unprotected labor reserve. They were then used by the power elite to divide labor movements, drive down wages, and provide mines, mills, and plantations with a pool of underpaid, overworked toilers. The virulent racism of the redneck sheriff and poor white farmer only served to bolster the profits of the bankers and owners, leaving the sheriff and the farmer not richer but secure in the knowledge that "at least I'm not a nigger."

When Angela Davis looked at Birmingham in the context of the *Communist Manifesto*, she uncovered the roots of black suffering.

> Images surged up in my mind of Black workers in Birmingham trekking every morning to the steel mills or descending into the mines. Like an expert surgeon, this document cut away the cataracts from my eyes. The eyes heavy with hatred on Dynamite Hill; the roar of explosives, the fear, the hidden guns, the weeping Black women at our door, the children without lunches...it all fell into place. What had seemed a personal hatred...became the inevitable consequence of a ruthless system which kept itself alive by encouraging spite, competition, and the oppression of one group by another. Profit was the cold and constant motive for the behavior, contempt, and despair I had seen.[3]

Marxism did not leave Davis simply with an analysis of America's problems, it empowered her with the prospect of revolution. By accepting communism at age sixteen, Angela Davis changed both herself and the world.

> The most powerful impact the *Manifesto* had on me was the vision of a new society...without exploiter and exploited...where no one would be permitted to own so much he could use his power to exploit other human

beings. The final words of the *Manifesto* moved me to an overwhelming desire to throw myself into the communist movement. 'The Communists disdain to conceal their views and aims. They openly declare that their ends can be attained only by the forcible overthrow of all existing social conditions. Let the ruling classes tremble at a communist revolution. The proletarians have nothing to lose but their chains. They have a world to win.'[4]

On February 1, 1960, black students in Greensboro, North Carolina, triggered the historic sit-in movement by refusing to leave the lunch counter in Woolworths. As a member of Advance, a Marxist-Leninist youth organization, Angela participated in solidarity rallies in support of the Greensboro sit-in. In Advance, Davis worked with Mary Lou Patterson, Phyllis Strong, Margaret and Claudia Burnham, and Harriet Jackson, all daughters of well-known black leaders in the Communist Party USA. After studying literature at prestigious Brandeis University, Angela Davis continued her education in France and Germany. Formal schooling did not preclude social action, and while in Europe, Davis supported the Algerian anti-colonial guerilla war and other anti-imperialist causes.

Davis's real commitment, however, lay with the Afro-American people. Her resolve to rejoin their struggle was intensified on September 9, 1963, when four black girls were murdered in the racist bombing of Birmingham's 16th Street Baptist Church. Denise McNair, Addie Mae Collins, Cynthia Wesley, and Carole Robertson had jumped rope, played house, and shared dolls with Angela's sister Fania. Now, white America deemed them unfit to live, scattering their dismembered bodies among the debris of their Sunday school classroom.

Upon completion of her European education, Angela returned to the United States to pursue a doctorate in philosophy at the University of California at San Diego (UCSD). As in Europe, Davis was not confined to the classroom and the library. She was a leader in the Free Speech movement and in the students' fight to bring a Third World College to UCSD. Moving on to the University of California at Los Angeles (UCLA) as a

Violent Coordinating Committee (SNCC), she was deeply involved with the struggle for democracy by Los Angeles' black community. Through the SNCC Davis met Franklin and Kendra Alexander, two members of the Communist Party USA. Franklin, Kendra, and Angela soon became leaders in the community's response to the slaying of Gregory Clark. The eighteen year-old Clark had been stopped by the police, allegedly for drinking while driving (although the cans on the floor were all soda cans). The police officers handcuffed Clark, and according to witnesses, shoved him to the ground where they unloaded their .38 revolvers in the back of his head.

The Clark murder was only a beginning for Davis's rise as a radical leader on the West Coast. Through the SNCC she worked with the Black Panther Party on community self-defense and on ending police brutality. Her most significant involvement, however, was with the Che-Lumumba Club. Founded by Charlene Mitchell (1968 Presidential candidate of the CPUSA), the Che-Lumumba Club was a militant, all-black collective of the CPUSA. The club provided Angela and other members with a forum to exchange ideas on radical black political action.

> I needed to become part of a serious revolutionary party. I wanted an anchor. I needed comrades with whom I could share a common ideology. I was tired of ephemeral, ad-hoc groups that fell apart when faced with the slightest difficulty...I turned over my fifty cents—the initial membership dues—to the chairman of the Che-Lumumba Club, and became a full-fledged member of the Communist Party.[5]

The club and the Black Panther Party developed political education classes for teenagers at a Los Angeles community center. Angela's class often had over two hundred students (many of whom had difficulty reading) who studied and discussed Lenin's *The State and Revolution* and other Communist literature.

Shocked by the popularity of Davis and her comrades, reactionary forces targeted selected movement leaders. Franco, a leader of the Black Panther Party, was found murdered in an alley. A few weeks later, Black Panther Party members Bunchy Carter and Jon Huggins were murdered by cultural nationalists on the UCLA campus. Panther and club members were harassed, arrested, and jailed on dubious charges. Even SNCC yielded to the anti-Communist movement, expelling club member Franklin Alexander from the L.A. SNCC for being a "Maoist Communist."

California's governor joined the assault on Angela Davis. Resurrecting a backward 1949 policy denying employment to Communists, Governor Ronald Reagan and the University Board of Regents tried to fire Angela Davis for her political beliefs. Like Paul Robeson before the House Committee on Un-American Activities, Angela told her adversaries, "Yes, I am a communist, and I will not take the fifth against self-incrimination because my political beliefs do not incriminate me, they incriminate the Nixons, Agnews, and Reagans. These men are the capitalist yes-men who have stolen the wealth of the world."[6] Progressive faculty and students held mass rallies in support of professor Davis, and Reagan and the Regents backed down.

* * *

George Jackson, John Clutchette, and Fleeta Drumgo, three black males in Soledad penitentiary, were charged with the 1970 murder of a white prison guard. Without evidence or witnesses, the state of California proceeded with the murder charge. Angela Davis saw their pictures in the newspaper and noted, "Their faces were so serene and strong, but their waists were draped in chains."[7] This image of young black men shackled like slaves moved Davis to work for their liberation. To Angela the case of the Soledad Brothers was similar to the 1931 Scottsboro Boys rape case or the ridiculous 1951 charge against W.E.B. DuBois. All three represented the government's attempt to crush black liberation movements through intimidation and terror.

Leading community demonstrations and campus rallies, Davis and her comrades in the Che-Lumumba Club committed long hours to the Soledad Defense Committee. Georgia Jackson (Jackson's mother), Inez Williams (Drumgo's mother), and Doris Maxwell (Clutchette's mother) rallied the committee with their powerful testimony of the misery, miseducation, and poverty of their sons' lives. The struggles of these middle-aged black women inspired Angela and the Defense Committee. Moved by their example, Davis became immersed in the campaign to free the Soledad Brothers. She later wrote,

> At UCLA I was fighting for my right as a black woman, as a Communist, as a revolutionary, to hold onto my job. In Soledad Prison, George Jackson, John Clutchette, and Fleeta Drumgo were fighting for their rights as black men, as revolutionaries, to hold on to their lives. Same struggle. Same enemies.[8]

When Angela finally met George Jackson she was impressed by his revolutionary fervor. Despite the chains, prison walls, and murder charge, George's optimism of the eventual liberation of Afro-America was infectious. She maintained a regular correspondence with George, and many of his responses were published in his classic revolutionary manifesto, *Soledad Brother.*

In two years Angela Davis had become the most prominent revolutionary Afro-American woman. Gregory Clark, Bunchy Carter, Jon Huggins, Che-Lumumba Club, the SNCC, the Black Panther Party, the Soledad Brothers, anti-Communist governors and regents, UCLA death threats, street rallies, political education classes—Angela's revolutionary energy was unmatched. In 1970, a shoot-out in a San Rafael courthouse would catapult her to international prominence.

Through the Soledad Brothers campaign, Davis met

the younger brother of George Jackson, sixteen year-old Jonathan Jackson. She noticed upon first meeting him that he was deeply committed to his brother's freedom. Davis later wrote,

> Jonathan wanted only to talk about George. All of his activities, all of his interests were bound up in some way with his brother in Soledad... The last time he had seen George on the 'free' side of the walls, he was a seven year-old. From that time... there had been visits overseen by armed guards in Chino, Folsom, San Quentin, Soledad.[9]

On August 7, 1970, Jon Jackson's zeal for his brother's freedom erupted into action. With guns drawn, young Jonathan strode into the San Rafael Courthouse during a trial for inmate James McClain. He and black inmates McClain, William Christmas, and Ruchell Magee tried to flee with two hostages. The guards opened fire, killing Jackson, McClain, Christmas, and one of the hostages. The San Rafael Courthouse shoot-out sent shock waves throughout the nation, and the FBI searched frantically for accomplices.

The FBI "traced" Jon Jackson's gun to Angela Davis, and that was all President Nixon and J. Edgar Hoover needed to convince the nation that San Rafael was only part of Davis's scheme to foment revolution in America. As an admitted Communist, she was a perfect suspect. Angela immediately made the FBI's Ten Most Wanted List, only the third woman in U.S. history to achieve that distinction. With hysterical bulletins about the philosophy professor being "armed and dangerous," the FBI and local police forces hounded Davis across the country.

Finally captured in a Howard Johnson Motel in New York, Angela was hauled off to prison. In jail her stature increased in the eyes of the black community, for many saw the allegations as an excuse to neutralize one of the most outspoken black radicals of that time. Nixon, meanwhile, congratulated the reactionary J. Edgar

Hoover for "setting this example for all other terrorists."

Angela's politics permeated the Women's House of Detention in New York. The poor, black, and Puerto Rican women there looked up to Angela as someone who, despite her education, remained committed to the oppressed. In the courtyards, lunch halls and laundry rooms, Angela conducted political education classes for female prisoners. Already victims of the "free market," the women in the House of Detention eagerly discussed the writings and theories of George Jackson, Mao, and Lenin. The philosophy professor who had lectured the children of California's middle class now taught New York's expendable lower class.

Prison life impressed upon Davis the rich legacy of black struggle for self-determination in America. While looking through several old books in the prison library, she noticed that Claudia Jones had checked out some of those same volumes. The courageous Claudia Jones, one of the greatest Afro-American Communists, had been imprisoned twenty years earlier for fighting the same enemy as Angela Davis. That Claudia Jones stood in her place at another time filled Angela with both a sense of history and a renewal of courage.

Although her spirits were lifted by visits from Communist Party member Charlene Mitchell and Henry Winston, she was unconsolable after hearing news of George Jackson's murder. In 1971, George Jackson (like so many other black men both in and out of jail), was shot in the back by a white law officer. The ultimate irony was George's posthumous acquittal one year later.

After two years of pretrial motions, jury selections, and the trial itself, in 1972 Angela was acquitted of conspiracy to kidnap and conspiracy to commit murder charges. Bettina Aptheker's book, *The Morning Breaks*, covers the details of the trial, from the vibrant support of the progressive community to the state's lies and treachery.

Davis continues her work for the liberation of black people through socialism. Still active in the Communist Party, Angela Davis inspires Afro-American activists with her fiery challenges to the racism and imperialism of the United States. Her commitment to black political prisoners continues with the National Alliance Against Racist and Political Repression, an organization founded by Angela and others, who knew George Jackson would not be the last "Soledad Brother."

Her most recent book, *Women, Race & Class*, addresses sexism and racism as extensions of capitalism. Outlining the history of black and white women in the labor, abolitionist, and suffrage movements, Angela's book is a testament to her own struggle on behalf of the oppressed. From a little black girl in Birmingham to the symbol of Afro-American resistance in the Sixties and Seventies, Angela Yvonne Davis's life demonstrates the power of revolutionary theory when embodied in one who is oppressed three ways: for her race, for her class, and for her sex.

> For me revolution was never an interim thing to do before settling down; it was no fashionable club with newly minted jargon or a new kind of social life—made thrilling by risk and confrontation, made glamorous by costume. Revolution is a serious thing, the most serious thing in a revolutionary's life. When one commits oneself to the struggle it must be for a lifetime.[10]

Lucy Parsons: The Forerunner

Born in 1853, Lucy Parsons was the first Afro-American woman actively involved in Socialist politics. From 1877, when she joined the Socialist Labor Party, to her death in 1942, Lucy Parsons agitated for the rights of labor, blacks, and women.

In her early years as an anarchist, Parsons demanded the abolition of all forms of political authority. In every city the police harassed her and often prevented her from addressing rallies and demonstrations. When her husband was arrested in the Chicago Haymarket Square Riot of 1886, Lucy Parsons went out on the circuit in defense of the demonstrators.

In the early 1900s, Parsons worked in the radical Chicago Working Women's Union and the Socialist

Labor Party, and was one of the first women to join the International Workers of the World (IWW). A key figure in national radical movements, Parsons recruited many of the women who later became leaders in America's labor and suffrage movements. At the founding convention of the IWW, Parsons dealt with the subjugation of women by noting, "wherever wages are to be reduced, the capitalist class uses women to reduce them."[11]

Deeply impressed by the accomplishments of the Bolshevik Revolution in Russia in 1917, Parsons soon became involved in the Communist Party-influenced International Labor Defense (ILD). While in the ILD Parsons organized and agitated for freedom for the Scottsboro Boys and young black Communist miner Angelo Herndon. In 1939, Lucy Parsons formally joined the Communist Party and spent the last years of her life building the CPUSA.

Capitola Tasker, Lulia Jackson, and Mabel Byrd

In 1934, four black women joined the U.S. delegation that traveled to Paris for the International Women's Conference. Capitola Tasker, Lulia Jackson, Mabel Byrd, and a woman representing the mothers of the Scottsboro Boys were leaders in various left movements in the United States. Byrd was elected one of the conference secretaries, and Tasker and Jackson stunned the conference with their eloquent testimonies about Afro-American struggles for human dignity.

Lulia Jackson was active in the bitter Pennsylvania miner strikes and was familiar with the violence perpetrated by the owners. When delegates at the convention called for a "peace resolution," Lulia thundered, "Ladies, it has just been said that we must not fight, that we must be gentle and kind to our enemies, to those who are for war. I can't agree with that. Everyone knows the cause of war—it is capitalism. We can't just give those bad capitalists their supper and put them to bed the way we do with our children. We must fight them."[12]

Capitola Tasker was a black sharecropper from Alabama whose moving testimony about racist repression of the black sharecroppers' union movement shocked the delegates. She compared the racist terror suffered by Afro-Americans with the fascism growing in Italy and Germany. Before leaving the conference to return to Alabama she said,

> When I get back to Alabama and go out to that cotton patch back of our little old shack, I'll stand there thinking to myself, Capitola, did you really go over there to Paris and see all those wonderful women...or was it just a dream? And if it turns out that it really wasn't a dream...I'm just going to broadcast all over Alabama all that I've learned here, and tell them how women from all over the world are fighting to stop the kind of terror we have in the South, to stop war.[13]

Louise Thompson: Communist in Harlem

As a Harlem Communist leader, Louise Thompson was active in both politics and culture. Educated as a socialworker, Thompson taught at Hampton Institute and came to New York under the prestigious Urban Fellow program. Racism and sexism denied Thompson the opportunities her edcuation promised, and while in Harlem she searched for a way to change the society that held her back. Her friend William Patterson, a member of the Communist Party U.S.A., encouraged her to study Marx and Lenin. Impressed with socialism's scientific analysis of capitalism and the program for revolutionary change, Louise Thompson joined the CPUSA.

She quickly emerged as a leader in the Harlem branch of the Party, and by 1930 her apartment became a forum where black intellectuals and activists discussed the Bolshevik Revolution and the Party's position on Afro-Americans in the South. Louise Thompson invited the artists and writers of the Harlem Renaissance to her home to meet Party members and discuss strategies for utilizing art to further the struggle.

In 1932, she went to the Soviet Union with a group of

black writers and actors who had been invited to make a film about black life in America. A few years later she and Langston Hughes formed the Harlem Suitcase Theater, a collective dedicated to "proletarian theater," worker solidarity, and the eventual victory of a Communist revolution. Louise also formed The Vanguard, a left-wing group that sponsored dance, theater, and music performances in Harlem.

In addition to her work in the arts, Thompson was involved in other Party activity in Harlem. Known throughout Harlem as "Madame Moscow" for her support of Russia, she formed the Friends of the Soviet Union to educate Afro-Americans on the progress of the Bolshevik Revolution. Louise also worked with Party leaders in ending job discrimination and demanding unemployment relief during Harlem's Depression years. Her main contribution, however, was in the arts, and for several years her work to combine leftist politics with black art influenced the Communist Party.

* * *

Claudia Jones: To Die Fighting

Claudia Jones, born in Trinidad, was one of the most respected members of the CPUSA. This young articulate woman joined the Communist Party after her involvement with them in the defense of the nine Scottsboro Boys. Soon after joining the Party she led the CPUSA's Women's Commission and led Harlem's Councils of the Unemployed.

Jones, like Harry Haywood, was a firm believer in the CPUSA's political theory of "Self-determination for the Black Belt South." This view held that blacks in the South constituted an oppressed nation, not just a discriminated race, and consequently had the right to self-determination. When Party Chairman Earl Browder dismantled the Self-determination position, Claudia Jones saw this as a betrayal of oppressed blacks in the South and bitterly challenged this view. She wrote that

Browder's view was "based on the pious hope that the struggle for full economic, social, and political equality for the Negro people...would be brought through reforms from the top."[14]

For Claudia Jones the slogan "Self-determination for the Black Belt South" represented a truly revolutionary sentiment that fueled the Party's work in the Scottsboro case, the Sharecroppers' Union, and their courageous organizing in the textile and steel mills of North Carolina and Alabama. Based on the legitimate Afro-American demands for land, equality, and freedom, Jones felt the Self-determination thesis was the only hope for black liberation in America.

Claudia Jones also worked to end the class, race and sex oppression of black working women. In an article entitled "An End To The Neglect Of The Problems Of Negro Women," Jones argued that only socialism could liberate black women from the stifling clutches of racism, male chauvinism, and exploitation. She eloquently described the leadership roles played by black women in southern sharecroppers' unions and the courageous leadership of Miranda Smith and Velma Hopkins in the North Carolina tobacco strikes.

A fiery advocate for the most abused sectors of the black working class, Jones paid particular attention to the plight of black domestic workers. She condemned her white Party comrades who preached revolution but exploited their maids and servants at home. She wrote,

> the continued relegation of Negro women to domestic work has helped to perpetuate and intensify chauvinism directed against all Negro women...The very economic relationship of Negro women to white women, which perpetuates 'madame-maid' relationships, feeds chauvinist attitudes and makes it incumbent on white women progressives, and especially communists, to fight consciously against all manifestations of white chauvinism.[15]

As an active Communist and militant defender of

sharecroppers, domestics, and laborers, Claudia Jones was declared a criminal during the frenzy of the late 1950s. Like several of her comrades, Jones was indicted under the fascist Smith Act and sentenced to prison in New York State. After ten months in jail she was released and deported to England as an "undesirable alien." She fell ill, and died soon after her arrival in England.

An uncompromising fighter for black liberation, Claudia Jones's life was consumed with struggle. When corporate America exploited black workers, she fought them. When the Party leadership backtracked on the Self-determination thesis, she fought them. When wealthy whites (even her Party comrades) abused domestic workers, she fought them. Articulate, courageous, dedicated, Claudia Jones fought whoever stood between the people and freedom. Indeed, her imprisonment, deportation, and early death demonstrated the lengths to which America would go in silencing this radical black woman.

Ericka Huggins: Poems and Revolution

Poet and Black Panther Party member Ericka Huggins was typical of the strong black women who joined the Party in the sixties. Outspoken and articulate, Huggins held the Los Angeles chapter together after her husband Jon was murdered along with Bunchy Carter at the UCLA campus. When she saw her demoralized comrades she shouted, "What's wrong with you all? We can't stop now. We've got to keep struggling."

Rebuilding her life after Jon's murder, Ericka moved to her hometown of New Haven, Connecticut with her two year-old daughter Mai. Ericka established herself as a leader in New Haven's black community and slowly built a local chapter of the Black Panther Party. Due primarily to her efforts, the New Haven chapter became known in the Black Panther Party for its dedicated cadre of female members.

In 1969, Bobby Seale came to New Haven to participate in the Panther movement there. Fresh from his courtroom encounter in Chicago where Judge Julius Hoffman ordered him to be chained and gagged, Seale attracted the attention of the FBI and the New Haven police. The national pattern of government repression against the Black Panthers was continued in New Haven when the police arrested Seale, Huggins, and twelve other members of the New Haven Black Panther Party for the murder of Panther Alex Rackly. Among those indicted for murder or conspiracy to commit murder were Frances Carter, Margaret Hudgins, Loretta Luckes, and Rose Smith, all women recruited into the Party by the zealous Ericka Huggins.

The six-month trial ended in a hung jury when it was discovered that the actual killer of Alex Ruckly was George Sams, an admitted police agent. During her time in prison, Ericka exchanged letters with Angela Davis, submitted articles to the Party newspaper and wrote revolutionary poetry. The prostitutes, school dropouts, and petty thieves who filled Niantic State Prison admired Ericka Huggins for her undying commitment to revolutionary change.

By 1971, the government's extermination of black radicals had reached horrifying levels. Break-ins, shoot-outs, mass arrests and other means of neo-fascist rule had decimated the ranks of the Panthers and other black revolutionary organizations. Ericka encouraged her party comrades, writing, "I get angered and saddened, and my thoughts are centered on the necessity for us to move swiftly and begin to change before it is too late, before too many of us have been ruled out, jailed or sucked into the vacuum of apathy."[16]

During these repressive years, Ericka's poetry from the grey walls of prison strengthened the Party and comforted her jailmates.

<pre>
                i am ericka
              22
                fuzzy hair
</pre>

>   droopy eyes
>   long feet
>   i love nature
>   i love people
>   love love
>   i am a revolutionary
>   nothing special
>   one soul
>   one life
>   ready to give it
>   ready to die[17]

In another, untitled, piece she wrote:

>   to other women in prison
>   don't let those silly fascists
>   pluck at your nerves...
>   smile and know
>   they are sad and completely
>   void of the love that
>   people like you possess
>   love, peace, strength
>   venceremos.
>   ericka[18]

The 1971 murder of New York City Panther leader Sam Napier inspired this poem by Huggins:

>   for sam a brother/ friend of the people
>   i remember now that sam used to call me
>   sweet sister
>   and his voice had a ring to it like music/
>   sort of a soft-fast-hardworking voice
>   (always a smile to it tho)
>   that's how his soul was—soft yet strong
>   fast, yet not by passing the
>   needs of the people/ the FREE-dom of the
>   people/hardworking—yes he was
>   the sweat engraved in the issues of our
>   paper—in good times/ hard, bitter bad times
>   his is not/ nor will be forgotten...
>   love for the people self less ness
>   seems as tho he was taken away so

> unnecessarily
> seems as tho we've got a lot to learn about
> this struggle of ours
> seems as tho this country, amerika, wants
> to wipe out all the samuel napiers
> jonathan jacksons
> bobby seales of the whole world
> seems as tho we have a lot of work to do
> love to give
> freedom to give
> Good brother...
> this may be said many times, but it
> is sincere—
> you will not be forgotten, we love you,
> sweet brother we love you/
> ericka[19]

Ericka Huggins, mother, poet, Party leader, and revolutionary, fought for her people despite her husband's murder, political imprisonment and police harassment. She describes how she became involved with the Panthers in this 1970 letter from prison:

> we...were disillusioned with the nothing that students were doing...i wanted to struggle in practice, not theory. the whole nationalist thing stunk. i was looking for something real...i remember reading...about the black panther party...[I] had to go and do something. amerika was destroying the people—we felt desperately the need to help.[20]

Sandy Smith: The Price of Freedom

After its brief flirtation with justice in the 1960's, America turned sharply to the right, unmercifully rolling back the economic and political gains of Afro-Americans, workers, Chicanos, and women. During the 1970s this reactionary political climate led to an increase in flagrant racist attacks. In Miami, black insurance agent Arthur McDuffie was beaten to death by six police officers for allegedly running a stop sign. In Los Angeles the elderly Eula Love was blown away by police for failing to pay a $22.07 gas bill. And in Greensboro, North Carolina, five members of the Communist Workers' Party (CWP) were murdered by the Ku Klux Klan during a 1979 anti-Klan rally. One of the dead was Sandy Smith.

Distressed by the mounting misery of her people, Sandy Smith left her studies at Bennett College to become a professional revolutionary. Smith helped found the national black student organization YOBU (Youth Organization for Black Unity) and assisted in organizing the Revolutionary Workers' League (RWL). In the RWL Sandy and her comrades fought for the freedom of the Wilmington Ten, worked to save black colleges, and organized black and white textile workers in the Cone Mills plant in North Carolina.

In the economic slump of the late Seventies, the Klan and other racist groups blamed blacks for the growing impoverishment of white workers. In Greensboro, the Klan held public rallies to whip up race hatred among unemployed and threatened white workers. Sandy Smith, the RWL and the CWP realized that revived racism would polarize Greensboro's labor movement and allow the mill owners to steamroll a divided union. Attacking this threat to the survival and progress of her people, Smith was among those who organized the militant 1979 anti-Klan rally at which she and four others were murdered. In keeping with America's lapses into fascism, the Klansmen who pulled the triggers on that February afternoon have since been acquitted.

Joanne Chesimard: Assata Shakur

A member of the leftist Black Liberation Army, Joanne Chesimard was hunted by the FBI throughout the 1970s. In 1979, Joanne was on the FBI's Most Wanted List as a result of her escape from prison. While in prison, she bitterly attacked the system that abused her people.

It should be clear, it must be clear to anyone who can think, see or hear, that we are the victims. The victims are not the criminals... as was proven by Watergate. They call us thieves and bandits. They say we steal. But it was not us who stole millions of black people from the continent of Africa. We were robbed of our language, of our gods, of our culture, of our human dignity, of our labor and of our lives. They call us thieves yet it is not us who rip off billions of dollars every year through tax evasions, illegal price fixing, embezzlement, consumer fraud, bribes, kickbacks, and swindles. They call us bandits, yet every time we walk into a store in our neighborhood we are being held up. And every time we pay our rent the landlord sticks a gun in our ribs.[21]

Women in Zimbabwe: Teurai Ropa Nhongo

In Africa it is difficult for women to play active roles in revolutionary struggles. Traditional peasant values and reactionary colonialism joined to consign women secondary roles in society. Despite these obstacles, thousands of African women have led struggles for the liberation of their nation and their sex. Although only one is discussed here, African women in Guinea-Bissau, Ghana, Angola, South Africa, Zimbabwe, and Mozambique have led guerilla forces, planned strikes, shaped policies, and fueled African liberation movements.

In 1966, the Zimbabwe African National Union (ZANU) initiated a guerilla war to end ninety years of white racist rule. Women in Rhodesia (the colonial name for Zimbabwe) led hard and sorry lives. Their land was taken away and they were forced onto arid, unproductive lots. Their sons were shipped to South Africa to slave in the mines while soldiers and settlers dominated their bodies, families, and children.

These women, however, were not passive spectators to the liberation wars; educated and uneducated, rural and urban, Zimbabwean women fought and died for national self-determination. The most popular of these militant women was Teurai Ropa Nhongo, a party leader and senior member of her guerilla unit. Nhongo's military valor during the *Chimurenga* (liberation war) has since become legendary. While pregnant with her first child, during a fierce battle with the Rhodesian army she went into labor and left the fray. After giving birth behind a tree, Nhongo wiped the baby clean, strapped him to her back, picked up her weapon, and returned to aid her comrades in battle.

After independence in 1980, Nhongo was elected to the executive council of ZANU and was appointed Minister of Youth, Sports, and Recreation. Nhongo believes that liberated Zimbabwe has significantly changed the lives of women. In an interview for *Black Scholar* she noted:

> Women suffer the added disadvantage of being a symbol of prestige and are often treated by men as little better than a commodity. Zimbabwean women are fighting hard to be treated as full human beings, rather than objects of pleasure or tools of labor.[22]

In 1982, Nhongo and thousands of other women successfully fought for passage of the Legal Age Act, which authorized women to manage their own affairs without the consent of others. Robert Mugabe's government also created the Ministry of Community Development and Women's Affairs to deal specifically with wife abuse, sex discrimination, child care, and other issues affecting Zimbabwean women. Mugabe said the ministry was created to ensure women "are not relegated to second-class citizenship in a land they helped to liberate."[23] In an amazing display of progressive legislation for an impoverished Third World country, Zimbabwe also passed the Industrial Conciliations Act which guaranteed women employees eighty-four days maternity leave and two half-hour periods during the day for breast-feeding.

Although Zimbabwe still suffers from the stifling legacy of a peasant society and the effects of ninety years of colonialism, the future is brighter than the past with leaders like Teurai Ropa Nhongo and with a Socialist government committed to women's rights.

In The Vanguard: Black Socialist Parties in the United States and the Caribbean

- **The African Blood Brotherhood**
- **Congress of Afrikan Peoples**
- **Maurice Bishop and the New Jewel Movement**
- **The Black Panther Party**

In The Vanguard:
Profiles of Black Revolutionary Parties

Lenin and the Bolsheviks demonstrated to the world the central role a vanguard party plays in leading a Socialist revolution. While Marxism holds that the working class is the reservoir of revolutionary sentiment, it is a cadre of committed individuals who learn from, struggle with, and lead the masses of people that make revolution a reality.

In the United States, the working class is a multinational collection of whites, blacks, Chicanos, Asians, and others. While theory would call for a multinational party, in many instances virulent racism among white workers precludes such unity.

Black Socialists, consequently, founded all-black parties as the vanguard and protector of the Afro-American working class. Cyril Briggs of the African Blood Brotherhood (ABB) and Huey Newton of the Black Panther Party restricted membership to blacks not to discriminate, but to link with that broad mass of Afro-American workers for whom whites, including white workers, represented the oppressor. Nonetheless, black Socialists did not neglect internationalism, and it is significant that both the ABB and the Congress of Afrikan Peoples were later absorbed into multinational revolutionary organizations.

The dynamics of revolutionary parties differed in the Caribbean, where black Socialist parties were pitted against black neocolonial leaders, not white racism. Consequently, in predominantly black Grenada, the New Jewel Movement was oppressed by black dictator Eric Gairy, and it fought his oppression with the same intensity that its brothers and sisters fought racism in the United States.

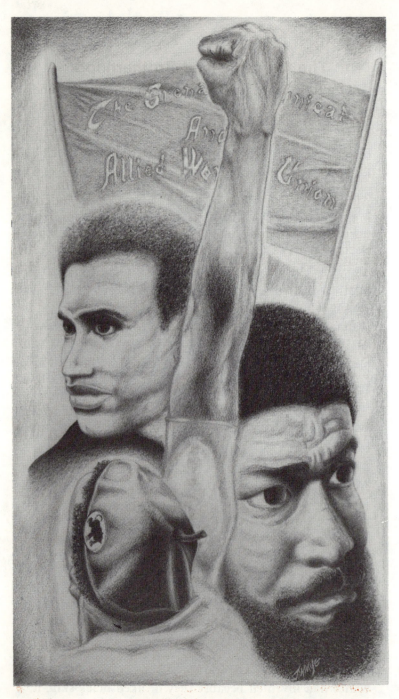

Self-Determination

The African Blood Brotherhood

In 1917, black revolutionaries Cyril Briggs and Richard Moore quit the Socialist Party because of its weak stand on black liberation. The Socialist Party felt blacks were no more exploited than their white counterparts, and consequently developed no specific program for dealing with segregation, lynchings, and disenfranchisement of the Afro-American worker. Although Briggs and Moore were West Indian immigrants, they knew enough of the poverty, unemployment, and abuse of black America to reject the Socialist Party's inertia.

At the same time, Briggs quit the *Amsterdam News* after the editorial board censored his anti-war editorials. In search of a vehicle for their radical expressions, Briggs and Moore founded the newspaper *Crusader*. At a time when Marcus Garvey's nationalism and Booker T. Washington's acquiescence were dominant themes in black America, *Crusader* and A. Philip Randolph's *The Messenger* advocated socialism as the solution to the ills of Afro-American workers. By 1918, the *Crusader* achieved a circulation of thirty-three thousand readers, evidence of black impatience with America's hypocritical democracy.

Briggs and Moore, both street-corner orators, worked in Harlem when Marcus Garvey's Universal Negro Improvement Association (UNIA) reached its zenith. While they were both attracted to UNIA's emphasis on black solidarity, Briggs and Moore believed that Garvey's separatism precluded alliances with progressive whites and obscured the real enemies of capitalism and imperialism. The two West Indians believed Garvey's statement that "capitalism is necessary for the progress of the world" left the black masses as permanent labor fodder for the western industrial giants.

Exploitation of Harlem by realtors, bankers, landlords, and factory owners convinced Briggs and Moore that racism was not simply an isolated idea that whites had invented because they disliked black skin; it was the logical outgrowth of an economic system that pitted humans against humans in the scramble for the few crumbs handed out by the rich and powerful. Since the only beneficiaries of racism were the owners and the wealthy, Briggs and Moore saw bigotry as a tool the ruling class used to keep black wages down, undermine labor unity and increase their bloated profits. Since capitalism was the enemy, it must be destroyed and a new system erected in its place. The militancy of the interracial International Workers of the World (IWW) and the example of the Bolshevik Revolution convinced Briggs and Moore that revolution was both necessary and possible.

In light of the need for revolutionary change, in 1919 Cyril Briggs and Richard Moore created the first black revolutionary organization in the United States, The African Blood Brotherhood (ABB). The Brotherhood began in Harlem, attracting West Indian and Afro-American intellectuals, organizers, and workers. The ABB was a secret cadre organization that included in its initiation rites the African fraternization ritual of mixing the blood of the applicant with that of the seasoned members, thereby sealing by sacred oath the loyalty of its members.

Every member of the Brotherhood was ranked in one of the party's seven degrees. The degrees represented stages of progress for ABB cadre. The first degree was for new members and the next five were granted according to educational progress and practical struggles in the service of the people. The seventh degree was for Superlative Service and was attained only by the Brotherhood's most selfless and dedicated members. All members, however, regardless of degree, had to believe in and practice the nine principles of the party.

1. A Liberated Race in the United States, Africa and elsewhere.
2. Absolute Racial Equality
3. The Fostering of Racial Self-Respect
4. Organized and Uncompromising Opposition to the Ku Klux Klan.
5. United Negro Front.
6. Industrial Development Along Cooperative Lines with the Profits evenly distributed among the people

participating.
7. Higher wages for Negro labor, shorter hours of work and better living conditions.
8. Education
9. Cooperation with other Darker Races and with Class-Conscious White Workers.[1]

The program of the ABB was undeniably influenced by Garvey and the UNIA. Nevertheless, Briggs, Moore and ABB members did not advocate black escape to Africa. They instead fought for black unity, alliances with progressive white workers, and bitter struggle for a new society right here in the United States.

In 1923, the African Blood Brotherhood had seven thousand members in fifty-six chapters in the Uniteds States and the West Indies, including one chapter of West Virginia coal miners. The largest chapters, however, were in Harlem and Chicago. In addition to Cyril Briggs and Richard Moore, the Harlem ABB membership included Harry Haywood, Otto Huiswood, Otto Hall, Grace Campbell, and Lovett Fort-Whiteman. When the Communist Party USA (CPUSA) recruited Afro-Americans in 1921-1922, Briggs and Moore were the first to join. The revolutionary experience of Brotherhood membrers was not wasted; Haywood, Hall, Huiswood, Campbell, Fort-Whiteman, Briggs, and Moore all became respected leaders of the CPUSA both in Harlem and in the United States.

The Chicago chapter was composed of black workers who were first organized into the Socialist Free Thought Society. Edward Doty, born in Alabama, was a labor radical and the leader of the Chicago Brotherhood chapter. His comrades, Herman Dorsey, Alexander Dunlap, Alonzo Isabel, Norval Allen, Gordon Owens, and H.V. Phillips, were familiar figures in radical black politics. The Chicago ABB organized black workers in the infamous Chicago stockyards and campaigned against the high rents black workers were forced to pay on the South Side. In Chicago, Doty also organized the American Consolidated Trades Council (ACTC), a federation of black trade unions formed to protect the black immigrant worker against harsh employers and racist AFL unions.

Nationally, the Brotherhood assisted the Communist Party in organizing the American Negro Labor Congress, a short-lived attempt to build a national link for black workers. ABB members were also active in the struggle to free the two dozen troops of the all-black 24th Infantry. While training to fight the Germans, members of the 24th were attacked (and one murdered) by racists in Houston. When the soldiers defended themselves, they were arrested and charged with attempted murder.

Although the ABB was Socialist, it promoted black solidarity in a time of growing Afro-American nationalism. Several disillusioned UNIA members left Garvey to join the ABB. The most notable UNIA member to join the Brotherhood was W.A. Domingo, a fiery Jamaican known in Harlem as one of the most militant street-corner speakers ever heard.

In a show of black solidarity, Cyril Briggs sought a united front between the UNIA and the ABB. In the early Twenties Garvey derailed attempts by Briggs and Moore to get the UNIA and ABB to work on a united front against the Ku Klux Klan and in support of organized labor. Relations eventually soured between the two organizations, with charge and counter-charge being hurled from one to the other.

By 1923, the African Blood Brotherhood ceased to exist and most members continued their revolutionary activities in the Communist Party USA. Cyril Briggs and the Supreme Council of the Brotherhood did not disband the Brotherhood out of failure; it was scuttled with the understanding that now the struggle would move to a higher level—that of a multinational party leading all workers toward a more just and democratic society. Even after the absorption of ABB members into the CPUSA, the Brotherhood's ideology had a long-term impact on the policy of the Party.

In 1918, Cyril Briggs noted that Afro-Americans were a "nation within a nation," and by the early 1920s the ABB promoted the right of black southern masses for self-government. In 1928, when the CPUSA took up the revolutionary slogan and program of "Self-determination for the Black Belt South," much of the impetus came from ex-Brotherhood member Harry Haywood.

Brotherhood members brought more than revolutionary theory to the Party; ABB cadre spearheaded Party work in the black community, and the incomparable Briggs and Moore led the way. Briggs edited the Party's Afro-American news service and served as the national secretary to the American Negro Labor Council, while Moore was president of the Harlem Tenants' League. George Padmore, Solomon Harper, and Grace Campbell also led chapters of the Tenants' League, which fought for lower rents and adequate repairs in the flats rented to black workers in Harlem. In addition, the eloquent Moore and W.A. Domingo founded the Harlem Educational Forum, a vehicle through which workers were exposed to socialism. Cyril Briggs was involved in other Party work, serving on the Party's executive committee in 1929 and directing CPUSA efforts among the unemployed and homeless in Harlem during the Depression. As the Depression decimated black families, Briggs thundered,

> Negro Workers! Where are the Negro businesses and professional class leaders in this terrrible crisis? What progress against unemployment has the NAACP, the Urban League...the UNIA? The Negro bourgeoisie does not put up a fight against Negro oppression for the reason that they have a stake in the system that oppresses us. They are the lap dogs at the table of the imperialists, demanding simply increased participation in the exploitation of the Negro masses."[2]

Cyril Briggs committed his entire adult life to building a revolutionary people's party. When he died in Los Angeles in 1966, the seventy-two year-old Briggs led the Party's West Coast Negro Commission. For a decade and a half, Cyril Briggs and Richard Moore worked together a hard as any two individuals have ever toiled for black liberation in America. By forming the African Blood Brotherhood, Briggs and Moore created the forerunner of the Revolutionary Communist League, the Black Panther Party, and every other organized expression of black revolutionary sentiment.

Congress of Afrikan Peoples and the Revolutionary Communist League

The Civil Rights Movement of the Sixties yielded to the Pan-African Movement of the Seventies. The militant nationalism of the Pan-Africanists sent shock waves through the liberal facade of American politics and linked Afro-American freedom fighters with Africa's anti-colonial wars.

The Congress of Afrikan Peoples (CAP) was at the forefront of the black nationalist movement of the 1970s. Founded in 1970 by Amiri Baraka (LeRoi Jones), and other black nationalists, CAP soon had seventeen chapters nationwide. Three thousand delegates representing two hundred and twenty Pan-African and nationalist organizations attended the founding convention and elected Amiri Baraka chairman of the Congress of Afrikan Peoples.

Active in "Stop Killer Cop" struggles and in electoral campaigns in Newark, St. Louis, and other cities, CAP also spearheaded the National Black Political Assembly where eight thousand black nationalists, leftists, intellectuals, writers, and politicians developed the 1972 Black Political Agenda. At the National Black Political Assembly Convention, delegates called for the release of black political prisoners, an end to FBI and CIA surveillance, the establishment of a minimum income for working people, and support for the African liberation movements in Guinea-Bissau, Angola, and Mozambique.

By 1974, Amiri Baraka and CAP's nationalism was challenged by the African socialism of Sekou Toure, Kwame Nkrumah, Julius Nyerere and Amilcar Cabral, and by the Marxism-Leninism of the Black Workers' Congress. In addition, the CAP-supported African Liberation Support Committee identified imperialism (not Europe) as the main enemy of Africa.

Direct experiences in the struggle for black liberation also moved CAP to the left. The continued impoverishment of the masses despite black electoral gains, the realization that the beneficiaries of racism were not white workers but the ruling class, and conflicts with black middle-class forces on united front issues led many in CAP, including Baraka, to reevaluate their black nationalism. It became increasingly clear to the leadership of CAP that black nationalism's emphasis on African traditions, black religions, male dominance, and black self-help (capitalism) could never liberate the masses of black workers. As Baraka noted in a 1975 article in *Black Scholar*, "black capitalism is profit for a few, only this few is black, but for the masses of people, no change at all...Where ever you find a superrace theory, you find a capitalist."[3]

In 1974, ideas developed through struggle and the lessons of Socialist revolutionaries in Africa moved CAP to study Marxism-Leninism and declare itself a Marxist-Leninist-Mao Zedong Party. In moving to the left, CAP struggled with local chapters and individual members over their past nationalism, male chauvinism, and the use of metaphysics and mysticism as a means of analyzing society. Baraka and CAP also developed a more international focus, supporting not only African revolutionary parties like FRELIMO, but non-black groups like the Palestinian Liberation Organization (PLO) as well.

In seventeen cities the Congress of Afrikan Peoples promoted Marxist-Leninist theory and practice, publishing the paper *Unity and Struggle* and organizing in auto plants, steel mills, foundries, and mines. CAP also addressed the particular concerns of black women by sponsoring African Women's Conferences in several cities.

Under the leadership of Amiri Baraka, the Congress focused on black revolutionary theater, music, and literature. CAP played a leading role in organizing black writers' conferences and formed the Anti-Imperialist Cultural Union, a multinational cultural workers' organization.

In 1976, CAP changed its name to the Revolutionary Communist League (RCL) and began an in-depth study of the *Selected Works of Mao Tse-Tung* and the *History of the Bolshevik Revolution*. This study led Baraka and the leadership of CAP to initiate closer ties with the black working class and make their concerns those of the RCL. Baraka later noted in a 1975 essay:

> Who would be interested in joining a socialist or communist party that says openly that your liberation ain't at the top of their agenda... We do not believe that socialism will scare the masses, because we were here in the '60s when the masses tried to burn this motherfucker to the ground."[4]

The commitment to black liberation was confirmed when, in 1976, the RCL advanced the Black Nation thesis abandoned by the Communist Party USA in the 1950s. Like the leadership of the African Blood Brotherhood in 1919, the RCL maintained that blacks in the South constituted not a race but an oppressed nation. This thesis held that Afro-Americans in the South had the right not only to equality and justice but also self-determination as a separate nation.

In 1979, the RCL merged with the League of Revolutionary Struggle (LRS) to continue the fight for black liberation through a multinational Communist organization. Like the African Blood Brotherhood in 1924, the RCL expanded from an all-black party to a multinational organization committed to both a Socialist America and an Afro-American nation in the Black Belt South.

The League's commitment to the Self-determination thesis ensured RCL members that black liberation would remain at the top of the organization's agenda. In addition, RCL leadership believed membership in the

League only strengthened the black liberation movement because it could now be coordinated with the struggles of workers, Chicanos, and Asians to win democracy and socialism in America. Through the League the black Communists of the RCL energized their movement by linking it with other struggles for democracy and by making it more difficult for the state to isolate and destroy their movement.

The League of Revolutionary Struggle, like the ABB in 1924 and the RCL in 1975, demanded "Self-determination for the Black Belt South." While the Democratic and Republican parties ignored the voting irregularities, miseducation, and poverty of the South, the League's 1984 Minimum Program of Struggle relating to Afro-Americans in the South demanded:

> —reorganization of the county lines of the South to end gerrymandering of the Black population, and end all restrictions on Black voting rights.
> —redistribution of the land of the big landlords and agribusiness to finally realize "40 acres and a mule" for Blacks.
> —an end to racist violence...
> —the right to Self-Determination for the Afro-American Nation...[5]

The League continues RCL's commitment to black culture, and LRS periodicals highlight revolutionary Afro-American music and literature. Whether on the cultural front or in the Black Belt, the black Communists who began a Pan-African struggle in CAP in 1970 continue to work to build a just and democratic society in the United States.

Maurice Bishop and Grenada's New Jewel Movement:
Forward Ever!

On March 13, 1979, forty-six cadre of the New Jewel Movement commandeered Grenada's radio station and subdued government soldiers in a nearby army barracks. This small band of revolutionary Grenadians shook the world much like Toussaint L'Overture and black Haitians did in 1791. Like L'Overture, whose black Haitian republic forced the French colonialists to their knees (it was the French defeat in Haiti that resulted in France's selling its colonial possessions, e.g., the Louisiana Purchase), Maurice Bishop and the New Jewel Movement alarmed neocolonialists in Washington and London with their talk of determining their own destiny, establishing "fraternal ties with the Cuban people," and participating in the non-aligned movement.

Grenada, the Spice Island, was home to the Carib and Arawak people until French and English conquerors exterminated them in the 1600s. English conquerors then decided this beautiful island of nutmeg, bananas, and cocoa would be most productive using slaves from Africa. Black slaves were dragged across the Atlantic, and Grenada was transformed into an island plantation where thousands of Africans sweated and died to profit a few white plantation owners. For three hundred twenty-four years, black labor enriched white capitalists.

English colonialism was replaced in 1967 by the corrupt neocolonialism of Sir Eric Gairy. For twelve years Gairy ruled Grenada through fixed elections with the help of his secret police, the Mongoose Gang. The Gang terrorized Grenadian activists, unionists, and reformers, and Gairy established ties with the American Mafia, Pinochet of Chile, and South Korean dictators. Gairy was the classic Third World neocolonialist dictator, creating a society where tourist dollars lined the pockets of a few cronies while the masses of Grenadians suffered from illiteracy, malnutrition, and unemployment.

By the time Bishop and the New Jewel Movement

overthrew Gairy in 1979, joblessness in Grenada was at forty-nine percent. Unemployment for women was at seventy percent, with the few who found work forced to choose between losing their job or submitting to sexual harassment and abuse. The economy, civil liberties, and opportunities were so wrecked that the black masses called their leader "Hurricane Gairy." The extent of Gairy's callousness was evident when he urged the United Nations to commit funds to study UFO's while his people went jobless and hungry. With finance capital running the hotels and the Mongoose Gang brutalizing the people, it appeared that Gairy would rule Grenada until his death. The people of Grenada, however, had other ideas.

Maurice Bishop returned from London to Grenada in 1970. Influenced by Julius Nyerere's socialism and C.L.R. James's independent Marxism, Bishop helped form the Movement for Advance of Community Effort (MACE) to celebrate African Liberation Day. A trained attorney, Maurice Bishop joined Kenrick Radix in defending Grenadian nurses arrested during a demonstration. For this and other defenses of Grenada's working people, Bishop soon became an immensely popular figure among the island's workers and peasants. Bishop later formed the Movement for Assemblies of the People (MAP), an organization dedicated to expanding democracy in Grenada. The inspiration for MAP, Bishop explained, originated from the Afro-American Black Power movement and the armed revolutions in Guinea-Bissau, Angola and Mozambique.

While Bishop organized MAP, Unison Whiteman and other Grenadians formed JEWEL, the Joint Endeavor for Welfare, Education, and Liberation. In March of 1973 MAP and JEWEL merged into the New Jewel Movement and developed a program for national independence and food, jobs, health, and employment for the people.

Later that year the New Jewel Movement established a People's Congress where Sir Eric Gairy was tried "in absentia" for crimes against the people and a general strike was called in protest of his policies. For this attempt at democracy, the Mongoose Gang viciously attacked Maurice Bishop, Unison Whiteman, and Sewlyn Strachan on what later became known as "Bloody Sunday." At another demonstration in 1974, the police shot and killed Maurice Bishop's father, Rupert. These and other incidents of repression forced the New Jewel Movement underground to study Marxism and to organize into a revolutionary party.

Despite vigorous opposition from Gairy and his goon squads, the New Jewel Movement continued to struggle with and for the working people of Grenada. In 1975, the Movement led a demonstration of fifteen thousand and in 1977 Bishop led a militant workers' rally calling for union recognition and political democracy. Finally, after seven years of strikes, demonstrations, sham elections, and Mongoose Gang repression, the New Jewel Movement advocated armed struggle and created the People's Revolutionary Army. It was this cadre of black Socialists who seized power from Gairy's corrupt machine and sought to build a new and productive Grenada from the ashes of colonialism.

In a radio address to the people immediately after the People's Revolutionary Army assumed power, Bishop said, "People of Grenada, this revolution is for work, for food, for decent housing and health services, and for a bright future for our children and great-grandchildren."[6] During the takeover only two people were killed, and while the Mongoose Gang was imprisoned by the People's Revolutionary Army, Sir Eric Gairy fled the country with as much wealth as he could carry. Empowered by the revolution, Bishop and the New Jewel Movement undertook the difficult task of reconstructing Grenada—not for the people, but with the people.

Within a month of the revolution the United States had already begun meddling in Grenada's affairs. Ambassador Frank Ortiz (soon to be recalled by the U.S. with the termination of diplomatic relations) warned Bishop, "We would view with displeasure the tendency on the part of Grenada to develop closer ties with Cuba."[7]

Aware that Grenada was to a large degree dependent upon tourism, Ortiz hinted the U.S. government would discourage visitors from the United States. In his final insult, Ortiz offered Grenada five thousand dollars if it would refuse ties with Fidel Castro and Cuba.

The New Jewel Movement refused, and in a radio address Bishop said:

> Sisters and brothers, what can a few $5,000 do? Our hospitals are without medicine...our schools are falling down. $5,000 cannot build a house or a health clinic. We feel forced to ask whether the paltry sum of $5,000 is all that the wealthiest country in the world can offer to a poor but proud people who are fighting for democracy, dignity, and self-respect based on a real and independent economic development...We intend to continue along an independent and non-aligned path...We are a small country, we are a poor country, with a population of largely African descent...and we definitely have a stake in seeking the creation of a new economic order which would assist in ensuring economic justice for the oppressed and exploited peoples of the world, and ensuring that the resources of the world are used for the benefit of all the people and not a minority of profiteers. Our aim, therefore, is to join all organizations and work with all countries that will help us to become more independent and more in control of our resources...Grenada is a sovereign and independent country, although a tiny speck on the world map, and we expect all countries to strictly respect our independence just as we respect theirs. We are not in anybody's backyard, and we are certainly not for sale...We would sooner give up our lives before we compromise, sell out, or betray our sovereignty, our independence, our integrity...or the right of our people to national self-determination and social progress.[8]

Once Bishop so brazenly defied U.S. imperialism, the New Jewel Movement became the constant victim of an American destabilization campaign that culminated in the 1983 invasion by U.S. Marines. Imperialist threats, however, did not diminish Bishop's zeal to create a new society in the West Indies.

The work to build a stable Grenada from the ashes of colonialism and Gairy's dictatorship was no easy task. The Central Committee and leadership of the New Jewel Movement, including Bishop, Unison Whiteman, Bernard Coard, Kenrick Radix, Don Rojas, Jacqueline Creft, Vincent Noel, Sewlyn Strachan, George Louison, Fitzroy Bain and others began the slow and deliberate process of rebuilding a land with a legacy of genocide, slavery, colonialism, and corruption.

When seen in the context of Grenada's enforced underdevelopment, the accomplishments of the New Jewel Movement from 1979 to 1983 are indeed impressive. Under Gairy, unemployment ravaged the island, leaving forty-nine percent of the people without work. By 1983, the New Jewel Movement had reduced unemployment to sixteen percent as Grenada became one of the few countries to grow economically during the slump of the early 1980s.

Sexual harassment of women was outlawed, and women workers were further protected by the Maternity Leave Law of 1980 which guaranteed three months leave. Trade unions, vigorously controlled under Gairy, were given new powers under Bishop. The right to strike was restored and companies had to recognize unions if fifty-one percent of the workers voted for representation. Public health care, free milk for children and the elderly, and a house repair program were instituted by the government.

Some of the biggest gains in Socialist Grenada were in education. As Prime Minister Maurice Bishop noted, "Perhaps the worst crime that colonialism left our country is the education system...because the way it developed...taught us self-hate and abandonment of culture, history, and values."[9] Three hundred years of colonialism left Grenada one secondary school. After two years under the New Jewel government the Grenadian people had constructed one school with plans for another. Under Gairy only three students went to study abroad, two children of the elite and Gairy's own daughter. In the "New Grenada," three years after the revolution, one hundred nine students, many children of peasants and the working class, were able to study abroad through government scholarships.

The most significant educational achievement was the abolition of illiteracy. In the past a literate population was not necessary since its only function was to produce profits for hotel owners, banana distributors and nutmeg firms. The New Jewel government created the Centre for Popular Education, a literacy program where thousands of agricultural workers, factory workers, clerical workers, farmers, and the unemployed learned to read. By 1981, the illiteracy rate had been reduced to two percent and the Centre began a comprehensive program to eliminate functional illiteracy as well.

Gairy destroyed popular rule through rigged elections and police terror. During the New Jewel Movement's brief administration, thousands of Grenadians worked in the mass organizations created by Bishop and his cabinet. Over six thousand women were members of the National Women's Organization, students joined the National Youth Organization, and hundreds of farmers participated in the Productive Farmers Union. In addition, people's councils were held in villages, workplaces, and schools all over the nation. These popular bodies provided a means by which the average Grenadian citizen could tell Maurice Bishop and other government representatives what they felt about the national budget, bus service, health care, and other social issues.

Bishop explained the relationship of the party to the people in his third anniversary address to the nation.

> As we begin the 4th year of our revolution it is very clear that the great strength of the revolution, first and foremost, lies in the unbreakable link between the masses and the party; between the masses and the government; between the masses and the state. This is what gives our revolution invincible force, because the masses see the party, see the government, see the state as theirs, not

something foreign or strange, or apart or isolated from them, but living throbbing entities that embody their aspirations, their interests, their hopes.[10]

After the United States insulted Grenada with its ridiculous five thousand dollar bribe, relations with Washington worsened with time. Bishop and the New Jewel Movement defied the U.S. by establishing ties with Cuba, declaring its solidarity with Puerto Rican independence, supporting liberation movements in El Salvador and South Africa, and aligning with the Nicaraguan Sandinista government.

A State Department memo cited other reasons why Washington should look unfavorably upon Grenada's militant black government. The State Department reasoned that since Grenadians spoke English, the revolutionaries could communicate directly with the U.S public. Even worse, a Socialist nation with a ninety-five percent black population could have a dangerous appeal to the thirty million Afro-Americans living in the United States. The latter point showed Washington's fear that black Americans inspired by the revolutionary example of Bishop and the New Jewel Movement could pose a serious threat to "domestic security."

For years Grenadians had yearned to build an international airport to make the island more accessible and spur the economy through tourism. When Cuban engineers and companies in western Europe began working on the airport at Port Salinas, Washington began a vicious smear campaign of lies and deception. Waving around unclear photos that allegedly displayed Grenada's "sophisticated military base," President Ronald Reagan claimed the airport would be a launching base from which Communists could attack the United States and its "Central American allies." The United States government and media both made wild accusations about the military buildup in Grenada, as though one hundred thousand poor Grenadian peasants were gearing up to invade two hundred fifty million Americans.

In a 1983 speech at New York's Hunter College, Prime Minister Maurice Bishop outlined the vicious maneuvers employed by the U.S. to destabilize and disrupt Grenada. Bishop noted that in 1981 U.S. Marines executed a mock invasion of a Caribbean island in an operation called "Amber in the Amberdines." This was obviously meant to create fear in the Grenadian people since their nation is often called "Grenada in the Grenadines." The prime minister also pointed out how Washington had pressured European countries and the International Monetary Fund into denying loans to Grenada.

In addition to economic destabilization, the U.S. government also slandered Grenada's plans for elections, spread lies to prevent tourists from traveling to Grenada, and continued the ridiculous propaganda about the "sophisticated military base." (Bishop replied to that charge by saying that if anyone found sophisticated equipment in Grenada, please let him know, since his poor country needed all the technology it could get.) By late 1983, many in the New Jewel Movement felt an attack by the United States was inevitable, though some believed the most wealthy nation in the world would never attack their small island nation. Grenada and the world, however, would soon find out how desperate Washington was to destroy the people's government in Grenada.

Finance Minister Bernard Coard was seen by many in the New Jewel Movement as the intellectual power in the party, a brilliant thinker with a firm grasp of Marxist-Leninist theory. In the early 1980s, Coard consolidated his power on the Central Committee, and by 1983, critisized Bishop's leadership for being too moderate. Charge and counter-charge followed, and eventually Coard persuaded the Movement leadership to place Bishop under house arrest. Whiteman and others loyal to Bishop resigned, leaving Coard and his coalition in charge of the government.

The masses of Grenadian workers and students continued to support Bishop, and when Coard's followers attempted to explain Bishop's arrest, they were booed and chased off the stage. Kenrick Radix and Fitzroy Bain led street demonstrations with hundreds of Grenadians shouting "No Bishop No Revo!" and demanding the prime minister's release. One crowd went to his house and freed him from his captors, and thirty thousand other Grenadians (thirty percent of the entire population!) waited in St. George's to see and hear their leader.

The Coard leadership panicked. In the madness that followed, soldiers separated Bishop and his comrades from the crowd and herded them over to Fort Rupert (named after Bishop's slain father). The soldiers, many believe under orders from Coard, then executed Maurice Bishop, Unison Whiteman, Norris Bain, Jacqueline Creft, Vincent Noel, Fitzroy Bain, Evelyn Bullen, Avis Ferguson, and Goty Robinson in a bloody climax to a struggle between the people's demands and Coard's ideological purity. Grenada was stunned. Fort Rupert could be seen from the hills of St. George and hundreds witnessed the massacre of the popular Maurice Bishop.

The Reagan administration was primed for an invasion, and used the massacre as an excuse to call out the Marines and Navy on a ten-square mile island (Grenada is the same size as Washington, D.C.). Reagan charged that Coard's government threatened the lives of American medical students in Grenada, although many students later testified that they were not endangered until after the invasion. The sight of six thousand U.S. Marines from the world's most powerful country invading impoverished Grenada again demonstrated western imperialism's disdain for black self-determination.

An entire volume could be devoted to the horrifying details of the Reagan administration's treacherous dealings with Grenada from 1980 to 1983. The U.S. continued to lie throughout the invasion: "Cuban soldiers" were actually construction workers, and "military arsenals" were really barns with a few old guns stacked in a corner. The illegal invaders of Grenada rounded up the remaining leaders of the New Jewel Movement, and a special detachment of Marines engaged in a rehearsed psychological program to make Grenadians accept the invaders as a "liberation army."

A few years of U.S. occupation enthroned capital and private property in Grenada; the reading schools and health clinics were gone, drug trafficking was rampant, and unemployment rose to twenty-five percent. The failure of the New Jewel Movement to deal with ideological conflicts and U.S. imperialism will be remembered in history as a tragedy for the people of Grenada.

Although Grenada must bear responsibility for the fracture of its party, many believe the Coard/Bishop controversy was created and exacerbated in the dark corridors of the CIA. Despite the destruction of the Grenadian revolution, Bishop and the New Jewel Movement awakened in many the possibility of making history instead of remaining pawns in history. It is this legacy which will someday be resurrected by the oppressed Africans in the United States, the Caribbean, and Africa.

> The revolution has reminded us that when we put our confidence in the people, when we are honest with the people, when we ... make it clear as a government that our intention is to address the basic needs and basic problems of our people, when we tell them that our intention is to stop looking outward for solutions from the metropolitan centers that have dominated and exploited us for so long but instead to begin to turn our eyes inwards to our country, to look at the problems ourselves, to try and find solutions for our problems based on our needs and based on our resources, that when these things are done a lot is possible. We have been amazed, we have been inspired, we have been encouraged by the tremendous unleashing of creativity and of energy by our people.[11]
>
> —Maurice Bishop, in a speech entitled "Forward Ever," given for the first anniversary of the Grenadian revolution.

Don Rojas, Maurice Bishop's press secretary, urged that the lesson of Grenada energize our future struggles.

In a 1983 interview he noted,

> We must let the positive symbols, achievements, and example of the Grenadian revolution continue to guide and inspire us as we press on with the struggle against imperialism and its handmaidens—racism, colonialism, neo-colonialism and fascism. We must not be demoralized by the tragic setbacks of October (1983)...Rather, we must strengthen our resolve, our optimism, and our confidence as we continue to call for the withdrawal of foreign troops from Grenada and for an end to U.S. colonization...We must demand an end to the campaign of harassment, intimidation, and victimization against the NJM...We should also condemn the reactionary campaign throughout the entire Caribbean to...crack down on every progressive force in the anti-imperialist and trade union movements. At the moment, we should put a lot of our energy into support work for our comrades in Nicaragua who face an imminent U.S.-backed invasion. Now is the time for unity of all revolutionary and progressive people around the world. It is a time to rise above sectarianism and come together in a broad anti-imperialist united front for peace, justice, and social progress.[12]

Black Panther Party: Revolutionary Suicide

Nothing was as galvanizing to the black community and shocking to the white community as the appearance in 1966 of the militant Black Panther Party. America in the 1960s was schizophrenic, hovering at the peak of liberalism on one hand, lapsing into the abyss of fascism on the other. The Black Panther Party was too much for either political wing; it was condemned by liberals and targeted for elimination by the reactionaries. In dealing with the Black Panthers, the FBI, the Justice Department, the courts, and local police agencies made a sham of America's civil liberties and pretensions of democracy.

Huey P. Newton was the founder, minister of defense, and heartbeat of the Black Panther Party. He emerged from the rough streets of Oakland's ghetto an illiterate, jobless, and angry young man. Newton's world mirrored the pain of Afro-America: unemployed men hanging around on street corners with brown paper bags; old women waiting for buses to take them to their maid work in the suburbs, children playing in alleys amid broken glass and abandoned cars. As a teenager Newton wondered, "I found it hard to understand how my father could work so hard yet have so little."[13] At an early age, Newton knew his people's poverty was not from a lack of hard work, but rather a lack of democracy and opportunity.

When Newton attended Oakland's Merritt Junior College (his older brother, Melvin, had taught him to read and write), he brought with him his concern for those trapped in the ghettos. Studies of Marxism and the Chinese revolution satisfied his hunger to find a solution to Afro-American suffering. He later wrote,

> It was my studies...that led me to become a socialist. The transformation from nationalism to socialism was a slow one. When I presented my solution to the problem of black people...people said, 'Well, isn't that socialism...I figured if that was socialism, then socialism must be a correct view. So I read more of the

works of the socialists and began to see a strong similarity between my beliefs and theirs. My conversion was complete when I read the first four volumes of Mao Tse-Tung to learn more about the Chinese revolution. It was my life plus independent reading that made me a socialist, nothing else.[14]

In 1966, Newton met Bobby Seale at a pro-Cuba rally and the two attempted to organize black students for community work. When it became evident that students at Merritt College would not go beyond "rap sessions," Seale and Newton proclaimed, "Later for you all, we're going to the streets." It was in the streets that Seale and Newton found an arena for revolution.

In Oakland, as in other American cities, Afro-Americans were routinely victimized by police officers. Blacks were stopped without cause, arrested without charge, and often murdered in cold blood by racist policemen. It was as though the southern lynch mobs had moved north and were now charged with keeping law and order in the black community. Huey and Bobby saw police brutality as the most visible and painful symbol of white domination.

Newton and Seale were compelled to do something; the question was, what? In searching for answers, they read and discussed Robert Williams's *Negros With Guns*, Frantz Fanon's *The Wretched of the Earth*, the speeches of Malcolm X, and the writings of Mao Zedong, Fidel Castro, and Ché Guevara. Mobilized by these and by the example of Robert Williams's shoot-out with the Klan in Monroe, North Carolina, Newton and Seale decided to confront police violence where it occurred, in the streets. In September of 1966, Bobby Seale, Huey Newton, and fifteen year-old Bobby Hutton founded the Black Panther Party of Self-Defense.

The three emerged from their study sessions with a patrol for self-defense—not for the police, but from the police. The sight of three black men with guns and lawbooks observing police arrests and informing people of their rights alarmed Oakland's power elite. Law enforcement agencies went into a frenzy over how to deal with this "uprising," but Afro-Americans all over Oakland muttered to themselves, "It's about time!" The sons and daughters of slaves and sharecroppers, long victimized by vigilante "justice" and police violence, saw the stand of Newton, Seale, and Hutton as a defiant move toward self-determination. Young black men and women, many unemployed or underemployed, flocked to join the Black Panther Party of Self-Defense.

The three party founders developed a formal structure for the Black Panthers to channel the energies of the new recruits. Meeting in the back room of an Oakland community center, Newton, Seale, and Hutton drafted what became the Party's program, the rallying point for thousands of Panthers all over the nation. "What We Believe," the party program, contains both the fulfillment of America's promised democracy and the elimination of murderous racism and heartless "free enterprise."

What We Believe

1. We believe that black people will not be free until we are able to determine our own destiny.
2. We believe that the federal government is responsible to give every man employment or a guaranteed income. We believe that if the white American businessmen will not give full employment, then the means of production should be taken from the business men and placed in the community...
3. We believe that this racist government has robbed us and now we are demanding the overdue debt of forty acres and two mules. [This] was promised to us 100 years ago as retribution for slave labor...
4. **We believe that if the white landlords will not give decent housing to our black community, then the housing and land should be made into cooperatives...**
5. We believe in an educational system that will give to our people a knowledge of self.
6. We believe that black people should not be forced to fight in the military service to defend a racist government that does not protect us. We will not fight and kill other

people of color in the world...

7. We believe that we can end police brutality in our black community by organizing black self-defense groups...dedicated to defending our black community from racist police oppression...

8. We believe that all black people should be released from the many jails and prisons because they have not received a fair and impartial trial.

9. We believe that the courts should follow the U.S. Constitution so that black people will receive fair trials...

10. 'We hold these truths to be self-evident, that all men are created equal, that they are endowed by their Creator with certain unalienable rights, that among these rights are Life, Liberty, and the pursuit of Happiness. That to secure these rights, Governments are instituted among Men, deriving their just powers from the consent of the governed, That whenever any Form of Government becomes destructive...it is the Right of the People to alter or to abolish it, and to institute new Government...Prudence, indeed, will dictate that Governments long established should not be changed for light or transient causes...But when a long train of abuses...evinces a design to reduce them under absolute Despotism, it is their right, it is their duty, to throw off such Government...'[15]

While black youth flocked to the party headquarters on 28th Street in Oakland, the highest powers in the state government sought to quell this Afro-American revolt. A California legislator introduced a bill prohibiting the Panthers from carrying guns in public. So specifically was it written for the party that it was known as the "The Panther Bill." Ironically, Newton, Seale, and Hutton used the bill to stage an act of defiance for which the Black Panther Party is most remembered.

On May 2, 1967, several armed Black Panthers assembled on the steps of the State Capitol building in Sacramento to protest the Panther bill. If patrolling the streets was shocking, the sight of young Panthers in black berets and leather jackets walking boldly into the citadel of white authority was frightening. Law and order governor and symbol of reactionary politics Ronald Reagan fled in fright at the sight of the approaching Panthers. Ever since slavery, the white capitalists' greatest nightmare has been the awful specter of armed black men taking over the seats of white power. On May 2, 1967, young men from Oakland ghettos made this nightmare a reality.

The May 2 rebellion launched the Oakland Black Panther Party into national headlines. If J. Edgar Hoover and the FBI thought Dr. Martin Luther King, Jr. was a troublemaker, this showing in Sacramento by arrogant armed blacks was too much. But white folks' "bad niggers" were heroes to the people, and young blacks in Philadelphia, St. Louis, Washington, D.C. and other major cities joined the Panthers in droves. Eventually thirty-five cities would be home to a chapter of the Black Panther Party for Self-Defense. The May 2 protest was a bold declaration of war against America's lingering racism and persistent exploitation, and as such attracted thousands of young warriors into the fight. Eldridge Cleaver, author of the best-selling *Soul on Ice*, was recruited into the party. Cleaver later became the party's resident writer, editing the newspaper *The Black Panther* and writing most of the essays on party theory.

With Newton as minister of defense and Seale as chairman of the party, the Black Panther Party continued police patrols, published its party organ, *The Black Panther*, and in 1968 began what it called "survival" programs. The most popular and successful survival program was the Free Breakfast for Children Project. As an interim measure "pending revolution," the free breakfast programs gave the party additional visibility and respect in the black community and allowed them to directly affect thousands of black children every day. The breakfast programs, party patrols, and newspaper sales only increased the popularity of the Panthers among Afro-Americans. In 1971, a secret FBI memo to President Nixon noted that 25% of blacks respected the Black Panther Party, including 43% of those under 21.

By 1969, the Black Panthers moved from self-defense

to a Marxist-Leninist ideology. This dramatic move traumatized white progressive circles and black nationalist organizations. Whites were disturbed that the Panthers had moved so far to the left, and black nationalists criticized their international focus. The Panthers, however, remained an all-black party. Minister of Defense Newton said, "The Black Panther Party is an all-black party because we feel as Malcolm X said there can be no black-white unity until there is black unity."[16]

The party's black unity stance led to alliances with Stokely Carmichael, H. Rap Brown, and the other leaders of the SNCC (Student Non-violent Coordinating Committee). This short-lived merger collapsed, however, when Carmichael condemned the Panther's alliance with the white radical Peace and Freedom Party. The Panthers, in turn, blasted SNCC's refusal to see class differences, stating:

> The Black Panther Party... will not fight capitalism with black capitalism, we will not fight imperialism with black imperialism, we will not fight racism with black racism. Rather, we will take our stand against these evils with a solidarity derived from a proletarian internationalism born of socialist ideology.[17]

Newton also added, "we don't suffer in the hangup of skin color, we don't hate white people, we hate the oppressor."[18] Like the African Blood Brotherhood fifty years earlier, the Black Panther Party linked black liberation with America's deliverance from the private ownership and accumulation of wealth. The Panthers condemned black nationalist organizations that, in the words of Minister of Defense Huey Newton, "Seek refuge by retreating into ancient African behavior and culture. The Black Panther Party has no need to go to 11th century Africa. We must deal with the dynamic present to forge a progressive future."[19]

Despite criticism from nationalist organizations, Newton, Seale, Cleaver, and other party leaders worked with the Puerto Rican Young Lords, the Chicano Brown Berets, the Chinese-American Red Guards, and the white

Young Patriots and Peace and Freedom Party. In 1968, the Peace and Freedom Party and the Panthers fielded Eldridge Cleaver, Kathleen Cleaver, and Huey Newton for political office. The Panthers also participated in anti-imperialist and anti-fascist conventions with white leftist groups, usually under the leadership of the vocal Eldridge Cleaver.

In 1970, the Black Panther Party joined with white leftists in sponsoring the First Revolutionary Constitutional Convention. The convention's aim was to rewrite the Constitution to include Chicanos, Puerto Ricans, Afro-Americans, white leftists, women, homosexuals, and Native Americans. While Black Panther participation demonstrated the party's ties with other groups, there were some leftist groups with whom the party did not associate. Eldridge Cleaver blasted both the Socialist Workers' Party (SWP) and the Communist Party USA (CPUSA). When the CPUSA told party leaders they should "Wait until the time is right and revolt with the CP and the masses," Eldridge countered, "[The CP] are nuthin' but hitchikers on the Black Revolution" an condemned them as "a white NAACP." Cleaver called both the SWP and the CPUSA "white mother country radicals" trying to lead from the rear.

The Black Panther Party saw itself as part of a worldwide revolt against colonialism and oppression. It supported the Palestinian struggle for land in the Middle East, and during the Vietnam War vigorously supported the North Vietnamese. As a representative of the black liberation struggle, Huey Newton visited North Vietnam, China, and other Third World nations. When moderate black leaders attacked Newton's position on Vietnam, he replied, "the government that kills in Jackson State is the same one that kills at My Lai."[20]

The Panthers' international focus did not obscure their struggles for Afro-America. In 1968 and 1969, the party called for a plebiscite for black Americans to decide whether or not they wanted a separate black nation in the United States. The party also demanded that United Nations observers come into America's ghettos to oversee police behavior toward black citizens. This call was consistent with Malcolm X's demand that the African, Asian, and Latin American nations in the U.N. join in solidarity against America's domestic racism.

With the frequent arrests, jailings, raids, and murders of Panther members, it is a wonder the group functioned at all, much less developed revolutionary theory. In his classic study on the role of Communist parties, Lenin, in *What Is To Be Done*, notes, "Without revolutionary theory there can be no revolutionary movement." Indeed, the fuel of the Panther movement was the anger of young blacks guided by theory developed by Huey Newton, Bobby Seale, Eldridge Cleaver, David Hilliard, and other leaders of the party.

By far the most significant Panther theory was the view on the "lumpenproletariat" as developed by Eldridge Cleaver's article "On Lumpen Ideology." To the Black Panthers, the most revolutionary segment of society was the lumpenproletariat, the street people: the pimps, prostitutes, hustlers, petty criminals, and unemployed who have nothing to lose with the overthrow of U.S. capitalism. Unlike most leftist parties, which believed the workers were the vanguard, the Panthers felt the lumpenproletariat was more radical than the workers and must be organized lest the state organize them against the revolution.

Newton and Panther leadership also developed the theory of Revolutionary Intercommunalism. Since the United States was an empire which economically dominated the entire world, the concept of nations no longer applied. What once were nations became interrelated communities, tied together by the economic interdependence created by U.S. imperialism. Reactionary intercommunalism, then, was U.S. imperialism operating in the communities of the world so that the resources and land did not benefit the community but rather a few rich individuals in the United States.

Revolutionary Intercommunalism occurred when the people seized the means of production and distributed the wealth justly among the countries of the world. U.S. dominance of the world was verified when Washington called Vietnam "a police action," much like the attacks on urban rioters in Newark were called "police actions." Since Revolutionary Communalism held that the U.S. was the economic and political center of the world, the Black Panther Party would wage war against U.S. imperialism at home while FRELIMO in Mozambique, the ANC in South Africa, and the PLO in Palestine hammered away at America's tentacles abroad.

This theory put the party in the vanguard of struggle not only for Afro-American liberation but for self-determination and equality for all the peoples of the world—a long way to come for an organization that began with three young black men tired of police brutality in the ghettos of Oakland. These and other revolutionary theories were taught to approximately three hundred party cadre in the Panthers' Ideological Institute in Oakland.

Other Communist and Socialist parties believed the Panthers had erred in their focus on the lumpenproletariat. It was the workers' class consciousness, they felt, sharpened by direct conflict and struggle with private capital, which provided the basis for sustained revolution. While the lumpen truly had no stake in society, their conditions forced them to view the enemy in more immediate terms, such as police in the black community. By organizing lumpen, the Panthers became fixated on confrontations with white police, ignoring struggles with the white landlords, white factory owners, and white bankers whose quiet but persistent, profiteering at the expense of Afro-Americans overshadowed violence by their police buffers.

Despite its shortfalls, the lumpen ideology provided the Panthers with a base in the black lower classes. And this is precisely what made the party so revolutionary. Many left wing parties consisted of bourgeois whites, while black nationalist organizations often were influenced heavily by middle-class blacks. The Black Panther Party, on the other hand, had a membership that was twice oppressed, Afro-Americans victimized by both race and class. Unlike many white leftist and black nationalist organizations, most of the membership of the

Black Panther Party had nothing to lose in the fall of American capitalism.

* * *

In August of 1967, five months after the Sacramento protest, Hoover and the FBI had seen enough of the Black Panther Party. Hoover issued a memo to FBI personnel directing them to "expose, disrupt, misdirect, and otherwise neutralize black nationalist groups."[21] Hoover also expanded the notorious Counter Intelligence Program (COINTELPRO) to "prevent the coalition of militant black nationalist groups which might be the first step toward a real mau mau in America...and prevent the rise of a black messiah."[22] In 1968, another Hoover memo claimed "the Black Panther Party, without question, represents the greatest threat to the internal security of the country."[23]

The FBI had a green light from the highest levels of American government to neutralize black revolutionaries, and COINTELPRO concentrated on the Black Panther Party. Of the two hundred ninety-five "authorized actions" against black groups from 1956 to 1971, two hundred thirty-six were directed at the Black Panther Party. Black Socialist Manning Marable lists a few of these treacherous tactics:

> ...all means legal or otherwise were permitted: telephone wire-tapping, sending anonymous or fictitious materials to members or groups, the use of paid informants to disrupt an organization...leaking damaging information on a leader to the media, creating phony organizations soley for disruptive purposes, and contacting the employers and neighbors of activists.[24]

When combined with the hostility of local law enforcement agencies, the official war against the Panthers took on murderous proportions. Some observers estimate that between 1966 and 1973 over one hundred Panthers were murdered by the police, their paid agents, or "provoked" individuals. Shoot-outs between the Panthers and "pigs" became commmon occurrences. Angela Davis noted that from 1967 to 1969, nineteen Panthers were killed and over one thousand arrested. Although most charges were eventually dropped, the arrests significantly disrupted Party leadership. With Newton, Seale, Hilliard, Cleaver and other leaders in and out of jail, Party operations were severely hampered. Minister of Defense Huey Newton was arrested fifty times in 1967 alone. Jail became a second home for many of the Panthers.

The extent of the shameful war against the Panthers is seen in the experiences of the three founders, Huey Newton, Bobby Seale, and Bobby Hutton. In 1967, Newton was stopped and assaulted by two Oakland police officers. A shoot-out followed in which one officer died, the other was wounded, and Newton was shot in the groin. In *Revolutionary Suicide*, Newton writes that he was unarmed and would not have confronted two armed officers on a dark Oakland street even if he were. Caught in the cross fire of what he saw as an assassination attempt against him, Newton was nevertheless charged with the murder of Officer Frey. Despite the lack of evidence and witnesses, Newton was convicted of voluntary manslaughter. For the next twenty-two months he lingered in a four-by-six cell in solitary confinement at Los Padres Men's Colony until public pressure and a conviction reversal released him. The campaign to "Free Huey" was one of the most sustained struggles of the Black Panther Party.

Chairman Bobby Seale, arrested several times in Oakland on flimsy charges, made national news with his arrest and trial as one of the Chicago Eight. Charged with inciting riots during the demonstrations at the 1968 Democratic National Convention in Chicago, the party chairman sought to defend himself before Judge Julius Hoffman. Seale was charged with sixteen counts of contempt of court for comments like "If I am consistently denied this right... by the judge of this court, then I can only see the judge as a blatant racist."[25]

In one of the most glaring examples of racism in the history of the American justice system, Judge Hoffman ordered the bailiffs to chain and gag Seale for the remainder of the trial. The image of Bobby Seale sitting motionless in the courtroom with his hands and feet shackled and his mouth covered is one of the most enduring symbols of black suffering and struggle in America.

After this debacle Seale went to New Haven, Connecticut to help Ericka Huggins lead a chapter of the Black Panther Party. Soon after his arrival, Seale was arrested with Huggins, Lonnie McLucas, Warren Kimbro, Rose Smith, and six other Party members for the murder of Black Panther Alex Rackley. They were eventually acquitted in 1971, the crime actually having been committed by a paid police informer. When Seale was released from prison that year, he went to Oakland and saw Huey Newton outside of prison for the first time since 1967.

Bobby Hutton, the third member of the founding trio, was murdered by the Oakland police department. At fifteen, Hutton was the youngest leader in the Party. Despite his age, "Lil' Bobby" was respected by the Party membership for his unwavering dedication to black liberation and his sensitivity toward black folk both in the Party and on the streets. On April 6, 1968, two days after the murder of Dr. Martin Luther King, Jr., a shoot-out occurred between dozens of Oakland police and Panthers at the Party headquarters on 28th Street. After ninety minutes of police shotgun blasts, tear gas cannisters and firebombs, Eldridge Cleaver, David Hilliard, and Bobby Hutton were led out from the headquarters. Cleaver describes what happened:

> The pigs told us to stand up... pointed to a squad car parked in the middle of the street and told us to run to it. I couldn't run... they snatched Lil' Bobby away from me and shoved him forward, telling him to run to the car. The most sickening sight. After he had traveled ten yards, stumbling and coughing in the smoke, the pigs let loose on him with their guns.[26]

Bobby Hutton, inspirational young leader of a national black political party, was mercilessly shot in the back by some sadistic police officers. The people's love for Lil' Bobby was demonstrated when five thousand Afro-Americans attended his memorial service. Children fed by Lil' Bobby, teenagers assisted by Bobby during a police shakedown, and hundreds of other angered blacks turned out to pay tribute to this Afro-American hero.

Offical repression of the Panthers did not end with Newton, Seale, and Hutton. On December 4, 1969, Illinois Party Chairman Fred Hampton and Peoria Party leader Mark Clark were brutally murdered by law enforcement agencies. Without warning or provocation police officers fired two hundred rounds of shotgun and submachine gun blasts into Hampton's Chicago apartment.

Although the police claimed they had been fired upon, evidence later showed that Fred Hampton was murdered in his sleep and that an informer had given the officers a floor plan of the apartment so they would know exactly where to fire at the sleeping Panthers. An inquiry into the murder by Ramsey Clark concluded that police conducted a "search and destroy" mission and that Hampton was killed by shots fired at close range while he was unconscious.

In 1968, Bunchy Carter and Jon Huggins were murdered on the UCLA campus by black cultural nationalists. Many believe the murder was provoked by FBI COINTELPRO skullduggery, which created animosity and spread lies about one group to the other. In April of 1969, the entire leadership of the New York chapter was arrested on charges of conspiring to bomb police stations and department stores. The New York 21, including Curtis Powell, Joan Bird, and Afeni Shakur, were acquitted of all twelve counts, but not before the Party was seriously indebted from court fees and hampered by a critical loss of leadership.

David Hilliard, the Party's national leader when Newton and Seale were incarcerated, was arrested several times in Oakland on ridiculous charges brought by panicky police officers. In 1969, he was arrested by fifty agents for threatening the life of the President. At an anti-war rally Hilliard had said, "We will kill any motherfucker that stands in the way of our freedom," later hinting that President Nixon might be one of those "motherfuckers."[27]

Emory Douglass, minister of culture, had his artwork and Party cartoons dragged before a congressional committee by Vice-president Spiro Agnew in an attempt to demonstrate the Panthers' violent tendencies. Other Panthers were likewise hunted. D.C. Cox, and Ray 'Masai' Hewitt were pursued by the police on various charges. George Jackson, author of *Soledad Brother*, was a leader of the Party (his expertise in guerilla tactics earned him the title of Field Marshal) who in 1971 was shot in the back by guards at San Quentin. Minister of Information Eldridge Cleaver, also arrested several times, eventually fled to Algeria after violating parole. Cleaver had become a marked man in California when he challenged Governor Reagan to a duel: "Mickey Mouse, I challenge you to a duel... and if you can't relate to that, right on. Walk, chicken, with your ass picked clean."[28] For many Panthers it seemed that selling newspapers and conducting "free breakfast" programs were made impossible because of the legal fees, "Free Huey" rallies, and incessant stream of funeral invitations.

The repression of the Panthers was no local phenomenon restricted to a few individuals. In 1969, *The New York Times* published a partial list of Panther statistics;

1968

Jan. San Francisco police, without warrant, raid the home of Eldridge Cleaver

Feb. Bobby and Artie Seale are arrested in their home without warrant. Charges of "conspiracy to murder" later dropped. Two other Panthers arrested near the Seale home at the same time are later released. By the time their charges were dropped, the other two had been killed.

April David Hilliard arrested. Charges later dropped. Bobby Hutton killed.
Denver police arrest three Panthers for "contributing to delinquency."
Charges later dropped.

Sept. Denver police arrest one Panther and kill another for

	alleged sniping. No one was injured.
	Colorado Chair of the Party arrested for arson. No evidence is produced and the charges were dropped.
Nov.	Eight San Francisco Panthers arrested on charges of shooting at police. All charges later dropped.

1969

April	New York 21 arrested. No one has a serious police record, no evidence produced, bail set at $2 million.
	San Francisco police, using tear gas, raid Black Panther HQ and arrest sixteen. Twelve are released and four charged with "illegal use of sound equipment."
May	Los Angeles police raid Party HQ and arrest eleven. All eleven released with no charges filed.
June	Chicago FBI raid Party HQ and arrest eight for "harboring a fugitive." No fugitive is found but police confiscate money, literature, and membership lists.
	Denver police raid Party HQ and arrest three. All three later released.
	Sacramento police raid Party HQ "in search of sniper." No sniper is found but police wreck equipment, food, and furniture.
July	Chicago police raid Party HQ and building is "totally destroyed."
Sept.	San Diego police raid Party HQ in search of suspect who is not found. Police seize weapons and ammunition.
	Los Angeles police kill Panther Walter Toure Pope, claiming he fired on them.
Dec.	David Hilliard arrested for threatening Nixon.
	Fred Hampton and Mark Clark murdered by Chicago police in massive raid.
	Fifty Los Angeles police raid Party HQ and are held off for two hours by three Panthers.[29]

As evidenced by the *Times* article, the campaign of brutality against the Panthers seems incredible. This vicious assault on human rights stands in sharp contrast to the partial treatment afforded the Ku Klux Klan and Nazi Party organizations, both of whom at this writing can hold rallies anywhere in the United States. While a party committed to black liberation becomes the victim of genocidal extermination, racist organizations continue to flourish. The repression of the Panthers illustrates clearly the illusion of American democracy. While all is quiet, radical books and protest flourish, but when the oppressed demand fundamental changes, not only are the books and rallies censored but the people themselves are neutralized.

By 1973, the Panthers were effectively silenced. Cleaver was in exile, Newton had gone into exile in Cuba, and Bobby Seale had entered Oakland's mayoral race as a progressive candidate. Death and jail claimed hundreds more.

In the early 1970s, Newton published *Revolutionary Suicide*, a book outlining the history of the Panthers. According to Newton, everyone commits suicide. "Reactionary suicide" occurs when you surrender and through apathy and self-destruction allow the system to determine your destiny. "Revolutionary suicide" is not a death wish; it is a strong desire to live in dignity, yet with an acceptance of the possibility of death in the struggle for black liberation and socialism. Arrayed against the armed might of Hoover's FBI and posse police departments, "revolutionary suicide" became the destiny of the Bobby Huttons, Sam Napiers, Fred Hamptons, and Bunchy Carters who simply wanted housing for the elderly, food for the children, education for the young, and justice, dignity, and jobs for the masses of Afro-American people.

*   Postscript   *

Repression against members of the Black Panther Party is not yet over. As of 1987, former Party leader Elmer Geronimo Pratt had spent seventeen years in prison for a murder he didn't commit. As deputy minister of defense in Los Angeles, Pratt secured the building in which eighteen Panthers held off three hundred L.A. police officers. Incensed, the FBI formed the "Pratt Task Force" to neutralize him. In 1970, he was charged with a murder in Santa Monica. The key witness later proved to be a police informer and the FBI wiretap logs which proved Pratt was in Oakland at the time mysteriously disappeared. He was convicted in 1972 and has been denied parole seven times. In a 1987 interview with *Unity*, Pratt remained hopeful; "A lot of beautiful brothers and sisters gave their lives for...freedom, and I lost many who were very close to me in that period, I was dedicated to certain things then, and have taken on their spirits to continue that struggle."[30]

Geronimo Pratt of the Black Panther Party

The Party of the Negro People: Communist Party USA, 1919-1944

- **Party of the Negro People**
- **Harry Haywood**
- **Angelo Herndon**
- **Henry Winston**

The Party of the Negro People: Communist Party United States of America 1919-1944

No political party in the history of the United States has demonstrated the depth of commitment to black liberation as did the Communist Party United States of America (CPUSA) from 1919 to 1944. Beginning with the infusion of black Socialists from the African Blood Brotherhood in 1922 and expanding with the 1928 adoption of the line "Self-determination for the Black Belt South," the CPUSA was involved in almost every major Afro-American struggle for jobs, voting power, educational opportunities, and protection against lynch mobs and police violence. Contrary to popular misconceptions, the CPUSA was not white, "left-wing missionaries" helping poor defenseless blacks; it was black intellectuals, artists, workers, sharecroppers, and students themselves striking a blow for the emancipation of their people from the treacherous grips of both racism and capitalism.

Whether in Harlem's Unemployment Councils during the Depression or in rural Alabama Sharecroppers' Unions, black members of the Communist Party set the standard by which future Afro-American revolutionaries are to be judged. For thirty years the Communist Party was so immersed in black struggle that thousands referred to it as the "Party of the Negro People." The Party was not a group of abstract theorists; it was a collection of individuals who marched with the oppressed, confronted racist police and endured firings and evictions for the people. Harry Haywood, Angelo Herndon, and Henry Winston are profiled here only as examples of the hundreds of black men and women who joined the CPUSA to create a free black nation and a just and Socialist America.

And Justice for All?

The Party of the Negro People

When African Blood Brotherhood (ABB) members Cyril Briggs, Richard Moore, Otto Huiswood, Harry Haywood, George Padmore and Otto Hall joined the CPUSA in the early 1920s (they held membership in both organizations for a while) the Party benefited from the talents of the most politically advanced black activists in the country. From the time ABB members joined the Communist Party, they assumed responsibility for the Party's work in Harlem.

Since Harlem in the 1920s was the center of Afro-American thought and culture, the work of the CPUSA there could impact blacks all over the nation. When Briggs, Moore, and others told the oppressed Afro-Americans about the progress of Lenin and the Bolsheviks in eliminating racism, unemployment, evictions, pogroms (lynch mobs), and landlords, many black Harlemites listened intently. Even with the popularity of Marcus Garvey and the United Negro Improvement Association, Afro-Americans in Harlem were deeply moved by the fearlessness and dedication of blacks in the Communist Party.

The first CPUSA organization specifically established for work among Afro-Americans was the American Negro Labor Congress (ANLC). Headed by Lovett Fort-Whiteman, the ANLC was formed to end discrimination in industry and integrate the lily-white trade unions. Fort-Whiteman, Richard Moore, Harry Haywood, H.V. Phillips and Edward Doty, all ex-members of the African Blood Brotherhood, organized ANLC chapters in several cities in the U.S. The AFL, however, opposed ANLC attempts to integrate unions and the formidable A. Philip Randolph (the most important black trade union figure of the period) refused to support the Congress. The ANLC, consequently, never flourished among black workers and was soon dismantled by the Party.

Nevertheless, in the early 1920s the Communist Party was distinguished by its commitment to opening unions to Afro-American workers. While other parties and organizations either practiced or ignored racism, the CPUSA uncompromisingly supported black workers' struggles with unions and employers.

James Ford, later a CPUSA vice-presidential candidate, exemplified the Afro-American workers attracted to the Party during this period. Ford joined the Party after the Communists in his postal union were alone in supporting his condemnation of labor racism. Although Ford was a graduate of Fisk University and a veteran of World War I, the only employment white society could offer this educated black veteran was a postal worker job in Chicago. Fiercely dedicated to the aims of the Party, the articulate Ford eventually became head of the International Trade Union Committee of Negro Workers, the Trade Union Unity League (TUUL), and the Harlem branch of the CPUSA. Several other blacks joined in the early 1920s due to the Party's support for black workers, including attorney William Patterson and inventor Solomon Harper.

Despite the recruitment of black cadre like Ford, Patterson, and Harper, CPUSA influence remained small until the Party's 1928 adoption of the revolutionary political line "Self-determination for the Black Belt South," as developed by the Communist International (Comintern). This view, based partially on Lenin's *National and Colonial Question*, held that blacks in the South represented an oppressed nation due to their unique historical experience in America.

Slavery, the Civil War, and the aborted democratic revolution of the Reconstruction created a distinct black nation in the South. As a nation, blacks were due more than reforms like integration and civil rights; Afro-Americans had the right to establish a government that reflected the deepest aspirations of the people. The Party taught, therefore, that Afro-Americans in the South had the right to secede from the United States, and if they seceded, to determine their own political and economic system.

The revolutionary nature of the Self-determination line is most clearly seen when contrasted with the violent methods employed by the white South to rob black workers and farmers of money, votes, and land. The political line of "Self-determination for the Black Belt

South" elevated the black liberation struggle to the top of the CPUSA's agenda. Cyril Briggs, Otto Huiswood, and Edward Welsh were elected to the Central Committee of the CPUSA as the Party marched boldly to the vanguard of black struggle. In 1928, the Party defiantly declared, "The Communist Party is the party of the liberation of the Negro race from all oppression,"[1] and in 1936 CPUSA leader Harry Haywood noted that many black workers commonly referred to the CPUSA as "the Party of the Negro People."

Black and white party cadre ventured South armed with the Self-determination slogan and a revolutionary fervor unmatched in U.S. history. In the South black farm workers were constant victims of drunken thugs, enforced starvation, and artificial debt. After the Reconstruction blacks were forced into a sharecropping and tenant farming system that differed from slavery only in degree.

In chapter 1 Hosea Hudson describes how he and his family were locked on the plantation by debts contrived by the landlord. Without tools, seed, or money, Hudson and millions of other Afro-Americans borrowed on credit from the landowners. At the end of the year, "squaring up" time, the landowner could always figure a way to hurl struggling black families back into debt peonage. This barbarous system was maintained by the most brutal violence imaginable. Lynch mobs whose ferocity matched crazed cannibals stood in the shadows to murder and maim any blacks (or whites) bold enough to challenge the system.

The viciousness of the South was matched by the courage of Afro-American Communists. Mack Coad was a powerfully-built steel worker and sharecropper who defied the Klan and racist vigilantes to organize Alabama's rural farmers into The Organization of the Sharecroppers' Union. Undaunted by threats of jail or lynching, Coad was almost beaten to death in Memphis for "agitatin' " and later fought the fascists in the Spanish Civil War. In 1931, however, he was engaged in a war of a different kind, that of embattled black sharecroppers fighting for survival against white landowners.

Union secretary Al Murphy, responsible for recruiting Hosea Hudson into the Party, assisted Coad in building the Sharecroppers' Union. Murphy had taught himself to read and by candlelight had absorbed the writings of Marx and Lenin. Fortified by bitter experiences and energized by revolutionary theory, Murphy walked from plantation to plantation convincing black farmers that their only hope lie in the creation of a radical union.

By late 1931 Mack Coad's and Al Murphy's extraordinary organizing efforts brought five hundred members to the Sharecroppers' Union. These five hundred, common Afro-American working folk, risked lynch mobs and Klan raids to recruit their neighbors, family, and church friends into a union which by 1933 had swollen to twelve thousand.

Typical of the black cotton farmers who helped build the union was young Estelle Milner from Camp Hill, Alabama. After reading the CPUSA's paper *The Southern Worker*, Milner excitedly ran to every black farm in her area with news of how Murphy and Coad defied racist violence to form the unions. She stirred up oppressed farmers who later formed the militant Camp Hill Sharecroppers' Union.

The Sharecroppers' Unions demanded a food allowance, the right to own a garden, nine months of school for their children, an increase in winter furnishings and an increase in plantation wages. Another key demand was freedom for the Scottsboro Boys, the nine black teenagers arrested for raping two white girls on an Alabama train. An obvious frame-up (both girls were prostitutes with dubious records) lacking evidence or witnesses, the Scottsboro Boys' case typified the brutality used by the South to terrorize blacks with legal (and illegal) lynchings.

The CPUSA and the Sharecroppers' Unions viewed freedom for the Scottsboro Boys as indispensable to the ongoing struggle on the plantation. As long as Afro-Americans were subjected to random violence, black workers could be terrorized into submission. Black organizers like Al Murphy, Mack Coad, Estelle Milner, Ralph Gray, and others faced death threats, harassment, and imprisonment in their persistent attempts to give black cotton workers a measure of self-determination on the white man's plantation. Black sharecropper Clyde Johnson said, "the union was popular among us because it gave us hope and protection... it gave us a voice."

This long awaited voice was not without cost. Furious that Estelle Milner and her comrades dared to challenge the "white man's empire," sheriffs and vigilantes attacked a union meeting at a black church in Camp Hill, Alabama in 1931. In the shoot-out that followed, whites murdered union leader Ralph Gray and wounded three other sharecroppers. When word spread that black sharecroppers fired back at the attacking sheriffs, the whites in Camp Hill went berserk. Organizing themselves into posses, five hundred whites launched "nigger hunts" to terrorize and murder black cotton workers. No one knows how many were killed, and four of the arrested sharecroppers disappeared from jail never to be seen again. Conservative elements of the black press and clergy joined the white racists by raising $1,500 in reward money for whomever would capture those "guilty of agitating our poor niggers." Mack Coad hid in the woods for weeks, a fugitive of the white man's hunting dogs and the black traitor's money.

The next year in Reeltown, Alabama, a white farmer tried to take away the livestock of black sharecropper Cliff James. A member of the Sharecroppers' Union, James refused and called some of his comrades to help him resist the landlord's robbery. James resisted forcible eviction, and the landlord called the sheriff to deal with these recalcitrant "niggers." The sheriff arrived surprised to find James and other Sharecroppers' Union members armed and ready to defend themselves. Two deputies were wounded and one sharecropper was killed in the ensuing gunbattle.

This armed black defiance sparked four days of riots and terrorism wherein white posses hunted down black farmers and their families like dogs. As with the Camp Hill massacre, an unknown number of Afro-Americans were killed. In a tragic display of race betrayal, black doctors at Tuskegee Institute turned in two wounded sharecroppers who had crawled there for treatment. Both later died on a cold damp floor in Kilby Prison, their wounds untreated and their lives extinguished by the black traitors to whom they crawled for help.

Black demands for justice on the plantation were not crushed by southern fascism. Eula Gray, the niece of murdered Ralph Gray, continued her uncle's legacy. A lively and eloquent leader, Eula Gray led the union through bitter struggles for pay, shelter and education. Ozzie Hart, leader of the Sharecroppers' Union in the 1940s, continued the tradition of sacrifice and struggle begun by Al Murphy and Mack Coad.

By 1940, fifty thousand black farmers were members of Sharecroppers' Unions, where they defied lynch mobs and race hate to demand dignity from the parasitic landowners. The Party also fought peonage and debt slavery through the Abolish Peonage Committee. Established in 1940, the Committee used court cases and media coverage to expose and outlaw peonage. By 1945, pressure from the CPUSA forced the Justice Department to actively pursue the abolishment of debt slavery in the South.

Black Communist Party members also helped found the Southern Negro Youth Congress in 1937. The Congress created a vehicle through which radical black youth could work directly for the immediate needs of the black southern worker and farmer. One of the first actions of the Congress was organizing Virginia tobacco workers for improved wages, benefits, and sanitation conditions. Congress leaders Henry Mayfield, Ethel Lee Goodman, Esther Cooper, Henry Winston, Louis Burnham, and Ed Strong led demonstrations, strikes, and other protests for black workers in the South. From 1937 to 1948 the Congress was involved in every major political struggle in the Black Belt South, including the establishment of the Southern Conference of Human Welfare. An unsegregated organization (rare in 1938), the Conference initiated several political reforms to improve the lives of both black and white farmers.

One of the moving forces behind the Southern Negro Youth Congress was the fiery and dynamic Ed Strong.

Uncompromising in his commitment to black liberation, Strong left the seminary to help build the Southern Negro Youth Congress and chair the Youth Committee of the National Negro Congress. When in the Fifties the CPUSA dropped the call for "Self-determination in the Black Belt South," Ed Strong, Claudia Jones and Harry Haywood loudly condemned that decision.

Maintaining that southern black farmers and workers constituted the most revolutionary group in America, Strong urged that the CPUSA not back away from its militant demand of self-determination. When he died of cancer a few years later, the Communist Party lost one of its most promising young leaders. With activists like Strong, the Congress is considered by many to be the ideological predecessor of the Student Non-violent Coordinationg Committee (SNCC) which led the Civil Rights sit-ins and protests and spawned leaders like James Farmer and Stokely Carmichael.

*   *   *

The South was not the only battlefield for the struggles of black Communists. At the same time the Party adopted the "Self-determination" position, Afro-America was engulfed with the rest of the nation in the misery, poverty, and unemployment of the Great Depression. The black community suffered from Depression-like conditions even during economic upswings; with the onset of bank failures, factory layoffs, and high prices, black urban misery reached new heights.

Alone in its commitment to Afro-American liberation, the CPUSA organized in Harlem, Chicago, and other cities with large black populations. By 1929, the Party had established several Unemployment Councils, militant interracial groupings of workers, the unemployed, and students which demonstrated for direct relief for the unemployed. The Councils formed defense squads which returned evicted tenants to their old apartments in defiance of the sheriff and landlord. In Harlem, Sam Brown, Leon Davis (who later founded the predecessor union to Local 1199), Louis Campbell, Arthur Williams, William Fitzgerald (an ex-Garveyite attracted by the Party's unemployment protests), Norma Smith and Hammie Snipes formed the core of those black workers who demonstrated for relief, marched on unemployment relief offices, and opposed the violent eviction of men, women, and children.

Many Unemployment Council leaders were themselves unemployed workers. While many were not members of the Communist Party, their dedication to the jobless and hungry was a powerful force on Harlem's political landscape. In Harlem alone, three thousand Afro-Americans were members of the Unemployment Councils by 1935. Almost daily in Harlem there was commotion in the streets and relief offices where unemployed blacks and whites demanded immediate assistance from the government. Since their labor created the wealth of the country, they argued, the unemployed were entitled to the basic necessities of life.

In Chicago, Councils of the Unemployed demanded relief for the jobless, unemployment insurance, free lunches for school children, moratoriums on evictions, and an end to employment and housing discrimination. In 1931, four black Unemployment Council members preventing the forced eviction of a 74 year-old black grandmother were killed by police. At a mass funeral organized by the Party and the Council, thirty thousand black and white workers marched down State Street. During the march, Chicago's "Red Squad" (a notorious police surveillance unit) mercilessly beat black Party member Harold Williams. Williams was hospitalized for weeks, and at unemployment rallies throughout the city Chicago police would yell to the marchers, "How's Williams doing?"

In New York, Chicago, Richmond, Birmingham, and other cities, Unemployment Councils won immediate relief for thousands of jobless, both black and white. Word quickly spread that if you needed someone to stand up for your rights, go to the Communist Party and their Unemployment Councils. One black mother when faced with eviction told her children, "Quick, go run and find the reds!" One Afro-American woman in Harlem described her experiences with the Party:

> ...in twenty-four hours they got me food to eat and made sure I would not be set outdoors. At first I was afraid whenever I went to the relief station I would try to tell the clerk I was hungry and break down and cry. But they soon got me out of that. They taught me to stand up and fight.[2]

Another black women added, "I stood in the rain for three days and the Home Relief Bureau paid no attention to me. Then I found out about the Unemployed Council... We went in there as a body and they came across right quick."[3]

The brunt of the work, struggle, and sacrifice was borne by the workers themselves. The Councils were not middle-class do-gooders spending a few hours in a relief line, they instead were unemployed men and women standing up to a system which used them when necessary and discarded them when desired. Hammie Snipes, a fearless Council leader who was respected by the people and given the most dangerous assignments by the Party, was typical of the caliber of militant workers attracted to the Councils.

In 1930, the Party replaced the struggling American Negro Labor Congress with the League of Struggle for Negro Rights (LSNR). The League's program reflected the newly adopted "Self-determination" thesis. LSNR leader Harry Haywood explained,

> The immediate program demanded abolition of all forms of discrimination, disenfranchisement, anti-marriage laws, and Jim Crow. It urged the establishment of a united trade union movement to include black workers... It called for mass violation of all Jim Crow laws, and 'death to the lynchers,' the banning of the KKK, and all extra-legal terrorist organizations, the liquidation of debts and mortgages of the poor farmers.[4]

In order to accomplish the immediate demands of the League, the Communist Party drew upon the talents of some of their most dynamic organizers and leaders. Ben Amis was elected national secretary, poet Langston Hughes was the president, and Harry Haywood served on the national council. Several cadre contributed articles to *The Liberator*, the voice of the LSNR.

Black League members demonstrated against racist employers, organized Afro-American workers for inclusion in lily-white unions, and led anti-Klan rallies. The League and its youth arm, the Young Liberators, supported Ethiopia's fight against Mussolini's invasion and worked to free the Scottsboro Boys and Party leader Angelo Herndon (jailed in Atlanta for organizing black and white workers).

Future black leaders of the Party were groomed in the Young Liberators. James Ashford, a selfless and dedicated communist, worked long hours to develop the League into an effective organization. Bonita Williams and Abner Berry were other dedicated cadre whose experience in organizing and revolutionary activity was forged in struggle with the Young Liberators.

Despite the activity of League chapters, it never developed into the united front the Party hoped. While there were many black organizations fighting Jim Crow and lynching, none were as radical as the LSNR. Consequently, no black organization risked working with the League for fear of being labeled "communist sympathizers." While mainline Afro-American groups called militantly for reform, they balked at revolution.

In 1936, the Party dissolved the League in favor of the National Negro Congress (NNC). The Congress was founded in Chicago as a united front of black labor, intellectuals, reformers, politicians, workers, and students. At the opening convention, five thousand delegates from five hundred eighty-five organizations representing 1.2 million Afro-Americans vowed to work on trade union, anti-imperialism, anti-lynching, and discrimination issues. NNC chapters smashed Jim Crow unions in many cities, helped lead a United Auto Worker strike in 1941, and worked with the Southern Negro Youth Congress in organizing black tobacco workers in Virginia.

The Congress attracted several brilliant black Communists. James Burnham, a college student who lead the fight for black history courses (in 1937!), Claudia Jones, the independent and fiery Party leader who fought for black women and domestic workers, and Howard Johnson, dancer at the Cotton Club and key Party link with Harlem's cultural community, were among the many black Communists who worked in the National Negro Congress.

When A. Philip Randolph quit as the leader of the NNC (Randolph complained about Party influence over the Congress), John Davis took over and was more receptive to the CPUSA. Davis said, "Blacks should not limit themselves to a particular economic system," and that the U.S. should shift "emphasis from protection of private property to protection of people from misery and poverty."⁵ Despite Davis's leadership, the Congress dissolved in the 1940s when the agents of government and big business pressured more moderate forces out of the Congress by charging it was dominated by "reds" and Moscow.

The struggle which catapulted the Communist Party into the forefront of the black liberation movement was the Scottsboro Boys case. When white sheriffs arrested the nine Alabama youths for rape, moderate black organizations like the NAACP were conspicuous by their silence. The Party, on the other hand, leapt into the fray through the International Legal Defense (ILD) and bitterly defended the Scottsboro Boys. (The ILD was a legal organization which fought for the rights of workers and blacks).

From the beginning the Party and the ILD maintained that the Scottsboro Boys were but victims of Southern terror tactics used to perpetuate white economic and political rule in the Black Belt. A victory for the Scottsboro Boys would be more than freedom for nine black teenagers, it would mark the early rumblings of an Afro-American nation asserting its independence from white economic domination. Without terror, white capitalists could not rule black labor. Black and white Communists led spirited mass protests and black mine workers, domestics, and sharecroppers knew the same forces conspiring to destroy the Scottsboro Boys worked to subvert justice and democracy for themselves.

Through Party agitation the courts indefinitely suspended the death penalties handed to the Scottsboro Boys. Several Afro-Americans joined the Communist Party after witnessing the zeal and determination with which the Communists pursued justice for the nine Alabama teenagers whom most of the country seemed ready to hand over to southern justice. Audley Moore, a black female party leader, was but one of the Afro-American activists who joined the Party when the CPUSA's commitment to black liberation was demonstrated in their work around "the Boys."

Black Communists were not confined to soley domestic issues. The National Negro Congress, Southern Negro Youth Congress, and League of Struggle for Negro Rights all participated in the anti-imperialist struggles of the 1930s. When Mussolini invaded Ethiopia, black Communists led rallies condemning Italy's attack and America's silence. One rally in Harlem attracted twenty-five thousand blacks and whites marching in unity against a war in which Italian tanks and planes attacked Ethiopian women and children. Afro-American Communists joined with Marcus Garvey and the UNIA on several occasions to protest the rape of Ethiopia.

Blacks also were involved in the Party's assistance to the Spanish people's fight against Franco's right wing revolution. Oliver Law, Oscar Hunter, sharecropper organizer Mack Coad, LSNR leader Harry Haywood, and Milton Herndon were among the black Communists who actually went to Spain to fight the Spanish fascists on the battlefield. To these courageous fighters, fascism in Spain and racism in America were flip sides to the same coin. Writer Langston Hughes and singer Paul Robeson went to Spain to inspire the International Brigades with songs and poems about struggle, sacrifice and socialism. Milton Herndon, brother of Party leader Angelo Herndon, was killed on the Aragon front.

Black women played crucial roles in building the CPUSA. Several black women overcame racism and sexism to profoundly impact Party work among Afro-Americans. In the 1920s cultural worker and educator Louise Thompson and trade union leader Maude White joined the Party and developed into powerful leaders. Thompson formed several organizations to promote party work through culture and White headed up the Party's Needles Trade Union. White was educated in the Soviet Union with Harry Haywood and returned home to organize black trade unions and Councils of the Unemployed.

When Party work increased in the black community after the adoption of the 1928 Self-determination slogan, several revolutionary black women joined the Party. Domestics, students, mothers, and workers played a leading role in Unemployment Councils, Ethiopian independence, hospital care, domestic worker rights, education, and housing. Bonita Williams, a formidable leader in the LSNR, also marched at the head of unemployment rallies in the streets of Harlem. In 1934, Williams led black working class women on a demonstration against the sudden escalation in food prices. This lively rally was an unprecedented display of the organized rage of Afro-American working women.

Audley Moore, born in Louisiana, organized in the ILD and was a staunch advocate for improving the education of Harlem's school children. Moore was a familiar figure at the Welfare Department, where she raised hell for her unemployed, homeless, and hungry sisters. Once a member of the UNIA, Moore left Garvey and joined the Party after seeing the Communists work for the Scottsboro Boys. In the book *Communists in Harlem During the Depression*, both Moore and Williams are described as having "down home eloquence which articulated the feelings of uneducated, underemployed, and abused black women."[6]

Rose Gaulden, a black nurse in the Harlem Hospital workers' union, led the fight to improve sanitation conditions and reduce the alarming number of infant deaths. One of her comrades wrote,

> "She came out of rural Georgia, and on occasion she would take to the step ladder on Lenox Avenue and keep a crowd in stitches... The politics was interspersed with humor in a rollicking homespun fashion, though at Party meetings she revealed a depth of thought beyond many of us."[7]

By far the most significant and extraordinary aspect of the Communist Party was its commitment to unity among black and white workers. In a country where the stench of racism fouled social, political, and economic relationships, the CPUSA boldly created a Party where black and white met together, marched together, organized together and fought together. The Communist Party was so recognized for racial equality and solidarity in the midst of America's rigid color-caste system that whites who associated with blacks were assumed to be Communists. Author Jessica Mitford noted, "FBI agents, seeking evidence of Communist Party affiliation, would routinely ask a suspects' neighbor and co-workers 'do Negroes visit their homes for meetings or social gatherings?' "[8]

White Communists did not earn the respect of Afro-American working people through rhetoric, it was forged in brutal battles against those capitalist and racist forces which decimated black working peoples. Several whites were murdered in the South for organizing black tobacco workers, cotton farmers, and sharecroppers. Isadore Dorfman, typical of the militant whites in the party, was savagely beaten by southern terrorists for organizing Afro-American workers.

The Party also demonstrated its commitment to black liberation and racial equality when in 1932 white member William Foster and black member James Ford ran for President and Vice-president of the United States. Standing on the platform of social insurance, immediate assistance to the unemployed, and the right of Self-determination in the Black Belt South, Foster and Ford contrasted sharply with the lily-white Republican and Democratic parties. The Party was vigilant in eliminating racism from within, and Harry Haywood describes in *Black Bolshevik* a Party trial held for a white comrade charged with racism. Minister and congressman Adam Clayton Powell, Jr., noted, "There is no group in America, including the Christian church, that practices racial brotherhood as much as the Communist Party."[9]

Despite the unified struggles of Afro-Americans and whites in the CPUSA, internal ideological differences and external persecution crippled the Party in the Forties and Fifties. The end of the Second World War brought the beginning of the global Cold War and domestic McCarthyism. America became obsessed with anti-Communist hysteria and witch hunts. "Reds" were hiding everywhere, and gains made by workers under Communist-influenced unions were rolled back as the state and big capitalists ruined the lives and families of hundreds of citizens. Communist organizations, radical unions, and even moderate groups were targeted by the House Committee on Un-American Activities.

The prime target of McCarthyism, however, was the Communist Party. In 1948, the FBI arrested the entire leadership of the CPUSA (The Foley Square 11) in New York for "conspiracy to advocate violence." In 1950, the McCarran Act made communism a conspiracy and Communists foreign agents. Many foreign-born Party members were deported, including Claudia Jones and union leader Ferdinand Smith. Hundreds more were prosecuted, fired from work, ostracized by neighbors, and publicly shamed. The Party was forced underground, and Harry Hayood estimates that the CPUSA lost contact with one-third of its entire membership.

In an attempt to restructure the Party, many revolutionary elements were abandoned. The entire southern branch of the Party was liquidated, and the CPUSA lost many of the black workers and farmers who became loyal cadre in the 1930s. The Sharecroppers's

Union was dissolved and the CPUSA created in its place a more moderate farmers' union.

For Afro-Americans, the most significant change was the Party's reversal on the question of Self-determination for the Black Belt South. Although Harry Haywood, Edward Strong, and Claudia Jones opposed the decision, James Jackson of the Central Committee led the move to abolish the "Black Nation" thesis. Jackson had joined the movement at sixteen, and was a leading member of the Southern Negro Youth Congress. Rising in the Party hierarchy, Jackson was an organizer in the auto industry and later the educational director of the CPUSA. During the Cold War he was indicted with the Foley Square 11 and went underground for five years as a refugee from political persecution.

In journal writings and convention speeches, Jackson argued, "blacks are not constituted as a separate nation, rather, they are a racially distinct people...(the) separatist orientation disorients the black movement and confuses white allies."[10] Arguing that the self-determination notion promoted black nationalism rather than black-white worker unity, Jackson and the leadership of the party dropped "Self-determination in the Black Belt South."

Despite the change in political line, black CPUSA members like William Patterson, Claude Lightfoot, and Henry Winston continued to offer Afro-Americans an alternative to the vicious system that produced for them both slavery and segregation. Patterson presented a booklet to the United Nations entitled "We Charge Genocide," and Lightfoot and Winston authored several books promoting Communism as the solution to black misery.

Black membership in the CPUSA peaked in 1938 when ten thousand Afro-Americans embraced communism. Like no other party, the CPUSA impacted millions of black miners, domestics, sharecroppers, tobacco stemmers, teachers, and children. Cyril Briggs, Richard Moore, Mack Coad, Al Murphy, Harry Haywood, Edward Strong, Rose Gaulden, Hammie Snipes, Claudia

Jones, Bonita Williams, and thousands of other Afro-Americans dedicated their lives to communism and the promise of black liberation.

Harry Haywood: Black Bolshevik

For sixty years Harry Haywood was one of the most important black Communists in America. Party leader, intellectual, political theorist, union organizer, author and committed revolutionary, Haywood began with the African Blood Brotherhood, served over thirty years in the CPUSA, and spent his last years in the Communist Party, Marxist-Leninist (CPML).

Harry Haywood was born in Omaha, Nebraska, the son of former slaves who had moved there from Tennessee. Haywood's grandfather killed an attacking Klansman while in Tennessee, and he took his entire family to Nebraska to escape racist retaliation. As a young boy in South Omaha, Harry, his brother, Otto and his sister Eppa (both of whom later joined the Communist Party) listened as their grandparents spoke of their sufferings as slaves. Displaying welts and cuts from whippings, Haywoods's grandfather would say, "Chillun, I got scars I'll carry to my grave."

Harry, Otto and Eppa soon learned that brutality against blacks was not confined to slavery or to the South. When Haywood was fifteen, his father was attacked and beaten by a gang of whites who threatened to kill him if they caught him again. Harry Haywood later wrote, "I remember vividly the scene that night when Father staggered through the door...His face was swollen and bleeding, his clothes torn and in disarray. He had a frightened, hunted look in his eyes."[11]

Forced by white violence to move a second time, the Hall family (Harry Haywood changed his last name when he joined the Communist Party) fled to Minneapolis, Minnesota. Haywood lamented, "Our whole world had collapsed. Home and security were gone. The feeling of safety... had proved elusive. Now we were just homeless 'niggers' on the run. The cruelest blow, perhaps, was the shattering of my image of my father."[12] The Halls were soon ravaged by racism. Real estate agents paid them nothing for their home, they couldn't earn enough in Minneapolis to live under one roof, and the family was split apart. In his first day at school, Harry was mocked by an entire classroom of whites singing plantation songs.

With the outbreak of World War I, Haywood joined an all-black Illinois regiment and sailed to France to fight the Germans. The racism that devastated the Hall family in Tennessee, Nebraska, and Minnesota reached Haywood in the battlefields of France. He uncovered a bulletin circulated by the U.S. Army among French officers and troops. The *Secret Bulletin Concerning Black American Troops* stated:

> Although a citizen of the United States, the black man is regarded by the white American as an inferior being...The black is constantly censured for his want of intelligence and discretion, his lack of civic...responsibility...(therefore) (1) We must prevent the rise of any pronounced degree of intimacy between French officers and black officers. (2) We must not commend too highly the black American troops. (3) Make a point of keeping the native population from 'spoiling' the Negroes.[13]

This infamous memo highlights the absurdity of black troops dying in France to save a "democracy" they never experienced at home. Haywood's unit, the 8th Illinois, fought several bitter battles against the Germans and lost hundreds of men to wounds, diseases, and bitter cold. Harry, like many other black soldiers on the front, saw several of his friends die in the mud and horror of France.

When peace finally came to Europe, the war did not end for Afro-Americans. While President Wilson mouthed pious platitudes about equality and democracy, racist white America sharpened their knives for the returning black soldiers. During the "Red Summer" of 1919, white terrorists rampaged through Chicago, dragging blacks from homes, trains, and stores slaughtering them in the streets. Haywood, who was living in Chicago at the time, hid from the frenzied mobs with other black war veterans.

When the Chicago Riot was over, thirty-eight people were dead, five hundred thirty-seven were injured, and one thousand were left homeless. Viewing the flames, casualties, and wreckage of racism, Haywood said:

> [This] was the great turning point in my life... My experiences in the Army and at home with the police left me totally disillusioned about being able to find any solution to the racial problem through the help of the government; for I had seen that official agencies were among the most racist and dangerous to me and my people... I began to see I had to fight; I had to commit myself to the struggle against whatever it was that made racism possible.[14]

Haywood's later experiences identified the forces behind racism. Otto Hall, Haywood's older brother, was a member of the African Blood Brotherhood and urged Harry, "You ought to quit reading those bourgeois authors and start reading Marx and Engels." His sister, Eppa Hall, was one of the first black women to join the Communist-influenced meat packing union at Swift Packing Company. She told Harry of the progressive whites she encountered and how the company's goon squads attacked white leftists like lynch mobs attacked southern blacks.

Chicago, like New York, was heavily influenced by Marcus Garvey's United Negro Improvement Association (UNIA). Haywood rejected Garvey's nationalism; he believed black nationalism offered the masses pride but no program, no method to liberate Afro-Americans from the economic clutches of private property.

Keenly aware of social events, Haywood also noticed that the white labor radicals of the 1920s were attacked more viciously by the state than was the UNIA. Strikers were attacked by Pinkerton Guards, mass arrests and deportations of suspected Communists were conducted under U.S. Attorney General A. Mitchell Palmer, and often the black middle class joined white capital in condemning workers' movements. Haywood wrote, (these events) sharpened my political perceptions... The racial fog lifted and the face and location of the enemy was clearly outlined. I began to see that the main beneficiaries of Black subjugation also profited from the oppression of poor whites, native and foreign-born. The enemy was those who controlled and manipulated the levers of power; they were the super-rich, white moneyed interests who owned the nation's factories and banks... These levers of power also controlled education, the media, the arts, and all law enforcement agencies. At the bottom of this pyramid and bearing its weight were the working people who toiled in the steel mills, the packing plants, the railway yards, and the thousands of other sweatshops. Lowliest among these were the blacks, pushed to the very bottom by the 'divide and rule' policy.[15]

Whenever time allowed, Haywood studied Marx's *Communist Manifesto*, Engels's *Origins of the Family, Private Property, and the State*, and John Reed's *Ten Days That Shook the World*. Fascinated by international revolts against colonialism, Haywood avidly read about Lenin and Trotsky in Russia, Sun Yat-sen in China, Ghandi in India, Sandino in Nicaragua, and Kadelli and Gumede of the African National Congress in South Africa. Energized by the anti-colonial struggles, Haywood searched for ways to join the war against capitalism. He wrote, "In the years since... the Army, I had come from being a disgruntled Black ex-soldier to being a self-conscious revolutionary looking for an organization with which to make revolution."[16]

Harry sought out his brother Otto and told him he was ready to join the Communist Party. Otto suggested instead that he join the African Blood Brotherhood, a secret all-black revolutionary organization formed for "immediate protection and ultimate liberation of Negroes everywhere." After a few months in the brotherhood, Haywood along with other members joined the Communist Party USA. He was profoundly influenced by his stay in the African Blood Brotherhood and later wrote:

I found my experience in the Brotherhood both stimulating and rewarding. In addition to learning a lot from the communists with whom I was associated, it was here I forged my first active association with black industrial workers. I found them literate, articulate and class-conscious, a proud and defiant group which had been radicalized by the struggles against discriminatory practices of the unions and employers.[17]

Haywood's work in the Party and the Brotherhood convinced him that socialism alone would bring culture, education, welfare, and work to the masses. After several months in the Party, he quit full-time work to become a professional revolutionary. He organized the Chicago chapter of the American Negro Labor Congress (ANLC), recruited black workers into the Party, and led marches against U.S. intervention in Nicaragua. Through his work, Haywood "was confident that we were building the kind of Party that would eventually triumph over capitalism."

In the early 1920s, Communist parties all over the world looked to the Soviet Union as the teacher and model for revolution. The CPUSA was no exception. In 1925, Harry Haywood was one of six U.S. Party leaders chosen by the CPUSA to receive theoretical and practical training at Moscow's University of the Toilers of the East Named For Stalin (Russian acronym is KUTVA). At KUTVA, Haywood studied Marxism-Leninism with cadre from Korea, Palestine, Algeria, China, Ireland, and South Africa. Haywood and other black students, including his brother Otto Hall, Lovett Fort-Whiteman (later the first head of the American Negro Labor Congress), Harold Williams, Jim Farmer, Jane Golden, and Maude White, spent hours discussing how to make the Bolshevik revolution a reality for Afro-Americans.

In 1927, Haywood was assigned to The Lenin School, the Communist International's (Comintern's) three year course for advanced Party cadre. It was as a student at The Lenin School that Haywood impacted the CPUSA's political line on its relationship with the Afro-American struggle. In preparation for the Comintern's Sixth

Convention, Soviet theoreticians were developing the thesis that blacks in the southern United States constituted a separate nation and had the right of self-determination.

As a respected Afro-American student and emerging party leader, Haywood was consulted on his views on the Self-determination theory. Haywood, like most other Communists in the United States, felt nationalism was a reactionary theory which divided workers, allowed monopoly capitalism to flourish to the detriment of the people, and led to inevitable wars for the domination of markets and resources.

After several discussions with Bolshevik leaders and black students, Haywood changed his opinion and eventually supported the Self-determination thesis. He differentiated between the reactionary nationalism of countries that use chauvinism to impose their will on others, and the progressive nationalism of oppressed racial groups struggling for a just society. Under Haywood's definition, the nationalism of Afro-Americans, Irish, and Nicaraguans opposed the same enemy of the international working class: monopoly capitalism.

At the Sixth Congress, Haywood argued that the evolution of the "Black Nation" began in slavery, when the liberties won in the Revolutionary War were not granted to the African slaves. This exclusion from America was heightened when after the Civil War the democratic reforms of the Radical Reconstruction were aborted by the vicious Hayes-Tilden Compromise of 1877. Without land, rights, or property, the Afro-American people became a colonial vassal state of the United States, with Wall Street and monopoly capitalism exploiting the Black Belt South as they would the colonies of Puerto Rico, Cuba, and Hawaii. The profits of northern bankers and insurance companies were guaranteed by the poor southern whites who forced down wages by dividing the working class movement. Self-determination for the black nation, then, would free Afro-Americans from economic exploitation and rob monopoly capitalism of a profitable "colony."

After bitter Comintern debates in which Harry Haywood emerged as the chief supporter of the Black Nation thesis, in 1928 the Sixth Congress of the Communist Party resolved to support Afro-American self-determination in the Black Belt South. An elated Harry Haywood wrote,

> This new line established that the Black freedom struggle is a revolutionary movement in its own right, directed against the very foundations of U.S. imperialism, with its own dynamic pace and momentum, resulting from the unfinished democratic and land revolutions in the South. It places the black liberation movement and the class struggle of U.S. workers in their proper relationship as two aspects of the fight against the common enemy— U.S. capitalism. It elevates the black movement to a position of equality in that battle.[18]

The significance of Harry Haywood's role in the CPUSA's adoption of the Self-determination line cannot be overstated. The thesis fueled the Party's courageous work in Sharecroppers' Unions, the defense of the Scottsboro Boys, and the development of thousands of militant black cadre. With blacks defined as a race, the Party could call for racial equality and black assimilation into America and be done with it. With blacks defined as a nation, however, the struggle was no longer against abstract racism but against "the very foundations of monopoly capitalism." While Harry Haywood did not single-handedly develop the Black Nation thesis, he certainly was its most influential proponent.

The Party rushed headlong into the task of organizing the Black Belt. A strike at the textile mills of Gastonia, North Carolina brought violent reaction from the mill owner and his henchmen. Nevertheless, the CPUSA served notice on finance capital that they were serious about changing forever the open season the owners had on wages, conditions, and lives of Afro-Americans.

Back in Moscow, Haywood was completing his study and preparing to return to the U.S. to join the struggle for black liberation. Before returning to the States, Haywood attended an international conference of labor unions held in Hamburg, Germany where he met several Afro-American party leaders: Helen McClain, a lively Philadelphia needle trades organizer; Ike Hawkins, courageous Pennsylvania coal miner; and the brilliant George Padmore were among the Afro-Americans who convinced Haywood of the Party's success in developing black cadre.

As soon as Haywood returned to America, the Party assigned him to help organize the League of Struggle for Negro Rights, the CPUSA's vehicle for realizing the goal of self-determination. Through the League, Haywood agitated, fought, wrote, organized, marched, and demonstrated for the freedom of the nine Scottsboro Boys due to be executed on a flimsy rape charge in Alabama. Black Communists Sol Harper, Ben Amis, Bob Minor, and Haywood thrust the CPUSA into the vanguard through the fervor and seriousness with which they waged the Scottsboro struggle. While whites prepared lynching parties, black ministers prayed and read scriptures, and the NAACP and reform groups claimed their hands were tied ("after all, they might be guilty"), these black Communists provided attorneys, raised funds, and led a furious defense in the courts and the streets to save the Scottsboro Boys.

* * *

In 1931, the Party-influenced Trade Union Unity League (TUUL) organized black and white miners to struggle against the brutal working conditions in western Pennsylvania's mines. The TUUL planned a massive strike and called in Harry Haywood to help develop the campaign. Ike Hawkins, leader in the militant National Miners' Union, ex-African Blood Brotherhood leader Richard Moore, and Harry Haywood assisted in the strike and rallied miners around the slogan "Fight Against Starvation!"

For twelve weeks forty thousand miners held out

against the Coal and Iron Police. Some of the strike leaders were killed and injured as the fascists attacked the strikers with machine guns, tear gas, and billy clubs. Widespread starvation and police terror, both instigated by the operators, finally broke the backs of the courageous workers.

Upon returning to New York, Haywood became the head of the Party's Negro Department, directing CPUSA work in the Afro-American community. Haywood was respected throughout the Party for his tireless work touring the South, training cadre, organizing unions, calling demonstrations. His name was mentioned whenever the Communist Party undertook a project for black liberation.

Haywood also tried to build the Communist Party in Memphis, Tennessee. Remembering that his grandfather had been run out of Tennessee, and Party leader and sharecropper organizer Mack Coad had been beaten almost to death by Memphis police, Haywood and the CPUSA planned a demonstration condemning the police murder of seventeen year-old Levon Carlock. Looking for an alleged black rapist of a white woman, the police stopped Carlock on a street corner as he waited for his new bride to get off work. They accused Carlock of the rape and kicked him down an alley where they savagely beat him and blew his brains out.

Haywood and the LSNR led demonstrations condemning the murder and calling for charges against the officers. With black moderate leaders begging for weak concessions before "the Reds agitate our community," the police brazenly chased the Party leadership out of Memphis.

Haywood was not discouraged by this failure. Still head of the Negro Department, he directed Party work in Chicago, New York, and other cities where the Councils of the Unemployed, the anti-war committees against the invasion of Ethiopia, and the newly formed National Negro Congress were active in the Afro-American community. In 1935, in Chicago, Haywood led demonstrations against the invasion of Ethiopia. Ten thousand black and white workers participated in demonstrations in which the Communist Party linked the fascist invasion of a sovereign African nation with the continued subjugation of black workers in the United States. The rally was brutally broken up by the Chicago police, and Haywood himself was beaten and kicked by "Chicago's Finest."

After running in a Chicago congressional election as a Communist candidate in 1936, Haywood was among those Afro-Americans who went to Spain to combat fascism on the battlefield. While in Spain, Haywood's leadership style was criticized and slanderous lies (the source of which are unknown) charging cowardice were spread among the CPUSA leadership. When he returned home, Haywood was removed from his post in the Party leadership amid dubious charges and exaggerated rumors. Embittered but not disillusioned, Haywood moved west where he established the Los Angeles chapter of the CPUSA. Haywood later joined the National Maritime Union, a revolutionary union where black and white workers showed solidarity with anti-colonial struggles around the world.

Although shunned by Party leadership, Haywood nevertheless opposed Earl Browder and James Ford's decision to abandon the Self-determination strategy. With the end of World War II and conciliatory gestures by Roosevelt and Stalin, the CPUSA moved more toward reform than revolution. Ford, by then leader of the Party's Negro work, believed that postwar economic progress and the peaceful expansion of democracy made the idea of self-determination obsolete. Consequently, the Party liquidated the radical Sharecroppers' Unions of the South and disbanded the ILD.

In a counterattack to this reversal, Haywood wrote the classic work on the "Black Nation" thesis, *Negro Liberation*. Financed in part by the vigilant Paul Robeson, *Negro Liberation* was a brilliant reaffirmation of the 1928 Party resolution on the Black Belt South. Haywood linked the plantation with imperialism, noting, "The tremendous profit garnered from Negro plantation work is similar to the imperialist tribute exacted from backward colonial labor—all of which goes to support a vast swarm of parasites on the back of the lowly soil cultivator."[19]

He goes on to detail the inner workings of the sharecropping system, and elaborates on how Wall Street and finance capital are the chief beneficiaries of what many see as random white violence in the South. Haywood argues brilliantly that Reconstruction sought to build the deepest aspirations of the Afro-American people: land reform, education, and political power. When northern capital and southern aristocrats combined to crush Reconstruction, the unfulfilled democratic land reforms became the basis of the Black Nation's claim to self-determination.

According to Haywood, the Black Belt South was to American robber barons what Mozambique was to Portugal and Kenya was to England, "an oppressed nation striving for national freedom against the main enemy, imperialism." In *Negro Liberation*, Haywood vigorously opposed the Party's shift in politics, noting that "... the right of self-determination for the Black Belt Negro... commits its proponents to the most consistent and unremitting fight for every democratic need of the Negro people."[20]

Haywood, Claudia Jones, and Edward Strong staunchly opposed the desires of CPUSA leadership (James Ford, Earl Browder, and James Jackson) to reform the Black Belt thesis. Despite the controversy, Haywood continued to work for the Party. He assisted in the defense of the Foley Square 11 (the arrest of the entire CPUSA leadership by the FBI), worked on William Patterson's book, *We Charge Genocide*, and taught revolutionary theory to many of the Party's younger cadre.

Despite his urgings that the CPUSA not abandon the black southern masses in the impending struggle for civil rights, the CPUSA formally abandoned the "Black Nation" thesis at the 1957 Party convention. Communist organizations formed around Afro-American work were dissolved. The League of Struggle for Negro Rights, Civil Rights Congress, Southern Negro Youth Congress, and the Council on African Affairs followed the Sharecroppers' Unions into oblivion.

The 1957 decision prompted Haywood to leave the Party after thirty-six years of revolutionary activity. During the 1960s, Haywood believed the Party's lack of a revolutionary political line prevented them from harnessing the energy of the Civil Rights Movement. He wrote,

> I believe that if we had had a revolutionary party in the sixties that much of the spontaneity and reactionary nationalism of the period could have been combatted. Undoubtedly, the ruling class would still have tried to split the Black Power movement, but the left wing would not have been nearly wiped out as an organized force in the black community. If the CPUSA hadn't liquidated communist work in the South and the factories, the sixties would have seen a consolidated proletarian force emerge in the Black Belt and the ghettos. The communist forces could have come out of the Black Revolt with developed cadres rooted in the factories and communities, with credibility among the masses.[21]

In his later years Haywood worked with the Communist Party Marxist-Leninist (CPML), an organization formed to recapture the revolutionary spirit of the CPUSA of the Thirties and Forties. Haywood helped guide the CPML through its early struggles, drawing on his vast experience in the CPUSA. In 1978, he published his classic work, *Black Bolshevik: Autobiography of an Afro-American Communist*, in which he details his education in Russia, the history of the Self-determination thesis, Party ideological conflicts, racist police brutality, the treachery of monopoly capital, his work in the African Blood Brotherhood, the National Negro Congress, and mine worker and maritime unions, and his vast experiences as an Afro-American Communist. Haywood's development of the Self-determination thesis, his writings, and his dedication to socialism rank him as one on the greatest Afro-American Communists who ever lived.

Angelo Herndon: Convert to Communism

After the Scottsboro Boys' case, the most dramatic legal battle of the 1930s was the Communist Party's defense of Angelo Herndon. A nineteen year-old black miner and member of the Communist Party, Herndon was arrested and jailed for organizing black and white unemployed in Atlanta. As with the Scottsboro Boys, Communist Party cells all over the nation held fundraisers, wrote telegrams, and rallied for Angelo Herndon's freedom.

Herndon's sufferings as a southern worker, detailed in his autobiography *Let Me Live*, provide graphic evidence of why he and other black workers sought to drastically change America through the program of the Communist Party. Born into a religious family in the South, the young Angelo Herndon experienced tragedies which shook his Christian faith and sent his family reeling into poverty. When Angelo was nine, his father died of miners' pneumonia. Herndon describes the sufferings of his poor family (five brothers and sisters), headed by an overworked underpaid black woman:

> Our poverty was appalling. I was terribly distressed by my mother's helplessness. She was a house servant to rich whites. They mistreated her. We hardly ever saw her, for she worked until midnight. Only on rare occasions did we see her, and the little affection that we got from her then had to suffice for a whole week's desolateness. She received ten dollars for her weekly allowance and was never paid overtime.[22]

At the mercy of southern mine, mill, and land owners, thirteen year-old Angelo and his brother Leo worked as coal loaders in Kentucky. The mine company they worked for was run like a slave camp, and Angelo, Leo, and other black boys were customarily cheated and abused. Angelo later wrote,

> On every pay day I found in my pay envelope an account of the deductions which the company made. These usually amounted to from ten to fifteen dollars (out of a

total salary of forty dollars). They were for baths (which I hardly ever got a chance to take), for school (I was only thirteen years old and certainly had no children), for medical insurance, hospital service, and supplies.[23]

When Herndon spoke out against this and other company scams, his white supervisor grabbed him and shouted, "You dirty little nigger, shut your trap and don't let me hear a sound from you again. You take what you get and be grateful for it. If you don't like it, get the hell out of here and see if you are treated better elsewhere."[24] Herndon found he was not treated better elsewhere. At the Goodyear Rubber Company in Alabama, Angelo recalled, "There were day and night shifts, and often I worked one shift after another. We worked like mules, slept like dogs in stinking tents, and ate rotten food. The discipline was that of an army camp..."[25]

Since black poverty and misery were everywhere, Herndon reasoned that the harsh conditions of Afro-American workers were not isolated incidents of bigotry. Even at a young age he discerned the cycle in which violence sustains economic exploitation. In his autobiography he noted how the sadistic lynching of Hayes Turner and his pregnant wife Mary was used to intimidate other blacks who might, like the Turners, dispute the fraudulent accounting of white landowners.

The violence of southern capitalism began to wear down Angelo Herndon. "I could see neither joy nor purpose in life," he wrote, "and my young spririt, only fourteen years of age, was weighted down by a burden of weariness hard to imagine."[26] For young Angelo, prayers and sermons did nothing to ease black suffering. While whites murdered, cheated, and exploited, Herndon was saddened that his people's only response existed in the shouts and songs of a Sunday service. Herndon's religious inertia soon changed.

> It was on a sultry evening in June, 1930. I was coming home from work with a friend when some soiled handbills ...caught my eye. I was startled by the headline, which read: 'Would you rather fight or starve?'

My friend and I sat down on a house step and began reading it. We read it over and over again, not believing our own eyes.[27]

Fascinated by this message of hope, Herndon attended the next meeting of Birmingham's Council of the Unemployed. Initiated by the Communist Party, the Unemployment Councils rallied black and white jobless to demand relief from the society to which they had already contributed so much.

At his first meeting, Herndon listened to black and white speakers link racism and unemployment to U.S. capitalism. Of all the speakers, black steel worker John Lindley had the biggest impact on the young Herndon. That night Lindley spoke of his struggles as a worker and an Afro-American:

> For eighteen years I worked at the Ensley Steel Mills...and now when I am no longer able to speed up and work like I used to, they have decided to get rid of me by throwing me out on the streets to starve, but I am one of those who will not take it lying down. I am going to fight for my rights, no matter how dear the price may be...There is only one way for us to free ourselves from this wage-slave system and that is by uniting both Negro and white workers into a fighting alliance. If you do not believe what I say, then why do they molest Negro and white workers when they meet together?[28]

Young Angelo Herndon was struck by these powerful words of a black elder, whose sufferings led not to prayers of humility and hopes for the afterlife but to radical action. Fascinated by the prospect of alleviating the agonies of his people, Angelo rushed up after the meeting and said, "I'm with you with all my heart and I would like you to put me down as a member." He now no longer prayed that his mother would not be degraded and abused; he chose to do something about it, and he diverted his energies from religious passivity to the practical struggles of the Unemployment Council. Angelo wrote of his "rebirth" in the Communist Party:

> The change of my viewpoint was almost fabulous, emerging from the urge to escape the cruelties of life in religious abstractions into a healthy, vigorous, and realistic recognition that life on earth, which was so full of struggle and tears for the poor, could be changed by the intelligent and organized will of the workers.[29]

Filled with revolutionary zeal, Herndon became a whirlwind of energy in the Unemployment Council. His life was totally transformed, and the sight of black and white southerners working together for economic justice led him to join the Communist Party.

> Up to the time I had met the Communists I did not know how to fight the lynchings of Negroes and Jim Crowism. I was bewildered, grief-stricken, and helpless. All of a sudden I found myself in an organization which fought selflessly and tirelessly to undo all the wrongs perpetrated upon my race. Here was no dilly-dallying, no pussyfooting on the question of full equality for the Negro people.[30]

All of Herndon's pent-up frustrations were now released through struggles with his comrades in the Party. As a volunteer organizer in the militant National Miners' Union (MNU), Herndon established four union locals in Alabama coal mines. He also organized longshoremen in New Orleans, sharecroppers in rural Alabama, and held demonstrations for the Scottsboro Boys. This revolutionary activity was not in an ivory tower, for Angelo was arrested, harassed, and beaten with fists, boards, and rubber hoses by the poor white sheriffs maintaining "order" for the parasitic robber barons of the South. When not in jail or the picket lines, Herndon kept up with revolutionary theory. "After the meetings I would go home...Then, while the whole household was asleep, I sat before a kerosene lamp reading the works of Karl Marx, Frederick Engels, and Lenin. I felt like Christopher Columbus discovering a new world."[31]

Herndon went wherever workers suffered. In 1932, the city of Atlanta cut twenty-three thousand families from the relief rolls and eliminated benefits for hundreds of other working class families. The specter of starvation and disease haunted Atlanta's unemployed. In response, Angelo Herndon and the Unemployment Council printed and distributed ten thousand leaflets calling for a demonstration. Herndon and his comrades demanded $4 per week for the families of the unemployed, no discrimination in distribution of benefits, and coal, shoes, and food for the poor of Atlanta.

In July of 1932, Herndon and one thousand black and white workers marched to Atlanta's relief office to demand immediate assistance. Officials were stunned by this unprecedented display of racial solidarity, and the next day the benefits were reinstated and six thousand dollars immediately allocated for the unemployed. Herndon later said, "It was a demonstration of the southern worker's power. Like a giant that had been asleep a long time, he now began to stir."[32]

The giant of southern reaction also began to stir. While on his way from the Unemployment Council's post office box, Herndon was arrested by Georgia sheriffs. Digging up an 1861 slave law, the grand jury charged him with "Attempting to Incite Insurrection...to incite insurrection and did make an attempt to induce others to join in combined resistance to the lawful authority of the State of Georgia."[33] Herndon's arrest for his struggles on behalf of black and white unemployed ignited protests from all over the nation.

The ridiculous charge of the state of Georgia against Herndon was matched only by the racist, anti-Communist preacher prosecuting the case. In his opening statement, Reverend Hudson declared, "This is not only a trial of Angelo Herndon, but of Lenin, Stalin, Trotsky...and every white person who believes that black and white should unite for the purpose of setting up a nigger soviet republic in the Black Belt!"[34]

In a primitive display of religious backwardness, Hudson proclaimed, "Send this damnable anarchistic Bolshiveki to his death by electrocution. God will be pleased and our daughters can walk the streets safely.

Stamp this thing out now!"³⁵ Throughout the trial Hudson's antics were condoned by a southern judge for whom racism and anti-Communism were also solemn creeds.

Opposing the prosecutor and judge was Ben Davis, a black attorney who had been born into a relatively wealthy Atlanta family. Although he was destined for a comfortable life in Atlanta's black middle class, Davis was attracted to communism by the Party's diligent defense of the Scottsboro Boys. He joined the Party and abandoned a life of relative leisure for one of struggling for the working people of America. Davis's bold defense of Herndon in the midst of the racist South is one of the great Afro-American battles for justice in the courtroom.

As the trial progressed, it became clear that Herndon was not charged with "inciting to insurrection" but with promoting equality and human dignity. Angelo Herndon recalled that,

> They (the prosecutors) questioned me in great detail. Did I believe that the bosses and government should pay insurance to unemployed workers? That Negroes should have complete equality with white people? Did I believe in the demand for self-determination of the Black Belt South—that the Negro people should be allowed to rule the Black Belt territory, kicking out the white landlords and government officials? That it wasn't necessary to have bosses at all? I told them I believed all of that—and more...³⁶

Davis pulled no punches in the trial. For his closing argument, he exhorted:

> Gentlemen of the jury, don't try to organize for better conditions, and—especially you who are unemployed—don't try to fight for bread for yourselves or your starving families; for if you do, Rev. Hudson will send you to the electric chair. According to Mr. Hudson, it is a crime to ask for bread... In the first place, Rev. Hudson doesn't know any more about Communism than a pig knows about a full-dress suit... The issue is simply this, consider

in your minds when you retire to the jury room whether you want to see a man burn in the electric chair because he had the courage to fight for the Negroes and whites who are hungry and without bread and jobs.[37]

Despite the brilliant eloquence of both Ben Davis and Angelo Herndon, the defendant was found guilty of insurrection and sentenced to twenty years in the penitentiary.

After the trial, Davis was whisked out of the South by the CPUSA. They did not want to see their talented comrade murdered by an angry southern lynch mob for his flagrant verbal assaults on Rev. Hudson. Davis went on to Harlem where he edited Party periodicals, wrote *Path to Negro Liberation*, and from 1944 to 1949 served two terms on the New York City Council. His autobiography, *Communist Councilman from Harlem*, discusses in depth his struggles for black liberation through the formal political arena. Davis later was one of the Foley Square 11 and served five years for "conspiracy to overthrow the government."

The ILD did not give up on Angelo Herndon, and after four years of hearings, re-hearings, appeals before the State Supreme Court, appeals before the Supreme Court, and retrials, Herndon was finally acquitted in 1936. After his release, Herndon, like Davis, went north and continued to work with the Communist Party USA.

*   *   *

The amazing transformation of Angelo Herndon from a frightened black Christian praying for freedom to a bold Afro-American Communist struggling with black and white workers for justice and socialism is indicative of the revolutionary potential of black workers. Those deluded into thinking that Afro-Americans are reluctant to advocate socialism should ponder the risks and death threats cadre like Herndon faced in their struggle to bring revolutionary change to the United States. Herndon should be remembered along with that galaxy of black heroes for whom revolution was not rhetoric, but a way of life.

> All my life I'd been sweated and stepped on and Jim-Crowed. I lay on my belly for a few dollars a week, and saw my pay stolen and slashed, and my buddies killed. I lived in the worst section of town, and rode behind the "Colored" signs of streetcars, as though there was something disgusting about me. I heard myself called 'nigger' and 'darky' and I had to say, 'Yes sir' to every white man...I had always detested it, but I had never known that anything could be done about it. And here, all of a sudden, I had found organizations...that weren't scared to come out for equality for the Negro people, for the rights of workers. The Jim-Crow system, the wage-slave system, weren't everlasting after all! It was like all of a sudden turning a corner on a dirty, old street and finding yourself facing a broad, shining highway...I felt then, and I know now, that the Communist program is the only program that the Southern workers, whites and Negroes both—can possibly accept in the long run.[38]

Angelo Herndon, 1934

Henry Winston: My Vision Endures

Henry Winston rose from a poor school dropout to the chair of the Central Committee of the Communist Party. Born in 1911 in Hattiesburg, Mississippi, by age eighteen Winston worked twelve hours a day to help his father feed their family. Moving on to Kansas City, Winston met members of the CPUSA at a street rally. Intrigued by their commitment to Afro-Americans at the mercy of brutal landlords and rampaging mobs, Winston began reading Karl Marx's *Communist Manifesto* and John Reed's *Ten Days That Shook The World*.

Empowered by Communist theory, Winston became a leader of the Kansas City Council of the Unemployed, where he led marches and demonstrations for coal, food, shelter, and money for families of the unemployed. As a member of the Young Communist League Winston was involved in the struggle for the Scottsboro Boys and led a delegation to Washington to demand employment and living wages for the jobless.

In 1933, the twenty-two year-old Winston joined the Communist Party. Realizing the potential for leadership in this young fighter from Mississippi, the CPUSA sent him to Moscow for political education. Like Harry Haywood before him, Winston returned to the U.S. with a revolutionary fervor that propelled him into the leadership of the Party. By 1938, at twenty-seven years old, Winston was elected to the Party's National Committee. He later was elected to the Central Committee where for several years he led party work in trade unions, sharecropper organizing, and anti-war demonstrations.

In 1948, the U.S. government initiated the infamous Cold War by arresting the entire leadership of the Communist Party under the infamous Smith Act. Passed in 1940, the Smith Act outlawed any organization or person that advocated the violent overthrow of the government of the United States. The act was used, however, against anyone who fought for the rights of working people and Afro-Americans. Of the eleven arrested by the FBI, three were black: Winston, Ben Davis, and James Jackson.

Charged with "conspiracy to advocate the overthrow of the government" at some future, unspecified date, the Foley Square 11 were tried under the largest police guard in New York history. At the trial Winston thundered,

> I am a Negro. I have experienced Jim Crow. I have seen lynchings. I have experienced segregation, brutality of every possible kind, insults and abuses, and have always searched for a program for my people that would liberate them from this type of oppression... This is my life, and I shall never forget the fact that the Communist Party was the first organization in this country which offered a program for my people as well as my class.[39]

The courts cared nothing for Winston's sense of justice, and sentenced him and the other defendants to five years in jail. The Party appealed the decision, and while Winston awaited the decision he continued to advocate his views with the publication of *What It Means To Be A Communist*. The Supreme Court upheld the conviction in 1951, but the Party hustled Winston, Jackson, and two others underground while the rest of the Foley Square 11 went to jail.

While in prison, Winston continued to lead the Party, but after several months he eventually turned himself in to serve his sentence. In prison Winston's health deteriorated but the authorities made no attempt to get him adequate medical care. The Party's Committee to Free Henry Winston, led by William Patterson, fought to force the prison to allow Winston to see a doctor. By the time medical help arrived, Winston had developed a brain tumor which severed his optic nerve and blinded him for life. Sightless and weakened, Winston nevertheless was possessed by one thought, "that of retaining my strength for the struggle."

In 1961, Henry Winston was pardoned and released by President Kennedy. In his first address to the Party, Winston demonstrated he lost none of his revolutionary fervor.

> I return from prison with the unshakeable conviction that the people of this great land, Negro and white, need a Communist Party fighting for the unity of the people, for peace, democracy, and socialism. I take my place in it with great pride. My sight is gone but my vision endures.[40]

Ten years of prison and his incurable blindness did not halt the struggles of Henry Winston. Throughout the Sixties and Seventies, he led the Party's electoral work, organized the CPUSA's campaign to free Angela Davis, and wrote several books, including *Strategy For A Black Agenda*. In 1966, the fiery Winston was elected National Chair of the Communist Party, and was key in the Party's decision to nominate Charlene Mitchell as its presidential candidate in 1968. As Chair, Winston worked fervently to maintain Afro-American membership in the Party, and at the 1975 National Convention, 28% of the delegates were black. Loss of sight or freedom did not deter Winston, and he remained a committed member of the party he believed was loyal to black liberation.

Incarcerated Revolutionaries

- **George Jackson**
- **Jon Jackson and Ruchell Magee**

Incarcerated Revolutionaries

So many black radicals have been jailed by reactionary governments that a separate chapter on incarcerated revolutionaries could include almost every black revolutionary in history. Bishop, Rodney, Du Bois, Robeson, Wright, Newton, Seale, Herndon, Claudia Jones, Baraka, Davis, Mary Ann Moultrie, Ngugi, Mondlane, Mugabe, Cabral, Nkrumah, Neto, and thousands of other black revolutionaries were either jailed or threatened with jail.

Rather than discuss all incarcerated black radicals, this chapter is reserved for those Afro-Americans who were imprisoned as "criminals," but once in jail embraced communism as a tool for analysis and action. While many middle-class intellectuals and activists discover socialism during relaxed conversions in plush college libraries, the black men discussed here learned of class struggle and economic justice while confined in concrete cages.

Afro-Americans are often jailed for petty crimes against property while the real criminals fly Lehr jets, vacation in the Bahamas, and cut shady multibillion-dollar deals. They are not ignorant of America's injustices, and their life in prison often increases their hostility toward a society whose punishments and rewards are based on race and class. Consequently, the black men who found in Marxism an outlet for their anger became the most dangerous black Communists, without a stake in the system and ready to die for liberation.

It was this commitment, exemplified in the great George Jackson, that made incarcerated revolutionaries so incendiary. Chains, bars, walls, barbed wire, dogs, guards, locks, and handcuffs could not contain the message of revolution advanced by George Jackson and his comrades in chains.

For the Love of Dignity and Freedom

George Lester Jackson:
Soledad Brother

George Jackson was the ultimate "renegade nigger": angry, bitter, caged, and revolutionary. Eyes peering out from behind the cell door, hands itching for a gun, a knife, a bomb—anything with which to wage revolution on those responsible for his people's misery. Once George combined his consuming rage with Communist theory, he was destined to die. The United States was leveling Vietnam, bombing Cambodia, funding Portuguese fascists in Angola and Mozambique, meddling in Iran, El Salvador, and Guyana, and could not afford to have a loudmouth black prisoner writing books about black, brown, and Asian Socialists waging war against white capitalists. He had to die.

"A brother from the streets," George Jackson had been in and out of trouble since he was a young boy growing up in Chicago's West Side projects. Roaming the mean streets of Chicago and later Los Angeles, George was a school dropout and petty criminal, the "typical" black urban male. At age fourteen he was arrested for purse-snatching. In 1960, the eighteen year-old Jackson was arrested for driving the car of some friends who had stolen $70 from a Los Angeles gas station. For this heinous and dastardly crime against property, young George received an indeterminate sentence of one year to life. (One year to life! Compare this with the lecture circuit, television appearances, and high consultant salaries of the crooked crew of Nixon, Agnew, Kissinger, Haldeman, Erlichman, Mitchell, Dean, Colson, and Liddy, who subverted democracy through Watergate and other crimes in the late Sixties and early Seventies).

George defied the prison system in the same way that he defied society. Soon after his incarceration, he was sentenced to two years solitary confinement for refusing to sit in the back of the recreation room. His defiance soon took more ominous directions, at least as far as the authorities were concerned. George read avidly, and what he read transformed his self-destructive behavior into a purposeful struggle for black liberation. He says in his book, *Blood In My Eye,*

> In prison I met Marx, Lenin, Trotsky, Engels, and Mao, and they redeemed me. I also met the black guerrillas (other revolutionary black prisoners) George Lewis, James Carr, W.C. Nolen, Bill Christmas, Tony Gibson, and others. We attempted to transform the black criminal element into a black revolutionary movement.[1]

As a petty hoodlum George stole pocket change from gas stations; as an incarcerated Communist, he now sought to transform the entire structure of American society.

On January 13, 1970, a fight broke out among black and white inmates in the yard at Soledad Prison. A white tower guard with a reputation for racism and marksmanship fired on the crowd. When the shooting was over, W.C. Nolen, Alvin Miller, and Cleveland Edwards were dead. Black inmates considered the murders an execution since all three prisoners were known as "black militants" who struggled for the rights of Afro-Americans at Soledad. The grand jury, however, ruled the killings "justifiable homicide," and the guard was hailed as a hero by racist inmates and guards.

Three days later, a white guard was found dead inside the prison, allegedly in retaliation for the cold-blooded executions in the prison yard. The next month, George Jackson, John Clutchette, and Fleeta Drumgo were charged with the murder of the white guard. These three, like the three murdered Afro-American prisoners, had a reputation for being "bad niggers" who did not "take shit" from prison authorities, racist guards, or white prisoners. But they were more than just angry black men; George, John and Fleeta were revolutionaries who sought to organize uneducated black prisoners into a "convict army of liberation." Although there was never any evidence linking them to the crime, the warden said Jackson "was the only one who could have done it." So began the celebrated Soledad Brothers case.

The other two Soledad Brothers, Fleeta Drumgo and John Clutchette, had received long sentences for crimes against property. At the time of the murder charge, both men were serving six-month to fifteen-year terms for burglary and robbery. Like George Jackson, Fleeta and John had changed from destructive criminals into radicalized black prisoners training themselves for the impending revolution.

Poor families, neglected schools, forgotten neighborhoods, and greedy landlords constituted their world, and Fleeta, John, and George learned early that America offered nothing except what they could take for themselves. "Acceptable" avenues to upward mobility were blocked, so the three struck out against society as criminals. Hangin' out, breakin' in, and dodging "the Man" became a way of life for these bitter products of American capitalism. Since Afro-Americans were no longer slaves, the U.S. discarded its black citizens through an insidious genocidal process that drowned youthful hopes in a sea of indifference, racism, and discrimination.

Fleeta, John, and George were like the thousands of young black men who even today fill America's jails. Afro-American poet Gil Scott-Heron writes that most black convicts are school dropouts with less than $50 on them at the time of arrest, "so only the poor and the ignorant go to jail." Like the hordes of young blacks that fill U.S. prisons, the Soledad Brothers were not born criminals, they were the products of a system that requires a permanent labor pool composed of those who can be hired in crises, drafted to fight in wars, and expended in accordance with the cruel dictates of the "free market."

In the regimented, zoo-like conditions of the penitentiary, Fleeta, John, and George uncovered the cause of and reason for their misery. Through discussion, group readings, and experiences both in and out of prison, the three came to see black subjugation in the context of a heartless capitalist system that generated profits for the few without regard for the needs of others. They read Malcolm X, the literature of the Black Panther Party, and the smuggled works of Marx, Lenin and Mao. In discovering socialism, the Soledad Brothers found out just who the real criminals were. In a letter to his father, George writes,

> Chew on this for a few moments...a colonizer, the original thief, a murderer for personal gain, a kidnapper-slaver, a maker of cannon, bombs, and poison gas, an egocentric parasite...trying to convey to us that we must adjust ourselves to his way, that we must learn to be like him.[2]

Socialism taught the Brothers how crime and incarceration are part of class struggle. Jackson wrote, "Crime is the result of the grossly disproportionate distribution of wealth and privilege. Imprisonment is an aspect of class struggle."[3] On a similar note, Fleeta Drumgo wrote to his family, "I am constantly thinking about the unemployment, underemployment, poverty, and malnutrition that are the basic facts of our existence...it is this that causes crime."[4] John Clutchette made the same point when he told an interviewer, "You won't find members of the ruling clique in places like this...you will find their victims."[5]

Even before the murder charge, George, Fleeta, and John were constant victims of official harassment, provoked violence, and repeated denial of parole and privileges. The only thing worse than a "nigger behind bars" was one who even in prison refused to capitulate to white supremacy. Walking around talking about the reactionary rich, genocide against blacks, and urban guerrilla warfare, the three became the scourge of the Soledad Prison authorities. George demonstrated his revolutionary insights when he wrote,

> The hypocrisy of American fascism forces it to conceal its attacks on political offenders by the legal fiction of conspiratory laws and highly sophisticated frame-ups. The people must learn that when one offends the totalitarian state, it is not an offense against the people of that state, but an assault upon the privileges of the privileged few.[6]

Fleeta Drumgo's writings also reveal why the authorities had to silence him.

> There's a growing awareness behind these walls, we're seeing through the madness of capitalism, class interest, surplus value, and imperialism, which the Gestapo system perpetuates. It is this we have to look at and understand in order to recognize the inhumanity inflicted upon the masses of the people here in America and abroad. As brother Malcolm X said, 'We as people, as human beings, have the basic human right to eliminate the conditions that have and are continuously destroying us.'[7]

In a letter home, John Clutchette demonstrated he had arrived at the same conclusions as his colleagues.

> In prison we are governed by the same system that excludes the human rights of the people, a system with no concern for the people's welfare...on the outside. Here on the inside the attitudes are more extreme, we are, like the people outside, forced into resisting force.[8]

Since the crime of murdering a prison guard carried an automatic death penalty, it is clear that the state sought to permanently eliminate these meddling black revolutionaries. While the iron-fisted repression of the Black Panther Party demonstrated the weakness of black revolutionaries on the outside, the incarcerated revolutionary was naked before the ruthless advances of the state. They could, like their three brothers in the Soledad Yard, be picked off like turkeys by a white racist guard. George wrote of this horrible condition,

> I am born to a premature death. A menial, subsistence wage-worker, odd-job man, the cleaner, the caught, the man under the hatches, without bail—that's me, the colonial victim. Anyone who can pass the Civil Service exam today can kill me tomorrow. I've lived repression every moment of my life....In every sense of the term, I'm a slave, of property.[9]

In another letter, George added,

> I've been hungry too long, I've been angry too often. I've

been lied to and insulted too many times. They've pushed me over the line from which there can be no retreat. I know they will not be satisfied until they've pushed me out of this existence altogether. I've been the victim of so many racist attacks I can never relax again. I can still smile now, after ten years of blocking knife thrusts, and the pick handles of faceless sadistic pigs, of anticipating and reacting for ten years, seven of them in solitary. I can still smile now, but by the time this thing is over I may not be a nice person.[10]

The Soledad Brothers were not alone. White leftists, the Black Panther Party, and black radicals like Angela Davis organized support groups under the slogan, "Save the Soledad Brothers from Legal Lynching." Rallies were held all over the nation to expose the racist murder charge and demand freedom for the Soledad Three.

Although the state used the murder charge to silence the Soledad Brothers, their plans went awry. Public support skyrocketed the Soledad Three into the national news, and inmates all over the nation were radicalized by the struggle of their brothers in California. George Jackson, the leader of the three, was catapulted into national prominence with the 1970 publication of his book of prison letters, *Soledad Brothers*.

Declared contraband in California prisons, *Soledad Brother* was a stirring documentary of a black man's revolt against racism and capitalist domination. Consisting of letters to his mother and father, his brother Jonathan Jackson, his attorney Fay Stendel, and Angela Davis, George Jackson's book was one of the most powerful manifestos to come out of the Black Liberation Movement of the Sixties and Seventies. The next year, George published *Blood In My Eye*, an outline of his theories on the strategies and tactics of guerrilla warfare, written while in solitary confinement. Appointed to Field Marshall in the Black Panther Party, author of two revolutionary books, and celebrated inmate-theorist, the imprisoned George Jackson was a powerhouse of Afro-American revolutionary thought.

Drawing on the black militancy of Du Bois and

Malcolm X and the communism of Lenin and Mao, George developed his own radical ideology. As a black urban male for whom "prison... looms as the next phase in a sequence of humiliations," George created a body of literature which must be studied by future generations of Afro-Americans. Of revolution, George wrote,

> It will not be allowed. That makes the true revolutionary an outlaw, the black revolutionary a doomed man.... To the slave revolution is an imperative, a love-inspired act of desperation.... Revolution builds in stages, it isn't cool or romantic, it is stalking and being stalked.[11]

Of capitalism:

> ...capitalizing on the next man's weakness has contributed to...man competing against man for the necessary things, for status symbols, for the power to suppress his competitors.... Our [Afro-Americans] change from an article of moveable property to untrained misfits on the labor market was not as most think a change to freedom from slavery, but merely to another kind of slavery.... Ever since slavery, our principal enemy is and must be isolated and identified as capitalism. The slaver was and is the factory owner, the businessman of capitalist America...It was the profit motive that built the tenement house and the city project. Profit and loss prevents repairs and maintenance. Free enterprise brought the monopolistic chain store into the neighborhood. The concept of private ownership of facilities that the people need to exist brought the legions of hip-shooting brainless pigs down upon our heads.... They're there to protect the entrepeneur.[12]

And on the ruling class:

> This is a huge nation dominated by the most reactionary and violent ruling clique in the history of the world, where the majority of the people just simply cannot understand that they are existing on the misery and discomfort of the world.[13]

In *Blood In My Eye* he writes:

> The minority ruling clique is engaging the people's vanguard for control of the masses. The ruling clique approaches the task with a 'what-to-think' program; the vanguard elements have the much more difficult job of promoting 'how-to-think'.[14]

Blood In My Eye also outlines the details of black urban guerrilla warfare. A victim of violence in prison and the streets, George Jackson had no pacifist illusions about "peaceful transitions to socialism" or the quiet evolution of full equality for Afro-Americans.

> Armed struggle is at the heart of revolution. If the problems of the people cannot be redressed because the necessary resources are in the hands of a relatively few families and individuals, it means we are going to have to seize this property.[15]

For Jackson, black misery mandated that the revolution begin as soon as possible. "We cannot wait," he cautioned, "until the generation that thinks of blacks as niggers and the rest of the world as gooks, chinks, spics, etc., has been educated away.[16]

As a black male intimately familiar with the ravages of racism, George believed the white working class was incapable of leading a socialist revolution. He believed the working class was divided into two parts: one "new pig class" of fascists, nationalist factory workers, construction workers, and the like; and a more progressive wing with students, teachers, and a few advanced blue-collar workers. To George, racism was "the most complex psycho-social by-product that private enterprise has manufactured, and obstacle to an united left."[17]

Like the Black Panther Party and the League of Revolutionary Black Workers, George Jackson believed the oppressed black masses would lead the transformation of America. Afro-Americans would be the urban shock troops who weakened the heart of America while Mozambique, Chile, and Korea tore away at the overseas tentacles of U.S. imperialism. At the center of George's vanguard party, however, was the black prisoner. "With the time and incentive these brothers have to read, study, and think, you will find no class more aware, more embittered, or dedicated to the ultimate remedy, revolution."[18]

A prisoner in the belly of the beast, without freedom, a job, a home, or a family, George had nothing to lose except his life. He was therefore determined to make war on the system that starved, miseducated, and killed his people.

> I don't want to die and leave a few sad songs and a hump in the ground as my monument. I want to leave a world that is free from pollution, racism, poverty, bigotry, wars, armies, and licentious economies.... If he [the white ruling class] prevails over me, I want something to remain, to torment his ass, to haunt him.[19]

Corporate profits, derived from domestic racism and global exploitation of Third World resources, could ill-afford a black prisoner who eloquently rallied the Afro-American underclass to socialism. On August 21st, 1971, George Jackson was shot in the back by prison guards who claimed he was attempting to escape. Eric Mann, in the book *Comrade George*, exposes the lies of the authorities and charges the state with plotting to assassinate this hero of black liberation.

George's death reverberated throughout black America, particularly in the prisons. At Attica State Penitentiary in New York, his assassination prompted the inmates to plan a demonstration for better living conditions and an end to harassment. After the inmates took hostages in order to negotiate with the authorities, Governor Nelson Rockefeller ordered in troops, and thirty-one prisoners were killed in the ensuing massacre.

The year after George Jackson's murder, the charges against the Soledad Brothers were dropped. The state had gotten its wish, George Jackson was gone. Nevertheless, Jackson had overcome miseducation, poverty, eleven years in prison (seven of them in solitary confinement), and murder plots to leave a legacy of revolutionary fervor from which future generations could benefit. "People are already dying who could be saved," he wrote. "Generations more will die or live poor butchered half-lives if you fail to act. Discover humanity and your love in revolution. Pass on the torch. Join us, give up your own life for the people."[20]

George Jackson, murdered at twenty-nine, remains a powerful symbol of Afro-American defiance against ruthless capitalism and racist oppression. Jackson was not an aberration or a misfit of society, he was rather, a reflection of both the immense suffering and militant rage of Afro-Americans. The Soledad Brother's greatness lies in his desire for revolutionary change and his willingness to die to make it happen.

> The black revolutionary is a doomed man. All the forces of counterrevolution stack up over his head. He is standing in the tank trap he has dug. He lives in the cross hairs. No one can understand his feeling but himself. From the beginning of his revolutionary consciousness he must use every device to stay alive. Violence is a forced issue. It is incumbent on him.[21]

> Dear father,
> ...you have worked hard and obeyed the laws but still have nothing. Is it idle dreaming for me to want an end to something like this?[22]

> I am an extremist. I call for extreme measures to solve extreme problems. Where face and freedom are concerned I do not use or prescribe half measures. To me life without control over the determining factors is not worth the effort of drawing breath. Without self-determination I am extremely displeased.[23]

> —*excerpts from the writings of George Lester Jackson*

The San Rafael Courthouse Rebellion: Jon Jackson and Ruchell Magee

George's younger brother Jonathan grew up in the shadow of his brother's life sentence. At seventeen, Jonathan lived and breathed the Socialist revoluton his older brother wrote about in his letters. In *With My Mind On Freeom*, Angela Davis writes of her amazement at the depth of Jonathan Jackson's commitment to freeing his mentor, role model, and brother, George Jackson. While his classmates in Pasadena, California worried about movies, dates and sports, Jonathan developed into a young warrior-revolutionary. His consciousness as a teenager was evident when he wrote, "We do 30% of the nation's work for 1% of the returns and a huge pool of us is always kept unemployed to reduce the value of the labor of those who are employed."[24] The repression of the Black Panther Party and the Soledad Brothers led him to observe, "We can't build a vanguard party without finding some way of staying alive...One fundamental problem remains, the survival of the vanguard political party."[25]

When his brother George was charged with murder while in prison, Jonathan's rage erupted. "I'm not waiting for them to attack a new part of Africa or Asia. I'm entering the war now."[26] On August 7, 1970, Jonathan Jackson walked into the San Rafael Courthouse, pointed guns at the guards, and calmly said, "All right, gentlemen, I'm taking over now." Unchaining San Quentin inmates James McClain, William Christmas, and Ruchell Magee, Jonathan Jackson gathered up four hostages for protection and attempted to flee in a van.

Jackson had planned to drive to a radio station where he would broadcast to America the lies, dirty tricks, and violence used against his brother and black inmates at prisons all over the nation. He never made it. Despite the hostages, the San Quentin guards went into a frenzy and shot up the vehicle. Jonathan and his comrades never fired a shot. One hostage (Judge Haley), James McClain, William Christmas, and the courageous young Jackson were killed in the gunfire. The black prisoners and Jonathan Jackson considered their brief moments of freedom to be reminiscent of the glorious Underground Railroad of years past, when black slaves stole liberty from the clutches of white plantation owners.

George loved his brother deeply, and wrote this tribute when he was told of his sacrifice:

> Man-child, black man-child with submachine gun in hand. he was free for a while. I guess that's more than most of us can expect. I want people to wonder at what forces created him, terrible, cold, vindictive, calm, man-child, courage in one hand, the machine gun in the other, scourge of the unrighteous—an ox for the people to ride![27]

It was in memory of Jon Jackson that Angela Davis later engaged in political struggles for black and brown prisoners. She wrote,

> Not to fight in this way was to leave Jonathan forever lying on the asphalt—lying there in his own blood as though he was where he belonged. Not to fight would be forever to deny him—all the young and unborn Jonathans—the beauty of lush green mountains instead of cold gray bars, the freshness of a trip to the seaside instead of a dismal journey into a Soledad Prison visiting room. A childhood full of smiles and nice toys and older brothers who are beautiful, strong and free...[28]

Ruchell Magee survived and was tried along with Angela Davis for conspiring to commit the courthouse rebellion. Like the Soledad Brothers, Magee was just one more uneducated brother for whom work, stability, and personal fulfillment were but fleeting illusions. At age thirteen in Louisiana, Magee was arrested (for attempted rape of a white woman in a state that regularly manufactured that charge to repress the black population) and worked like a slave on the prison chain gang. He survived the brutality of Louisiana State's Angola Penitentiary, and at age twenty-three the unskilled and illiterate convict was released and moved to Los Angeles. Scratching out a living washing dishes and cars, Magee was again arrested for possessing ten dollars worth of marijuana. In a bizzare case, Magee was also charged with kidnapping for sitting in the car of someone with whom he had had an argument.

Since there was nothing productive Magee could do (funny how blacks became expendable after slavery—for more on that phenomenon, read Sidney Wilhelm's *Who Needs The Negro*, and Samuel Yette's *The Choice: The Issue of Black Survival In America*) he might as well be locked up where he could not endanger law-abiding, tax-paying citizens.

Magee wanted to plead not guilty for both the petty drug charge and his kidnapping frame-up, but the court-appointed attorney disagreed and filed a guilty plea. Magee protested and was beaten and gagged. When the dust settled, Ruchell Magee had an indeterminate sentence of one year to life for possessing ten dollars of marijuana and for "kidnapping."

To white America, Magee was just another "nigger in jail," an "ignorant" criminal (his I.Q. score in Louisiana was 78) who threatened property rights and white womanhood. For seven years Magee languished in San Quentin. Rather than acquiesce to white supremacy, Magee struck back with a fury. In the midst of the emasculation of prison, he taught himself to read and became versed in constitutional rights. When Magee wrote the courts for the transcript of his trial, he found several inconsistencies and deliberate doctoring of the file. "For seven years," he wrote in a letter, "I have been forced into slavery on a flagrant racist slave conviction, where the pigs have used any and all types of falsehood to avoid releasing me."[27]

During the trial of Magee and Angela Davis, the media attempted to portray a sickening "Beauty and the Beast" syndrome: Magee the ignorant, virile brute, and Angela the attractive, educated professor. Magee and Davis did not allow these portrayals to divide them, and they supported each other throughout the trial. Although Ruchell Magee and Angela Davis were eventually acquitted, Magee's imprisonment and trial are sad reminders of how black lives are ruined by this unending American nightmare.

Revolutionary Giants

- **Paul Robeson**
- **W.E.B. Du Bois**

Revolutionary Giants: Paul Robeson and W.E.B. Du Bois

In the history of black activism, Paul Robeson and W.E.B. Du Bois stand out brilliantly for their undying love for black people and their length of service to socialism and the working masses. In one hundred thirty-two years, Robeson and Du Bois did more to promote peace, justice, and democracy than any other two persons in American history.

Paul Robeson in the theater and W.E.B. Du Bois in the classroom were incomparable talents committed to both excellence and justice. Despite their greatness, America's racism and anti-communism refused to recognize the talent of Paul Robeson and the genius of W.E.B. Du Bois. The two were not only the wrong color, they also made the mistake of siding with the world's oppressed.

Robeson and Du Bois could have become self-absorbed elitists who left the masses to fend for themselves. Yet each risked their careers and livelihoods with their uncompromising commitment to social equality and world peace. Robeson's name is absent from theater history, and Du Bois's writings seldom receive the attention they deserve. This is no accident; it is instead the result of a concerted effort to suppress the contributions of two men whose ideas were considered too dangerous.

Despite harassment, blacklisting, trials, sabotage, and character assassination, both Du Bois and Robeson stood up to reactionaries in America and the world. When their hairs were gray and bodies weakened, Robeson and Du Bois continued to cast their lot with exploited workers, even at the expense of their own health and careers.

Limited Liberty

Paul Robeson: Artist of Revolution

One can argue that Paul Robeson was one of the most gifted human beings ever to have lived. Yet natural talents for personal gain meant nothing to him. For this great black revolutionary, talents were merely the means by which he could fight for human dignity, world peace, economic equality, and racial solidarity throughout the world. Singer, actor scholar, attorney, writer, author, athlete; all such roles and titles were secondary to his stated purpose in life, that of a struggler for the freedom of Africa, Afro-Americans, and the international working class. From 1919 to 1976, Robeson championed Welsh miners, Spanish freedom fighters, Afro-American auto workers, Ethiopian peasants, southern sharecroppers, Jamaican farmers, and anyone else in search of freedom from colonialism, militarism, and racism.

For Paul Robeson, blackness was not a box in which he was confined; it was the vehicle through which he reached out to the entire world. For him, internationalism was no abstract theory. Paul Robeson spoke twenty languages, absorbed himself in the traditions and customs of the working people of Wales, Albania, Nicaragua, Nigeria, the Soviet Union, and dozens of other nations, and refused to rest until all were free.

Yet, his internationalism did not consume his blackness or his commitment to African independence and Afro-American liberation. He believed appreciation for African history would be the basis for black progress both in the United States and in Africa. During his twelve year stay in London (1927-1939), Robeson supported white workers from London, Birmingham, Ireland, and Wales. At the same time he learned of the West African Student Union (the group to which Kwame Nkrumah and other future African leaders belonged).

Rather than choose the cause of oppressed white workers over the struggle for African independence, Robeson combined the two into a synthesis of revolutionary socialism and black militancy which propelled him to the forefront of every social issue for the rest of his life. "In my music, my plays, my films," he wrote, "I want to carry this central theme, to be African."[1] To this sentiment Robeson added,

> Even as I came to feel more Negro in spirit, or African as I called it then, I also came to feel a sense of oneness with the white working people who I came to know and love. The belief in the oneness of humankind, about which I have often spoken in concerts and elsewhere, has existed within me side by side with my deep attachment to the cause of my own race.[2]

Although the purpose of Paul's stay in England was to advance his acting career, he soon became absorbed in the sufferings of London's factory workers, shipbuilders, and miners. He joined the Unity Theater, a cultural arm of the British Labor Party that employed Welsh miners and British workers to deliver Socialist messages through the medium of theater. Robeson also met C.L.R. James, the black Marxist scholar who said of Paul, "To have spent one hour in his company was something you remembered for days, and if I had to sum up his personality... I would say that it was the combination of immense power and great gentleness."[3] Despite government harassment, Robeson acted in the Unity Theater, demonstrated for employment and food, and wrote about African history and independence.

While in England, Robeson heard West African students and English workers talk excitedly about the gains of Russia's Bolshevik Revolution. In 1934, he went to see for himself. While in the Soviet Union, Robeson saw how the Yakuts and Uzbeks, once classified as backward people by the Czar, "were leaping ahead from tribalism to modern industrial economy, from illiteracy to the heights of knowledge."[4]

Within twenty-five years the Yakuts and Uzbeks had moved from an inert peasantry to self-determined peoples running their own factories and directing their own theaters and universities. These impressive accomplishments convinced Robeson that the socialism that allowed a previously oppressed minority in the Soviet Union to develop could aid the Afro-American quest for liberation. In Moscow, black Communist Party member William Patterson told him of the struggles of the American Communist Party (CPUSA) to free the Scottsboro Boys in Alabama. Soviet progress and the struggles of the CPUSA at home only increased his desire to return to the United States.

After visiting the Soviet Union, Robeson went to Spain in 1938 to help the freedom fighters battle Franco's fascism. Like several Afro-Americans in the Communist Party (Mack Coad, Milton Herndon, and others) Robeson went to Spain because of his "devotion to democracy." He later elaborated on his decision:

> As an artist I know that it is dishonorable to put yourself on a plane above the masses, without marching at their side, participating in their anxieties and sorrows, since we artists owe everything to the masses... morever, I belong to an oppressed race, one that could not live if fascism triumphed in the world. My father was a slave, and I don't want my children to become slaves.[5]

At a rally of Spanish workers and peasants demanding land reform and workers' rights, Paul delivered his famous Manifesto Against Fascism.

> Every artist, every scientist, must decide now, where he stands. He has no alternative. There are no impartial observers. Through the destruction, in certain countries, of man's literary heritage, through the propagation of false ideas of national and racial superiority, the artist, the writer, the scientist, is challenged. This struggle invades the former cloistered halls of our universities and all her seats of learning. The battlefront is everywhere. There is no sheltered rear. The artist elects to fight for freedom or slavery. I have made my choice!... The history of the era is characterized by the degradation of my people. Despoiled of their lands, their culture destroyed, they are denied equal opportunity of the law and deprived of their rightful place in respect of their

fellows. Not through blind faith or coercion, but conscious of my course, I take my place with you. I stand with you in unalterable support of the lawful government of Spain...[6]

The sufferings of the people of Spain only reminded Paul Robeson of the agony of Afro-America and rekindled the desire he felt in Moscow to return home. He wrote:

> ...[Spain] was a major turning point in my life. I met the working men and women of Spain who were heroically giving the last measure of devotion to the cause of democracy...and it was the upper class—the landed gentry, the bankers, the industrialists, who had unleashed the fascist beast against their own people...As an artist, as a Negro, as a Friend of Labor, there should be plenty for me to do at home, so I returned in 1939.[7]

As he did in England, Spain, and Russia, in America Robeson balanced career goals with his struggle for socialism. When he was not playing Othello on Broadway, or singing "Ol' Man River" in Hollywood movies, Paul freely gave his energies and talents to auto worker unions, the Communist Party, the Foley Square 11, women's rights, world peace, the Chinese revolution, civil rights, African independence, Ethiopian freedom fighters, tobacco workers in North Carolina, maritime workers in Seattle, and any other cause that promoted human dignity.

In 1937, Paul Robeson and Max Yergan established the Council on African Affairs, an organization committed to African liberation. At the Council's 1944 conference, Robeson, Dr. Alphaeus Hunton, Dr. W.E.B. Du Bois, Kwame Nkrumah, and other black leaders developed the following revolutionary program for the Council:

1) To give concrete help to the struggle of the African masses.
2) To disseminate accurate information about Africa.

3) To prevent American loans and guns from being used to crush the freedom struggle of Africans and other subjected peoples.
4) To strengthen the alliances of progressive Americans, black and white, with the peoples of Africa and other lands in the common struggle for world peace and freedom.[8]

In 1955, after eighteen years of existence, the Council on African Affairs was hounded into oblivion by the mad dogs of McCarthyism. Nevertheless, it served as the model for the African support groups of the 1960s and brought to the fore pertinent news about African liberation struggles.

The Council was just one of Paul Robeson's many projects. In Harlem he was a tireless worker for the Communist Party, and his resonant voice was often heard at Party benefits, rallies, and demonstrations. Rather than hoard his earnings as an actor, Robeson donated funds to numerous causes, including the publication of Harry Haywood's *Negro Liberation* and Langston Hughes's Harlem Suitcase Theater.

The Council on African Affairs and the CPUSA did not consume all of Robeson's boundless energy. In the Forties and Fifties he supported Progressive Party candidates, spoke out against the Korean War, founded the journal *Freedom*, worked in U.S.-Soviet friendship societies, and was on call for labor union strikes, rallies, and fundraisers anywhere in the country. Mine workers, longshoremen, domestics, tobacco workers, sharecroppers, and other workers were captured by the powerful songs and words of Paul Robeson as he struggled with them for human dignity against the bosses.

For these activities, Robeson earned the hatred of the buffers of U.S. imperialism—the police, the FBI, the State Department, and the blindly patriotic wing of the American public. As early as 1936, the establishment offered him permanent employment in Hollywood if he would end his assault on American injustice. In the 1940s, Paul Robeson was everything the government despised: a militant Afro-American linked with the workers and colored races of the world, fighting with radical American labor unions and promoting the progress of the Soviet Union.

Even worse for the U.S. government, Robeson's international reputation diminished their ability to blatantly silence his irritating calls for justice. His popularity prevented, at least for a while, the iron-fisted tactics used against the Communist Party from 1948 to 1955, and the Black Panther Party from 1966 to 1973.

American reactionaries waited like vultures for Robeson to say or do something they could distort and use against him. Speaking before the World Congress of Partisans of Peace in 1949, Robeson said, "It is unthinkable that the American Negro would go to war on behalf of those who have oppressed us for generations, against a country [the Soviet Union] which in one generation has raised our people to full dignity of mankind."[9] The American right went berserk, and newspaper editorials, radio programs, and government spokespersons proclaimed Robeson a traitor. The government also brought forth several "Negro spokesmen" who vowed Afro-American loyalty to the U.S. and gushed of black eagerness to prove that loyalty by fighting wherever and whomever the government wanted.

When Robeson returned to the United States, he was greeted by seven thousand black and white workers at a Harlem welcome-home rally. In an amazing speech titled, "For Freedom and Peace," Robeson struck back at "buck-dancing Negroes" and government repression.

> And I defy any part of an insolent America, however powerful; I defy any errand boys, Uncle Toms of the Negro people, to challenge my Americanism; because by word and deed I challenge this system to the death; because I refuse to let my personal success, as part of the fraction of one percent of the Negro people, explain away the injustices to fourteen million of my people; because with all the energy at my command, I fight for the right of the Negro people and other oppressed labor-driven Americans to have decent homes, decent jobs, and the dignity that belongs to every human being!... What a

> travesty is this supposed leadership of a great people! And in this historic time, when the people need them most. How Sojourner Truth, Harriet Tubman, Fred Douglass must be turning over in their graves at this spectacle of a craven, fawning, despicable leadership, able to be naught but errand boys...and stooges and cowardly renegades...Let them get their crumbs from their Wall Street masters. Let them snatch their bit of cheese and go scampering rat-like into their holes.[10]

In the same speech Robeson linked the rape of Africa with northern oppression and southern racism.

> They will shoot our people down in Africa just as they lynch us in Mississippi...For who owns the plantations in the South? Metropolitan Life—yes, the same Metropolitan Life Insurance Company that owns and won't let you live in the Stuyvesant Town flats in New York...We do not want to die in vain any more on foreign battlefields for Wall Street and the greedy supporters of domestic fascism. If we must die, let it be in Mississippi or Georgia! Let it be where we are lynched and deprived of our rights as human beings![11]

For such audacity Robeson bore America's fascist fury. Later that year he was attacked in Peekskill, New York, when he tried to perform in a concert for labor unions and working people. The crowd of twenty-five thousand supporters was attacked by a vicious mob of racists and reactionaries whose ignorance was ignited by incendiary statements in the press. The Peekskill riots were an embarrassment to U.S. "democracy" as rampaging mobs attacked innocent people, turned over cars and buses, and seriously injured one hundred and forty-five people.

Like vultures encircling their wounded prey, the reactionaries began to close on Paul Robeson. In 1950, the State Department revoked his passport due to "the applicant's frank admission that for years he has been politically active in behalf of independence of the people of Africa."[12] For a global artist whose livelihood depended upon travel, this amounted to economic strangulation. This fascist move was coupled with a concerted attempt among theater producers, entertainment moguls, and concert hall owners to blacklist Robeson from domestic performances. Consequently, Robeson's annual income plummeted from $104,000 in 1949 to $6,000 in 1950.

The next year the State Department charged him with "espionage" for his sponsorship of the World Peace Appeal, which called for an end to the Korean War. This was only part of a multi-pronged strategy hatched in the higher echelons of the U.S. government to isolate and neutralize this great Afro-American artist and lover of peace.

From 1950 to 1957 the State Department conspired to influence public opinion against him, discourage foreign governments from honoring him, prevent his employment abroad, and discredit him by trotting out black leaders to condemn him.

This treachery was evident when in 1951 the U.S. ambassador to Ghana suggested that a credible Afro-American write an article condemning Robeson. A few months later the organ of the NAACP carried a "hit piece" on Robeson which the ambassador circulated in Ghana to show Africans that "their hero" was unpopular in the United States. Fascist manipulation in full swing!

Robeson did not back off from his South Africa-style banning. He unflinchingly continued his assault on U.S. imperialism abroad and worker exploitation and racism at home. At his passport hearing in 1955, the State Department charged that "during his concert tours abroad [Robeson] had repeatedly criticized the conditions of Negroes in the United States." To this he replied, "So what! I have criticized those conditions abroad as I have at home, and shall continue to do so until those conditions are changed."[13]

The State Department also used his remarks sent to the 1955 Bandung Conference of Third World nations as an excuse to deny him a passport, He said;

> If other nations of the world follow the example set by the Asian-African nations, there can be developed an alternative to the policy of force and an end to the threat of H-bomb war. The people of Asia and Africa have a direct interest in such a development since it is a well-known fact that atomic weapons have been used only against the peoples of Asia... Throughout the world all decent people must applaud the aims of the Conference to make the maximum contribution of the Asian and African countries to the cause of world peace.[14]

While a passport denial kept him out of the global anti-colonial movement, it did not hinder his activities at home. When the National Negro Labor Council (NNLC) was formed in 1951, Paul Robeson was in the vanguard of this nationwide mobilization of black workers against repression, racism, and monopoly capitalism. At the NNLC's 1952 Conference, Robeson's speech, "The Battleground is Here," ignited the delegates. "No," he thundered,

> I can never forget the 300-odd years of slavery and half-freedom; the long, weary, and bitter years of degradation visited upon our mothers and sisters, the humiliation and Jim Crowing of a whole people. I will never forget that the ultimate freedom and the immediate progress of my people rest of the sturdy backs and the unquenchable spirits of the coal miners, carpenters, bricklayers, sharecroppers, steel and auto workers, cooks, stewards and longshoremen, tenant farmers and tobacco stemmers—the vast mass of Negro Americans from whom all talent and achievement rise in the first place. If it were not for the stirrings and militant struggles among these millions, a number of our so-called spokesmen with fancy jobs and appointments would never be where they are... My advice to this 'top brass' leadership of ours would be, 'you'd better get back with the Folks'—if it's not already too late. I'm glad I never left them. Yes, the faces and tactics of the leaders may change every four years... but the people go on forever. The people—beaten down today, yet rising tomorrow: losing the road one minute, but finding it the next; their eyes always fixed on the star of true brotherhood, equality, and dignity—

the people are the real guardians of our hopes and dreams. That's why the mission of the Negro Labor Council is an indispensable one.[15]

In 1958, Paul published *Here I Stand*, a powerful autobiography of his struggles against racism and colonialism. *Here I Stand* blasts the McCarthyism that haunted him and ends with an urgent and eloquent plea for "collective Negro action" to end racism and Jim Crow in the United States. Naturally, America's media—the press, radio, bookstores, reviewers, and distributors— ignored the book. In an amazing show of reactionary unity, not one white commercial publisher reviewed Paul Robeson's book. After thirty years of work in the public eye as a college All-American football player, a concert singer, and an actor, Paul Robeson and his book were buried by a nation bent on crushing Afro-American dissent.

Despite the boycott of his book, Robeson still reached thousands of Afro-Americans and workers. Through *Freedom* (the journal that later became the voice of the NNLC), Robeson's column "Here's My Story" pounded away at injustice and urged black workers forward in their struggle. Robeson wrote articles on "China's Freedom and the Negro;" "U.S.A. and the Union of South Africa (U.S.A.);" and in 1954, long before the anti-war movements of the Sixties, Robeson condemned U.S. support of French colonialism in Vietnam. He called Ho Chi Minh the "Toussaint L'Overture of Vietnam," and wrote,

> Vast quantities of U.S. bombers and tanks and guns have been sent against Ho Chi Minh and his freedom fighters: and now we are told that it may be 'advisable' to send American GI's into Indo-China in order that the tin, rubber, and tungsten of Southeast Asia be kept by the 'free world'—meaning white Imperialism.[16]

Again linking oppression overseas with that at home, Robeson wrote, "What business did a black lad from

Mississippi or a Georgia sharecropping farmer have in Asia shooting down the yellow or brown son of an impoverished rice farmer?"[17]

For Robeson, art was a weapon of resistance. In 1952, he sang before thirty thousand workers in the Mine, Mill, and Smelters' Union. In 1954, he sang for the film, "Song of The Rivers," which was banned in the United States for its condemnation of colonialism. Robeson's stirring renditions of Welsh miner songs, Russian peasant songs, music from the Spanish Civil War, and Negro spirituals demonstrated the commonality of worker resistance. For most people, however, it was "Ol' Man River" that moved and inspired. As his political awareness increased, Robeson changed the original fawning lyrics to words of militant self-respect. The conclusion, which originally ended in passive acceptance of defeat, was changed to the triumphant, "I must keep fightin', until I'm dying."

Theater was also a vehicle of revolutionary expression. As head of the Performing Arts Division of the NNLC, Robeson performed for tobacco, auto, and mine workers in solidarity concerts all over the country. For Robeson, art was not a cerebral experience separated from life. Art was life, and in the hands of progressives and working people it was a reflection of and catalyst for the people's struggle for justice.

It was inevitable that during the Cold War Robeson would be hauled before the House Committee on Un-American Activities. Unlike some of the others, however, Robeson refused to quiver or break. When the Committee asked him why he did not move to Russia, Robeson replied, "Because my father was a slave, and my people died to build this country, and I am going to stay here and have a part of it just like you. And no fascist-minded people will drive me from it. Is that clear?"[18]

When it was clear the House Committee and other forces of repression could not silence Robeson, the state continued its systematic campaign to wipe his cultural accomplishments from history. Despite being a two-time All-American, he was omitted from the College Hall of Fame (the only two-timer not to be inducted). Although from 1925 to 1960 he was one of the most famous concert singers in the world, he is absent from most books on music. He acted in ten major plays, and his *Othello* had record-breaking runs on Broadway, but theater texts are silent on his greatness. From 1932 to 1939, Robeson was in eight major movies. However, one might never know it, for much of the footage and many newsreels have mysteriously vanished.

Despite these setbacks and his failing health, Robeson would not be silent. At the height of the government's war on him Robeson stated, "My labors in the future will remain the same as they have in the past, in the antifascist struggle, and struggling for working people."[19]

Robeson was the consummate Afro-American Socialist, his popularity among black working people was matched only by white America's and the black bourgeoisie's disdain and fear of him. For the black middle class he was too far "out there," praising the Soviet Union, bad-mouthing the United States, and stirring up trouble among the dispossessed. He displeased much of the black middle class with comments like, "The Negro problem cannot be solved by a few of us getting to be doctors and lawyers."

Although illness curtailed his revolutionary activities from 1959 until his death in 1976, with the strength that remained Robeson worked incessantly for the creation of a world in which lynch mobs, multi-national corporations, atomic wars, and exploited miners would become obsolete, the artifacts and relics of museums and history books. No Afro-American revolutionary artist in the future can work to transform U.S. society without doing so in the spirit and legacy of the great Paul Robeson. May we never forget him!

> ...my deep conviction that for all mankind a socialist society represents an advance to a higher stage of life— that is, a form of society that is economically, socially, culturally, and ethically superior to a system that is based upon production for private profit.[20]
>
> —*Paul Robeson,* Here I Stand, *1952*

W.E.B. Du Bois: The Soul of Black Folk

William Edward Burghardt Du Bois stands as the most significant fighter for Afro-American liberation in the history of the United States. Du Bois's shadow is cast from slavery (he was born three years after the Civil War), through Reconstruction, Jim Crow and lynchings, past two World Wars separated by the lean dark years of the Great Depression, and up to the height of the Civil Rights Era (he died on the day of the historic March on Washington in 1963). W.E.B. Du Bois was involved in innumerable struggles against racism and imperialism from 1888 to 1963, a full seventy-five years of dedicated labor in service to the oppressed of the world.

During that time he distinguished himself as the radical's radical and the scholar's scholar, setting a standard by which all intellectual activists are judged. Author, organizer, teacher, lecturer, editor, and freedom fighter, Du Bois has no equal in either scholarship or passion for black liberation. You cannot talk about integration, Pan-Africanism, U.S. socialism, black scholarship, the NAACP, Reconstruction, the Harlem Renaissance, Afro-American studies, the slave trade, African history, or the peace movement without paying tribute to this great Afro-American freedom fighter.

* * *

Du Bois was born in Great Barrington, Massachusetts, to a family which had been free ever since Du Bois's grandfather was released in 1780 for service in the Revolutionary War. While completing his education at Fisk, Harvard, and the University of Berlin, Du Bois also learned about southern bigotry, northern racism, and European militarism and radicalism. Du Bois believed a liberated people knew their history, and he sought to aid this cause by writing his doctoral dissertation on slavery. Later published as a book, *The Suppression of the African Slave Trade* was the first comprehensive look at American reluctance to end the bloody trade in human cargo.

As a professor at Atlanta University (1896-1910), Du Bois hosted annual conferences dedicated to a long-term study of the American Negro. At a time when white academia treated blacks little better than monkeys, W.E.B. Du Bois used scholarship to analyze and solve the dilemmas of the Afro-American people. Yet, his conferences were not the private domain of the learned, for Du Bois drew both from students and local farmers and workers in his research.

In 1905, Du Bois and several progressive blacks and whites formed the Niagara Movement. When the Movement leaders became shackled by moderation and caution, Du Bois left and helped found the National Association for the Advancement of Colored People (NAACP) in 1909. As a leader in the NAACP, Du Bois rewrote Afro-American history, attacking lynching, challenging the accomodationism of Booker T. Washington, and guiding the organization through an era of virulent white supremacy.

By far his most lasting contribution to the NAACP was as founder and editor of its journal, *The Crisis*. By 1920, *The Crisis* had reached a circulation of one hundred thousand, enough for almost one-tenth of the Afro-American households in the United States. Workers, writers, students, teachers, domestics, and sharecroppers read Du Bois's articles regularly, and countless numbers of black Americans were inspired by his militant calls to action.

Unlike many of the black leaders in the NAACP, Du Bois was not merely concerned with domestic discrimination. Since 1910, his sense of justice for Afro-Americans had been sustained by a belief in socialism. He came to believe that racism did not exist in isolation, but rather it was the logical conclusion of a system that pits race against race for the private accumulation of goods. He believed, "there is not enough for everyone to have two automobiles; not enough for everybody to have a country villa, but enough for everyone to have sufficient to eat and to wear, and comfortable, sanitary housing."[21]

Du Bois's advocacy of socialism sprung from his conviction that it would liberate his people from the agony of America. In 1929, the Socialist Party held that blacks did not require any particular emphasis since they were simply another race of exploited workers. In response Du Bois thundered, "If American socialism cannot stand for the American Negro, then the American Negro cannot stand for socialism."[22] For Du Bois and the black Socialists who followed him, socialism was not an ultimate truth. It was rather a strategy that was useful only to the extent that it liberated Afro-Americans from poverty and exploitation.

Afro-America was not his sole concern, for socialism expanded his field of vision far beyond the United States. Through it he reached across the seas to Mother Africa, birthplace of his ancestors and site of the worst forms of European colonialism. In 1900, 1919, 1921, and 1945, Du Bois was a central figure in the famous Pan-African Conferences held first in England and later in Africa. The 1945 conference was by far the most significant, with Du Bois and former CPUSA leader George Padmore joining young African students Kwame Nkrumah and Jomo Kenyatta. The '45 conference went beyond rhetoric, with many of the participants evolving into African nationalist leaders.

At a time when Africa seemed helpless before European missionaries, rapacious trading companies, and frenzied army generals, Du Bois wrote of the revolutionary role Africa would play in world events. In 1915, his article "The African Roots of War" declared that the prime cause of World War I was the clash of European imperialists over the control of African resources. He later published the classic book *The World and Africa*, where he argued that the legacies of the kingdoms of Egypt, Ethiopia, Mali, Songhay, and Ghana formed the basis for the resurgence of African nationalism and the inevitable defeat of parasitic colonialism. *The World and Africa* is brilliant history as well as a coherent strategy for African liberation. Through his organizational efforts and Pan-African writings, Dr. Du Bois was a forerunner of the explosive African nationalist movements after 1945.

Concurrent with his work on the international scene,

Du Bois remained a central figure in the Afro-American fight for justice. For Du Bois, literature was both sword and shield; a sword to attack the enemies of black America, and a shield to defend them from racist attacks. In 1903, Du Bois wrote *The Souls of Black Folk*, perhaps one of the greatest works in Afro-American (and American) literature. *The Souls of Black Folk* is a poetic and powerful treatise on the conditions of black America, as well as an assessment of strategies for liberation.

Du Bois blasts Booker T. Washington's moderation, analyzes the militant undertones of the slave spiritual and early black music, and makes observations on black life in America which are amazingly relevant today. Many major black militants and intellectuals have been affected by *The Souls of Black Folk*. Angela Davis and A. Philip Randolph both cite *Souls* as one of the texts that most affected their thinking about Afro-American struggle.

In 1935, Du Bois's article, "Negro Nation within the Nation," outlined the influence of black folk on United States history. At that time, most white Americans, from those in the White House to those on the shop floor, believed blacks had contributed nothing to human advancement. Tottering under the weight of this venomous racism, even Afro-Americans doubted alleged reports of black contributions. Despite the unbelievers, Du Bois's article outlined the four major black contributions to American life: The gift of toil; black music, where "the rhythmic cry of the slave...stands today as the sole American music;"[23] the literary and cultural contributions of Claude McKay, Paul Robeson, and others; and the spirit of democracy, since it is black folk who remind America that "liberty and justice for all" is not.

In 1927, Du Bois was a key figure in the Harlem Renaissance, the cultural explosion in which black art, music, literature, and dance burst on the national scene as expressions of Afro-American vitality. His militant writings and work in the NAACP urged many of the black writers and artists of the period to stay rooted in the masses of black workers and peasants.

Early in his career, Du Bois believed a "Talented Tenth" would lead the race to equality. He changed this view when it became evident that the black middle class was too selfish and compromising to lead the movement. As a Socialist, Du Bois developed the perspective that history is made by the people themselves. Nowhere is this view more evident than in his classic work, *Black Reconstruction in America*. Subtitled *An Essay Toward a History of the Part Black Folk Played in the Attempt to Reconstruct Democracy in America*, *Black Reconstruction* is truly one of the most remarkable historical works in the English language. Since the author was both black and Socialist, his view of Reconstruction is vastly different from standard American history.

Through seven hundred pages Du Bois meticulously argues that the black ex-slaves of Georgia, Alabama, Mississippi, Tennessee, and elsewhere created from the ruins and racism of the South a democracy previously unknown in that region. He says that it was the revolutionary sentiment of the black masses; the abused, tortured, and hunted ex-slaves, that fueled such radical concepts as free public education, land redistribution, and social programs for blacks as well as poor whites.

Du Bois also argues that the black worker was the sole cause for the Civil War, and it was their General Strike ("tools and guns in the hands of black slaves") during the war that enabled the North to defeat the South. Unlike historians who call slavery "a mistake," Du Bois claims that it was systemic to U.S. capitalism. He writes, "the black worker is part of that vast and dark sea of labor in India, China, the South Seas, and all Africa; in the West Indies and Central America and the U.S.—that great majority of mankind on whose bent and broken backs rest today the foundation stones of modern industry."[24]

Du Bois' *Black Reconstruction* is truly revolutionary history, with chapter titles like "The Black Worker," "The White Worker," "The Planter," and "The Counter-Revolution of Property" loudly proclaiming his Socialist perspective. Du Bois shows how the forcible suppression of the South's ruling class (he notes that this group, 7% of the South's population, dominated America, comprising eleven of the first sixteen presidents, seventeen of twenty-eight Supreme Court Justices, and fourteen of nineteen attorney generals) was similar to the Marxist view of the dictatorship of the proletariat. Du Bois believed that black troops and Union soldiers in the South were similar to Marx and Lenin's teachings, that in the early days of revolution the worker's political power could be maintained only by rigorous military control over the reactionary ruling class.

The revolutionary changes ushered in by black workers empowered by Reconstruction were tremendous. Bills providing free public education to both black and white alike (according to Du Bois, "Public education for all at public expense was, in the South, a Negro idea")[25]; ballot boxes available to all regardless of color or property; and the opening of juries to include blacks and poor whites, are a few examples of black democracy. Du Bois also focuses on the internationalism of the newly freed slaves, noting that black Congressmen opposed restrictions on Chinese immigration and supported federal relief for the Cherokee Indians.

Despite gains in education and politics, the ex-slaves' demand for land was consistently sabotaged. Both the northern capitalists and the southern reactionaries bitterly opposed any radical redistribution of land. While the North applauded (at least superficially) black political power, it saw the promise of "forty acres and a mule" providing the ex-slaves with the means by which to escape the orbit of white capitalist control. Without land, social legislation was incomplete, for blacks would remain economically dependent on racist landowners.

Northern capital believed a democratic Black Belt South would not serve their investments well. Consequently, the white elite in both the North and South aborted this valiant experiment in democracy. In the chapters "The Counter-Revolution of Property" and "Back to Slavery," Du Bois notes how "Profit, income, uncontrolled power in My Business for My Property and for Me"[26] replaced black rule in the South in 1877. The treacherous Hayes-Tilden compromise of 1877, where the South cast votes for Hayes in exchange for the removal of northern troops, effectively returned Afro-Americans to the "good ol' days." Northern neglect and southern lawlessness thrust blacks from power and forced them into feudalistic conditions of tenant farming, sharecropping, and peonage, a true counterrevolution.

Du Bois points out how Reconstruction's gains were overturned by mob violence, rampant murder, flagrant election fraud, segregation, and disenfranchisement. He wrote that the overthrow of Reconstruction was no isolated incident, it signaled the genesis of the United States as a "reactionary force that was the cornerstone of our imperialism of the 1890's." The disenfranchised blacks of the South were the domestic counterparts to exploited Cuban, Philipino, Haitian, and Hawaiian workers abroad.

In his final chapter, Du Bois pays tribute to the courageous black men and women of Reconstruction: "They descended into hell (slavery), and in the third century they arose from the dead, in the finest effort to achieve democracy for the working millions which this world had ever seen."[27] Thus ends Du Bois's fine treatise on the power not of the educated elite, but of the black worker.

Unlike many for whom age brings conservatism, Du Bois grew more radical as he grew older. The same man who in 1917 supported U.S. involvement in World War I became an anti-war activist during World War II. His interest in Pan-Africanism, peace, and socialism put him at odds with the more conservative leadership in the NAACP. He was eventually ousted in 1948, and his last speech to them demonstrates how far to the left he was from his "Negro" colleagues.

> We have grown in the habit of regarding colonial questions as comparatively unimportant and far removed from our immediate domestic interests. We can easily correct this tragic error, if we remember that we have spent thousands of millions of dollars and killed millions of human beings... mainly because of jealousy

and greed arising primarily over the control of labor, land, and materials of colonial peoples...Of the dollar that you pay for a box of chocolates, the cocoa farmer in West Africa gets three cents...We are part of colonial exploitation, whenever we buy a pound of coffee and pay the machine three times as much as the man who raises it...Every leading land on earth is moving toward some form of socialism, so as to restrict the power of wealth, introduce democratic methods in industry, and stop the persistence of poverty and its children, ignorance, disease, and crime.[28]

While the NAACP sought judicial and legislative solutions to overt racist acts like lynching, school segregation, and housing discrimination, W.E.B. Du Bois believed blacks should build a society better than the one into which they sought to integrate. Such progressive thinking was too much for the narrowly-focused NAACP, and after thirty-eight years of service, Du Bois was kicked out of the organization.

In 1948, Du Bois joined Paul Robeson in heading up the Council On African Affairs. These two revolutionary giants agitated for the cause of Africa and campaigned against U.S. support of brutal colonialism in Rhodesia, the Congo, and elsewhere. Robeson and Du Bois were so persistent that in the late 1940s the Attorney General included the Council on his "subversive organization list."

During the height of the Cold War against the Soviet Union abroad and suspected "Communists" at home, Du Bois's promotion of peace and disarmament earned him the disdain of America's right wing. As a participant in the Cultural and Scientific Conference for World Peace in 1949, Du Bois was one of the prime movers of the Stockholm Appeal to abolish nuclear weapons around the world. When he helped found the Peace Information Center (PIC) in 1951, the eighty-three year-old Dr. Du Bois became a hot target for McCarthy's committee and Hoover's FBI. Under his leadership, PIC was dedicated to global disarmament and often organized opposition to the warlike policies of Washington.

In 1951, in one of the great travesties of American

justice, an elderly black professor was hounded by the iron-fisted anti-Communists of the most powerful nation on earth. Despite protests from black intellectuals and workers and white progressives, Du Bois was indicted for "failing to register as an agent of a foreign power."

Although he was eventually acquitted, the government continued to harass him. His mail was tampered with, black newspapers were warned not to speak highly of him, and his travels in Europe, Africa, and the United States were closely monitored by the State Department and the FBI.

But again, like the great Paul Robeson, Du Bois was not swayed. Before his trial, he and his wife traveled across the nation to raise funds for his legal defense. A speech before fifteen thousand people in Chicago showed that sixty years of struggle had not squelched his militancy.

> Why is it, with the earth's abundance and our mastery of natural forces, and miraculous technique; with our commerce belting the earth; our goods and services pouring out of our stores, factories, ships, and warehouses; why is it that nevertheless most human beings are starving to death, dying of preventable disease, and too ignorant to know what is the matter, while a small minority are so rich that they cannot spend their income?[29]

During his trial Du Bois was abandoned by the black middle class, many of whom turned their backs on a man they considered duped by Moscow.

> I have discovered that a large and powerful portion of the educated and well-to-do Negroes are refusing to forge forward in social leadership of anyone, even their own sick people, but are eager to fight social medicine for sick whites and sicker Negroes; are opposing trade unionism not only for white labor but for the far more helpless black worker; are willing to get rich not simply by shady business enterprise, but even by organized gambling and the dope racket.... Other Negroes of intelligence and prosperity had become American in their acceptance of

exploitation as defensible and in their imitation of American 'conspicuous expenditure.' They proposed to make money and spend it as it pleased them. They had beautiful homes, large and expensive cars and fur coats. They hated 'communism'...as much as any white American.[30]

Du Bois's trial taught him a lesson in black subjugation. He learned firsthand the sufferings of the Scottsboro Boys, the Soledad Brothers, and the thousands of other blacks whose lives have been crushed in America's legal lynch mobs. He wrote:

> What turns me cold in all this experience is the certainty that thousands of innocent victims are in jail today because they had neither money, experience, or friends to help them. The eyes of the world were on our trial...but God only knows how many who were innocent as I and my colleagues are today in hell. They daily stagger out of prison doors embittered, vengeful, hopeless, ruined. We protect and defend sensational cases where Negroes are involved. But the great mass of arrested or accused black folk have no defense. There is a desperate need to oppose the national racket of railroading to jails and chain gangs the poor, friendless and black.[31]

In the late 1950s, Du Bois visited both the Soviet Union and the People's Republic of China. He left these two countries even more convinced that socialism alone would liberate Afro-Americans and Africa. Watching the Chinese people build their emaciated nation from the ashes of western and Japanese exploitation, Du Bois said, "Never have I seen a nation which so amazed and touched me as China." On Du Bois's ninety-first birthday, the Chinese government broadcast his radio address to the world.

> Behold a people, the most populous nation on this ancient earth, which has burst its shackles, not by boasting and strutting, not by lying about its history and its conquests, but by patience and long suffering, by blind struggle...She aims to make men free. But what men?

> Not simply the mandarins but including the mandarins; not simply the rich but not excluding the rich. Not simply the learned, but led by knowledge to the end that no man shall be poor, nor sick, nor ignorant, but that the humblest worker as well as the sons of emperors shall be fed and taught and healed and that there emerge on earth a single, unified people, free, well and educated. You have been told, my Africa, my Africa in Africa and all your children's children overseas; you have been told and the telling so beaten into you by rods and whips, that you believe it yourselves, that mankind can rise only by walking on men; by cheating them and killing them; that only on a doormat of the despised and dying can a British aristocracy, a French elite, or an American millionaire be nurtured and grown. This is a lie...Speak China, and tell your truth to Africa and the world.[32]

After the visit to China, Du Bois was invited to live in Ghana by Kwame Nkrumah. Soon after arriving there, the lifelong Socialist formally enrolled as a member in the Communist Party. In his book *The Autobiography of W.E.B. Du Bois*, he boldly asserted,

> I have studied socialism and communism long and carefully...I now state my conclusion frankly and clearly. I believe in Communism. I mean by communism a planned way of life in the production of wealth and work designed for building a state whose object is the highest welfare of its people and not merely the profit of a part....I know well that the triumph of communism will be a slow and difficult task, involving mistakes of every sort. It will call for progressive change in human nature...I believe this possible, or otherwise we will continue to lie, steal and kill as we are doing today.[33]

In Ghana, Du Bois pursued a project he planned since 1909, the publication of the *Encyclopedia Africana*. A monumental work on the history, arts, people, and destiny of Africa, the *Encyclopedia Africana* was to serve as the foundation of a one hundred year program of study of Africa. Du Bois never completed the project. In 1909, racism and lack of funds halted his work; in 1963, death ended Dr. Du Bois's dream.

The greatest of warriors, Dr. W.E.B. Du Bois died at age ninety-five. Du Bois touched the lives of millions of people around the world with his selfless commitment to liberation for Afro-Americans and for the colored peoples of the world. It was fitting that this great Afro-American should die as a Communist and be buried in one of the first African nations to free itself from colonialism.

The hundreds of speeches, articles, books, lectures, meetings, protests, conferences, rallies, petitions, demonstrations, essays, and organizations initiated by Du Bois stand as a brilliant legacy of truly the seminal revolutionary figure in Afro-American history: William Edward Burghardt Du Bois. No one who is free today from imperialism, colonial rule, racist violence, or capitalist exploitation can celebrate that freedom without paying homage to the black professor who graced the earth for nearly a century.

> "We cannot talk of Dr. Du Bois without recognizing that he was a radical all of his life. Some people would like to ignore the fact that he was a Communist.... It is time to cease muting the fact that Dr. Du Bois was a genius and chose to be a Communist."[34]

Dr. Martin Luther King, 1968

Beyond Rhetoric: Armed Revolutions in Africa

- **Amilcar Cabral and the PAIGC**
- **FRELIMO and Mozambique**
- **Angola**
- **Zimbabwe**

Beyond Rhetoric: Armed Revolutions In Africa

Perhaps the most misunderstood figures in history are the African revolutionaries. Racism, anti-Communist hysteria, and cultural ignorance will not allow the white elite to admit Africans can wage independent revolutionary struggle. Usually, revolutionaries in Zimbabwe, Guinea-Bissau, Mozambique, and Angola are portrayed as blood-thirsty terrorists who indiscriminately murder fellow Africans in an attempt to bring Soviet rule to Africa.

This chapter is one small attempt to correct this distortion of history and briefly describe the harsh conditions that Amilcar Cabral, Samora Machel, and Agostinho Neto attempted to correct through armed struggle.

Cynics see the problems of Africa and bemoan the failure of revolution. People pampered in the relative comfort of the West cannot imagine the economic, social and cultural context in which the African revolutionaries attempt to establish socialism. Hundreds of years of debilitating colonialism superimposed on a peasant society can not be magically transformed into progressive socialism by the wave of the hand.

The African Socialist is confronted with two dilemmas: first, leading the people's war against the oppressors; and second, building a just society from the ruins of war and colonialism. When one looks at the context of their struggle and the enemy they fought against, African Socialist revolutionaries are truly remarkable figures. Their determined struggle to win bread, land, and justice from the richest and most technologically advanced nations of the world serves as an inspiration and model for future revolutionary movements.

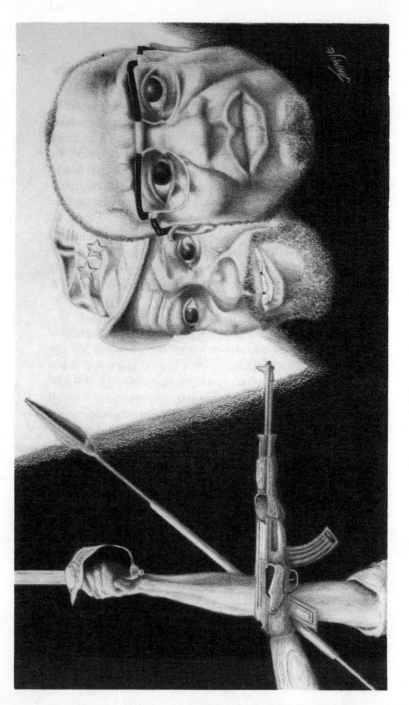

Beyond Rhetoric: Revolution

Amilcar Cabral: Messenger of Revolution

People familiar with the anti-imperialist struggle in Africa consider Amilcar Cabral of Guinea-Bissau to be one of the world's most outstanding theoreticians and practitioners of revolutionary struggle. A brilliant teacher, Cabral trained most of the leading cadre of the Partido African da Independencia da Guine e Cabo Verde (African Party for the Independence of Guinea-Bissau and Cape Verde Islands, known also as the PAIGC). His teachings, both oral and written, focused on the liberation of women, anti-elitist education, public health, and participatory government. The story of Amilcar Cabral, the PAIGC, and the ordinary workers and peasants of Guinea-Bissau is an example of how leadership, a revolutionary party, and people's struggles can transform a society.

Portuguese colonialism was the ultimate in parasitic exploitation. Labor and resources were sucked out of Guinea-Bissau without regard to the cost in human lives, and Portugal's sole concern was its annual profit and loss statement. Every African in Guinea-Bissau over fifteen had his or her salary taxed twenty-five percent for services that were never received; education was used to create an elite class of assimilated Africans; ninety-nine percent of the population was illiterate; sixty percent of African infants died before age one; and there was only one doctor for every forty-five thousand people.

This cruel system was enforced by a Portuguese secret-police force known as Internal Police for Defense of the State (PIDE). If the populace showed any resistance to Portuguese domination, rice exports were increased until there was a domestic shortage. From 1942 to 1947, thirty thousand Africans on Cape Verde Island (off the coast of Guinea-Bissau) died from state-controlled starvation.

Amilcar was born on Cape Verde in 1924, and as a young man went to Lisbon to become an agricultural engineer. While in Portugal he was targeted by the police for supporting anti-colonial movements and for his associations with other militant African students.

Mario de Andrade and Agostinho Neto of Angola, and Marcelinos dos Santos and Eduardo Mondlane of

Mozambique, were among the future revolutionary leaders of Africa that Cabral worked within Portugal. They formed study groups and political action organizations to "re-Africanize" themselves and prevent the Portuguese from separating them from the masses.

These study sessions worked, for when the comrades returned to their native lands, all of them risked life and security in service for the masses of African people. When Cabral returned to Guinea-Bissau as an agricultural engineer, he was exiled to Angola by the Portuguese for speaking out against colonial rule. In exile, Cabral joined his comrade Agostinho Neto in establishing the Popular Movement for the Liberation of Angola (MPLA).

Exile in Angola did not diminish Cabral's love for his own people. When he returned to Guinea-Bissau, Cabral worked again as an agricultural engineer. Through this job he analyzed the class nature of Guinean society and formulated his ideas on African self-determination through proper use of the land. Cabral's movements were not accidental. He later told PAIGC cadre at a Party seminar:

> So it is not by chance that I went to Guinea. It was not material hardship that drove me back to my native land. Everything had been calculated step by step. I had enormous potential for working in any of the other Portuguese colonies, or even in Portugal. I gave up a good position in the Lisbon agronomy centre...It was thus to follow a calculation, the idea of doing something, to make a contribution to arouse the people to struggle against the Portuguese. And I did this from the first day I set foot in Guinea.[1]

On the night of September 19, 1956, Amilcar Cabral, Aristides Pereira, Luiz Cabral, Julio de Almeida, Elisee Turpin and Fernando Fortes met secretly to establish the Partido Africana da Independencia—African Party of Independence, or PAI. (The name was later changed to African Party for the Independence of Guinea and Cape Verde, or PAIGC.)

Without money or mass support, outnumbered by

heavily armed Portuguese, and harassed by PIDE agents, these six Guineans boldly resolved:

> The time has come to prepare our people to take on a decisive epoch of their history—that of struggle for our political liberation; it will only succeed by mobilizing all the offspring of the motherlands without distinction as to sex, tribe, or color. It will be the struggle of all Guineans and Cape Verdians dedicated to the search for happiness for all the offspring of these two countries. But to engage in struggle our people need direction. It is the Party which must be organized in a clandestine manner with the aim of eluding the police vigilance by the colonialists.[2]

The founders of PAIGC believed that the workers of the urbanized port of Bissau would form the strength of the Party, and Cabral and his comrades organized African dock workers under cover of darkness. Energized by these efforts, the workers of Bissau went on several successful strikes in 1959. The ship owners and the colonial government soon tired of these troublesome antics. During a strike on August 3, 1959, Portuguese troops massacred fifty unarmed African dock workers at the port of Pidjiguiti. Many of the one hundred wounded strikers taken to the hospital after the attack inexplicably disappeared.

This crushing blow to the base of PAIGC forced Cabral and his comrades to reassess their tactics. Party headquarters were transferred to neighboring Conakry, capital of Sekou Toure's Guinea, and Cabral shifted PAIGC's focus from the urban workers to the peasants in the Guinean countryside. To the PAIGC, the sheer numbers and torturous conditions of the peasants made them the "principal physical force of the national liberation struggle." Although factory workers, dock workers, teachers, and civil servants were not neglected, PAIGC recruited rural peasants to build the Party.

Training the masses revealed the genius of Amilcar Cabral. Assuming the task of training the first Party mobilizers, Cabral imbued illiterate peasants, disillusioned youth, and abused urban workers with the awareness that they could change history through collective struggle. From 1959 to 1961, Cabral trained over one thousand Party cadre, forging Balante, Fula, Mandjak, Mandinka, and Pepal into a solid force of revolutionary Guineans. Urging men and women from peasant backgrounds to replace metaphysical thinking with scientific analysis, Cabral said, "Do not confuse the reality you live in with the ideas in your head." Cabral taught new members:

> Keep always in mind that the people are not fighting for ideas, for the things that are in anyone's head. They are fighting...for material benefits, to live better and in peace, to see their lives go forward, to guarantee the future of their children. National liberation, war on colonialism, building of peace and progress—independence—all that will remain meaningless unless it brings a real improvement in conditions of life.[3]

Those whom Cabral taught in turn went out to recruit and teach others. Antonio Bana, a Party militant killed in action in 1963 at age thirty, exemplified the oppressed Guineans who formed the core of the PAIGC. "At the beginning of my life," Bana says,

> I worked in Bissau as the white man's boy. I worked with a lot of whites, but none of them ever hit me because I knew the answer to living with them: work well and don't talk back to them. One day a friend came to me and we got talking. He said there was a Party. I didn't know what a Party was. So this comrade explained this Party was for getting independence, for fighting against the Portuguese, for the liberty of the people, for winning a new life. Well, I knew all right that the Portuguese had kicked our people around...We asked this comrade questions. We felt the same things, but not clearly. Now he explained everything quite clear. We met again, several times, that's how I became a volunteer in the fight against the Portuguese. Since then I've done everything I could for the Party. The Party can count on me. I worked for the Party and I listened to Cabral speaking...My job was to mobilize people. I used to hold little meetings among the folk I knew...and explain that the time had

some to fight for being free, and that the PAIGC was fighting for this, later on I was sent, I and others into the countryside to mobilize the peasants.[4]

When Antonio Bana and his comrades were sent "into the countryside," they talked with peasants like Sala N'tonton, a farmer from Quinara. N'tonton wrote of his encounter with PAIGC cadre.

> I was a farmer and our village was a poor one. We'd pigs and chickens. The Portuguese bought these, but gave us bad prices. We had to pay a lot of taxes without ever seeing the benefit of them. Where was the school? The clinic? That was the time a comrade from the Party came to our village. He began talking about how things were and what we had to do to put things right. I listened to him. I knew he wasn't telling lies. I knew things were like he said, I'd seen it for myself. I joined the Party after that.[5]

Young exuberant cadre like Antonio Bana and Sala N'tonton infused the PAIGC with the vigor necessary to wage armed struggle against the Portuguese. But vigor was not enough. A visit by Cabral to the People's Republic of China resulted in armed support from Mao Zedong and Zhou Enlai. In February, 1961, Angola's MPLA foreshadowed armed rebellion in Guinea-Bissau with an attack against Portuguese troops in Luanda.

In August, 1961, on the second anniversary of the massacre at Pidjiguiti, Cabral and the Party published the "Proclamation of Direct Action."

> The African Independence Party; proclaims August 3, 1961, as the date of the passage of our national liberation struggle from the phase of political struggle to that of national insurrection, to direct action against the colonial forces; declares that all its militants and cadres are mobilized for direct action in the national liberation struggle.[6]

Later that year, Cabral sent the Portuguese government a letter demanding "immediate self-determination or the Party would answer with violence the violence of the Portuguese...and by all means possible completely eliminate colonial domination."[7] The Portuguese responded to Cabral's letter by arresting two thousand union and nationalist activists, burning "suspect" villages, and massacring dozens of innocent Africans with Nazi-like brutality.

In early 1963, many of the cadre trained by Cabral at Conakry struck the first armed blow for national liberation with an attack on the Portuguese barracks at Tite. This bold offensive marked the beginning of a ten-year war with an openly fascist nation backed by treacherous support from the NATO alliance (western Europe and the United States). Nino Vieria, Osvaldo Vieria, Antonio Bana, Constantino Texeria, Domingos Ramos, Armando Ramos, Babo Keita, Rui Djassi, Francisco Mendes (all of whom were among the best and most disciplined Party field commanders), Rafael Barbosa (later chair of the Party and jailed for six years by the colonialists), Aristides Pereira (Cabral's closest colleague during the War of Liberation), and Amilcar Cabral led several successful attacks on Portuguese troops. After six months of fighting, the PAIGC controlled fifteen percent of the countryside.

In 1964, two significant events further strengthened the PAIGC in the eyes of the Guinean masses. For seventy-five days on the island of Como, PAIGC troops engaged the Portuguese army in some of the heaviest fighting of the war. Despite Portuguese reinforcements and military superiority, PAIGC cadre routed three thousand Portuguese soldiers and handed Lisbon a crushing colonial defeat. The victory at Como greatly enhanced the reputation of the PAIGC, and hundreds of peasants and workers joined the Party.

The second significant event in 1964 was the Party's first congress. The victories of 1963-1964 increased the terrritory under Party control and swelled the ranks of the PAIGC. Consequently, Cabral and the leadership saw the need to reorganize the Party and to develop structures for administering the liberated territories. At the 1964 congress, Cabral's theoretical and political genius again made a lasting imprint on the Guinean struggle for independence. At his suggestion, the nation was divided into administrative zones and districts, with each area headed by a Party committee. Known as local action committees, they were to consist of five elected members, of which two had to be women. This inclusion of Guinean women in positions of power was not accidental. Mozambican revolutionary Samora Machel (a contemporary of Cabral) noted, "...in the same way as there cannot be a Revolution without the liberation of women...the liberation of women cannot succeed without the victory of the Revolution."[8]

By ensuring that women serve on the local action committees, Cabral boldly attacked the backward sexist views of the patriarchal society he was attempting to transform. The sight of women leading troops, chairing meetings, and making decisions broke sharply with the traditions where women worked and suffered in silence. Carmen Pereira, a member of the Party's executive committee and a cultural leader in Guinea-Bissau's southern region, was symbolic of the Guinean women whose courage in war and reconstruction moved the struggle forward.

The 1964 congress also made the local action committees responsible for administering the politics, health care, education, and economics of the liberated areas of Guinea-Bissau. This move gave peasants a voice in their own affairs, and was the first real attempt at democracy in Guinea-Bissau. Through the local action committees the Party made notable accomplishments in the liberated areas. Medicines previously unavailable were obtained for the peasants, thousands learned to read and write, farming tools and technology were freely shared with rural families, and aspirations long muted shaped the political direction of the nation.

The Party's work in the liberated zones was even more remarkable in the context of Portugal's brutal counterattacks. With support from NATO, Portugal used napalm, herbicides, incendiary bombs, terrorism, torture, and other barbaric means to break the national revolution of Guinea-Bissau. When the war of liberation first began in 1963, Portugal had ten thousand troops in Guinea. By 1972, this number had swelled to eighty-five thousand, nearly one colonial soldier for every ten Guinea civilians.

Support from NATO and even the Vatican, which sent money to Portugal, prolonged the valiant struggle of the PAIGC. In 1972, the NATO alliance sent Portugal five hundred million dollars worth of jets, gunboats, helicopters, and napalm, creating the obscene spectacle of the amassed military might of the western "democracies" arrayed against the bravery, determination, and sacrifices of Cabral and the peasants and workers of Guinea-Bissau.

In 1968, Portugal began a reconquest campaign which included superficial reform to counter the Party's successful transformation of the liberated zones. Cabral dubbed this "smiling and bloodshed," and continued to lead Party military assaults on the Portuguese. In 1971, the PAIGC held its First People's National Assembly, with delegates attending from liberated zones in Guinea-Bissau. By 1972, the PAIGC controlled seventy-five percent of the nation while the Portuguese military was confined to isolated rural military bases and the city of Bissau.

The 1971 assembly, again led by Secretary-General of the Party Amilcar Cabral, declared Guinea-Bissau and Cape Verde as sovereign states under the leadership of the PAIGC. This was confirmed when a special mission of the United Nations toured the country and verified that indeed the PAIGC was the "sole legitimate representative of the people of Guinea-Bissau." The United Nations mission was a direct result of the brilliant speeches Cabral had made before that body in the 1960s.

Despite the United Nations decision, military victories, and improvements in the liberated zones, Cabral and his comrades still had a long road ahead in 1972. Heavy casualties among the leading cadre of the Party hampered their ability to move forward, and the challenge of transforming an impoverished peasant nation into a progressive Socialist society was a monumental task. Military struggle against the Portuguese was only half the battle, for Cabral also had to organize the construction of a new society.

Cabral and the PAIGC did not want to leave intact the parasitic system which allowed exploiters to feed off the labor of the workers and the peasants. He told an audience of Afro-Americans, "We want in our country this, to have no more exploitation of our people, not by white people or by black people. It is in this way we educate our people, the masses, the cadre, the militants."[9] Cabral, the leader of the Party and the Messenger of Revolution, believed that both Portuguese colonialism and the traditional Guinean order must yield to a new social order. He taught Party cadre:

> A lot of people think that to defend African culture we have to defend the negative things in our culture, but this is not what we think. While we scrap colonial culture and the negative aspects of our own culture, we have to create a new culture, based on our traditions and respecting what the world has conquered for mankind.[10]

Cabral balanced lofty revolutionary teachings with daily struggles among suffering masses of his people. In *No Fist Is Big Enough To Hide The Sky*, Basil Davidson describes a meeting between Cabral and village peasants.

> Cabral speaks, 'I am saying goodbye to you... You have been brave in the face of bombardments. You have not abandoned your village. On the contrary, you have opened new rice fields, and that is great encouragement to us... So we have a lot to do this coming year. Already you have given a fine example with rice... Shortly we will send you a trained man who will help you to grow more, so as to have a better diet, not only rice.' Cabral talks for three quarters of an hour and as though he had just had a good night's sleep. In fact I know that he walked twenty-five miles yesterday and spent the night huddled in a canoe. After he stops there is a debate. Six or seven men and women speak. A tall young man in a blue and white striped gown apologizes for some of the committee members who are absent: they had to come from a distance, they couldn't arrive in time... He says the anti-

aircraft guns have helped, they can't knock out those planes but they give the people courage. That's why more rice is being grown than last season...But there is one problem: why don't the People's Shops [stores organized by the PAIGC for African peasants] have palmoil and palmnuts. They should do this. A debate follows. Cabral says the installing of these shops has not been easy, needs time to iron out the shortcomings. But after all the people are paying no taxes to the PAIGC...Pascoal intervenes to explain the principle of buying oil and nuts is in fact agreed and put into practice. Cabral comments that this is one thing on which he's obviously out of touch...

An old man arises with an elder's dignity. He says that he supports the Party. Living under the Portuguese was like living in a cave. Now, since the Party came, the Portuguese are afraid, things are different... 'We didn't think it could be different. Party work and Party talk: it's like a big lie at the beginning. But in the end it's the real truth.'

He is followed by a youngish woman who begins with slow ceremony, rewinding her cloth so as to ensure that the baby on her back is safe and comfortable. She is N'kanha, and she is chairman of the village committee...She compares the Portuguese with the ant...'They come and bite us, but we will soon chase them into the sun.'

The meeting ends and rifle distribution begins. Who can handle a rifle? About fifteen peasants stand up. Cabral hands out the rifles one by one, embraces each recipient, says a few words.[11]

The greatness of Cabral as a revolutionary leader is evident when one contrasts this village encounter with his famous lecture on "National liberation and Culture," his remarkable teachings of PAIGC cadre, and his numerous speeches before other governments and revolutioanry organizations. Although an internationally recognized revolutionary theorist, Cabral could nevertheless commune and struggle with the common working peasants of the Guinean countryside. On one day he could march through the swamps and rice fields of Guinea-Bissau with African peasants, and the next day address the United Nations on the social and economic progress of his country's liberated zones.

An example of why his revolutionary theories inspired anti-colonial struggles is the clarity of thought in his 1970 speech, "National Liberation and Culture."

> The value of culture as an element of resistance to foreign domination lies in the fact that culture is the vigorous manifestation, on the ideological or idealist level, of the material and historical reality of the society that is dominated...Culture is simultaneously the fruit of a people's history and a determinant of history...[12]

Cabral, the Messenger of Revolution for the people of Guinea-Bissau and Cape Verde, and the ideological pacesetter for the PAIGC, had long been marked for death by the western imperialists and Portuguese fascists who benefited from colonial rule. In 1970, Portuguese agents fired a bazooka at his home, barely missing his wife Anne Marie and their two children. (Contrast this barbarism with the PAIGC policy forbidding attacks on Portuguese civilians. The policy stated, "The Portuguese people are not our enemies, our enemies are the imperialists and soldiers of imperialism.")

Portuguese treachery did not end with their failed bazooka attack. In 1973, African traitors trained by PIDE were sent to disrupt the revolution by pitting ethnic groups against each other and by murdering Amilcar Cabral. On January 22nd, 1973, these Portuguese lap dogs surrounded Cabral in front of his home and shot him while his wife looked on in horror. Bleeding, Cabral struggled to his feet, only to fall again in a blaze of gunfire from the murderous lackeys. Cabral's brutal murder stunned the nation. His memory, however, inspired the revolution to move forward. In his last speech to Party cadre, Cabral said, "No crime, no power...or demagoguery of the criminal Portuguese aggressors can halt the march of history, the irreversible march of our people toward the independence, peace, and progress, to which they have a right."[13]

Robbed of their leader, the PAIGC continued to fight Portuguese colonialism, stepping up attacks on military units and continuing the medical, literacy, agricultural, and political services in the country's liberated zones. In 1974, a people's coup in Portugal deposed the fascist government, and later that year Portuguese troops withdrew from Guinea-Bissau and Cape Verde.

Amilcar Cabral and thousands of other committed Africans died in the ten-year PAIGC war with the Portuguese aggressors. Their vision and energy was missed when the PAIGC began rebuilding their nation from the ashes of colonialism. Nevertheless, the struggles in Guinea-Bissau and Cape Verde demonstrated to the world that people led by a revolutionary party can defeat the military power of those whose sole aim is the continued exploitation and subjugation of others. Although the workers, peasants, teachers, students, and Party militants were left with the monumental task of building a nation from the wreckage of a war-ravaged economy, a weak industry, an illiterate population, and the sabatoge and ethnic divisiveness promoted by traitors and mercenaries, it was much preferred to Portugese colonialism.

> The building of our country is not going to come from heaven. Everybody has to do work...What fills us with pride is our unity, now indestructible, forged in war.[14]
> —*Amilcar Cabral, in a speech in a Mandinka Village*

FRELIMO and the Mozambican Revolution

When the Mozambican people routed the Portuguese colonialists in 1975, they ended five hundred years of exploitation. At the 1884 Berlin Conference, European parasites greedily divided the African continent among themselves, and Portugal was granted Angola, Mozambique, and Guinea-Bissau. In Mozambique, Portugal leased large tracts of land to multinational corporations who completely dominated the lives and and of African farmers. One company leased sixty-two thousand acres in what became their own slave camp. In *The Struggle For Mozambique*, Eduardo Mondlane describes these conditions;

> The African found himself dispossessed not only of his political power and his land, but also of the most rudimentary rights to control his own life. He could be treated virtually like a slave; forced to leave his home and family to work almost anywhere, for excessively long hours...[15]

Africans under Portuguese rule had no rights or protection. Fascist troops created mass hunger by forcing African peasants to plant cotton for exports instead of the traditional staple crops. In a system similar to Afro-American sharecropping, the Mozambicans were herded into the fields at harvest time, forced to sell their crops at low prices, and left to fend for themselves during the rest of the year. Famines, soil erosion, and starvation were common as bloated capitalists filled their pockets with the benefits of African labor.

Rita Mulumba, later a militant with FRELIMO (Frente de Libertacao de Mozambique, or Liberation Front of Mozambique) recalls how she

> ...worked the fields growing cotton, We didn't want cotton, but we were forced to grow it...If we refused to grow cotton, they arrested us, put us in chains, beat us and then sent us away to a place from where one often didn't come back.[16]

Whether on cotton plantations, tea estates or in domestic work, Mozambicans suffered from colonial brutality. Describing her job as a maid, Teresinha Mblale says:

> I had to start early in the morning and work through till sunset, often into the night as well. I didn't get a meal there. My boss hit me and insulted me. If I broke a glass, they hit me and shouted at me, and at the end of the month I did not get paid.[17]

Portugal's brutal repression carried with it the seeds of its own destruction. The African spirit of resistance and yearning for self-determination was embodied in Samora Machel, military leader of FRELIMO and later president of the People's Republic of Mozambique.

Born in 1933 in Xilembene, Machel developed an early political consciousness. He wrote:

> My political education began not from writings in books, not from reading Marx and Engels, but from seeing my father forced to grow cotton for the Portuguese and going with him to the market where he was forced to sell at a low price... Gradually I saw that nothing would help but collective action. A man on his own could not acheive anything...the consciousness of being oppressed...began to have its effect, as well as ideas of independence.[18]

Machel was not alone. In Mozambique's northern regions Mzee Lazaro Karandame led a cooperative farming movement which challenged the foundation of Portuguese colonialism. These brave Africans refused to grow cotton and instead cooperatively planted maize and beans for local consumption. Mozambican students joined the growing people's struggle with the formation in 1949 of the Nucleo de los Estudiantes Africanas Secundarios de Mocambique (Nucleus of African Secondary Students of Mozambique, or NESAM).

In Mozambique's towns and backcountry, students in NESAM agitated for independence from the colonialists. The Portuguese secret police, PIDE, banned NESAM and arrested its leaders, closed down its headquarters, and sabatoged its activities. Despite Portuguese repression, NESAM was the training ground for many of FRELIMO's future leaders, including Eduardo Mondlane (co-founder and first party chair) Joaquim Chissano (party leader and eventual president of Mozambique), Mariano Matsinhe, Josina Muthewba, and hundreds of other Mozambican miltiants.

The Portuguese and their corporate colleagues were not ready to relinquish the potential for profits because of a few illiterate farmers and rebellious students. Portugal struck back in 1960 with one of the bloodiest atrocities in colonialism's sordid history.

The Portuguese governor of Cabo Delgado invited African farmers to a mass meeting in Mueda to discuss agrarian reform. When they arrived, the governor asked the crowd if anyone wanted to address the colonial officials. Those African farmers who raised their hands were immediately arrested by PIDE agents. Angered at this betrayal, the Mozambican peasants demonstrated and demanded the farmers be released. Portuguese troops hiding nearby opened fire on the unarmed farmers, and six hundred Mozambican men, women, and children were massacred. Teresinha Mblale, later a military leader of FRELIMO, recalls: "I saw how the colonialists massacred the people of Mueda. That was when I lost my uncle. Our people were unarmed when they began to shoot."[19]

The massacre at Mueda sent shock waves through the cities and villages of Mozambique. Portugal answered cooperative movements and student rallies with shocking violence. The people of Mozambique needed a revolutionary vanguard to lead an armed rebellion, but who would lead it?

Eduardo Chivambo Mondlane's early years, like Samora Machel's, Teresinha Mblane's and thousands of other Mozambicans', were shaped by Portuguese repression. As a young boy, he watched PIDE agents throw his mother in jail because her sons in South Africa's diamond mines did not return a portion of their earnings to Portugal's colonial treasury. (All three of Mondlane's brothers eventually died in South African mining accidents.)

His mother never succumbed to Portuguese terror, and every day she made young Eduardo repeat the names of his ancestors who died fighting the Portuguese. As Eduardo performed his daily salute, this young black child slowly developed a compelling desire to change the system which brought so much misery to his mother and the millions like her.

As a founding member of NESAM, Mondlane demonstrated leadership and organizational abilities which became legendary in Mozambique. After several years of service in NESAM, Mondlane left Mozambique to pursue his education in Lisbon. Despite studying in Portugal, he did not leave the struggles of his people. Mondlane and the Mozambican poet Marcelino dos Santos joined Amilcar Cabral (Guinea-Bissau), Mario Pinto de Andrade and Antonio Neto (Angola) in formulating strategies and tactics for the eventual liberation of their homelands.

Mondlane later left Lisbon to complete his education in the United States at Oberlin College and Northwestern University. Eduardo Mondlane became a lecturer, earned a doctoral degree, and worked as a consultant with the United Nations. Nevertheless, he left the relative ease of life in America to return to the land of peasant massacres, malnourished children, and forced labor. Influenced by the teachings of Julius Nyerere of Tanzania on the need for "total transformation" in Africa, Mondlane returned ready to give his life for the liberation of his motherland.

While in the United States, Mondlane worked for all three Mozambican liberation movements. Upon returning in 1962, he called the leaders of the three movements together for a meeting in Tanzania. At this historic gathering, Mondlane, Silverio Nungu, Mzee Lazaro Karandame, Jonas Namashula, Chai Chai, Mateus Muthemba, and Marcelino dos Santos fused the three organizations into FRELIMO, the Liberation Front of Mozambique.

Laying aside ethnic, tactical, and political differences, these African leaders declared as their motto, "Prepare the People for Revolution!" In deciding its priorities, FRELIMO declared that the Mozambican revolution could become a reality only by creating a literate population and by the cultural and social development of Mozambican women. This revolutionary call for literacy and women's rights in the midst of international imperialism was a measure of the latent but radical demands of the Mozambican people.

Although he had been away from Mozambique for

several years, the eloquent Eduardo Mondlane was elected Chairman of FRELIMO. With the standing order of "Respect the people, help the people, defend the people," Mondlane sent the cadre of the Party out into the Mozambican countryside to "organize and mobilize the peasants as the main force" of revolution.

Like their revolutionary comrades in Angola and Guinea-Bissau, FRELIMO spent its first years preparing the common working folk for revolution. From the northern provinces where PIDE and vigilantes enforced slave-like conditions, to the squalor and poverty of African shantytowns around Lourenco Marques (later named Maputo), FRELIMO cadre moved quietly among the people, listening, explaining, and slowly building a party able to crush Portuguese colonialism. FRELIMO member Gabriel Mauricio Nantimbo recalls:

> I was in a state of servitude, but I didn't know it. I thought that was just how the world was. I didn't know that Mozambique was our country. The books said we were Portuguese. Then about 1961 I began to hear other things...FRELIMO began operating in our zone. Some comrades explained about it and I wanted to join. By the end of 1962 even the government felt that the Party was growing, and they started a great campaign of repression, arresting and torturing everyone they suspected. Many preferred to die than betray their comrades. The Party gained strength. The leaders explained the truth to us, taught us our own strength.[20]

Empowering the peasants, workers, and students of Mozambique was the primary task of Mondlane and the other leaders in FRELIMO. "I joined FRELIMO," said Party recruit Joaquim Maquival, "because our people were exploited...The Party told us that we and no one else are responsible for ourselves."[21]

On September 25th, 1964, Eduardo Chivambo Mondlane issued this statement from the leadership of FRELIMO:

> Mozambican people, in the name of all of you,

> FRELIMO today solemnly proclaims the General Armed Insurrection of the Mozambican people against Portuguese colonialism for the attainment of complete independence.[22]

Later that evening, Nangade Diaca and Montequez Chai led other militants from FRELIMO on an armed attack against the Portuguese at Cabo Delgado. The crack of gunfire at Cabo Delgado was for the Mozambican people the first sound of freedom. Mozambican peasants who for years had seen their families destroyed, sons tortured, and daughters raped, cheered the news of FRELIMO's attack. Few African peasants wished for suffering and war, but five centuries of slavery and repression could not be wished away.

In 1964, FRELIMO had but two hundred and fifty trained soldiers. Although this number increased to eight thousand by 1967, by then the Portuguese army had grown to forty thousand. FRELIMO had other enemies as well. As in Angola and Guinea-Bissau, NATO (including the United States) generously provided the colonialists with sophisticated weapons of destruction. Boeing 707's, napalm, cluster bombs, and toxic defoliants were used to terrorize Mozambican men, women, and children in the "liberated zones" controlled by FRELIMO.

In the midst of this continous rain of death, FRELIMO military units tried to meet the social, economic, and cultural needs of the peasants. Like the PAIGC under Cabral in Guinea-Bissau, FRELIMO refused to collect taxes from the peasants, provided grassroots political structures for the people, established educational and medical clinics, and armed the people to protect themselves against roving bands of Portuguese soldiers. Culture reflected the armed struggle. Poet and FRELIMO leader Marcelino dos Santos wrote:

> Today's mission
> comrade
> is
> dig the basic soil of revolution
> make the people strong,
> with a bazooka.[23]

The Mozambican people were transformed by the very act of armed struggle. Ethnic differences faded when FRELIMO's cadre were engaged with the vicious colonialists in a life and death struggle. Military commander Samora Machel wrote:

> All Mozambicans who joined FRELIMO during the armed struggle passed through Nachingwea training camp; this was the filter and mould of consciousness...When we arrived, we brought with us vices, defects, egoism, elitism. We destroyed these negative reactionary values...We entered Nachingwea as Makondes, Maucuas, Nianjas, Rongas, Senas, we came out Mozambicans.[24]

The war also forever changed the lives of women in this traditional peasant society. Crushed between Mozambique's backward views toward women and the calculated strategy of the Portuguese to oppress African women, Mozambican women suffered immeasurably. The African women who had worked eighteen hours a day, kept families together when the men were taken away by police, and suffered sexual abuse, now picked up machine guns and hand grenades to free themselves and their nation. Eduardo Mondlane wrote:

> By accepting women into its ranks, the army has revolutionized their social position. Women now play a very active role in running popular militias. Through the army, women have started to take responsibility in many areas...In fact they do a great deal of important work in mobilizing the population. When a women's unit first visits a village which is not sufficiently involved with FRELIMO, the sight of armed women who get up and talk in front of a large audience causes great amazement.[25]

Typical of these "amazing" women was Rita Mulumbua. She recalls her days in the struggle:

> I am with Ajuas, Nyanjas, Makondes...I believe this is very good; before we did not think of ourselves as a single

nation; FRELIMO has shown us that we are one people. The struggle has transformed us. FRELIMO gave me the chance to study. The colonialists didn't want us to study. In this detachment we train in the morning and in the afternoon I go to study... FRELIMO wants us to study so that we should know, and in knowing we understand better, we fight better, and will serve our country better.[26]

FRELIMO's armed struggle, its role in liberating women, and its services in the liberated zones, were fueled by Socialist ideology. Party Chair Eduardo Mondlane wrote:

I am now convinced that FRELIMO has a clearer political line than ever before. The common basis which we had when we formed FRELIMO was hatred of colonialism and the belief in the necessity to destroy the colonial structure and to establish a new social structure. But what type... no one knew... At present FRELIMO is much more socialist, revolutionary, and progressive than ever, and that tendency is more in the direction of Marxism-Leninism. Why? Because the conditions of life in Mozambique, the type of enemy we have, does not give us any other alternative.[27]

Led by Eduardo Mondlane, FRELIMO cadre like Rita Mulumbua, Joaquim Machival, and the eight thousand other African fighters faced forty thousand Portuguese troops armed with the latest in murderous war technology. Already outnumbered and outgunned, in 1969 FRELIMO suffered the staggering loss of its beloved leader.

Always a target of treacherous murder plots, Mondlane had once said, "They are determined to kill me. I guess sooner or later they will. But I am not worried anymore. We really do have a collective leadership. FRELIMO, The Movement, is greater than any one man. They don't understand that."[28]

On February 3, 1969, Mondlane was assassinated by Portuguese agents in Dar es Salaam. He opened a package addressed to him which detonated, instantly killing the leader and inspirational figure of the

Revolution. News of his death elicited gleeful laughter from Portuguese imperialists who rubbed their bloated bellies in anticipation of continuing their rape of Mozambique.

The mournful guerrillas of FRELIMO knew they had gone too far to quit. Fighting with reckless abandon (a FRELIMO bulletin noted, "Our enemies must not forget that the guerrilla fighter returns to battle with increased rage when he has seen a comrade fall."[29]) they stung the Portuguese with military defeats in Tete and Zambezi. Under the brilliant military leadership of Samora Machel, FRELIMO crossed the Zambezi River and astonished the Portuguese with their rapid advance. Western nations frantically shipped bombs to the Portuguese, and in 1970 sixty-three thousand tons of bombs were dropped on the peasants and children of Mozambique.

FRELIMO had to fight internal battles as well. The Party vice-chair and successor to Mondlane was Uriah Simango, a Mozambican nationalist who promoted elitism and exploited the peasants in his liberated zones. Although Simango was the legal successor, many FRELIMO cadre did not want to compromise the revolution with an exclusive nationalism and divisive elitism. In a bitter internal struggle Samora Moises Machel was elected chair of the Party.

If Mondlane was the heart and soul of FRELIMO, Machel was the muscle. After joining the Party in 1962, he was one of the first to go to Algeria for military training. A quick learner and brilliant strategist, Machel mastered the military works of Vietnam's General Giap and China's Mao Zedong and quickly rose to the top of FRELIMO's military. Since the military provided social, health, educational and political benefits to the liberated zones, Machel's role increased and he became a driving force in Party ideology and direction. Born of poor peasants in Xilembene, Machel remained a man of the people. As Barry Muslow writes in *Samora Machel: An African Revolutionary*,

> Throughout the protracted armed struggle, he was to

> lead from the front, setting the pace of marches across the endless kilometers of sparsely populated Niassa Province, through the heartland of FRELIMO's liberated areas on the Mueda Plateau. But not just walking, all the time discussing the problems of the zone with the local people who gave their support... Talking and walking, sometimes all day and half the night.[30]

This revolutionary fervor multiplied in the company of other FRELIMO cadre, and by 1974 the outnumbered, outgunned, poorly armed militants of the Party brought the Portuguese agents of western imperialism to their knees. In June of 1975, FRELIMO declared an end to five hundred years of foreign domination and proclaimed the founding of the People's Republic of Mozambique.

Not willing to replace white capitalism with black capitalism, Machel, Marcelino dos Santos, Joaquim Chissano, Jorge Rebelo and the other members of FRELIMO's Central Committee found building the nation as difficult as winning the war.

A committed Marxist-Leninist, Machel called on his war-weary Mozambicans to help rebuild their beloved country. "The launching of the struggle and the victories we have won reveal concretely that there is no such thing as fateful destiny, we are capable of transforming society and creating a new life."[31]

With these words, Machel and FRELIMO formed the Grupos Dynamizados (dynamizing groups), grassroots political action groups that served as a link between the Party and the people. Formed in villages, factories, schools and offices, the Grupos Dynamizados mobilized people to collectively address the massive problems created by centuries of neglect and exploitation.

Portugal left a nation of nine million people with fifty doctors, ninety percent illiteracy, a shattered economy (from decades of compulsory growth of export crops), an infant mortality rate of sixty percent, and a life expectancy of thirty years.

The Grupos Dynamizados joined with the Organization of Mozambican Women (the OMW was a national women's group actively engaged in national reconstruction), to establish rural health clinics, and literacy training programs. In weekly meetings the people of Mozambique discussed worker-peasant alliances, recurring tribalism, and other concerns obstructing the forward motion of their village and nation. Marcelino dos Santos noted, "The Grupos Dynamizados created a sense of confidence in the oppressed masses and helped convince them that they had the capacity to transform Mozambique."[32]

In 1977, FRELIMO formally declared itself a Marxist-Leninist vanguard party. At the 1977 Party Congress, President Machel noted:

> Ideology is always the creation of a specific struggle by a people and its revolutionary classes. Ideology becomes a reality when it is taken up and experienced by the broad masses, when theory is renewed and materialized in day-to-day practice of struggle.[33]

The experience of the masses in both the liberation war and national reconstruction confirmed what Eduardo Mondlane had written several years earlier, that the revolutionary demands and bitter enemies of the Mozambican people left them no option but Marxism. Samora Machel and FRELIMO intensified their war to rebuild their country. Families were relocated from filthy shantytowns built by the Portuguese, education was declared both free and public, and health care was nationalized. Focusing on medical care, President Machel said, "The rich man's dog gets more in the way of vaccinations, medicine, and medical care than do the workers on whom the rich man's wealth is built."[34]

Dogs of another kind still existed both within and without the country. Not everyone was enthralled with the move toward socialism. Corruption, sabotage, and ethnic divisions sapped the reconstruction of its vitality. The United States and South Africa, the world's bastions of racism, funded the counterrevolutionary Mozambique National Resistance (MNR). The MNR collected the most reactionary elements of Mozambique into one terrorist organization bent on destroying the People's

Republic of Mozambique. MNR land mines, their burning of villages, and the destruction of Mozambique's infrastructure are reminders of capitalism's unwillingness to allow Africans to determine their destiny outside western control. These attacks, financed by Washington and South African fascists, continue even today.

Machel declared war on traitors and proclaimed, "We say that after the sacrifices and the bloodshed we cannot permit new parasites to come and feed on our sweat."[35] In the midst of reconstructing their impoverished nation, Mozambicans are forced to expend precious dollars fighting terrorists. Natural famines, destruction of capital equipment, and foreign debt made the Mozambican revolution a most difficult road. Despite these obstacles, Machel continued to awaken the irrepressible spirit of the people to defeat their enemies.

> Underdevelopment is not due to lack of resources. It reflects man's ignorance in using his existing resources and man's passive acceptance of his situation of wretchedness. Mozambican society carries the dead weight of the fatalist resigned legacy of peasant society... We know that in our hearts and minds there is determination capable of transforming the old world into a new world.[36]

The enemies of the people persist. On October 19, 1986, Samora Moises Machel was killed in a mysterious plane crash over South Africa. The African National Congress and several other groups blamed racist South Africa for the "accident." Indeed, evidence has surfaced that the South African racists used electronic equipment to veer the plane off course into a mountain. It would not be surprising, as the apartheid system has always looked with fear upon nine million Mozambicans shaping their own destiny.

Despite the loss of Mondlane and Machel, the strength of the common folk continues and the revolution lives. The conclusion of John Saul's *A Difficult Road: The Transition to Socialism in Mozambique*, captures the vitality and stuggles of revolutionary Mozambique:

I can remember dinners with Eduardo Mondlane, FRELIMO's first president, and long conversations with Marcelino dos Santos...And I can remember Samora Machel visiting my house...on the back of Jorge Rebelo's motorcycle—to talk of the war; of information and support work, still a long way from victory but well on the road, a vibrant and inspiring figure. I remember the palpable feeling of "people's power" in the liberated areas of Fingoe, where women revelled in their ability to speak up publicly for the first time and all shared a sense of freedom; I remember the unrestrained emotion of the rain-soaked crowd as the new Mozambique flag went up in the National Stadium a few minutes after midnight, June 25, 1975, and I remember how moved I was later when...Machel and dos Santos, freshly installed in office, embraced in triumph; I remember the intense concentration of my students in the evening course on Marxism at FRELIMO's party school, cadres bone-tired after a full day's work but dedicated to mastering the tools which would help to see a transition to socialism in their country; I remember the creative and self-critical atmosphere alive in the impressive new conference hall at the Fourth Congress as FRELIMO fought, against lengthening odds, to keep its revolution alive.

To have seen a people making its own history, freeing itself from a morally bankrupt and viciously oppressive colonialism and then launching an impressive project of humane and egalitarian social reconstruction, is a moving experience, to be allowed, as an outsider, to share in these struggles in some small way is more than moving, it is inspiring.[37]

Angola: The Grieved Land of Africa

Angola is the living embodiment of all that is wrong with capitalism. Capitalism's search for cheap labor and new resources at the expense of human needs has created in Angola a nation in sorrow. From the beginning, Angola's encounter with Europe was marred by unimaginable anguish. Between 1482 and 1858, nine million Angolans were shipped like cattle to work the fields of Brazil for their Portuguese masters, and millions of other Angolans were sent to the West Indies and North America. Those who remained in Angola did not escape suffering. For five centuries Angolan peasants were brutalized, intimidated, and exploited by greedy European entrepreneurs.

Liberation from Portugal did not bring peace to the embattled farmers, workers, students, and peasants of this blood-soaked land. Reactionary nationalist movements fueled with guns and moral support from racist South Africa and the United States tore the nation apart. The Angolan people became pawns in superpower conflicts as Cubans fought South Africans and America and Russia played tug-of-war with Angola. Despite this tragic history, the people survive and move forward. The men and women who work the factories and the ports, who raise the children and work the land, relentlessly struggle to transform Angola into an economically just and Socialist society.

The Angolan people's aspiration for a better way of life was dramatically symbolized by the late Antonio Agostinho Neto. Physician, poet, revolutionary, party leader, and president, Neto dedicated his life to improving the living conditions of all Angolans. Although he was able to go abroad and study medicine in Lisbon, Neto never forgot his roots and the suffering masses. He joined fellow Angolan Mario Pinta de Andrade and Guinean Amilcar Cabral in all-night sessions where they discussed, argued, and developed strategies on how to bring revolutionary change to their countries.

From 1952 to 1960, Neto was arrested several times for his anti-colonial activities. Portuguese jails did not crush his spirit, and during one prison term in 1956, he, Andrade, and other Angolans formed the Movimiento Popular de Libertacao de Angola (Popular Movement for the Liberation of Angola, or MPLA). Founded by a few idealistic students in the putrid stench of a Lisbon prison, the MPLA became the revolutionary vanguard and irrepressible hope of the Angolan people.

While in Lisbon, Neto also gained a reputation in literary circles for his poetry. He was hailed as one of the new breed of brilliant young African writers, and several of his poems were published. His works, however, were not about abstractions; they were clearly linked to the suffering masses and the impending struggle for change in Angola. In his book *Sacred Hope*, Neto wrote:

> To the houses, to the farms
> to the beaches, to our fields
> we will return
>
> To our lands
> red of coffee
> white of cotton
> green of corn fields
> we will return
>
> To our rivers, our lakes
> to the mountains, to the forests
> we will return
>
> To the freshness of the mulemba
> to our traditions
> to the rhythms and the bonfires
> we will return
>
> To the beautiful Angolan country
> our land, our mother
> we will return
>
> We will return to Angola
> liberated, independent Angola[38]

In 1960, Neto was released again from prison in Lisbon and he returned to his native land of Angola. The colonial authorities, however, were not elated by his arrival. Later that year he was arrested by PIDE, publicly flogged, and thrown in prison. Crowds from Neto's village of Bengo were outraged at the humiliation of their brilliant leader and hundreds demonstrated for his release outside the jail. Furious at this blatant affront to colonial authority, the Portuguese fascists murdered thirty demonstrators and burned the village to the ground. The imperialists increased repression all over Angola, and a cotton worker strike in the Malange district was met with bombs and napalm as thousands of striking Angolan peasants were murdered.

When Neto was released from prison, it was clear the Portuguese had no intentions for a peaceful settlement and he immediately began preparing the MPLA for war. On February 4, 1961, MPLA cadre attacked Luanda prison in a bold display of African resistance. Boldness, however, was not enough, and the assault failed when forty MPLA soldiers were killed. Vengeful Portuguese struck back, and vigilantes joined the army and PIDE in a mass campaign of murder and intimidation. MPLA leaders were tracked down and murdered, armed white lynch mobs massacred Angolans in Luanda shantytowns, and repression reached genocidal proportions in the countryside, where fifty thousand Angolan men, women, and children were killed under the watchful eye of NATO, South Africa, and the United States.

Neto, Mario Andrade, Viviato Cruz, Lucia Lara and other leaders of MPLA convened to reassess the direction of the revolution. Their dreams of a quick coup were shattered by the ferocity of Portuguese repression. Neto and his comrades in the MPLA decided to go underground, where they could recruit impoverished workers in secret and organize peasants without PIDE harassment.

Under cover of darkness, using every subterfuge and trick available, courageous Angolan workers, students, and militants recruited others into the MPLA. Neto's brilliant leadership revived the MPLA after the 1961 disaster, and for the next five years MPLA cadre quietly built the Party from the brainchild of a few imprisoned intellectuals to a powerful force for the people of Angola.

The MPLA was not alone. Holden Roberto of the National Front for the Liberation of Angola (FNLA) and Jonas Savimbi of the National Union for the Total Independence of Angola (UNITA) both fought Portuguese colonialists. Unfortunately, while the MPLA attempted to bring together Angola's diverse peoples, both UNITA and the FNLA were based on a narrow nationalism which pitted Angola's ethnic groups against each other. Although all three played a role in defeating the Portuguese invaders, vast ideological differences prevented the unity sought by Neto and other MPLA leaders. (In fact, by the early Seventies UNITA and

FNLA almost exclusively fought each other and the MPLA.)

Angola was home to six million Africans, and while most were Mbundu, Bakonga, Kimbundu, and Ovimbundu, there were over one hundred smaller ethnic groups in the Angolan interior. The fascists of Portugal and their NATO, South African, and U.S. bankrollers cruelly exploited this demograhic diversity to their calculated advantage. Through planted rumors, arms sales, and indiscriminate terror, the seeds were planted for civil war in Angola. In Angola, the interests of black nationalism and western imperialism became one. The authors of *Angola: In The Front Line*, note,

> FNLA's strategy for power was one of simple domination by one tribe, the Kikongo. That domination would be facilitated by American arms and support. After independence a capitalist economy was planned, run by the multinationals with ample rewards for those Angolan leaders who would be signing the contracts.
>
> UNITA's strategy was based on Ovimbundu tribalism, and a return to the halcyon days of Ovimbundu prosperity. The key to UNITA's capitalism was the multinationals...and peace with racist South Africa.
>
> MPLA alone, sought real independence and non-alignment, and thus needed to build a strongly united nation. Only the MPLA was committed to resolving the tribal and racial problems, with working-class and peasant interests a priority.[39]

The CIA, South Africa and the Portuguese supported the nationalism of UNITA and the FNLA, much like the Klan supported the Afro-American nationalism of Marcus Garvey in the 1920s. "Independent" black nationalist states were easier to exploit than non-aligned Socialist African nations with ties to other progressive countries. With nationalism, the Portuguese and other western capitalists could have the dual benefit of exploiting ethnic differences and reaping neocolonial profits. The United States, NATO, Portugal and South Africa had no intention of allowing the Socialist MPLA control Angola's oil, uranium, cobalt and chrome.

MPLA Poster

The ultimate indictment of the FNLA and UNITA is the millions of dollars they received both from Pretoria and Washington's CIA. Holden was on the CIA payroll as early as 1962 and Savimbi followed with funds from the CIA and South Africa in 1966. How could an African liberation party claim to represent the aspirations of the exploited Angolan masses with their pockets dripping with blood money from the Nazis of racist South Africa?

Despite these differences and the deliberate terror of the Portuguese, Neto led the MPLA into armed rebellion in 1966. Leaping beyond their traditional ethnic base among the Mbundu people, MPLA cadre fanned out in the countryside and recruited thousands of peasants into their war for the liberation of Angola. Three thousand MPLA troops fought in guerrilla attacks against fifty thousand Portuguese troops, and often the colonialists were assisted when soldiers from UNITA and the FNLA attacked MPLA units. (This treachery began as early as 1961 when Roberto's Union of the Peoples of Angola, the predecessor of the FNLA, murdered Tomas Ferreira and 21 MPLA guerrillas.)

From the early 1960's to the war's end in 1975, the people of Angola were victims of atrocities committed not only by the Portuguese but also by FNLA and UNITA soldiers who used torture and terror to intimidate the Angolan peasants. Antonio Agostinho Neto led the MPLA in several battles, winning the respect of the Angolan people and chasing the hated Portuguese from many villages and towns.

Neto of course was not alone in battle, and Hoji Ya Henda exemplified the bravery and skill of the MPLA. Henda joined the struggle as a teenager, and his courage in battle and devotion to liberation catapulted him into the military leadership of the MPLA. During the height of African revolutions in the 1960s and 1970s, Henda and Amilcar Cabral were viewed as symbols of the African Revolutionary. Henda was killed in action in 1968 and he is currently honored in Angola every year during Youth Day.

Women were also instrumental in winning the war for the MPLA. After the war, Maria Eugenia Neto wrote:

> Women contributed enormously—supporting guerrillas, transporting food, taking care of children, and carrying arms. We've just inaugurated a monument in Luanda...and one of the women in the statue is carrying a big parcel on her head with weapons on it with a child on her back...this really was the way it was.[40]

Without the popular support enjoyed by the MPLA, UNITA and the FNLA resorted to lootings, rape, and mayhem in an effort to build a following among the Angolan people. While the MPLA constructed military health services and literacy clinics in Angola's backcountry, several villages were burned and the people massacred by vicious UNITA or FNLA troops.

Savimbi and Roberto often assisted the Portuguese against the MPLA, and in fact, after the war the MPLA discovered correspondence between Savimbi and the Portuguese on how to defeat the MPLA and explaining how they would share power after MPLA's defeat.

Meanwhile, the MPLA took the initiative on the ideological front. While UNITA and the FNLA called on the Angolan people to concentrate solely on eliminating the white man (and the MPLA), Neto and the MPLA taught the more complex reality that the real enemy was not so easily identified. In a famous 1970 speech titled "Who Is The Enemy...What Is Our Objective?" Neto said:

> In my opinion, the national liberation struggle in Africa cannot be separated from the present context in which it is taking place; it cannot be isolated from the world. A workers' strike in England, the imposition of fascism on the Chilean people or an atomic explosion in the Pacific are all phenomena of this same life...Hence the need to see the problem clearly and provide clear answers to the following specific questions: Who is the enemy? What is our objective?...I wish to emphasize that neither is it true that Angola is dominated only by Portugal...For example, Great Britain and the United States of America...are competing for the domination of our people and the exploitation of the wealth that belongs to us...Therefore, if we say that Portugal is the manager of a series of socio-economic deals, we will see that it is not our principal enemy but merely our direct enemy...The

enemy of Africa is often confused with the white man...To answer our question, we would say that the enemy is colonialism, the colonial system, and also imperialism, which sustains the former, to the point of being the principal enemy...I shall therefore go on to say that national liberation must be a stage for the achievement of a vaster form of liberation, which is the liberation of man. If one loses sight of this idea, dynamism disappears and the essential contradictions in a country remain...The preoccupation of Africa with making the liberation struggle a racial struggle of blacks against whites is not only superficial, it is reactionary...To pose the question as black against white is to falsify the question and deflect us from our real objective. What do we want? An independent life as a nation in which economic relations are just both between countries and within the country.[41]

With this political line, Neto and the MPLA raised the liberation struggle from the narrowness of race war to an international perspective where Angolans, Afro-Americans, Chileans, and other Third World folk fought for both survival and self-determination. While Angolan nationalists prostrated themselves before the god of blackness and ancient Africa, the MPLA linked hands with the oppressed all over the world and fought the real enemy, monopoly capitalism. With this ideology and the fierce military leadership of cadre like Nito Alves and Hoji Ya Henda, the MPLA emerged as the most powerful party in Angola.

But Angola's suffering was not easily assuaged. When a ceasefire was called in 1974, U.S. President Nixon scurried about like a frantic rat trying to form a government consisting of Roberto's FNLA, Savimbi's UNITA, and the remaining Portuguese settlers. The MPLA was to be excluded and the majority of the Angolan people ignored. Although a fragile transition government was formed between the MPLA, UNITA, and FNLA, President Nixon's Operation Tarbaby combined Angolan nationalism with CIA manipulation to assure more black bloodshed.

In March of 1975, FNLA troops and Portuguese

settlers viciously attacked MPLA headquarters and murdered several party leaders. The MPLA was under seige, surrounded by FNLA forces in the north (supported by Zaire and the CIA) and by UNITA troops in the south and east (aided by South Africa, Zambia, and the CIA). Ex-CIA agent John Stockwell notes that his former employer spent $31 million on FNLA and UNITA operations against the MPLA. To further the international conspiracy against Angola, South African troops from Namibia invaded Angola from the south. This second war of independence was fought with both savagery and bravery, as the irresistible will of the workers and peasants of Angola defeated attempts to turn their nation into a playground for international powers. Backed by Cuban troops, in 1976 the MPLA soundly defeated both nationalist groups and chased the South Africans back to Namibia.

By 1977, the MPLA declared itself a vanguard party, espoused socialism as the eventual goal of the revolution, and set about the tremendous task of rebuilding Angola. The problems created by two hundred years of corporate control (DeBeers: diamonds, Krupp: iron ore and Gulf: oil), fifty years of fascism, bloody civil wars, ethnic dissensions, well-financed destabilization programs, external invasions, and a ruined economy (the Portuguese even burned Luanda's electrical and water plans and student's school records) awaited the battle-weary cadre of the MPLA. In this context, Neto wrote,

> It is necessary that the Party be built up that it constitute the backbone...of the nation. Where there is no Party, where the militants are not placed under strict discipline, where the leaders are not bound by revolutionary principles...there the enemies penetrate easily, and instead of independence we will have neo-colonialism.[42]

Neto was right. Diligence became the Party watchword as year after year Angola was victimized by South African bombings and UNITA terrorist raids. In 1978, South Africans killed six hundred Angolans and Namibians at Cassinga, and no city or village was safe from UNITA's terrorism.

This shameful treachery continued even into the 1980s, when the increasingly reactionary Jonas Savimbi was hailed by President Ronald Reagan and America's right wing as a "hero and a savior." Needless to say, the interests of Ronald Reagan are not the interests of an Angolan peasant. Reagan also sent UNITA $77 million, and in 1986 Savimbi used some of these funds to plant land mines along rural paths to blow legs and arms off of struggling Angolan peasants. To add to Angola's economic woes, South African attacks continued, and between 1976 and 1981, $914 million worth of agriculture, hospitals, petroleum, and fishing was destroyed by the racists. (This destruction occurred after the 1975 war!)

The fight for Angolan liberty was dealt another blow when Antonio Neto died of cancer in 1979. Fighter for liberty for twenty years, chair of the MPLA from 1962 to his death, and first president of Angola, Neto symbolized African resistance. The context of his struggle and the harsh conditions which he and his Angolan comrades endured cannot be overstated. Neto and the MPLA exemplify the tenacity and persistence of the African Socialist. Not resting while their people suffered, determined to be free, Neto and the MPLA battled the Portuguese, the United States, NATO, South Africa, Angolan traitors, and whoever else stood in the path of national liberation.

Zimbabwe: Chimurenga!

The African nation of Zimbabwe arose from the ashes of racist Rhodesia. Closely allied with South Africa, Rhodesia treated black Africans with the same disdain as their cousins to the south. In both countries, a well-armed white minority sapped the black majority of its labor power and human dignity.

For centuries the African peasants of Zambesia (original name of Rhodesia) produced enough food to feed themselves and their neighbors. This changed, however, when insatiable capitalists Cecil Rhodes and the British South Africa Company descended on the Shona and Ndebele peoples. Like packs of wild animals, English soldiers and speculators murdered, jailed, and imprisoned all those Africans who stood between them and the diamond and gold mines of Zambesia. A trail of maimed and broken black bodies marked the path Cecil Rhodes cut through Zambesia.

The extent of English domination was evident when the African nation was renamed Rhodesia, after the man who brought misery and death to millions of Shona and Ndebele. Rich in resources and cheap (forced) labor, Rhodesia became a plantation for the Africans and a paradise for the "enterprising" English. Peasants accustomed to self-sufficiency on their own land were forced off their farms by huge hut and poll taxes invented by the colonialists to create large starving labor pools for the British South African Company. Herded into migrant worker shacks, shantytowns, and mining camps, the African people lived in squalor and anguish.

The vacant lands left behind by the Africans were greedily consumed by English speculators. By the 1920s, seven thousand white farmers owned half of the farmland in Rhodesia, with the other half divided among eight hundred thousand African peasants. The average white farmer in Rhodesia sat on six thousand acres of the best land in the country, land that was once divided among hard-working African families. This pattern continued to the 1970s, when two hundred seventy thousand Europeans owned forty-five million acres.

The power of the Rhodesian military, the crippling effects of colonial education (education for servitude which taught Africans to despise themselves and adore the English), and corporate exploitation still could not quench the spirit of resistance among the Shona and Ndebele peoples. The desire for independence was intensified when black Rhodesians watched their brothers and sisters take up arms in Algeria, Guinea-Bissau, Angola, and Mozambique.

Under the leadership of Ndabaningi Sithole the Zimbabwe African National Union (ZANU) followed FRELIMO, the PAIGC, and the MPLA by mobilizing and educating exploited peasants. From 1964 to 1966, Sithole and other leading cadre of ZANU went from village to village spreading the message of self-liberation through armed struggle and sacrifice. Ernest Maunga, a ZANU guerrilla, used peasant traditions and customs to organize the Zimbabwean masses. As he explained:

> The Zimbabwean peasants had all-night meetings called 'pungwes'. Although the 'pungwes' were traditional community celebrations handed down from generation, we used the occasion to explain to the people the aim and struggle of ZANU for the liberation of our country. Through the songs and stories of the people we politically educated and recruited hundreds of Africans into the struggle, This was one of our most effective mobilization tools.[43]

In April of 1966, the military wing of ZANU, the Zimbabwean African National Liberation Army (ZANLA), launched its first armed attack on Rhodedian troops at Sinoia. All seven guerrillas were killed in a stunning setback to the liberation forces. Visions of a quick ZANU victory gave way to a more realistic analysis of the strength of the white military and of their resolve to cling to the goodies of capitalism's slave camp. Headquartered in Mozambique, ZANU cadre were influenced by FRELIMO's Socialist tactics, and they returned to the village *pungwes*, mining camps, and shantytowns to build a party capable of both defeating the well-armed Rhodesians and leading a liberated Socialist nation.

In 1972, the legendary Josiah Tongogara led thirty cadre in the first major attack on Rhodesian troops since 1966. Tongagara, a military leader in ZANLA, was revered by the African peasants for his bravery in combat and his brimming confidence in the inevitability of victory. The revolutionary optimism generated by Africans like Tongogara countered the sadism of white Rhodesians trying to maintain their bloody regime.

The long-awaited *Chimurenga* (liberation struggle) had finally arrived. Everywhere African peasants talked excitedly of independence. Young men and women emerged from mine shafts, tea plantations, and cotton fields to take up arms in the *Chimurenga*. Even those Africans not in the army were involved, feeding the soldiers, hiding guns, and directing pursuing white troops down wrong roads. Black Africans waged a cultural struggle as well, as Jamaican reggae and Thomas Mapfumo's *Chimurenga* songs inspired exhausted soldiers to move forward.

ZANU militants were also exhorted to continue the fight by their leader, the chair of the party, Robert Gabriel Mugabe. Born in 1924, Mugabe was just one of the millions of African workers who awaited the day when they could expel the racists and assume control of their own destiny. Mugabe attended school in South Africa where he met Nelson Mandela, Oliver Tambo and Robert Sobukwe. Moved by their resolve to abolish South African apartheid, Mugabe returned to Rhodesia to confront the enemies of his people. For his bold speeches and writings on African self-determination, Mugabe was jailed for ten years by Premier Ian Smith and his fascistic government. From 1960 to 1970, Mugabe languished in prisons, separated from his family and removed from the struggle. A decade of prison only hardened his resolve to win African liberation. When Mugabe was released in 1970, he went immediately to Mozambique to lead ZANU's preparation for the *Chimurenga*.

While ZANU embodied the hopes of the Shona people, the Zimbabwe People's Union (ZAPU) under Joshua Nkomo led the Ndebele people's struggle. By the late Seventies, both organizations had carved out large liberated zones where they eliminated the poll and hut taxes and provided health, education, and farming assistance. The Rhodesians and their friends in the United States and South Africa became desperate. In 1974, forty percent of Rhodesia's budget was spent on machine guns, helicopters, bombs, and tanks. Unwilling to lose a white capitalist ally, the United States and South Africa funneled millions of dollars in weapons to

Rhodesia.

The Rhodesian government implemented a brutal internal resettlement program which uprooted entire villages into concentration camps and indiscriminately machine-gunned anyone, including women and children, who resisted. Thousands of Africans died from this terrorism, but nothing could crush African resistance.

When FRELIMO freed Mozambique from the Portuguese in 1975, Rhodesia was suddenly bordered by three black African nations (Botswana, Zambia, and Mozambique). Time was running out on Rhodesia, and in 1978 Ian Smith tried to appease the African people by holding a sham election in which moderate black Bishop Muzorewa was elected president. This token appointment did not satisfy peasants who for ten years had watched sons, daughters, fathers, and mothers die in the flames of war. One black face at the top of a white capitalist administration was not their idea of revolutionary change, and the war continued.

With victory in sight for the African revolutionaries, England, the United States, and South Africa urged a compromise between Ian Smith and the forces of Mugabe and Nkomo. It was agreed that majority rule guaranteed by open elections would begin in 1980. White capitalist governments heavily subsidized the campaign of Bishop Muzorewa and anticipated a big victory. The people of newly-created Zimbabwe, however, had other plans. Mugabe and ZANU received eighty-three percent of the vote, and ninety years of colonial rule ended.

As in other struggles for liberation on the continent of Africa, winning the armed war was only the beginning of struggle. Many of the best leaders and organizers were killed in the fourteen-year *Chimurenga*, as twenty thousand Africans died fighting well-armed and often sadistic white Rhodesians. In addition, ZAPU and Joshua Nkomo felt cheated out of their place in leading the country, and the troops of the two parties often clashed. Mugabe and his young nation were also faced with building socialism in a country devastated by war and hampered by subtle economic sabotage used by western nations who hate to see Africans think or act for themselves.

Faced with massive problems in productivity, electrification, literacy, and health, Zimbabwe nevertheless has made significant gains since independence. The lives of women have dramatically improved, and the government has sought to provide every citizen with education, medicine, and shelter.

Culture, used in the *Chimurenga* as a weapon of struggle, was also part of the national reconstruction. In Harare (the capital) and in the rural areas, Minister of Education Dzingayi Mutumbuka sponsored cultural events that conveyed messages of self-reliance and social responsibility.

One of the leading African countries in the non-aligned movement, Zimbabwe is often condemned by the United States for its outspoken criticism of U.S. imperialism. Despite threats of sanctions and economic blackmail from Washington, the Harare government has continued to criticize events like the invasion of Grenada, U.S. aid to the Nicaraguan Contras, support of racist South Africa, and the 1986 attack on Libya.

Life in Zimbabwe is still hard, there is still much illiteracy, poverty, and disease. The future, however, is certainly brighter than the past ninety years of racist colonialism. Building an African Socialist nation in the midst of western reactionary politics, sitting next to the last bastion of racism in Africa, Robert Mugabe, ZANU, and the people of Zimbabwe face a monumental struggle. If their resolve during the bloody fourteen-year was any indication, it is a struggle they will win. *Chimurenga* continues!

Writers and Revolution

- **Langston Hughes**
- **Richard Wright**
- **Amiri Baraka**
- **Writers from the Caribbean**
- **Ngugi wa Thiong'o**
- **Revolutionary Writer in Retrospect**

Writers and Revolution

For Afro-American, Caribbean, and African revolutionary writers, culture is as much a weapon in the liberation struggles as arms or political power. With them there is no "art for art's sake." Rather than produce mindless volumes and diversionary diatribes on diet fads, money-making schemes, or abstract poems, the black revolutionary writer is rooted in the tragedies and triumphs of the black working class. The black writer has no time for sonnets and sunsets. The pain of Kenyan peasants, Newark's unemployed, or Haitian sugar cane cutters compels them to write both of the present agony and the future possibility of revolutionary change.

In writing for the people, the black writer is not paralyzed by despair, but instead is energized and sustained by the revolutionary yearnings of the masses. The black writer is not flustered by Mao Zedong's query, "Art and literature for whom?" Baraka's essays, Wright's short stories, Ngugi's plays, Roumain's articles, and Hughes's poems answer Mao's question with a resounding, "For the black masses!"

So indispensable is black revolutionary literature that where revolution is, there is the writer. George Jackson's *Soledad Brother*; W.E.B. Du Bois's *Black Reconstruction*; Antonio Neto's *Sacred Hope*; Walter Rodney's *Grounding With My Brothers*; Paul Robeson's *Here I Stand*; Marcelino dos Santos's unpublished poems; and hundreds of articles and pamphlets by black writers both transform and are transformed by the peoples' movements. As the people move, so moves the literature, and the literature becomes energized and moves the struggle even further, thereby completing the revolutionary link between the writers and the masses.

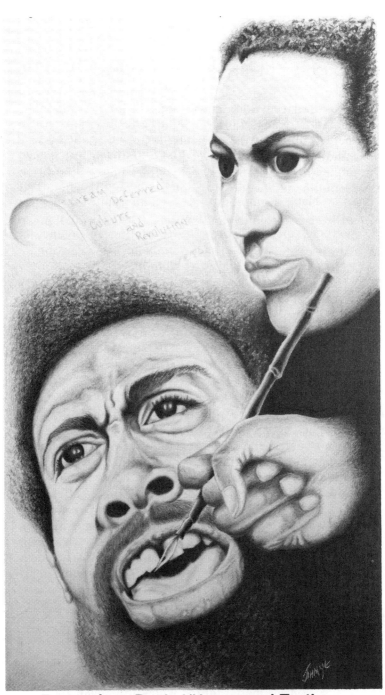

Expressions Denied/Unexposed Truths

Langston Hughes: Good Morning, Revolution

Langston Hughes is undoubtedly the greatest Afro-American writer in history. Master of the poem, weaver of the short story, brilliant playwright, controversial essayist, Langston Hughes, in his long and prolific career, captured the spirit of black folk. Unknown to many however, is that for many years Langston Hughes wrote as a black Communist in a white capitalist society. Arguably, his radical works are the most moving and powerful of his career. The revolutionary potency of Hughes's writings is seen vividly in his collection of poems, *Good Morning, Revolution*.

Born in 1902 in Joplin, Missouri, Hughes moved with his mother to Cleveland in 1916. It was there that Hughes first learned of socialism. His Polish classmates celebrated the overthrow of the Czar by the Bolsheviks in 1917, and they encouraged young Langston to read John Reed's *Ten Days That Shook The World*. Familiar with the daily oppression suffered by Afro-Americans, Langston Hughes was impressed by the Bolshevik claim to build a society "free of racism and landlords."

Hughes moved to New York to pursue college and a writing career, and he was profoundly influenced by the vibrancy and struggles of black Harlem. When he later worked as a seaman on a shipping liner, Hughes was moved by the horrifying poverty and abuse suffered by blacks both in the Caribbean and Africa. As an impressionable young black writer, he felt a burning desire to tell of the agony of his people, whether in Georgia, the Congo, or Jamaica. In his early poem "Negro," published in the NAACP's *The Crisis* and in his book *The Weary Blues*, Hughes writes:

> I've been a slave:
> Caesar told me to keep his door-steps clean
> I brushed the boots of Washington
> I've been a worker:
> Under my hand the pyramid arose.
> I made mortar for the Woolworth building...
> I've been a victim:

> The Belgians cut off my hands in the
> Congo
> They lynch me now in Texas...[1]

In linking Belgian colonialism with American racism, Hughes demonstrated a global perspective and Socialist internationalism which permeated his later works.

Exposure in *The Crisis* and literary journals catapulted Langston Hughes into a leading role in Harlem's cultural renaissance of the 1920s. Hughes joined Countee Cullen, Jean Toomer, Alain Locke, Claude McKay, Duke Ellington, Paul Robeson, Zora Neal Hurston, Aaron Douglas, Wallace Thurman, and others in creating a cultural movement which would impact black music, literature and art for years to come. For the first time black artists were able to openly protest America's racism through their writings and songs. Near the end of the Harlem Renaissance, however, Hughes moved beyond racial "protest poetry."

In 1929, the Great Depression reduced white workers to the longtime level of black workers and left Afro-America in unbelievable squalor and poverty. With millions unemployed, hungry and homeless, the Communist Party United States of America (CPUSA) led the unemployed in marches and demonstrations for food, coal, and shelter. Langston Hughes was impressed with the Party's sincerity and their efforts to alleviate the suffering of homeless workers and hungry children. Despite protests from his white literary patron (Charlotte Mason), Hughes's poetry soon reflected the militancy of the CPUSA. When forced to choose between revolutionary poetry or white financial support, Hughes chose revolutionary poetry.

Hughes thundered into 1931 with a poem in the leftist journal *The New Masses* called "Merry Christmas."

> Ring Merry Chistmas, Africa
> From Cairo to the Cape!
> Ring Hallelujah! Praise the Lord!
> For murder and for rape...

> Ring Merry Christmas, Cuba!
> (While Yankee domination
> Keeps a nice fat president
> In a little half-starved nation.)[2]

"Merry Christmas" was the beginning of a proliferation of works devoted to black workers, colonized toilers, and the bitter struggles of the Communist Party USA. Langston Hughes decided that his poetry was not for entertainment, but for articulating the muted but revolutionary demands of the Afro-American working class.

During the CPUSA's defense of the Scottsboro Boys, Langston Hughes wrote and published the pamphlet *Scottsboro Limited* to raise money for the Party's efforts. Hughes also lectured across the country on the significance of Scottsboro as a glaring example of the South's use of violence to keep black sharecroppers in economic bondage.

In his lecture, "Southern Gentlemen, White Prostitutes, Mill-Owners, and Negroes," Hughes notes that it is the greed of the mill owners that forces white women into prostitution (the two white girls who charged rape in the Scottsboro Case were both prostitutes) and sends black teenagers to the electric chair. In 1931, Hughes visited the Scottsboro Boys in Kilby prison and read to them from his play, *Scottsboro Limited*. The Scottsboro Boys, so typical of the young black men brutalized by the racist South, with fear in their eyes and the specter of lynch mobs or the electric chair clouding their future, listened as Langston Hughes read:

> Mob voices:
> Quick Quick Death there!
> The chair! The electric chair!
> 8th boy:
> No chair!
> Too long my hands have been idle
> Too long my brains have been dumb
> Now out of the darkness
> The new Red Negro will come:
> That's me!

No death in the chair!
Boys (rising):
   No death in the chair!
Red voices:
   NO DEATH IN THE CHAIR!
Red voices:
   No death in the chair!
   Together we'll make the world clean and fair.
8th Boy:
   Too long we have stood
   For the whip and the rope
Red voices (in deep chorus):
   Too long! Too long!
8th Boy:
   Too long we have labored
   Poor, and without hope.
Boys:
   Too long!
Red voices:
   Too long!
8th Boy:
   Too long we have suffered
   Alone.
Boys:
   But not now!
Red voices:
   No, not now!
8th Boy:
   The hands of the red world
   Are our hands too!
Red voices:
   The hands of the red world are you!
8th Boy:
   With all of the workers.
   Black or white,
   we'll go forward
   Out of the night.[3]

Hughes ends this moving piece with the Scottsboro boys and the "red voices" (Communist Party) shouting, "All hands together will furnish the might, Rise from the dead, workers, and fight!"[4]

Hughes also was involved in the CPUSA's electoral work. In 1932, during the presidential campaign of Communist Party members James Ford and William Foster, Hughes urged black support for their ticket with a prose-poem that urged, "Arise ye wretched of the earth, you black ones everywhere—hungry, underpaid, ragged in Cleveland, Detroit, Atlanta, Los Angeles, denied the rights of man—give your votes to Foster and Ford...Karl Marx said it could not last forever—the brutality and stupidity of capitalism..."[5]

In 1932, Langston Hughes and Louise Thompson led twenty Afro-Americans to Moscow to make a film depicting the realities of black life in the United States. Although the film was never produced, the trip allowed Hughes to visit Russia beyond Moscow. Like Robeson and Du Bois, Langston Hughes was stunned by the progress Uzbekstan (a Russian racial minority) made under Soviet socialism. As a correspondent from Russia for *The Chicago Defender* and other black newspapers, Hughes's accounts of Soviet progress intrigued Afro-American readers. In the NAACP's *The Crisis*, Hughes called Uzbekstan "The Land of Before and After."

> Before the Revolution, emirs and khans, mullas and beys. After the Revolution, the workers in power. Before, one-half of one percent of the people literate. Now, fifty percent read and write.... Before no theaters, no movies, no modern culture. Now, national art encouraged and developed everywhere.[6]

In *The Chicago Defender*, Hughes wrote:

> A few years ago a great Negro woman YWCA worker, Juliette Derricotte, known all across America, had died in the South because after an automobile accident, no hospital along the road where she was injured would admit her because she was not white...Nothing like that goes on in the Soviet Union...In the Soviet Union nobody need fear...since all basic human needs, health care, jobs, child care, education, are planned for by the State for the benefit of all the people...Naturally I have been asked the question, 'Well, if you like Russia so much, why don't you stay?' Here is my answer...because

this is my home, the USA...It is mine, faults and all—
and I had rather stay here and help my country get rid of
its faults, race prejudice, economic inequalities, than to
run away.[7]

We can only guess at the effect these words had on black workers as they compared Soviet progress with America's lynching trees and tenant farms.

While a just society seemed within Russia's grasp, America to Langston Hughes and millions of other Afro-Americans remained a cauldron of grief. The only flicker of hope for black workers lay in the militant demands and courageous sacrifices of the CPUSA. Hundreds of black workers, from Hosea Hudson and Mack Coad in Alabama to Harry Haywood and Bonita Williams in Harlem, fought bitterly for Afro-American liberation through the CPUSA. Unemployment Councils, Sharecroppers' Unions, and radical black trade unions created the hope that indeed change could come to America. Hughes's classic "Good Morning, Revolution" reflected this sentiment.

>Good Morning, Revolution
>You're the very best friend
>I ever had...
>You see.
>The boss knows you're my friend
>He sees us hangin' out together
>He knows we're hungry and ragged,
>And ain't got a damn thing in this world.
>And are gonna do something about it...
>The boss's got all he needs, certainly,
>>Eats well
>>Owns a lotta houses
>>Goes vacationin'
>>Breaks strikes
>>Runs politics, bribes police
>>Pays off Congress,
>>And struts all over the earth—
>But me, I ain't never had enough to eat
>Me, I ain't never been warm in winter.
>Me, I ain't never knows security—
>All my life, been livin' hand to mouth,

> Hand to mouth.
> Listen Revolution,
> We're buddies, see...
> We can take everything
> factories, houses, arsenals...
> And turn 'em over to the people who work...
> That's our job!
> I've been starvin' too long
> Ain't you?
> Let's go Revolution![8]

Hughes later published the powerful "The Same," and his controversial "Goodbye, Christ," in a leftist journal for the black working class called *The Negro Worker*. His works in *The Negro Worker* were intended to reach distressed black workers with the hopeful message of revolution. Hughes sought to tell his toiling brothers and sisters that they were not alone, that they, in fact, were part of a global collection of workers who through disciplined struggle could destroy capitalism. The internationalism Hughes displayed in his earlier works ("Lament for Dark Peoples" and "Negro") is even more apparent in "The Same":

> It is the same everywhere for me:
> On the dock at Sierra Leone,
> In the cotton fields of Alabama,
> In the diamond fields of Kimberley,
> On the coffee hills of Haiti,
> The banana lands of Central America
> The streets of Harlem,
> and the cities of Morocco and Tripoli
> Black:
> Exploited, beaten, and robbed,
> Shot and killed.
> Blood running into
> > DOLLARS
> > POUNDS
> > FRANCS
> > PESETAS
> > LIRE...[9]

In "Goodbye, Christ," a poem later read into the Congressional record by Joe McCarthy to demonstrate Hughes's "anti-Americanism," Hughes wrote:

> Goodbye,
> Christ, Jesus, Lord, God, Jehova
> Beat it on away from here now.
> Make way for a new guy with no religion at all—
> A real guy named
> Marx Communist Lenin Peasant Stalin Worker Me...
> Don't be so slow about movin'!
> The world is mine from now on[10]

Hughes also wrote other poems containing stinging criticisms of capitalist dehumanization and calls for worker revolt. They include, "Ballad of The Landlord"; "Let America Be America Again" (one of his most recited works); "Christ In Alabama"; the sarcastically powerful "Letter To The Academy"; "Memo to Non-White Peoples"; "Advertisement for the Waldorf-Astoria"; "Tired"; "Ballad Of Lenin"; "Revolution"; and many others. At the 1934 Communist Party convention Hughes read his celebrated piece, "One More 'S' In the USA," where he deals with the ruling class's use of race hatred to keep workers down, the role of war in expanding capitalist markets and bankrolling the corporate giants, and the need for worker struggle.

Hughes was not an ivory tower poet; his revolutionary poems were sustained by practical work in the black liberation movement. In 1933, he was elected president of the CPUSA's League of Struggle of Negro Rights. In 1936, he and Richard Wright developed the National Negro Congress's cultural program in an attempt to give black workers a voice through art and literature. For several years Hughes organized writer conferences which clarified the artists' role in anti-colonial, labor, and black movements. Langston Hughes was also an integral part of the growing global network of progressive writers. Through international writers' conferences Hughes met with Pablo Neruda of Chile, Jacques Roumain of Haiti,

Leon Damas and Leopold Senghor of West Africa, and other radical Third World literary figures.

For poems like "Good Morning, Revolution" and "The Same," Hughes was hailed nationally and internationally among progressives as a poet of the proletariat, a man whose literary talents were at the disposal of the Alabama sharecropper, the Harlem street-sweeper, and the Chicago steel worker. Communism had linked Hughes to the working masses. He became so convinced that the CPUSA held the solution to black misery that he wrote, "The Daily Worker [the Party's paper] is the only voice in the United States that consistently calls for the complete liberation of the Negro masses. Every Negro receiving a regular salary should subscribe and share it with his unemployed neighbors."[11]

Communism's internationalism carried Langston Hughes far beyond the boundaries of black America. During the Spanish Civil War Hughes went to Spain to report on the people's war against Generalissimo Franco's fascism. Hughes paid particular attention to black CPUSA members who fought in Spain to stop the advance of creeping fascism. He wrote of black martyr Milton Herndon, brother of Atlanta CPUSA leader Angelo Herndon, who was killed at Fuentes del Ebro fighting the same enemy his brother fought in the South. In tribute to the heroic resistance of the Spanish people and the International Brigades that fought on their side, Hughes wrote the powerful poems, "Air Raid: Barcelona"; "Moonlight in Valencia: Civil War"; and "Hero-International Brigade."

Hughes later traveled to China when Mao Zedong and the Chinese Communist Party were fighting both Japanese imperialism and Chinese reactionaries. While in China he wrote, "I was constantly amazed in Shanghai at the impudence of white foreigners drawing a color line against the Chinese, in China itself."[12] He also noted that the horrible lot of millions of Chinese peasants was manufactured and sustained by foreign economic control. Rampant narcotics, prostitution, crime, oppression, and poverty were all consequences of China's helplessness before the great capitalist powers of the world. Hughes, however, saw radical change on the horizon with the growth of the Chinese Communist Party under Mao Zedong and Zhou Enlai. He captured the revolutionary fervor of the Chinese Communists with his stunning poem, "Roar, China."

> ...so they came with gunboats.
> Set up concessions
> Zones of influence,
> International settlements.
> Missionary houses,
> Banks,
> And Jim Crow Y.M.C.A.'s.
> They beat you with malacca canes
> And dared you to raise your head[13]

The poem then describes racist repression and forced child labor, and closes with the triumphant:

> Smash the iron gates of the Concessions!
> Smash the pious doors of the missionary houses!
> Smash the revolving doors of the Jim Crow Y.M.C.A.'s!
> Crush the enemies of land and bread and freedom!
> Stand up and roar, China!
> You know what you want!
> The only way to get it is
> To take it!
> Roar, China![14]

When the Chinese Communists seized power in 1949, Hughes was electrified by the prospect that their victory would propel the Afro-American liberation struggle. "What is happening in China is important to Negroes, in fact, to people of color all over the world, because each time an old bastion of white supremacy crumbles its falling weakens the whole Jim Crow system everywhere."[15]

No liberation struggle escaped the scathing pen of Langston Hughes. Through literature he agitated for release of jailed Party leader Angelo Herndon and Haitian Communist writer Jacques Roumain, and supported migrant workers in California. By the late

1940s, however, the spreading Cold War chilled even the writings of Langston Hughes. In 1948, he was branded a Communist as the Senate read "Goodbye, Christ" and "Put One More 'S' In The USA" into the Congressional Record.

The FBI hounded Hughes, and as a professional writer dependent on publication for survival, government harassment eroded his livelihood. In 1953, he was dragged before McCarthy's Committee on Un-American Activities where he was given a bitter choice. Hughes could defend his radical verse, in which case he would be censored, unpublished, and unemployed; or he could apologize for his past mistakes and continue with his literary career. Unlike Paul Robeson, who practically told McCarthy and his neo-fascist colleagues to go to hell, Hughes backtracked from his earlier militancy. He told the Committee that many of those works were the observations of an objective artist, and that he did not necessarily believe in the revolution and struggle expressed in his poems and essays.

Despite his recantation, Hughes was not spared the government's wrath. Many of his works were banned abroad and in several states. He was dropped from the lecture circuit and many of his revolutionary poems and writings fell out of print. Although in the 1960s Hughes wrote several powerful protest poems against racism and injustice, none approached the stunning power of his revolutionary works.

Despite his fall before the House Committee, Hughes nevertheless remains a classic example of a writer whose link with the toiling masses of the world allowed him to accurately reflect and popularize the struggle of the working class. Whether he was writing about the obscene contrast of the rich and poor ("Advertisement at the Waldorf-Astoria"), the freedom struggle of Spanish peasants ("Air Raid: Barcelona"), or the bond between Afro-American workers and colonized folk around the world ("The Same"), Hughes described the struggle as it was and pointed the way to a new world to come.

I can't write exclusively about roses and moonlight; for sometimes in the moonlight my brothers see a fiery cross and a circle of Klansman hoods. Sometimes in the moonlight a dark body sways from a lynching tree—but for his funeral there are no roses...When poets stop talking about the moon and roses and begin to talk about trade unions, color lines, and colonies, somebody calls the police.[16]

Richard Wright: Black Boy

Richard Wright fused the pain of growing up black in Mississippi with the revolutionary theory of the Communist Party USA to produce the most potent Afro-American literature of the Twentieth century. Raised on a plantation in Natchez, Mississippi, Wright's childhood years were marred by lynch mobs, segregation, and sharecropping. White racism and economic hardship left in their wake a trail of broken black bodies and shattered families, and Wright's family was no exception. Several experiences—his father's desertion, his mother's terminal illness, the long days of hunger, his uncle's lynching, and the lifeless orphanage (Wright's early years are brilliantly described in his autobiography *Black Boy*) created a sensitive black man groping for an answer to Afro-American misery.

Moving north to Chicago, Wright found that racism and black poverty had preceded him. Chicago was a bustling town, and the young aspiring writer was deeply affected by Garvey's nationalism, communism, and the profound suffering of black workers. Working odd jobs, Wright himself suffered and was often forced by hunger to wait in Chicago's bread lines for food. Distressed by the persistence of black agony both north and south, Wright's interest was piqued when he "saw black men mounted upon soap boxes at street corners, bellowing about bread, rights, and revolution."[17]

Black Chicago Communists like Bob Ware, Joe Gardner, Ed Williams, and Jack Tilford impressed Wright with their uncompromising commitment to black working-class families. Consequently, when his friend

Abraham Aaron invited him to the CPUSA's John Reed Club for writers and artists, the young black Mississippi writer attended. After reading the literature given him by club members, Wright was stunned. He later wrote:

> I lay on my bed, and read the magazines and was amazed to find that there did exist in this world an organized search for truth of the lives of the oppressed and the isolated. When I had begged bread from the officials, I had wondered dimly if the outcasts could become united in action, thought, feeling. Now I knew it. It was being done in one-sixth of the earth already. The revolutionary words leapt from the printed page and struck me with tremendous force. It was not the economics of Communism, nor the power of the great trade unions, nor the excitement of underground politics that claimed me; my attention was caught by the similarity of the experience of workers in other lands, by the possibility of unifying the scattered but kindred peoples into a whole. It seemed to me that here at last, in the realm of revolutionary expression, the Negro experience could find a home.[18]

For Wright, the seemingly isolated misery in Mississippi shacks and Chicago tenements became inseparably connected with the struggles of peasants and workers all over the world. He was no longer a single angry black writer in search of a solution; Wright joined the John Reed Club and the Communist Party and became part of the international movement to build a just and Socialist world.

Revolutionary Communist theory—precise, directed, and rooted in the working masses—empowered the writings of Richard Wright. Where once he wrote only of black misery as it was, communism compelled him to write also of life as it could be. His 1934 poem in the leftist journal *New Masses* is a powerful synthesis of the black experience and revolutionary theory.

> I am black and have seen black hands,
> millions and millions of them—

They were tired and awkward and calloused
and grimy covered with hangnails,
And they were caught in fast-moving belts
of machines and snagged and smashed and
crushed...
And then black hands held trembling at the
factory gates the dreaded lay-off slip,
And black hands hung idle nd swung empty
and grew soft and got weak and bony
from unemployment and starvation...
I am black and have seen black hands,
millions and millions of them—
Reaching hesitantly out of days of slow
death for the goods they had made, but the
bosses warned that the goods were private
and did not belong to them,
And the black hands felt the cold steel bars
of the prison they made, and in despair
tested their strength and found that they
could neither bend nor break them...
And the black hands fought and scratched
and held back but a thousand white hands took
and tied them,
And the black hands lifted palms in muted
and futile supplication to the sodden faces
of mobs in wild revelries of sadism,
And the black hands strained and clawed
and struggled in vain at the noose that
tightened about the black throat,
And the black hands waved and beat
fearfully at the tall flames that cooked and
charred the black flesh...
I am black and have seen black hands
Raised in fists of revolt, side by side with
white fists of white workers,
And some day—and it is only this which
sustains me—
Some day there will be millions and
millions of them,
On some red day in a burst of fists on a
new horizon![19]

Wright's work in the CPUSA was not confined to poetry. He also wrote and edited Party papers, led a union in Chicago, supported Communist political candidates, lectured on revolutionary culture at the National Negro Congress Convention, and worked with black writers like Langston Hughes and Margaret Walker to clarify the role of radical Afro-American artists in relation to the people's struggle.

Anxious to tell black workers of the dedication of Afro-American Communists, Wright attempted a profile of black CPUSA members entitled, *Heroes: Red and Black*. American patriotism and propaganda distorted the goals of socialism, and Wright believed Afro-Americans would flock to the Party once they saw the commitment of black Communists.

David Poindexter, a black migrant from the South who led unemployment marches and was one of the Party's most influential organizers, was the first CPUSA leader Wright sought to interview. Richard Wright visited Poindexter several times and was deeply moved by his vision of a democratic and socialist America. Unfortunately, Wright's project ended abruptly when paranoia seized some Party leaders who feared Wright's interviews may be used by the police to identify and jail "suspected Communists."

Wright's zeal to produce art for revolution was not dampened, and he went on to write the powerful trilogy, *Uncle Tom's Children*, *Black Boy*, and *Native Son*. Written in the 1930s and 1940s, these works are moving accounts of Afro-Americans' struggles for human dignity in a nation where they had been kept as scapegoats for hard times and as labor reserves for good times. Wright's books were so powerful that even public horror at his Communist affiliation did not diminish their power.

Although some Party leaders criticized his depiction of black workers and farmers, Wright saw his work as the vehicle by which the black experience reached the Party and white workers. "The Communists," Wright felt,

> had oversimplified the experience of those whom they sought to lead. In their efforts to recruit the masses, they had missed the meaning of the lives of the masses, had conceived of people in too abstract a manner. I would try to put some of that meaning back, I would tell

Communists how common people felt, and I would tell common peoples of the self-sacrifice of the Communists who strove for unity among them.[20]

It was Wright's ability to "tell...how common people felt" that made him one of America's greatest writers. In *Uncle Tom's Children*, a collection of short stories, Wright conveys in unforgettable fashion the suffering and despair of black folk in the South. *Down By The Riverside*, one of the short stories in the collection, powerfully depicts black helplessness before a merciless flood and callous racists. *Fire and Cloud*, another of the stories, reflects Wright's Marxism when the Rev. Daniel Taylor says, "We gotta git wid the people."

His moving autobiography, *Black Boy*, draws upon the poverty, fear and hunger of Mississippi to bring to public light the harsh lives of Afro-Americans. One unforgettable passage on a reunion with his father reads,

> A quarter of a century was to elapse between the time when I saw my father...and the time I was to see him again, standing alone upon the red clay of a Mississippi plantation, a sharecropper, clad in ragged overalls, holding a muddy hoe in his gnarled, veined hands—a quarter of a century in which my...consciousness had become so violently altered that when I tried to talk to him I realized that, though ties of blood had made us kin, though I could see a shadow of my face in his face, though there was an echo of my voice in his voice, we were forever strangers, speaking a different language, living on vastly different planes of reality. That day...I was overwhelmed to realize that he could never understand me or the scalding experiences that had swept me beyond his life and into an area of living that he could never know.[21]

Wright's most controversial work, *Native Son*, uses the explosive character Bigger Thomas to expose blacks' burning desire for revenge created by years of humiliation. *Native Son* was criticized by many CPUSA leaders for its "non-revolutionary" portrayal of the black masses and its somewhat unfavorable depictions of its fictional Party characters. Wright countered with a letter in the *Daily Worker* which read, "*Native Son* shows that even for the great Party which has challenged America on the Negro question as no other party, there is much, much to do, and above all, to understand."[22]

Despite America's racism and CPUSA disputes, Richard Wright became the standard by which other black writers were judged. His 1937 essay, *Blueprint for Negro Writing*, has become a guidepost for Afro-American, Caribbean, and African revolutionary writers.

> The Negro writer who seeks to function within his race as a purposeful agent has a serious responsibilty...a deep, informed, and complex consciousness is necessary; a consciousness which draws for its strength from the fluid lore of a great people, and moulds this lore with the concepts that move and direct the forces of history today....The Negro writer is being called upon to do no less than create values by which his race is to struggle, live and die.[23]

After the publication of *Native Son*, Wright was increasingly criticized by Party leaders over what they believed were bourgeois influences in his writing. They believed Wright portrayed black workers as simply creatures of oppression devoid of class consciousness and revolutionary demands. Wright, however, contended that *Black Boy*, *Native Son*, and *Uncle Tom's Children* depicted black life as it is so that the Party could understand those they sought to organize for revolutionary action. These differences became irreconcilable, and in 1942 Wright resigned from the Communist Party.

Although Wright left the CPUSA he never denied the Party's impact on his life. "I owe my literary development to the Communist Party and its influence, which shaped my thoughts and creative growth. It gave me my first full bodied vision of Negro life in America."[24] One of his biographers noted, "although he left the U.S. Communist Party, he did not abandon Marxism-Leninism or class analysis."[25]

Cut loose from the protection the Party provided against government intrusion, Wright nevertheless attempted to continue his literary career. The FBI harassed him at every turn, and at one point even considered jailing him for his "subversive activities." J. Edgar Hoover received several memos concerning Wright, including one which stated, "this literature, subtle and inflammatory, can cause more harm than bomber squadrons."[26] In another secret memo, agents wrote, "His interest in the problems of the Negro is almost an obsession."

Government repression and racist publishers soon forced Wright to go into self-imposed exile in Paris, France. Like many creative black expatriates, such as Dexter Gordon, Wright found greater acceptance abroad than at home. Since Paris was the capital of France's colonial empire, many African intellectuals and leaders studied there before returning to their liberation struggle. As an internationally known writer and radical, Richard Wright advised many of these young revolutionaries. Some of them, like ex-CPUSA member and Pan-Africanist George Padmore, became close friends of Wright.

In 1956, Wright was one of the prime movers in the First Congress of Negro Artists and Writers. The Congress featured writers like Aime Cesaire, Frantz Fanon, Leopold Senghor, and Cheik Anta Diop, and used Wright's *Blueprint for Negro Writing* as the focal point for discussion. As a revolutionary patriarch, Richard Wright became an inspiration for young African writers fighting for independence from colonialism.

In his later years, Wright wrote *American Hunger*, *Black Power*, and *White Man, Listen*. Despite his departure from America several years earlier, Richard Wright was still subjected to FBI, CIA, and State Department harassment. Addison Gayle, in *Richard Wright: Ordeal of a Native Son*, recounts the sordid details of wiretaps, mail tampering, and rumor-mongering conducted by U.S. officials against this radical black writer. Exiled from his land and harassed by agents, Richard Wright died in Paris in 1960 at age fifty-two. Some believe Wright was poisoned by the CIA due to his stature among African revolutionaries.

His books and memory could not be erased, however, as successive generations of Afro-American, Caribbean, and African writers use *Black Boy*, *Blueprint for Negro Writing*, and his other works as examples of revolutionary writing. During the eight years Wright was a member of the CPUSA, revolutionary theory, the power of the working class, and the promise of socialism's ultimate victory infused his novels with a vitality rarely found in American writing. When Wright left the Communist Party in 1942 he did not leave his people, and until his death in 1960 Richard Wright used the pen as a sword to free Africans and Afro-Americans from economic bondage and racist oppression.

> As anyone with common sense could guess, I was a communist because I was a Negro. Indeed the Communist Party had been the only road out of the Black Belt for me. Hence the Communist Party had not been simply a fad, a hobby, it had a deep functional meaning for my life.[27]

> I do not believe, that the aim and goal of human life is to be found in individual happiness...or in moral piety....The most meaningful moments...I have gotten from this world have been in either making an attempt to change...life...or in watching with sympathy the efforts of others to do the same. For that reason I am a card-carrying Communist.[28]

Amiri Baraka: Voice of the Black Nation

Amiri Baraka (formerly Leroi Jones), the fiery cultural nationalist of the 1960s, is now one of the foremost black Marxist-Leninists in America. During the height of the Black Power/Civil Rights Movements, Amiri Baraka was a moving force in the black nationalist trend of that struggle. Active in Newark politics, Baraka and his grassroots supporters helped propel Kenneth Gibson into the mayor's chair. As one of the founders and the chair of the Congress of Afrikan Peoples (CAP), Baraka carried the message of Pan-Africanism, black nationalism, and cultural renaissance to ghettos and colleges all over the nation. CAP led community protests against police brutality, supported African liberation struggles, and organized black students and activists for political work.

Despite his effectiveness as a movement organizer, Baraka's most potent weapons in the liberation struggle were literature and culture. As a poet, playwright, essayist, jazz critic, and novelist, Baraka's writings urgently demanded justice for Afro-Americans and promoted culture as a means both of survival and revolution. His books *Blues People* (1963) and *Black Music* (1967) were the first to put Afro-American music, jazz and blues in particular, in the social context from which they arose. According to Baraka, black music was not "invented" by musical geniuses, it grew out of the sufferings and struggles of Afro-Americans through slavery, sharecropping, Jim Crow, and lingering racism. But jazz was not simply a recollection of the past. Baraka viewed the revolutionary sounds of Pharoah Sanders, John Coltrane, Albert Ayler, Sonny Murray, Sun Ra, Ornette Coleman, Archie Shepp and others as reflections of the sentiments of Afro-Americans for justice and democracy *now*.

In addition to his jazz books, Baraka hosted black poetry festivals, wrote the plays *The Dutchman*, *The Slave* and *The Toilet*, a book of essays called *Home*, and organized black writers on the East Coast through the nationalist Spirit House in Newark. During the eruptions of the Sixties, Baraka's writings captured eloquently the spirit of black resistance. Baraka emerged from the Sixties and Seventies as the poet of black rebellion. Despite his tireless energy on behalf of Afro-Americans, Baraka's nationalism often excluded from his field of vision the power of Afro-American workers and the dynamics of class struggle.

After the Sixth Pan-African Congress in Tanzania in

1975, however, Baraka and other leaders in the CAP abandoned "skin nationalism" and advanced the view that only a multinational working class guided by scientific socialism could eliminate imperialism, monopoly capitalism, economic exploitation and racism.

At the Tanzania congress, Baraka reevaluated nationalism in the light of Amilcar Cabral's struggle against Portuguese colonialism. Baraka saw in Cabral's writings that NATO support and Portuguese brutality were not fueled by racism; they were motivated by a system that required Guineans to suffer and die so that wealthy individuals and multinational corporations could increase their already bloated profits.

This view was borne out in practice, as CAP leadership recalled how their black unity line often faltered when faced with black bourgeois opposition to the demands of black workers. In other words, class struggle, not race hate, was the moving force of history.

A 1975 issue of *Black Scholar* carried a position paper in which Baraka outlined his transformation to a Communist revolutionary.

> Capitalism is a system that brings profits for a few, by maintaining the poverty of the masses. The color black does not change it!.... the liberation of the black masses in the United States is impossible without the total annihilation of capitalism. We say our ideology is scientific socialism, specifically, as practiced and theorized by Marx, Lenin and Mao Zedong, but we are rich with the experience of the black liberation movement's history, and have studied and been enriched by the struggle and practice of men like Du Bois, Garvey, Malcolm X, Nkrumah, Toure, Cabral, without whose work the words of Marx, Lenin, and Mao would mean little.[29]

In 1979, CAP merged with the League of Revolutionary Struggle (LRS) to form a multinational organization committed to building a Communist party in the United States. Baraka, later elected to the Central Committee of the LRS, wrote, "Countries want independence, nations want liberation, and the people, the people want revolution!" marking the merger of CAP with the League.

> ...Witness our motion here
> our courageous building
> from smaller to larger, from larger
> to
> formidable, from
> formidable, to ascendant to
> obviously irresistible. From the people
> themselves
> we draw our strength, Unite Revolutionaries
> Unite, for in that struggle for
> Revolutionary Unity is won the heart of the
> masses, the advanced are won to Communism!
> And so we build...[30]

Baraka's already potent view of the revolutionary nature of black culture was infused with a powerful class analysis. As a nationalist, his art reflected the radical demands of Afro-Americans, regardless of class; as a Socialist, Baraka's art mirrored the revolutionary sentiments of oppressed black workers. According to Amiri Baraka, the black artist had a responsibility to be more than "black." As Mao Zedong stated in his *Talks at The Yenan Forum on Literature and Art*, black art is revolutionary only to the extent that it speaks to and of the working class.

Baraka's 1984 book, *Daggers and Javelins*, contains speeches, articles, and essays which clearly illuminate the role of the artist in building a revolutionary movement. In the essay, "*Not Just Survival: Revolution*," Baraka notes,

> ...art is apologia for one particular class or another....There is no art that is above the views and needs or ideology of one class or another, although the rulers pretend that art is classless and beyond political definition, but such a line is itself a bourgeois ideology of art for art's sake. That is why we must make an art that serves the great majority of people.... For whom do we

write: for the people, for the revolutionaries, but also for the generations to come reared under...socialism, and eventually communism. Yes, our art must be a weapon of revolutionary struggle; otherwise it is...a distraction, an ornament the imperialists wear to make a gesture toward humanity.[31]

In *Daggers and Javelins*, Baraka lays out the historical legacy of revolutionary Afro-American art, analyzing the works of Langston Hughes, Richard Wright, Aime Cesaire, Ngugi wa Thiong'o, Harry Haywood's *Black Bolshevik*, W.E.B. Du Bois's *Black Reconstruction*, William Wells Brown's *Clotel*, and works by Afro-American, Caribbean, and African writers. His review of black culture's role during the 1960s is important in that he was a participant in struggle.

> We were warriors pure and simple, trying to burn the whiteman's playhouse down, but our petty bourgeois class base, lack of a communist Marxist-Leninist revolutionary party, lack of study, and domination by the reactionary lines of cultural nationalism turned us around....and many of us have yet to recover.[32]

Like Harry Haywood before him, Baraka believed the Communist Party United States of America's liquidation of the "Self-determination for the Black Belt South" thesis was a mistake which doomed the black revolution of the 1960s to the errors of cultural nationalism. The LRS, in fact, currently holds to the Self-determination thesis and Baraka articulately promotes the argument that Afro-Americans in the South constitute a nation requiring both self-determination and democracy.

Many of Baraka's poems and essays are found in the League's publication, *The Black Nation*, a journal of Afro-American thought which Baraka edits. *The Black Nation* expresses clearly Baraka's view that revolutionary change without culture is impossible. Essays like "Class Struggle In Music," revolutionary dramas by Langston Hughes, visual art by Tom Feelings and Vincent Smith, dub poetry by black English socialist Linton Kwesi Johnson are examples of the militant culture featured in *The Black Nation*.

Baraka continues to write and perform his own poetry. In the 1981 album *New Music, New Poetry*, Baraka joins saxophonist David Murray and drummer Steve McCall in a brilliant combination of Afro-American music and poetry. The poems "In The Tradition," "Against Bourgeois Art," and "Strunza Med" are potent works capturing the essence of art "for the people."

Through his work in the LRS and *The Black Nation*, Baraka continues the radical tradition of David Walker and reinterprets it for the present to mobilize artists and activists toward revolutionary struggle.

Writers from the Caribbean: Aime Cesaire and Jacques Romain
Aime Cesaire

Black poet and activist Aime Cesaire was born in 1913 on the island of Martinique, a French colony in the West Indies. In the 1930s Cesaire went to Paris on a scholarship where his zeal for Martinique's independence was further ignited by the radical black writers he met there. Afro-American poets Langston Hughes and Claude McKay taught Cesaire that militant poetry was a vital part of liberation struggles.

Afro-American poetry was not all that influenced Cesaire in Paris. The French capital was alive with Third World intellectuals and leaders who used French education as a springboard from which to wage independence movements in their native lands. Ho Chi Minh, Zhou Enlai, Leopold Senghor, Leon Damas, and Jacques Romain were among those that convinced Cesaire that colonialism's days were numbered.

In the late 1930s Cesaire joined a group of leftist writers, Senghor and Damas included, that published the literary journal *Legitime Defense*. After a few issues, *Legitime Defense*, became the primary vehicle through which Cesaire and his comrades attacked imperialism's insidious use of culture to create passive colonial subjects. The authors of the journal were also influenced by the Negritude Movement, a Caribbean "Harlem Renaissance" which promoted black cultural resistance. According to Cesaire, that movement created "an awareness of being black...of taking charge of one's destiny as a black."[33]

Cesaire believed the Third World needed a revolutionary ideology to overthrow colonialism, and while in Paris he became a member of the French Communist Party. He later noted the decision to become a communist was based on the struggles of other black writers like Langston Hughes of the United States and Jacques Romain of Haiti. During this time Cesaire continued to write poetry, including the widely read *Return To My Native Land*.

In 1945 Cesaire returned to Martinique to practice the socialism he learned abroad. He was quickly absorbed in Martinique's struggle for self-determination and was elected to the National Assembly as a Communist Party deputy. Cesaire later clashed with the French Communist Party, condemning their refusal to allow Martinique to establish its own Party and their unwillingess to condemn French brutality in Algeria. It appeared to Cesaire that European communists were afflicted with the same chauvinism the Party fought against, and he formally resigned from the French Party. He later wrote,

> It's neither Marxism or Communism I repudiate; the use certain people have made of Marxism and Communism is what I condemn. What I demand of Marxism and Communism is that they serve the black peoples not that the black people serve Marxism and Communism. Philosophies and movements must serve the people, not the people the doctrine and the movement....A doctrine is of value only if it is conceived by us and for us, and revised through us.[34]

Cesaire remained committed to black liberation. In 1950 he wrote the famous *Discourse On Colonialism* in which he exposes the sheer brutality of capitalism gone wild in the colonies. *Discourse On Colonialism* evolved into a classic which did much to shape the emergent Third World view of western imperialism.

Security? Culture? The rule of law? In the meantime I look around and wherever there are colonizers and colonized face to face, I see force, brutality, cruelty, sadism, conflict, and in a parody of education, the hasty manufacture of a few thousand subordinate functionaries.... Between which there is room only for forced labor, intimidation, pressure, the police, taxation, theft, rape, compulsory crops...brainless elites, degraded masses. No human contact, but relations of domination which turn the colonizing man into a classroom monitor, an army sergeant, a prison guard, a slave driver.

My turn to state an equation: colonization = 'thingification.'

They talk to me about progress, about 'achievements', diseases cured, improved standards of living. I am talking about societies drained of their essence, cultures trampled underfoot, institutions undermined, lands confiscated, religions smashed, magnificent artistic creations destroyed, extraordinary possibilities wiped out.[35]

Like radical black writers Langston Hughes and Richard Wright, Cesaire combined his writings with political action. After he broke with the French Communist Party, he founded *Le Parti Progressiste Martiniquais* (The Progressive Party of Martinique, PPM). He was also involved in international writers' conferences where for several years Third World writers and artists focused their energies on national liberation and democratic movements.

His literary career continued, however, as he produced the 1961 biography of Haitian revolutionary Toussaint L'Overture, and a 1967 play (*Un Saison au Congo*) about the betrayal and assassination of African revolutionary Patrice Lumumba. Through his lectures, (Cesaire taught and influenced revolutionary theorist Frantz Fanon), writings, and political work, Cesaire became one of the most respected activists in the Third World.

Jacques Romain

Haitian political activist, Afro-Caribbean writer, friend of Langston Hughes founder of the Haitian Communist Party; Jacques Romain exemplifies the defiant black writer whose commitment to the liberation of his people is more important than royalty checks and public acclaim. Born into a politically prominent family, Romain sacrificed his royal connections and bound himself to the suffering peasants and workers of Haiti.

In the late Twenties he was the chief organizer in the Communist Party's underground work among abused sugar cane workers and the starving unemployed. Haiti was indeed an island of misery. Mulitnational corporations extracted sugar and labor from the island and kept the descendants of Africa in stark poverty. Neocolonial dictators, invasions by United States Marines, and flagrant repression of peoples' movements forced Romain to organize by cover and shield of darkness. In this harşh cauldron of misery, where Romain's black brothers and sisters ranked among the poorest, most illiterate, and sickest in the world, he declaried, "Communism is the only way to change the social and economic conditions of the Haitian masses."[36]

Like Langston Hughes and Richard Wright, Romain combined communist ideology with revolutionary literature. He edited the journal *La Revue Indigene* which utilized oral folklore from the Haitian peasants and his anti-colonial essays to attack the horror created by rapacious "free enterprise." His writings caused a stir in Haiti, and Romain was jailed several times between 1928 and 1933. In 1934 he was arrested and sentenced to a three-year term in a rigged trial. The jailing of Jacques Romain for fighting for Haiti's oppressed is typical of the lengths to which monopoly capitalism will go to maintain their stranglehold on Third World resources. After his release three years later Romain was silenced by constant harassment from the Haitian strongmen who dominated the lives of the peasants. Nevertheless, until his death Romain wrote of and believed in the ultimate victory of the hungry masses of Haiti. Romain's impact on Haitian politics and black liberation is evident in Langston

Hughes' appeal for his release from prison.

> Jacques Romain, poet and novelist of color, and the finest living Haitian writer, has just been sentenced...for circulating a French magazine of Negro liberation called *Cri des Negres*. Jacques Romain...is one of the very few upper-class Haitians who understands the plight of the oppressed peasants of his island home and who has attempted to write about and to remedy the pitiful conditions of 90 percent of the Haitian people exploited by the coffee monopolies and by the manipulation of foreign finance in the hands of the National City Bank of New York. As a fellow writer of color, I call upon all writers and artists of whatever race who believe in the freedom of words and of the human spirit, to protest immediately...for the unmerited sentence to prison of Jacques Romain, one of the few, and by far the most talented, of the literary men of Haiti.[37]

Ngugi wa Thiong'o: Decolonizing the Mind

As a prolific writer, novelist, playwright, and teacher, Ngugi wa Thiong'o of Kenya is one of the most brilliant critics of neocolonialism on the African continent. Each of his literary works is a blow against those forces preventing the African people from determining their own destiny. For Ngugi, literature is not a means by which he can reap personal awards, it is a tool at the disposal of Kenyan peasants in their struggle for self-determination.

Ngugi was influenced by Mwangi Kariuki's 1963 book *Mau Mau Detainee*. Mwangi's book describes the bitter sufferings of the Kenyan masses which led to the Mau Mau Land and Freedom Army's war against English colonialism. Completely devoted to the Kenyan people, Mwangi once noted that "Kenya [is] a country of 10 millionaires and 10 million beggars." Mwangi was murdered by neocolonial agents in 1975, and since his death Ngugi's writings have followed the radical tradition of *Mau Mau Detainee*.

Ngugi's novels, *Weep Not Child*, *The River Between*, and *A Grain of Wheat*, established him as an important

African literary voice. His later works, however, were openly revolutionary. Ngugi was deeply moved by the Mau Mau's ten-year armed struggle. *Mau Mau Detainee* convinced him that the people's aspirations, expressed in song and on stage, were crucial to revolutionary change. During the early years of Mau Mau warfare, the British conquerors commissioned "nice Christian plays about prodigal sons and forgiving fathers" in an effort to teach Kenyans valuable bourgeois lessons in obedience. The masses had other plans, however, and Ngugi wrote,

> some students rebelled against the cult of Shakespeare...and started writing their own plays in Kiswahili....In the forests and mountains, the Mau Mau guerrillas continued their patriotic dances, songs, and theatre with one main theme: death to British imperialism, bury the white imperialist and his black running dogs. Well, their theatre called a dog a dog and not by any other name.[38]

Although the Mau Mau helped defeat English colonialism, Ngugi believed Jomo Kenyatta's neocolonial government was British imperialism in blackface. For Ngugi, the demands of the Mau Mau were compromised by Kenyatta and only socialism could fulfill them. Revolutionary Mau Mau culture was revived by Ngugi and the Kenyan peasants when they established the dynamic Kamiriithu Community Education and Cultural Center. Ngugi described the role of Kenyan peasants in building Kamiriithu in his book, *Writers In Politics*.

> This group in 1977 produced Nhasshika Ndeednda (I Will Marry When I Want) by Ngugi wa Thiong'o and Ngugi wa Mirii, the first modern play in one of Kenya's languages. The actors were all peasants and workers from Kamiriithu village, they designed and built an open-air stage in the centre of the village, and they collaborated in the evolution of the script as well as in the directing. In the process they broke with the hitherto accepted theatrical traditions. For instance the reading and discussion of the script was done in the open with the village audience helping in the selection, and all the rehearsals for four

months were done in the open with an ever increasing crowd of commentators and directors. The dress rehearsal was done to an audience of over one thousand peasants and workers. When finally the show opened to a fee-paying audience, the group performed to thousands of peasants and workers who often would hire buses or trek on foot in order to see themselves and their lives and their history portrayed in a positive manner. For the first time in post-independence history a section of the peasantry had broken out of the cruel choice that was hitherto their lot: the Bar or the Church. And not the least, they smashed the racialist view of peasants as uncultured recipients of culture from beneficent foreigners.[39]

Afraid that such cultural independence would make the peasants difficult to control, the neocolonial government of Kenya (that is, controlled by London and western financial interests) closed down the Kamiriithu Center. A few months later, Ngugi was detained without trial and imprisoned in Kamithi maximum security prison. In his book *Detained: A Prison Writer's Diary*, Ngugi describes his detention as the standard neocolonial reaction against those writers and intellectuals who dare cast their lot with the masses.

In a neo-colonial country, the act of detaining patriotic democrats, progressive intellectuals and militant workers speaks of many things. First it is an admission by the detaining authorities that their official lies labeled as new philosophy, their pretensions often hidden in three-piece suits and golden chains, their propaganda labeled as religious truth...their nationally televised charitable handouts and breast-beating before the high altar, their high-sounding phrases and ready-to-shed tears at the sight of naked children fighting it out with cats and dogs for the possession of a rubbish heap; that these and more godfatherly acts of benevolence have been seen by the people for what they are: a calculated sugar-coating of an immoral sale and mortgage of a whole country and its people to Euro-American and Japanese capital for a few million dollars in Swiss bank accounts and a few token shares in foreign companies.[40]

Ngugi saved his harshest critique for those who conspired to close the Kamiriithu Center.

> The comprador bourgeois could have their golf, polo, cricket...their horse and motor-races; their royal hunt; their German, American, French, English, Italian theatre, cinema, music, and concerts; their swimming pools and expensive sauna and massage clubs; their choice of expensive drinks after an easy day's work; their gambling casinos and striptease joints with white nudes imported from Soho, Las Vegas and Stockholm; their endless cocktail parties with the participants featured in the socialite pages of *Viva*, *The Daily Nation*, and *Chic*; but the peasants with clods of clay had no right to a theatre which correctly reflected their lives, fears, hopes, dreams, and history of struggle; had no right to their creative efforts even in their own backyards. The foreign imperialist church with its eternal call for submissive trust and blind obedience, and foreign-owned breweries of mass soporiferous drinks were now their only legalized cultural alternatives.[41]

Rather than crush this spirit of resistance, detention sharpened Ngugi's views on the revolutionary role of African writers. He believed that the African workers and peasants were the main force of social change, and that the task of the writer was to capture through literature the vibrancy of their struggle. In his book, *Homecoming*, Ngugi wrote,

> While we were at our bourgeois schools and universities searching for truth in books written for us by our imperialist conquerors, the peasant masses, those women I once heard sing, had collectively rejected the white seizure of the land.
> It was they who fought for Uhuru. It was the united strength of the peasants and the workers that made British imperialists retreat....I believe that African intellectuals must align themselves with the struggle of the African masses.[42]

Ngugi's 1975 lecture on "Writers In Politics" brilliantly portrays the role of writers in neocolonial Africa.

> The fundamental opposition in Africa today is between imperialism and capitalism on one hand, and national liberation and socialism on the other; between a small class of native 'haves' which is tied to international monopoly capital and the masses of the people.... Faced with these contradictions, the African writer can often retreat into individualism, mysticism, and formalism: such an African writer who often can see the shortcomings of the neo-colonial economies, the consequent distortion of values, the fascism in so many neo-colonial ruling classes, is at the same time scared of encountering socialism as an alternative social system. He is scared of the possibility of the working class and the peasantry controlling the productive frces... To avoid the two alternatives—the continuation of a neo-colonial status quo and the violent overturning by the masses—he makes a cult of Africanness, of Blackism, of the dignity of the African past... or he becomes cynical and laughs at everything equally....
>
> What the African writer is called to do is not easy: it demands of him that he recognize the global character of imperialism and the global character... of the forces struggling against it to build a new world.... He must write with the vibrations and tremors of the struggles of all the working people in Africa, America, Asia, and Europe behind him. Yes, he must actively support and in his writing reflect the struggle of the African working class and its peasant class allies for the total liberation of their labor power. Yes, his work must show commitment, not to abstract notions of justice and peace, but to actual struggle of the African peoples to seize power and hence be in a position to control all the forces of production and hence lay the only correct basis for peace and justice.[43]

Although particularly interested in the struggles of Kenyans and Africans, Ngugi uses literature to bridge the gap between Kenyans and their brothers and sisters in the United States and the Caribbean. In his book, *Homecoming*, Ngugi pays tribute to Caribbean writers and activists George Padmore, C.L.R. James, and George Lamming for their commitment to black liberation. In *Writers In Politics*, Ngugi includes a brilliant analysis of Afro-American writers in an essay titled, *The Robber and the Robbed*. He notes that Afro-American literature consists of two antagonistic images, one that mirrors the values of the Robbers and the ruling class (Phyllis Wheatley, Booker T. Washington, etc.,) and the other embodying the consciousness of the Robbed (Frederick Douglass, George Jackson, etc.,).

Despite detention and harassment, Ngugi continues his fiery cultural resistance to accommodation and neocolonialism. In 1981, Ngugi and Kenyan peasants revived the Kamiriithu Community Theatre. As they were preparing the set for the first act of the musical play *Maitu Njuqira* (about Kenyan labor battling repressive owners in the 1920s), three truckloads of troops arrived and burned the outdoor theater to the ground. In *Barrel of a Pen: Resistance to Repression in Neo-Colonial Kenya* Ngugi notes sarcastically that the same government that torched the people's theater subsidized the telecast of colonialist Elspeth Huxley's reactionary autobiography.

Barrel of a Pen is one of Ngugi's most recent works and one of the clearest indictments of neocolonialism ever published. Through his essays and his plays *The Trial of Dedam Kimathi* and *I Will Marry When I Want*, Ngugi hammers away at the conditions that grind working people into the dust. In the play *The Trial of Dedam Kimathi*, the detained Mau Mau leader tells the judge:

> I despise your laws and your courts. What have they done for our people?
> What?
> Protected the oppressor. Licensed the murders of the people.
> Our people,
> whipped when they did not pick your tea leaves
> your coffee beans...
> Murdered when they didn't rickshaw
> your ladies and gentlemen.
> I recognize only one law, one court:
> the court of those
> who fight against exploitation
> The toilers armed to say
> we demand our freedom.
> That's the eternal law of the oppressed,
> of the humiliated, of the injured,

the insulted.
Fight! Struggle! Change!⁴⁴

In the play *I Will Marry When I Want*, Giaccamba the factory worker tells Kiguunda the peasant,

> The question is this: Who owns the factories?
> Who benefits from the industries?...
> Have you ever seen any tycoon sweating?
> Except because of overweight...
> Look at yourself
> Look at the women farm laborers.
> Of those that pick tea leaves in the plantations.
> How much do they get?
> Five or seven shillings?
> What is the price of a kilo of sugar?
> Five shillings?...⁴⁵

Unmoved by government repression, Ngugi remains committed to the working peasants of Kenya. Their struggle is his struggle, and his drama, essays and novels belong to them. As a Marxist writer, Ngugi followed the teachings of Mao Zedong concerning art: "The first problem is, literature and art for whom?.... With us, literature and art are *for the people*."⁴⁶

The Revolutionary Writer in Retrospect

Black Socialist writers give peoples' movements expression. The long-muted voices of Georgia sharecroppers, Kenyan peasants, and Haitian farmers explode in the pens of Langston Hughes, Ngugi wa Thiong'o, and Jacques Romain. It is as the people's voice that the black writer becomes so dangerous to the system. Wright's exile, Hughes's trial, and Ngugi's detention are vivid examples of the state's fear of writers linked with the working class.

But revolutionary writers are dangerous for another reason. Not only do they articulate the desires of the people, they also lift diffuse struggles from wandering spontaneity by providing direction and focus. Revolution is not accidental; it is a purposeful movement where workers' demands are channeled by both Socialist theory and a Socialist party. The black Socialist writer both expresses the sentiments of working folk and points the movement in the right direction. When seen in this context, the repression of black writers, whether in Haiti, Kenya, or Harlem, is clearly understood. The path chosen by radical black writers is not an easy one, but in light of the suffering masses, it is the only one.

Scholars in Service to the Masses

- Walter Rodney
- C.L.R. James

Scholars In Service To The Masses

Bourgeois culture has transformed serious academic inquiry from a meaningful analytical tool into an often irrelevant preoccupation. Scholars have developed a guild mentality where pursuit of a Ph.D. is a sacred super-ethereal event and much academic inquiry has no connection to the hardships of the unlearned. Consequently, academicians have become the new priesthood, unscathed by earthly struggles and immune to external criticism. Universities have fallen prey to this mentality, and schools noted for their "prestige" are also noted for their absence from the common affairs of life.

Black Communist scholars, however, scoff at such foolishness. For them, study and struggle are reverse sides of the same coin. Without study and analysis, the liberation movement becomes scattered and repeats past mistakes. Without work among the people, study creates inapplicable theory and useless platitudes.

The penetrating works of Walter Rodney and C.L.R. James were not sterile theories concocted by isolated scholars; they were the works of men completely immersed in the sufferings of working people. Rodney's struggles in Guyana's Working People's Alliance and C.L.R. James's work among Afro-American sharecroppers imbued their study with vigor and realism.

For Rodney, James, George Padmore, and W.E.B. Du Bois (Du Bois and Padmore are discussed in other chapters), historical research and scholarly pursuits served one purpose: to understand society so that through practice and struggle they could change society. For these scholars, knowledge was immaterial if it could not correctly interpret the past, analyze the present, and point a clear path to a better future.

Scholars of Modern Politics and Social Change

Walter Rodney: Revolutionary Scholar

Few people in history have combined revolutionary scholarship and grassroots organizing with the same intensity as Walter Rodney. Whether in Jamaica, Tanzania, or Guyana, Rodney's classroom and library extended into the alleys and rubbish heaps where black children played, the corners where unemployed men stood, and the shacks where women fought to hold together impoverished families. From 1964 until his tragic assassination in 1980, each of Rodney's activities, whether study (he produced forty scholarly articles on Africa during this period) or practice, was completely devoted to Black Liberation. For Walter Rodney, academic inquiry was valid only to the extent it assisted the liberation struggle of Chicago steelworkers, Jamaican banana farmers, and Tanzanian peasants.

Born in 1942 in the West Indian colony of British Guiana, Rodney was exposed to class struggle at a young age. His father was a leader of the multiracial People's Progressive Party (PPP), and as a teenager Rodney distributed leaflets and heard thousands of hours of political discussions in his home. He later wrote, "without knowing anything about class, I knew there were certain kinds of Guyanese one did not give a PPP manifesto."[1]

Increasingly interested in black struggles for equality, Rodney studied history at the University of the West Indies in Jamaica and later earned a doctorate in African History from the University of London. While in England, Rodney's perspective of class struggle and black revolution was sharpened when he joined other West Indian students in study sessions with the brilliant Trinidadian Marxist C.L.R. James.

James urged his students to study the Marxist-Leninist classics *State and Revolution* and *What Is To Be Done*, and to analyze the conditions from which they arose. James told his eager students that the black revolutionary scholar must not accept blindly what worked in Russia or China. He taught that they must study for themselves the causes of black subjugation and develop theories which could become dynamite in the hands of the working masses.

Energized by James's tutelage, Rodney accepted a position as a history professor at the University of the West Indies in Jamaica. Rodney, however, was no ivory tower intellectual handing down sacred knowledge to the groping masses. While in Jamaica he confounded university and government authorities by hanging around the Rastafarians and unemployed poor in Kingston's slums. After his formal university lectures he was often seen teaching history in Kingston's rubbish dumps and shantytowns. In these street sessions Rodney was both teacher and student, and he later wrote,

> I got real knowledge from them, and when you get that, you know you get humility because look who you are learning from. The system says they are nothing, they are illiterates, the dark people of Jamaica. And you get confidence too, you get confidence from an awareness that our people are beautiful.[2]

Humility and service, first learned among Jamaica's poor, became hallmarks of Walter Rodney's career. The lessons he learned in Kingston's garbage dumps were later compiled in the remarkable little book, *Groundings With My Brothers*. Rodney notes in this book that the only way for the black scholar to escape the stifling "Babylonian Captivity" of bourgeois culture is by "attaching himself to the activity of the black masses."

Rodney was impressed by the Afro-American Black Power movement, and in 1968 he participated in the famous Congress of Black Writers held in the United States. In his lecture, "African History in Service to the Black Revolution," Rodney clearly defined the role of history and the historian. "The acquired knowledge of African history," he said, "must be seen as directly relevant but secondary to the concrete tactics and strategy which are necessary for our liberation."[3] He also noted that incorrect understanding of African history acted "as a drag on revolutionary action in the present epoch." He urged the writers and scholars at the Congress to destroy the falsehoods of African history and join without reservation the daily struggles of black working people.

The neocolonial Jamaican government never trusted Rodney's excursions into Kingston's shantytowns. During his trip to America, Jamaica issued an order declaring Rodney an "undesirable foreign element" and expelling him from the country. His articles and essays were banned, and any mention of Walter Rodney brought suspicion and government surveillance.

His passion for African studies and liberation, however, was undiminished, and Rodney left for Socialist Tanzania to continue his research into the black condition. FRELIMO from Mozambique, MPLA from Angola, and ZANU from Rhodesia all planned their revolutions from Tanzania's capital city, Dar es Salaam. While these African movements impressed Walter Rodney, it was Amilcar Cabral and the PAIGC in Guinea-Bissau that most influenced him. Cabral's penetrating anaylsis of Marxism interpreted for the specifics of Africa's struggle inspired Rodney's continuing search for revolutionary truth.

Tanzania also provided a base from which Rodney could develop conclusions to free Africa and her children in the United States and the Caribbean. This study resulted in the work for which he is most famous, *How Europe Underdeveloped Africa*. Written when Rodney was merely thirty years old, *How Europe Underdeveloped Africa* is a brilliant summary of how capitalism and colonialism retarded Africa's economic development and left a continent in shambles. Rodney's book was published in 1972, at the height of Afro-American protest movements and African liberation struggles, and it provided black revolutionaries with a guide to action. Even today, no discussion of Africa is complete without referring to Walter Rodney's *How Europe Underdeveloped Africa*.

Although Rodney's research showed European colonialism responsible for Africa's troubles, he maintained that the solutions lie with the African people.

The question as to who, and what, is responsible for our underdevelopment can be answered at two levels. First, the answer is that the operation of the imperialist system bears major responsibility by draining African wealth and making it impossible to develop more rapidly the resources of the continent. Second, one has to deal with those who have manipulated the system and those who are either agents or unwitting accomplices of said system.... None of these remarks are intended to remove the ultimate responsibility for development from the shoulders of Africans. Not only are there African accomplices inside the imperialist system, but every African has the responsibility to understand the system and work for its overthrow.[4]

How Europe Underdeveloped Africa is rich both in scope and data. The author begins with an overview of the economic systems of ancient and medieval African nations. The heart of the book, however, is the thesis that European appropriation of African resources and labor (slaves) interrupted Africa's normal course of development and irreparably destroyed economic progress. He notes that when Belgium, France, England, Italy and Germany colonized Africa they stifled inter-African trade and destroyed any possibility of a unifying infrastructure. By forcing African nations to be dependent upon London, Paris, Brussels and Berlin, European imperialism inhibited interdependence and cooperation between bordering nations. For example, Ghana as the appendage of London had more in common with England than with neighboring Guinea (which incidentally, was an appendage of Paris).

For Rodney, slavery's most harmful legacy was its theft from Africa of one hundred million creative and contributing human beings. Using the great Zulu leader Shaka as an example, Rodney writes,

> Had Shaka been a slave to some cotton planter in Mississippi or some sugar planter in Jamaica, he might have had an ear or a hand chopped off for being a 'recalcitrant nigger', or at best might have distinguished himself in leading a slave revolt.... On a slave plantation

Shaka would not have built a . . . Zulu state—that much is certain.[5]

Slavery's other contribution was to provide cheap labor, new markets, and higher profits to the barons of the Industrial Revolution. He notes how Barclays, Lloyds of London, Unilever, and other major companies were capitalized with profits from this bloody human cargo. Rodney also notes that western profits from Africa's diamonds, bauxite, iron ore, and gold created a situation where "Surplus from Africa was used to offer a few benefits to European workers to make the latter less revolutionary."[6]

In his analysis of colonialism's machinery, Rodney shows how colonial education, enforced monoculture (the procedure by which self-sufficient African societies were forced to grow export crops for the profit of European companies), and military repression combined to destroy Africa's normal path toward social and economic development. Indeed, Rodney notes that the ultimate effect of colonization was the removal of the African masses from history; in other words, the workers, peasants, youth, and women of Africa were unable under colonization to determine their own destiny and thereby make their distinctive historical imprint upon the world.

At the heart of Rodney's analysis of African underdevelopment is a stinging critique of capitalism and its offspring, individualism.

> It is a common myth within capitalist thought that the individual through drive and hard work can become a capitalist. In the U.S.A., it is usual to refer to an individual like John D. Rockefeller, Sr., as someone who rose from rags to riches. To complete the moral of the Rockefeller success story, it would be necessary to fill in the details on all the millions of people who had to be exploited in order for one man to become a multimillionaire. The acquisition of wealth is not due to hard work alone, or the Africans working as slaves in America and the West Indies would have been the wealthiest group in the world.[7]

In 1974, Walter Rodney decided to practice the lessons of *How Europe Underdeveloped Africa* in his native Guyana. Rodney had not lived there for over a decade and the political landscape had changed tremendously. In 1966, Forbes Burnham and the People's National Congress (PNC) was elected with help from the CIA and the British Secret Service. American and English investors needed the reactionary PNC to minimize the influence of the PPP and its Marxist leader, Cheddi Jagan.

Burnham's "cooperative socialism" was belied by rampant corruption, militarization, and terror. The Afro-Guyanese and Indian workers, however, refused to submit passively to the authority of Burnham. Although Rodney could have remained in Tanzania to lecture and write, he nevertheless returned home to struggle with his people.

Upon his arrival Rodney was welcomed and hired as a history professor at the University of Guyana in Georgetown. It was not long, however, before Burnham and the PNC realized that Rodney was serious about people's struggle. Burnham's regime could ill-afford a radical scholar talking about workers' rights and independence from neocolonial puppets, so Rodney's university appointment was rescinded. Unruffled, Rodney remained in Guyana. Vincent Harding, et al., explain in the Introduction to *How Europe Underdeveloped Africa* why Rodney stayed in Guyana.

> He had set himself two major tasks, both consistent with his ... role as a black intellectual who was committed to the liberation ... of his people. Both required his presence in Guyana. The first was to develop a major multi-volume work on the history of the working class in his country. The second task (and this was all-encompassing) was to immerse himself in the contemporary life of those same people and search with them to find a way to resist the power of a government that had clearly betrayed their hopes and their trust, a government that now stood in the way of their development."[8]

For the next several months, Walter Rodney was either studying Guyana's history in the public library or talking with and listening to the workers of Georgetown. He also taught African and Guyanese history to working people who could not afford college but who thirsted for the identity and self-respect gained through knowledge of their past. Between street and library, factory and archive, Walter Rodney became increasingly popular among the common folk of Guyana.

His study of past workers' struggles and his conversations with Guyanese fishermen, canal-builders, and domestics led Walter Rodney to help found the Working People's Alliance (WPA) in 1974. Established to improve the lives of working class Guyanese, the WPA was consciously a multiracial organization which recruited the descendants of both Africa and India. While Burnham sought to consolidate his rule by fanning racial divisivness, Rodney and the WPA promoted a class solidarity that recognized the unique contributions of each culture and viewed capitalism as the enemy of both national liberation and class unity.

The WPA was not Walter Rodney's abstract "position paper;" it was the concrete voice of Guyana's oppressed Africans and Indians. Co-founder Eusi Kwayana, a leader in the African Society for Cultural Relations with an Independent Africa, had a history of black nationalist activities in Guyana. Other WPA leaders, like Moses Bhagwan, Joshua Ramsamm, Clive Thomas, Rupert Roopnaraine, and Maurice Omawale represented African and Indian workers in a healthy atmosphere of mutual respect. Despite the scholarship of Rodney and the multicultural leadership, the main force of the Working People's Alliance was the Guyanese workers. Tired from long days in the fields, estates, factories, and foundries of Guyana, hundreds of laborers worked through the night building the WPA.

Rodney, when not recruiting members and leading meetings, continued with his research. While *How Europe Underdeveloped Africa* dealt with the life of a continent over centuries, in Guyana Rodney focused his work on a specific nation.The fruit of his research, *A History of the Guyanese Working People, 1881-1905*, combines both theory and practice. While his days were filled with meetings, marches, rallies and teachings, Rodney's nights were spent in libraries and archives digging up the lost history of past people's struggles. In perfect symmetry Rodney's daily struggles fused his research with vigor and meaning, and his studies clarified and focused the direction of the people's movements.

Unlike standard histories, Rodney's *History of the Guyanese Working People* does not focus on the deeds and misdeeds of the dominant class. Instead, Rodney wrote Guyana's history from the perspective of those who built the nation but were denied a share in its wealth. Colonial Guyana was literally submerged in the Atlantic Ocean. African slaves and later Indian indentured servants were used to build dikes, canals, and rivers around which the European settlers could erect their coastal estates and plantations. In this context, Rodney notes that brutal forms of control were used to extract labor from the workers. Like Afro-American slavery, beatings, whippings, and murders were common. After slavery was outlawed, the Africans wasted no time in demanding full inclusion into the society.

When the Africans became too rebellious, the planters and government curbed their bargaining power by importing thousands of Indians as indentured servants. The lives of Indian servants mirrored the slavery from which the Africans had just escaped. Nevertheless, as Rodney pointed out both in his *History of the Guyanese Working People* and in WPA meetings, the ruling class attempted to control the workers by generating competition and division between the Africans and the Indians.

In George Lamming's Introduction to *History of the Guyanese Working People*, he points out that while Rodney promoted African history and culture, that appreciation and understanding was not exclusive. It was, rather, a foundation from which Africans could join workers of other races, in this case Indian, to topple the walls of capitalist exploitation. When juxtaposed with his work in the WPA, Rodney's writings become more than academic theory; they are a strategy for liberation verified by the daily struggles of Guyanese workers.

When the WPA was small, Burnham and his cohorts could afford to ignore it and pretend it did not exist. Rodney and the African and Indian workers, however, would not be forgotten. In 1979, the WPA declared itself a party and openly challenged the corruption of the PNC. Rodney boldly condemned Burnham,

> The PNC...practices miltarization, manipulation of race, institutionalization of corruption, extension of political repression, distortion of revolutionary concepts...and allows reproduction of the petty bourgeois as a class in the midst of declining material standards for the vast majority and simultaneous with the accelerated expropriation of surplus by the multinational corporations.[9]

The open defiance of Rodney and the WPA outraged the PNC. In 1979, the leadership of the WPA was arrested for allegedly setting fire to a government building. Rodney, Karen DeSouza, Rupert Roopnaraine, Maurice Omawale, and Kwame Apata were tried for arson, but the government's flimsy case was so badly handled that the charges were eventually dropped. The message of repression, however, was clear. Later that year, WPA's newspaper *Dayclean* was banned, and WPA meetings were disrupted by members of what the workers called "Rent-a-thug," hired henchmen used by Burnham to terrorize citizens.

During this period of flagrant repression many of Rodney's Afro-American friends urged him to leave Guyana. He replied, "I must participate in the struggle for the transformation of the people and society; I can not leave just because I have ready access to the means of escape. It is imperative that I stay here."[10] Rodney clarified his commitment in a later speech;

> None of us is mindful of the threat that is constantly posed. We don't regard ourselves as adventurers or

martyrs or potential martyrs, but we think there is a job to be done, and at a certain point in time we have to do what has to be done.... We do not set out to get the best of our workers and revolutionaries killed just so that we can write poetry to celebrate them. When they are lost, they are lost, it's an irreparable loss and may in fact qualitatively affect the development of the struggle.[11]

Despite the courage of Walter Rodney and the black and Indian workers of WPA, violent PNC attacks continued. In 1980, WPA sypmathizer Rev. Bernard Drake was stabbed to death in full view of the police. Later that year, WPA leaders Ohene Koama and Edward Dublin were savagely murdered by Guyanese police. Dublin had been a petty criminal preying on Guyanese citizens when his involvement with Rodney and the WPA redirected his energies into the Working People's Alliance. Dublin soon emerged as a tireless Alliance organizer and was deeply admired by youngsters from working-class families. In a tribute to Dublin, Rodney told a gathering of the WPA, "The revolution is made by ordinary people, not by angels, it is made by people from all walks of life, and more particularly the working class who are in the majority. And it is a sign...of revolutionary transformation when street force members are developed into fighting cadre of a political movement."[12] In the same speech Rodney affirmed the WPA's willingness to endure the violence of Burnham, "As the brothers on the street say, 'I man ire' and 'I man dread', which simply means that whatever pressure may be going down, we are determined to resist."[13]

The murder of Dublin and Koama were but part of a larger pattern of PNC terror. Public meetings were cancelled, and Rodney often slept in different homes to thwart threatened assassination attempts. The frenzied, bloody hands of neocolonialism finally caught up with the brilliant black scholar. On June 13, 1980, Rodney picked up a walkie-talkie from a WPA "member" and drove away to test it. Government murderers detonated a bomb hidden in the walkie-talkie and Rodney was instantly killed. Committed Socialist, true man of the working people, brilliant scholar, dedicated organizer, Rodney was brutally murdered by a system which benefited from the exploitation of working people. Capitalists in London, Washington, and Paris breathed sighs of relief with the elimination of yet another black troublemaker.

Despite murders, false arrests, wire-taps, and other government intrusion, Rodney was devoted to the people to the very end. One of his colleagues wrote:

> On the night of his murder police barged into his home in search of incriminating materials. Spread out on the dining room table was the latest project he was working on; one of five children's stories designed to help kids understand that regardless of race, they were all equally Guyanese with a common history of exploitation, common class interests, and a common stake in a transformed future.[14]

Rodney was dead, but his labors were shouldered by others in black liberation struggles all over the world. Although a Guyanese, he connected black struggles in Georgetown with those in Los Angeles and Dar es Salaam. One of Rodney's most important theories was his view of the impact of Africa on Afro-Americans and Afro-Caribbeans.

> To the extent that the African struggle advances and that continent is freed from the web of capitalism and imperialism, to that extent the impact on the Caribbean, and in particularly, the black people in the U.S. is likely to be decisive.[15]

Walter Rodney was clear about his role as a writer and scholar. "I seek to publish as simply and cheaply as possible... to try and reach Africans who wish to explore further the nature of their exploitation, rather than satisfy the standards set by the oppressors."[16] Rodney did not research and write for academic acclaim and tenured positions; his was truly a history in service to black revolution. He did not use his degrees and books as platforms from which to sneer down upon the toiling masses. Rather, with an unparalleled humility and uncompromising dedication to common folk, Rodney lived his advice to black scholars and "linked himself with the activity of the masses."

Historian-revolutionary. Revolutionary-historian. No black struggle for freedom can move forward without deference to the works and struggle of the great Walter Rodney.

> Our will to struggle has not in any way been lessened. On the contrary, today we feel stronger than ever. We feel more confident than ever, not simply in our own capacity, because that would be incorrect. We feel more confident because of the demonstrative ability and capacity of the people, of all.[17]
>
> —*Walter Rodney, in his last public speech, one week before his assassination.*

> He must have touched something pretty deep when old East Indian women walked barefoot twelve miles behind the coffin of a black man.[18]
>
> —*Guyanese newspaper, 1980*

C.L.R. James: Marxism and Black Liberation

Cyril Lionel Robert James was born in Trinidad in 1901, two generations removed from slavery. The small island of Trinidad could not contain his talents, so James left to write and study in London. Initially interested in writing about sports and fiction, James was soon absorbed in the struggles of London's working people. Their demands for economic justice and democracy took on greater significance when James realized the same forces that abused workers in London's textile mills and docks also impoverished his fellow Trinidadians.

Employed as a writer and lecturer, in his spare time

James studied Marx, Lenin, Stalin, and Trotsky. It was the workers, however, who most impressed the brilliant Trinidadian writer. "My socialist ideas," he wrote,

> had been from books, and were rather abstract. These humorously cynical working men were a revelation that brought me down to earth. After I met them I read [Leon Trotsky's] *History of the Russian Revolution*...at the end of reading the book in 1934, I became a Trotskyist.[19]

The Bolshevik Revolution moved James from study to action. He became an active member and organizer in the Independent Labor Party (ILP), led strikes of English workers, and worked with the unemployed for immediate relief. Continuing his work among the miners, millers, and dock workers of London, James left the stagnating ILP to lead the more militant Revolutionary Socialist League (RSL). While in the RSL, James edited the newspaper *Fight*, and soon distinguished himself as one of the most important Marxist theorists in England.

In England, James the Trotskyite met Paul Robeson, the legendary Afro—American Socialist. Although the two differed politically (Robeson supported Stalin and the Soviet Union while James followed the exiled Leon Trotsky), Robeson and James worked together to promote socialism among Africans and their descendants in the diaspora. James also met George Padmore, a fellow Trinidadian who was a leader in both the Communist Party USA and the Pan-African movement. James, Padmore, and Robeson spent hours working to develop strategies to liberate their people from the ravages of racism and economic exploitation.

As a Marxist, James emphasized worker solidarity; as a black Trinidadian associated with Padmore, Robeson, and other black radicals, he passionately believed in African liberation. Home of his enslaved grandmother, mother of black people all over the world, Africa became a central point of C.L.R. James's socialism. During a period when Africa was viewed as a savage "dark continent," void of cultural and social value (save that conferred by the Europeans), James and his comrades proudly called themselves "Africans."

When Mussolini and his brown-shirted fascists invaded Ethiopia, James helped organize the International African Friends of Ethiopia (IAFE). Demonstrating a commitment beyond rhetoric, James told the Abyssinian (Ethiopian) embassy in London he was ready to go to Ethiopia to fight. He later wrote that he wanted to fight "on the African field where one of the most savage battles between capitalism and its opponents is going to be fought for many years...Given the fact that I am Negro and interested in the African revolution, it [joining the armed struggle] is well worth the attempt."[20] Before James could enlist, the Ethiopians were crushed by Mussolini's tanks and planes.

Ethiopia's defeat did not diminish James's zeal for African independence. In 1937, James, Padmore, and African expatriates formed the International African Service Bureau (IASB). Many in the IASB, including Padmore, Jomo Kenyatta, and Eric Williams (author of *From Columbus To Castro* and prime minister of Trinidad between 1962 and 1981) argued for nonviolence. James, however, was convinced that the tentacles of capitalism would not release their hold on African labor and resources because of prayers and sit-ins; the violence of imperialism could only be defeated by the violence of an armed revolution. James did not believe King Leopold in the Congo, Cecil Rhodes in Rhodesia, and Mussolini in Ethiopia would be moved by pleas of mercy from African workers and peasants.

James's advocacy of violent revolution also found expression in his scholarly work. During the period he argued for armed rebellion, James backed his views with the publication of his classic *Black Jacobins*. Published in 1938, *Black Jacobins* was a penetrating Marxist view of the 1791 revolt of black Haitian slaves under Toussaint L'Overture. Consistent with his radical political views, *Black Jacobins* was a literal declaration of war against imperialism in Africa, colonialism in the Caribbean, and capitalism in the United States.

The central thesis of *Black Jacobins* was James's view that history is written by exploited workers (or slaves) who rise up to destroy the chains of oppression. James wrote, "Those black Haitian laborers have given us an example to study" and believed the lesson of the slave rebellion was its spontaneous revolutionary impulse. Noting that "one does not need education or encouragement to cherish a dream of freedom,"[21] James wrote *Black Jacobins* with the conviction that the black masses had within themselves the capacity to create an autonomous liberation movement to overthrow the ruling class. Without the benefit of revolutionary theory or a revolutionary party, James wrote that the Haitian slaves successfully completed a class revolution and implemented a model of Lenin's "dictatorship of the proletariat" to maintain rule over reactionary French planters.

Black Jacobins also provides illuminating insights into the legendary black leader Toussaint L'Overture. James notes how L'Overture overcame French, British, and Spanish treachery to mold the slaves of San Domingo (colonial name for Haiti) into a powerful black liberation army. James details how L'Overture, Dessalines, Christophe and the black masses of Haiti transformed Caribbean and world history by chasing the French colonialists off the island and creating the first free black republic in the West. So devastated was France by the loss of her prosperous colony that Paris was forced into the infamous Louisiana Purchase; practically giving away to the United States all the land between the Mississippi and the Rocky Mountains.

Despite the greatness of L'Overture, James wrote that his class privileges (L'Overture was an educated house servant) created a "limit beyond which he could not go." James believed that L'Overture was more willing to compromise with the French bourgeois than would an African slave embittered by the sadistic whippings characteristic of Haitian plantations. (James's description of colonial brutality boggles the mind.) Indeed, L'Overture was murdered by the French after he had agreed to meet for peace talks. In criticizing L'Overture, James criticized his own class. "For that reason," writes Cedric Robinson in *Black Marxism*, "he

[James] was to insist often that the revolutionary masses must preserve to themselves the direction of the revolutionary movement, never deferrring it to professional revolutionaries or parties."[22]

With his brilliant analysis of the conditions and struggles of the Haitian masses, C.L.R. James provided future generations with a history of black revolution and a blueprint for future action. Indeed, in the tumultuous 1960s, with FRELIMO and MPLA guerrillas fighting Portuguese fascists in Africa and Afro-Americans rebelling in the streets, *Black Jacobins* was widely read by movement leaders in the Third World and black America.

After the publication of *Black Jacobins* James moved to the United States, where he studied U.S. society and continued his revolutionary writings and party work. He was still a leading figure in the international Trotskyite movement, and he assisted the Socialist Workers Party's (SWP's) program among American labor. In 1942, James moved to southeastern Missouri and organized black and white sharecroppers against plantation exploitation. Under the pen name J. Meyer, James wrote articles like "Down with Starvation Wages in Southeast Missouri," which argued that a progressive and integrated union was the only hope for starving workers in their struggle against greedy property owners.

From his experience in Missouri and his writings on the Haitian revolution, James developed the view that the black masses were the most militant sector of society. He and Trotsky disagreed on this issue, and eventually James left the SWP and formed his own party, the Worker's Party. He later moved to Detroit where he led study circles for future black Marxist leaders Grace Lee and James Boggs. Several other intellectuals and activists participated in these study circles, and many historians believe the radical teachings of C.L.R James laid the groundwork for the League of Revolutionary Black Workers.

These study circles allowed James to sharpen his revolutionary theory and inspired several brilliant works on Marxism and black liberation. In 1939, he published *A History of Negro Revolt*, and followed that with *Notes On Dialectics*. *Notes* was a masterpiece of Socialist theory, analyzing labor movement history and citing the failures and successes of Socialist revolutions. Although it was not widely read for thirty years, *Notes* was James at his scholastic finest, searching incessantly for an authentic socialism in opposition to Stalin, Trotsky, trade union bureaucrats, and U.S. capitalism. In addition to many novels, plays, and short stories, James also wrote *World Revolution* and *A History of the Third International*, two books on the international communist movement.

During this period James further developed the theory over which he clashed with Leon Trotsky, that of the autonomous black liberation movement. In a classic 1948 article titled "The Revolutionary Answer to the Negro Problem in the United States," James clarifies his view on the spontaneous militancy of Afro-Americans. In James's own words, the article "is a clear political programme which summarized the political attitudes...which I had placed before Trotsky in 1938."[23] After participating in black workers' struggles in Missouri and Detroit and researching African resistance movements, James concluded:

> The real leadership of the Negro struggle must rest in the hands of organized labor and of the marxist party. This is the position held by many socialists... We, on the other hand, say something entirely different. We say, number one, that the Negro struggle, the independent Negro struggle, has a vitality and a validity of its own....number two, that this independent Negro movement is able to intervene with terrific force upon the general social and political life of the nation, despite the fact that it is waged under the banner of democratic rights....number three, and this is the most important, that it is able to exercise a powerful influence upon the revolutionary proletariat, that it has a great contribution to make to the development of the proletariat in the United States, and that it is in itself a constituent part of the struggle for socialism.

In this way we challenge directly any attempt to subordinate or push to the rear the social and political significance of the independent Negro struggle for democratic rights. That is our position. It was the position of Lenin thirty years ago.... The Negro people, on the basis of their experience, approach the conclusions of marxism. First of all, on the question of imperialist war. The Negro people do not believe that the last two wars... are a result of the need to struggle for democracy. On the question of the state, what Negro... believes that the bourgeois state is a state above all classes, serving the needs of all the people? They may not formulate their beliefs in marxist terms, but their experience drives them to reject the shibboleth of bourgeois democracy.... The Negro struggles in the South are not merely a question of struggles of Negroes. It is a question of the reorganization of the whole agricultural system in the United States.[24]

In the same article James writes that the ex-slaves during Reconstruction, Afro-American sharecroppers in the Southern Tenant Farmers' Union, and militant black auto workers at the River Rouge Ford Plant are examples of the spontaneity of black radicalism. He also noted that almost every black organization "is dominated by the idea that each organization must in some manner contribute to the emancipation of the Negroes from capitalist humiliation and from capitalist oppression."[25] James concludes this powerful article by noting that "[Negro] hatred of bourgeois society and their readiness to destroy it when the opportunity should present itself, rests among them to a greater degree than in any other section of the population in the United States."[26]

James's powerful theory of black revolt and his work in study circles and with Missouri tenant farmers did not go unnoticed by the Cold War fascists. By 1952, the United States government declared C.L.R. James to be an "undesirable alien" and deported him to England. His imprint on Detroit, however, could not be erased, and his teaching later sparked movements like the League of Revolutionary Black Workers and the Black Workers' Congress.

James stayed in England for five years, and later moved to his home country of Trinidad to help Eric Williams rebuild the island from the debacle of English colonialism. He participated in Williams's People's National Movement Party and edited the paper *The Nation* until he and Williams split over the question of allowing U.S. military bases on the island. He started the Workers' and Peasants' Party in Trinidad and later divided his time between England and the United States, teaching philosophy and revolutionary theory.

James also continued with his writing. His experiences in London, Detroit, and Trinidad further strengthened his resolve to develop a revolutionary theory which, when put into practice, would correct mistakes made in other movements. In 1958, he wrote about the 1956 Hungarian Revolution in *Facing Reality*. Two years later, James published *Modern Politics*, a series of lectures presented at the Trinidad Public Library. These brilliant lectures represented James's theses on the historical development of civilizations and the Socialist theory necessary to end capitalist exploitation and its concomitant degradation of the human character.

Beginning with ancient Greece and running through the Middle Ages, the French Revolution, the Bolshevik Revolution, the World Wars, and current society, James traced human progress from slavery through capitalism. Socialism was on the horizon, he urged, and the path was through spontaneous revolutionary movements.

> (1) All development takes place as a result of self-movement, not direction from external forces. (2) Self-movement springs from and is the overcoming of internal antagonisms within an organism, not the struggle against external foes.[27]

James wrote of human life: "The end toward which mankind is inexorably developing by the constant overcoming of internal antagonisms is not the enjoyment, ownership, or use of goods, but self-realization, creativity."[28] In order to change into a place where all can realize their potential, James urged that people know their history and the potential for socialism. In the conclusion of *Modern Politics*, James writes,

> Properly encouraged and given a sense of history and a sense of destiny...[people] will do all they now do for war, for the sake of improving the normal life and the relations of human beings. But this will come only when people are their own masters.
>
> That for me is what Marxism is, and we must not be afraid, we must not think because we are small and insignificant that we are not able to take part in all that is taking place. The first thing is to know. Anyone who tries to prevent you from knowing, from learning anything, is an enemy, an enemy of freedom, of equality, of democracy.... Marxism is the doctrine which believes that freedom equality, democracy are today possible for all mankind. If this course of lectures has stimulated you to pursue the further study of Marxism, we will have struck a blow for the emergence of mankind from the darkness into which capitalism has plunged the world.[29]

In his later years, James published several other books on Pan-African revolt and socialism. In 1967, he published *The History of Pan-African Revolt*, a brief overview of African, Afro-Caribbean and African resistance to slavery and colonialism. He explains how L'Overture, Garvey, Kimbangu, Mau Mau, and Nyerere have all provided lessons for future generations seeking justice from the ruins of racism and capitalism. Focusing more on African independence in his later years, in 1977 he published *Nkrumah and the Ghana Revolution*.

Whether writing or organizing, C.L.R. James was the most important black Marxist thinker of his time. An innovator in Marxist theory, James is the seminal figure in radical black politics on three continents (Europe, Africa, North America). He is chiefly responsible for linking Marxism with black social resistance, and almost every revolutionary black intellectual has been profoundly influenced by the work of C.L.R. James. The League of Revolutionary Black Workers, Maurice Bishop and Grenada's New Jewel Movement, Walter Rodney, George Padmore and his Pan-African movement, socialist scholar Manning Marable and countless other black radicals have been challenged and inspired by the works of the incomparable C.L.R. James.

The Kingdom Is At Hand
Black Socialist Preachers

- **Rev. George Washington Woodbey**
- **Rev. George W. Slater**
- **Other Black Socialist Preachers**

The Kingdom Is At Hand: Black Socialist Preachers

The Black Church in America has produced some of the most important leaders in Afro-American life. Nat Turner, Richard Allen, Denmark Vesey, David Walker, Bishop Henry M. Turner, Rev. Adam Clayton Powell, Dr. Martin Luther King Jr., and Rev. Jesse Jackson are among the many leaders who flourished in the fertile soil of the Black Church. Despite their efforts, for the most part the church has focused on spiritual concerns and the afterlife, leaving the misery of the masses to be healed on Judgment Day. Bible studies, choir rehearsals, "poor saints" offerings, and Sunday services are often more important than massive unemployment, poor schools, infant mortality, and police violence.

A few black preachers, however, believed that Judgment Day was *now*, and that it was within their power to eliminate poverty and exploitation. Although religion often dulled the fervor of the oppressed to change society's inequities, these black preachers maintained that socialism alone could produce the equality, justice, and democracy promised by the coming Kingdom of God.

Rev. George Washington Woodbey, Rev. Theodore Holly, Rev. R.C. Ransom and Rev. George Slater are but a few of the black ministers whose gospel was empowered by class struggle and revolutionary politics. It was their radical precedent that paved the way for the Civil Rights Movement of the Fifties and Sixties and the Rainbow Coalition of the Eighties.

Religion/Man Is One

Rev. George Washington Woodbey

The most famous of all the black Socialist preachers is the Rev. George Washington Woodbey of the African Methodist Episcopal (AME) church. Born a slave in Johnson County, Tennessee in 1854, Woodbey moved with his parents to Nebraska after the fall of slavery. In Nebraska, young Woodbey saw both the pulpit and the ballot box as vehicles through which he could influence the lives of his fellow ex-slaves. Since neither the Republican or Populist Party could match Woodbey's radicalism, the young preacher joined the Socialist Party. A successful minister, prolific writer, and street orator, Woodbey soon became the leading Afro-American Socialist in the United States.

Woodbey was well-known for his political views in both Nebraska and Los Angeles, but it was in San Diego that Woodbey gained a national reputation as the "Great Negro Socialist Orator." Between 1902 and 1908 Woodbey was jailed several times for leading street corner rallies and for distributing his revolutionary pamphlets and books. At several demonstrations in San Diego, Rev. Woodbey was attacked by the police and more than once was hospitalized for severe injuries. Long before the riots of Newark, Watts, and Detroit, Woodbey recognized the role police forces, militia, and the National Guard would play in protecting property at the expense of human life. He wrote; "In the days of chattel slavery the masters had a patrol force to keep the Negroes in their place and protect the interests of the master. Today the capitalist uses the police departments for the same purpose."[1]

In 1912, Rev. George Washington Woodbey was at the center of a bitter "free speech" battle in San Diego. Woodbey, Socialist Party leaders, and the International Workers of the World (IWW) irritated San Diego's elite with their endless strikes and demostrations.

At the urging of millionaire sugar capitalist and streetcar franchise owner John D. Spreckels, the City Council prohibited street rallies within a forty-nine block area in downtown San Diego. In defiance of the law,

Woodbey, the Socialists and the IWW continued their public protests. Police and vigilantes brutally assaulted the speakers in a manner so horrifying that the governor's investigator wrote,

> I have visited Russia and while there, have heard many horrible tales of high-handed proceedings and outrageous treatment of innocent people at the hands of despotic and tyrannic Russian authorities.... It was hard for me to believe that I was still not sojourning in Russia, conducting this investigation there, instead of in this alleged 'land of the free and home of the brave.'[2]

Rev. Woodbey was almost murdered one night by vigilantes hiding near his home. All-night protection by members of the Free Speech League (the coalition organized to oppose city restrictions on street rallies) prevented yet another cold-blooded murder of a black revolutionary. Woodbey's courage in battling millionaires, the police, the city council and vigilantes catapulted him to prominence among American leftists.

While Woodbey was a leader in San Diego's Socialist Party, he served as the pastor of the Mount Zion African Methodist Episcopal Church. He was eventually removed from his position by the church hierarchy because "he loosened up his flock with the Bible, then finished his sermon with an oration on Socialism."[3] It appeared that the AME church could pray for the poor but was not willing to march with them.

Police repression and the loss of his ministry did not dismay the radical Rev. Woodbey. As a member of the executive committee of California's Socialist Party, Woodbey ran for state treasurer on the Party's 1912 ticket. Acquainted with the horrors of both slavery and racism, Woodbey ignited several Party conventions with his passionate demands. At the 1908 convention he was one of the first to oppose a Party proposal supporting immigration restrictions against the Chinese. He thundered,

> I am in favor of throwing the whole world open to the

inhabitants of the world. There are no foreigners, and cannot be unless some person comes down from Mars. It would be a curious state of affairs for immigrants for the descendants of immigrants from Europe themselves to get control of affairs of this country, and then say to the Oriental immigrants that they not come here.

Now listen: It seems to me that if we take any stand opposed to any sort of immigration that we are simply playing the old ...trick of the Democrats and Republicans and will gain nothing by it. I believe it is opposed, as I understand it, to the principles of international Socialism.[4]

His eloquence in favor of Chinese immigrants was a testimony to the solidarity this ex-slave had for other oppressed people of color. In growing from an enslaved teenager on a Tennessee plantation to a profound spokesperson for international solidarity, George Washington Woodbey exemplifies the power of socialism in the hands of the dispossessed.

Despite his street corner eloquence and his convention floor proclamations, Woodbey's prolific writings were his most significant contributions to black struggle. Intended to recruit blacks into the Socialist Party, Rev. Woodbey's self-published books explained socialism in terms poorly educated workers could understand.

His first book, *What To Do And How To Do It: Socialism vs. Capitalism*, was published in San Diego in 1903. Its dedication reads;

> This little book is dedicated to that class of citizens who desire to know what the Socialists want to do and how they propose to do it. By one who was once a chattel slave freed by the proclamation of Lincoln and now wishes to be free from the slavery of capitalism.[5]

What To Do And How To Do It is written as a conversation between a mother and son. To the mother's astonishment, the son has become a Socialist. The son explains that the poverty and hunger of the black and white masses is an inevitable consequence of a system where "the capitalist, who is not a producer, furnishes nothing except as he takes it through rent, interest and profits from the worker."[6]

The son then elaborates on socialism's economic justice, how the wealth produced by workers will finance the health, education, cultural, transportation, and recreational needs of all the people. After noting that Socialists will come to power through the ballot box (this was fourteen years before the Bolshevik Revolution), the son explains how Socialists would expropriate private property. When the mother questions the justice of the rich returning more to the government than poor people, the son says, "the man who turns over a large amount of capital created by labor which he did not do by his own hands, only turns over what he has taken from the man who has nothing to turn over."[7]

The son then describes to his mother Karl Marx's theory of surplus value. Using data from the 1900 census, the son explains that each American worker produced an average of $2,451 in goods but only received an average of $437 in wages. The capitalist earned $2,014 in surplus value per worker—money consumed by one individual instead of distributed among the people for health, food, and shelter.

Socialism's promise of economic equality, women's rights, and racial tolerance begins to attract the mother. Her intriguing discussion with her son ends with, "Well, you have convinced me that I am as much of a slave now as I was in the South, and I am ready to accept any way out of this drudgery."[8]

In 1904, Rev. Woodbey published *The Bible and Socialism*, a conversation between two preachers in which one shows the other how the Bible's Old Testament condemnations against the rich are an indictment of capitalism. When the other pastor asks, "Is this not the land of liberty?" the Socialist preacher thunders:

> Land of liberty, indeed! Where a man can't live on the earth without buying or paying rent to someone else. Cannot work for bread to feed his family without the consent of someone else, and even then only by giving up the larger part of his products to some one who does nothing. Is that what you call liberty? Go and tell these bruised ones in mine, field, and factory that Christ came to set them free in this life.[9]

When the capitalist preacher praises the rich for their generous donations to the poor, the Socialist preacher counters, "Charity, at best, simply means to give back to the worker when in a pinch of hunger a small pittance of what he has produced and been robbed of through profit on his labor; on goods; or by rent, or interest."[10]

Before the elections of 1908, Rev. Woodbey published a pamphlet titled *Why The Negro Should Vote the Socialist Ticket*. In it he urges: "All other parties have abandoned the Negro, and if he wants an equal chance with everyone else, he can get it no other way than by voting the Socialist ticket."[11] In a plea for class unity, Woodbey writes, "We poor blacks and whites have fought, and while we have fought, the capitalists have been taking everything from the both of us."[12]

He then describes for his black readers how life would be under a Socialist government.

> Under socialism, when we build a railroad, it will belong not to some Vanderbilt or Gould, but to the people. And when we ride on that railroad, or use, it, we will not have to pay a profit to the capitalist. And when the public owns all the mines, shops, factories, railroads, etc., and when we all have an equal voice in management, there will be a job for everybody, both black and white.[13]

In 1910, Rev. Woodbey published *Distribution of Wealth* in which he assails the enforced poverty of the working masses. Woodbey calls the new Socialist government the "Cooperative Commonwealth" in which the clothes, food, and shelter produced by the people will be available for use by the public, much like parks and streets. He claims that once the Cooperative Commonwealth is established, future generations of schoolchildren would read about capitalism and "shudder at the barbarism of the past."

Several blacks were recruited into the Socialist Party by the indefatigable George Washington Woodbey. Whether demanding food for the unemployed on the streets, explaining socialim in his writings, or defending Chinese immigration. Rev. Woodbey combined Marx and Jesus into tireless work on behalf of the oppressed.

Rev. George W. Slater

During the Panic of 1907, Rev. George Slater of Chicago attempted to aid unemployed black families by establishing grocery cooperatives through his church. This failed, however, when food manufacturers and distributors harassed Slater and sabotaged this threat to their profit margins. The Reverend was astonished that owners and growers would be more interested in making money than in preventing starvation.

Soon after this bitter lesson in merciless "free enterprise," Slater heard Rev. George Washington Woodbey at a Socialist Party street-corner rally in Chicago. He later wrote,

> For years I have felt there was something wrong with our country. I heard Comrade Woodbey...he showed me plainly the trouble and the remedy. From that time on I have been an ardent suporter of the Socialist cause...I saw that the tenets of Socialism were the solution of our problem; the ethics of Jesus in economic action, the solution of the poverty question with its attendant evils; the making possible of a practical brotherhod; the solution of the more serious phases of the so-called race problem.[14]

Slater believed the hunger, poverty, and despair he witnessed during the 1907 depression would be abolished under socialism. He therefore dedicated himself wholly to bringing socialism to the Afro-American people. He did not view this as a small task, and in a 1908 article in the *Chicago Daily Socialist*, Slater wrote, "Comrades, during this year I have set myself the task of reaching 1,000,000 colored people with the great message of Socialism."[15]

Slater exchanged his Christian gospel for the "good news" of socialism, and in order to reach black America he wrote and published the booklet, *Blackmen, Strike for Liberty*. *Blackmen* fervently advocated that an infusion of blacks into the Socialist Party would sweep the Socialists into power and allow them to build a society based on cooperation and justice. Slater distributed his booklet wherever blacks gathered; and at street demonstrations, church services, and strikes, the Socialist minister could be found selling his work for five cents a copy or giving it to those who could not afford to pay.

In 1908, Chicago's blacks lived under horrid conditions. Thousands had come north after slavery, and, with no skills or education, were abused, exploited, and even murdered. Rev. Slater attacked the foundation of this racist exploitation through his articles in the *Chicago Daily Socialist*. In one article, "The Cat's Out," he said:

> When you produce $6.80 a day you get only $1.20. Well, who gets the remainder—$5.60 of the money which you just have earned.... It is reported that Mr. Rockefeller's income is over 100 million dollars. There are over 80 millions of men, women, and children in the United States. By this you see that Mr. Rockefeller alone earned over a million dolars for every man, woman, and child.[16]

Seventeen years before A. Philip Randolph and the Brotherhood of Sleeping Car Porters, Slater exposed the degrading working conditions of sleeping car porters in his article, "Pullman Porter Pity." He wrote, "The Pullman porter is nothing more than a slave, working when and where they want him to work and getting for his labor only what they see fit to give him."[17]

In a 1909 article titled "Tillman vs. Tillmen," he attacked the fraudulent deal that enabled Senator Ben Tillman to swindle seventy thousand dollars in real estate for one hundred and forty-seven dollars. Slater wrote that under socialism, crooked deals that enriched racist politicians while their black constituents starved would not be tolerated.

Rev. Slater's church became a regular meeting place for the Socialist Party and striking workers. In 1912, he founded the Negro Socialist Literature and Lecture Bureau as another vehicle for promoting socialism among oppressed Afro-American workers.

Through his article, pamphlets, lecture bureaus and speeches, George Slater inspired numerous blacks and whites with the possibility of a Socialist America. Slater received many letters from people who read *Blackmen, Strike for Liberty* and said the book helped them understand and fight the mercilessness of capitalism. Rev. George Slater, like Rev. Woodbey before him was committed to creating the Kingdom of God on earth, right now.

Other Black Socialist Preachers

Rev. James T. Holly wrote "Socialism from a Biblical Point of View," a 1892 article which attacked the excesses of European imperialism. He wrote:

> The so-called Christian and civilized powers of Europe, assembled in a den of thieves which they styled an international conference, have deliberately parceled out Africa among themselves. The tens of millions of the masses in each country of Europe have been reduced to mere animal's fare; the hundreds of millions of India have had their life's blood sucked out of them; opium poison has been injected into the veins of the hundred millions of China at the point of the bayonet; and all this to fill the bottomless coffers of avaricious millionaires.[18]

In 1896, the talented black preacher Rev. Reverdy C. Ransom published the article "The Negro and Socialism," in which he argues that "when the Negro comes to realize that socialism offers him freedom of opportunity to cooperate with all men upon terms of equality in every avenue of life, he will not be slow to accept his social emancipation."[19] In the same article Ransom describes how

> socialism in a broad and general sense rejects the doctrine of selfishness which rules the present social order and affirms that altruism is a principal sufficient to govern the relations of men in the sense it is opposed to individualism and does not regard society as composed of an army of warring atoms, but believes the social system to be the best in which the interests of the individual are made subordinate to the interest of society, while allowing freedom for the highest development of his own personality.[20]

While Booker T. Washington and other black capitalists praised the virtues of free enterprise and private initiative, Ransom and his fellow black Socialist preachers would not let society forget about the millions upon whose backs rested the "self-made" millionaires. Ransom wrote, "The present social order with its poverty and vast reserve army of unemployed cannot be accepted as final, as the ultimate goal for which ages have been in travail."[21]

Ransom, Holly and the black preachers that followed them found the Bible's call for justice embodied in socialism. Christian duty was not discovered in the quiet chapel, it was waiting in the tumultuous streets where men and women struggled, sweated, and cried.

African Socialism

- **Kwame Nkrumah**
- **Patrice Lumumba**
- **Sekou Toure**
- **Julius Nyerere**
- **Frantz Fanon**
- **George Padmore**
- **Stokely Carmichael**
- **Abdul Babu**
- **Nelson Mandela**

African Socialism

Africa, according to early Marxist thought, lacked the industry and urban proletariat required to make the transition from capitalism to socialism. Marx and some of his successors believed that Africa's agrarian societies could not move into socialism without first developing a ruling class, factories, exploited workers, labor unions, and the other contradictions inherent in capitalism. European imperialism, however, changed this Marxist theory of revolution.

The suffering spawned by European companies, banks, armies, missionaries, and entrepreneurs instilled in African liberation movements a militant anti-capitalist ideology. Free enterprise had gone wild in Africa. Images of starving Mozambican children, limbless Congolese peasants, and overtaxed Rhodesian farmers totally discredited capitalism as an option for Africa.

Once independence was won, the problems faced by African nations were colossal. Ethnic differences exacerbated by Europe's "divide and rule" philosphy, an economy destroyed by war, and an economic and educational network designed to benefit the few and exploit the many were but a few of the monumental problems inherited by the people of independent African nations.

Where agrarian African societies had fed and clothed themselves, they were now thrust into the international capitalist network and subjected to the whims of the free market. At the same time, illiterate peasants were faced with building a just and Socialist society from the ruins of African feudalism and European colonialism. It is in this context that several leaders and peoples chose African socialism, Pan-Africanism, and Marxism-Leninism as the means to African liberation.

The Rock/African Socialism

Kwame Nkrumah and Ghana

In 1957, Ghana became the first African nation to free itself from the grasp of European colonialism. By the 1960s, Ghana symbolized the growing clamor for self-determination of colored peoples around the world. Ghana's freedom, however, did not come without a bitter struggle.

Kwame Nkrumah was the embodiment of the Ghanaian people's resistance movement. Born in 1909 in the village of Nzima in Ghana, Nkrumah moved to the United States in 1935. He lived in America for ten years, studying, teaching, and preparing himself to eventually return home. Nkrumah's personal fortunes never obscured his memories of Ghana's sufferings, and he wrote, "When I was a student in the United States I was so revolted by the ruthless colonial exploitation of the people of Africa that I knew no peace."[1]

Nkrumah met C.L.R. James in the U.S. and began reading Hegel, Marx, Lenin, and Garvey. Although the Communists taught Nkrumah of class struggle and revolution, it was Marcus Garvey that fired his enthusiasm about African liberation.

In 1945, Nkrumah combined black nationalism and communism in his pamphlet, *Toward Colonial Freedom*. Although he had been away from Africa for ten years, *Toward Colonial Freedom* catapulted Nkrumah into the leadership of the expatriate African community. He wrote,

> The imperialist powers need the raw materials and cheap labor of the colonies for their own capitalist industries. Through their system of monopolist control they eliminate native competition, use the colonies as a dumping ground for their surplus goods... It is from this that the African peoples must constantly strive to free themselves... This [freedom] can only be achieved by the political education and organization of the colonial masses.[2]

In 1945, Nkrumah went to London to pursue a legal career and prepare himself to return to his beloved country. Later that year, Nkrumah, W.E.B. Du Bois, George Padmore, and several African nationalists organized the famous Fifth Pan-African Congress in Manchester, England. This congress, attended by two hundred delegates from all over the black world, proved to be the ideological catalyst for future African liberation movements. While past congresses consisted of non-African theorists discussing position papers, the Fifth Congress brought together African nationalists and revolutionaries. Jomo Kenyatta, representatives from South Africa's ANC (African National Congress), and trade union leaders joined other African delegates in discussing and planning their own liberation. As congress recorder, Nkrumah emerged from Manchester as the spokesperson for African nationalism. The congress's declarations, he wrote in his autobiography, *Ghana*,

> asserted the determination of colonial peoples to be free and condemned the monopoly of capital and the use of private wealth and industry of personal profits alone. They made a stand for economic democracy as being the only real democracy and appealed to colonial people everywhere—the intellectuals, the professional classes and the workers—to awaken to their responsibilities in freeing themselves...from the clutches of imperialism...As the preponderance of members attending the Congress were African, its ideology became African nationalism—a revolt by African nationalism against colonialism, racialism, and imperialism in Africa—and it adopted Marxist socialism as its philosophy.[3]

After the congress, Nkrumah and other West Africans in London formed the Circle, a group committed to implementing the mandates of the Manchester Congress. The Circle's goals were:

> to maintain ourselves and the Circle as the Revolutionary Vanguard of the struggle for West African Unity and National Independence...To support the idea and claims of the All West African National Congress in its struggle to create and maintain a Union of African Socialist Republics.[4]

This was not the idle chatter of academicians and theoreticians; the young West African men who met in London's cafes, parks, and churches were plotting ways in which Africa would be snatched from the multinational corporations and returned to the people.

In 1947, the moderate United Gold Coast Convention (UGCC) invited Nkrumah to Ghana to assist their challenge to British rule. Nkrumah, eager to work for the freedom which he had discussed so often, accepted the offer and returned to Ghana later that year. By 1948, Nkrumah had become such a nuisance to colonial rule that he was imprisoned by the English. He was released in 1949, but soon found the UGCC too cautious in their demands for self-determination.

Nkrumah left the UGCC and formed the more militant Committee on Youth Organization (CYO). From that base, Kwame Nkrumah and other Ghanaian nationalists founded the Convention People's Party (CPP). Sixty thousand Africans gathered to hear Nkrumah at the CPP's founding rally. After condemning the vacillation of the UGCC, Nkrumah asked, "Then may I break away from any leadership which is faltering and quailing before imperialism and colonialism and throw in my lot with the chiefs and people of this country for full self-government NOW?"[5]

With this resounding beginning, Nkrumah and the CPP challenged both English colonialism and UGCC reformism. Although the older generation of UGCC intellectuals and elitists smugly thought of themselves as the undisputed leaders of black Ghana, Nkrumah aligned himself with the workers, women, farmers, and youth of Ghana and created a powerful political movement. In 1950, The CPP launched the Positive Action Movement, a series of boycotts and strikes protesting British reluctance to grant self-government for Ghana. Nkrumah and other CPP leaders were arrested and jailed for "sedition." From prison Nkrumah continued to lead the Party, secretly mailing directives scribbled on toilet paper.

To quell the people's demands, Britain held elections in which Ghanaian people were given limited governing powers. Although Nkrumah was still imprisoned, the people of Ghana overwhelmingly elected him to the National Assembly. In each election after that, the CPP increased its representation in the Assembly. The CPP's voting power in the Assembly and their labor power, evidenced by strikes and boycotts, soon overwhelmed English colonialism. In 1957, England reluctantly granted independence to Ghana, and one hundred thousand people watched Nkrumah lower the Union Jack and raise the red, green, and gold flag of independent Ghana.

Ghana was the first independent nation in Africa, and her early years were consumed by the problem of surviving in an environment where surrounding colonial powers did all they could to sabotoge this bold effort at African self-determination. If by example Ghana could prosper under African rule, European colonialism would be immediately rejected by the rest of Africa. Drawing from tactics discussed in the cafes and on the street corners of London, Nkrumah nationalized the economy and established ties with other Socialist countries. Pan-Africanism and dreams of a West African Union led Prime Minister Nkrumah and Sekou Toure of Guinea to forge an alliance between their two countries.

In 1963, Nkrumah published *Africa Must Unite*, an urgent call for African unity as the only protection against foreign domination. Two years later he wrote the classic, *Neo-Colonialism: The Last Stage of Imperialism*. Patterned after Lenin's *Imperialism, the Highest Stage of Capitalism*, Nkrumah's book exposed how American Zinc, the Anglo-American Corporation, consolidated Gold Fields, and other corporations disrupted African progress despite national independence. The book eloquently analyzed how high interest rates, the Peace Corps, missionaries, and AFL-CIO lackeys enslaved the "free" African countries. Nkrumah's critique of western intrusion was so sharp that the United States withheld a $35 million aid package after its publication.

Despite his calls for African unity, Nkrumah did not neglect Ghana. During his administration a United Nations report noted that Ghana spent more on education per capita than any other Third World nation. Ghana's poverty continued, however, and many peasants and workers became dissatisfied with unfulfilled promises. A sluggish economy and persistent poverty contrasted with Nkrumah's hopeful speeches, and foreign economic subversion wreaked havoc on Ghana's industry.

Internal turmoil and external pressures to abandon socialism finally led to a 1966 coup which ousted Nkrumah and sent him reeling into exile in Guinea. The nationalized rubber fields were turned over to Firestone, and the neocolonialism with which Nkrumah was so familiar returned in force in Ghana. The failure of Ghana's revolution did not destroy Nkrumah and he continued working for the eventual victory of Pan-Africanism.

In 1969, he published *Handbook of Revolutionary Warfare*, a book that urges a Socialist Africa unified under the banner of Pan-Africanism. In the chapter "Strategy and Tactics," Nkrumah lays the foundation for the All-African People's Revolutionary Party (AAPRP). This Party, according to Nkrumah, will be the vehicle through which African nations crawl from the abyss of poverty and miseducation into the brilliance of unity and socialism. Despite the failure of Pan-Africanism and socialism in his own nation, Nkrumah continued to believe that through organization and education Africans would unite for a strong and prosperous future.

Patrice Lumumba: The Star of Africa

> The whole world surprised, wakes up in panic
> To the violent rhythm of blood, to the violent rhythm of jazz
> The white man turning pallid over this new song
> That carries the torch of the people through the dark night
> The dawn is here my brother! Dawn! Look in our faces,
> A new morning breaks over our old Africa[6]

Patrice Lumumba's powerful poem exemplifies his revolutionary zeal and desire to create a new society from the ashes of African feudalism and western imperialism. Nothing old, nothing borrowed, but a new African society in which fulfilling employment, adequate shelter, stimulating education, and uplifting culture is available to all the people of the continent.

Lumumba's Congo was one of the most abused colonies in Africa. Belgian corporations and politicians operated one of the largest and bloodiest slave camps in history. Africans were forced off traditional farm lands and marched at gunpoint into the Congo's rubber forests to enrich Belgian corporate parasites. Resistance was met with savagery; hands and feet were severed, torture was commonplace, and sadistic murders were used to strike fear into the Congolese people. Belgian rule was solidified as the colonialists created animosity and strife between the Congo's two hundred ethnic groups.

In 1925, Patrice Lumumba was born to a poor peasant family in the village of Onalua. Lumumba's zeal for freedom was fired by conversations with Congolese workers and studies in African history and international socialism. From 1948 to 1956, the impassioned Lumumba founded and led a number of organizations dedicated to Congolese liberation. In the early 1950s, Lumumba called for a joint Belgian-Congo state. Over the next few years Lumumba became increasingly radical and soon became the most eloquent spokesperson for complete Congolese independence. Lumumba inspired suffering peasants and rubber workers with forceful poems and scathing articles in the newspaper *Uhuru*.

In 1958, the thirty-three year-old Patrice Lumumba founded the Congolese National Movement (MNC) in order to "use every means to liberate the Congo from imperialist domination." The first challenge facing the MNC was to resolve the ethnic divisions inflamed by Europeans frightened of Congolese unity. Calling tribalism "our most dangerous internal enemy," Lumumba's speeches, articles and rallies urged Africans to link arms for the overthrow of foreign oppression. The second challenge of Patrice Lumumba and the MNC was to build solid ties with Congolese workers and peasants. Lumumba wrote, "We know some Congolese are well off, but they are in the minority, meanwhile, we are concerned with the majority."[7] Convinced that the demands of workers and peasants would move the struggle forward, Lumumba also wrote, "[the people] want to advance more rapidly than we [the leaders] do."

In 1960, after years of strikes, boycotts, and demonstrations by the MNC and other liberation forces, the Belgian government granted independence to the Congolese people. At the liberation ceremony, Lumumba gave one of the most illuminating speeches in African revolutionary history.

> No Congolese... can ever forget that we have gained our independence through struggle, a daily persistent, idealistic struggle, a struggle in which we were undaunted by privation, suffering or great sacrifice, nor by the blood shed by our people.... We are proud of this struggle, of tears, of fire, to the depths of our being, for it was a noble and just struggle, and indispensable to put an end to the humiliating slavery which was imposed on us by force.
>
> This was our fate for eighty years of a colonial regime; our wounds are too fresh and too painful still for us to drive them from our memory. We have known harassing work, exacted in exchange for salaries which did not permit us to eat enough to drive away hunger, or to clothe ourelves, or to house ourselves decently, or to raise our children as creatures dear to us....
>
> We have seen our lands seized in the name of allegedly legal laws which in fact recognized only that might is right. We have seen that the law was not the same for a white and for a black, accommodating for the first, cruel and inhuman for the other....
>
> Who will ever forget the massacres where so many of our brothers perished, the cells into which those who refused to submit to a regime of oppression and exploitation were thrown? All that, my brothers, we have endured.
>
> But we...tell you very loud, all that is henceforth ended.... Together, my brothers, my sisters, we are going to begin a new struggle, a sublime struggle, which will lead our country to peace, prosperity, and greatness. We are going to establish social justice and make sure everyone has just remuneration for his labor.

We are going to show the world what the black man can do when he works in freedom, we are going to make of the Congo the center of the sun's radiance for all of Africa.⁸

A few days later Lumumba was elected by the people to be the prime minister of a hopeful and independent Congo. Belgium, the United States, and other NATO nations did not share the Congolese people's joy over Lumumba's speech. They saw in his passionate adherence to self-determination a significant loss in revenue and economic control. When Lumumba nationalized several key industries and told NATO its bases were no longer welcome in the Congo, a slander campaign was started by the agents of western imperialism. Lumumba was called a Communist and vicious lies were spread among the Congolese people. Devious lackeys of the West offered the radical prime minister millions of dollars (for his personal use) if he would end nationalization and democracy.

Unmoved by slander or bribery, Lumumba continued to work for socialism and equality in the Congo. Where bribery and lies failed, terror took over. Opposition leaders directed by Belgian colonialists and America's CIA illegally removed Lumumba from office. Public outcry was muted by a slander campaign against the prime minister. He was imprisoned and weeks later was taken from his cell, beaten with machine gun butts and hobnail boots, and shot on a desolate farm in northern Congo. The plot to murder Lumumba took on international implications when the U.S. Senate uncovered CIA files which said Lumumba was a "grave danger," and noted his assassination was "an urgent and prime objective."⁹

The CIA, Katanga secessionists (the mineral-rich province of Katanga sought to be independent from the Congo at the urging of Belgian agents), and European mercenaries murdered one of the most brilliant young African leaders of the 20th century. Once again, the West could not tolerate a radical African leader choosing to live outside the orbit of its insidious economic control. The murder of Lumumba represents the most flagrant example of western capitalism's willingness to kill anyone who stands in the way of continued profits.

> To my children whom I leave and whom perhaps I will see no more, I wish that they be told that the future of the Congo is beautiful and that it expects from them, as it expects from all Congolese, to accomplish the sacred task of reconstruction of our independence and sovereignty; for without dignity there is no liberty, without justice there is no dignity, and without independence there are no free men.
>
> No brutality, mistreatment or torture has ever forced me to ask for grace, for I prefer to die with my head high, my faith steadfast, and my confidence profound in the destiny of my country... History will one day have its say, but it will not be the history that Brussels, Paris, Washington, or the United Nations will teach.... Africa will write its own history.... Do not weep for me, my dear companion. I know that my country, which has suffered so much, will know how to defend its independence.[10]
>
> *Letter from Patrice Lumumba to his wife Pauline, written from Camp Hardy prison a few weeks before his murder on January 17, 1961*

Sekou Toure and Guinea

Sekou Toure was born to a poor Guinean peasant family with a rich history. Toure's grandfather, Alamamy Samoury, was a legendary resistance leader who died fighting the French invaders. Unlike the many African leaders who studied abroad, Sekou Toure was educated by the struggles of Guinean trade unions. His roots therefore, were never in the country's elite, but among the common laborers and peasants. Sekou Toure was influenced by the French Communist Party's Confederation Generale du Travail (CGT), a federation of trade unions in France. Toure believed, however, that Guinean independence would come only when Africans created their own organization.

In 1947, Sekou Toure helped organize the Parti Democratique de Guinee (Democratic Party of Guinea, or PDG), a coalition of various Guinean trade unions and ethnic groups. Through Toure's charismatic leadership, the PDG recruited thousands of dock workers, factory workers, laborers, and peasants into the Party.

Chinweizu notes in *The West and The Rest of Us:*

> The PDG leadership decided that the major objective was to make their party into a party of the masses. General proclamations against colonialism and big business, and considerations of foreign policy, had no chance of mobilizing the masses for whom these issues did not represent anything concrete. Their objective, therefore, was to create and reinforce the trade-union movement on the basis of struggle over bread-and-butter issues, especially the struggle against discrimination in salaries, social rights, etc.[11]

By addressing concrete needs of Guinea's workers and peasants, and recruiting across ethnic lines, the membership of the PDG grew rapidly. Foula, Soussou, Toma, Baga, Malinka and other groups joined in Toure's quest to bring economic justice and overthrow colonialism. In 1953, Toure led a general strike which lasted two months, broke the economic dominance of

French capitalists, and established him as the undisputed leader of the Guinean people.

For Sekou Toure, time spent organizing the elite was time wasted. It was the working class that held the power to bring about revolution in Guinea. He wrote: "Trade Unionism is a faith, a calling, an engagement to transform fundamentally any given economic and social regime, always in search for the best and the beautiful and the just."[12]

The largest campaign of the Party, and the one that made the PDG the hope of the people, was a bitter struggle against abusive village chiefs. The French colonial administrators had transformed the village chiefs into a privileged class that served as a buffer between them and the hungry masses. The chiefs were propped up as village leaders and given authority to collect taxes in exchange for pacifying the people with their religious spookism and fatalistic myths. Crazed with power, many chiefs invented taxes for every occasion, some even financing trips to Mecca and elsewhere from taxes levied against birth, death, and every imaginable circumstance in between.

The PDG mobilized the masses by promising that if elected they would reduce the powers of the chiefs. The Guinean people responded, and in the 1957 elections, the PDG swept into power, winning fifty-eight of sixty seats in the Assembly. The PDG used their political muscle to limit the powers of the village parasites and to implement tax reforms which allowed the people to pay taxes to the government in exchange for social services.

The French were alarmed at the popularity of Sekou Toure's reforms, and in 1958 they gave all of their African colonies the option of joining a French West African commonwealth or receiving complete independence. While the Ivory Coast, Senegal, and Niger all opted for the "security" of their white masters in Paris, the people of Guinea voted a resounding "no."

The vote in Guinea's national referendum was 1,136,000 for freedom, 57,000 for neocolonialism. Speaking on behalf of Guinea's workers and peasants,

Sekou Toure told Charles de Gaulle, "We, for our part, have a first and indispensable need, that of our dignity. There is no dignity without freedom. We prefer poverty in freedom to riches in slavery."[13]

He could not have known the extent of France's desire to see his country suffer. Angered at the Guinean ingrates, the De Gaulle government went berserk. Teachers, doctors, and technicians were withdrawn. Medical supplies were burned, phones were ripped out of the walls, light bulbs were crushed, and electric wires slashed. Anything that might help the Guinean people, no matter how small, was destroyed. At the same time, the French offered their "grateful" colonies economic assistance to advertise the fruits of loyalty to France.

Despite French sabotage and treachery, Toure, the PDG, and Guinea did not collapse. When France turned its back, Guinea turned to Ghana and the Soviet Union for assistance. President Toure urged the workers forward with a renewed sense of self-worth. He proclaimed, "If you are a laborer, say to yourself that you are the equal of Mr. Sekou Toure; if you are a farmer say to yourself that you are the equal of Mr. Sekou Toure, above any minister, above any public servant."[14] Far from bemoaning the departure of the Europeans, the Guinean masses sang:

> Good-bye Europeans
> Good-bye Europeans
> And without a grudge
> I, myself, am not offended
> Good-bye everyone to his own home
> Without any fuss
> Good-bye provided you disturb us no more
> Let him follow you
> He who believes you indispensable[15]

In the early years of his administration, Sekou Toure nationalized the economy in an attempt to build a distinctive African socialism in Guinea. He broke with the French Communist Party, noting that the rival European leftist ideologies (Marxism-Leninism, social-democracy, and Trotskyism) had no relevance to the needs of Guinean workers. Consequently, Toure and his cabinet set out to build a unique African socialism which addressed the specific needs of the Guinean masses.

Sekou Toure and Kwame Nkrumah of Ghana emerged as Africa's Socialist rebels. The liberation movements in Guinea-Bissau, Angola, and other countries established headquarters in Conakry (Guinea's capital), and Toure was one of the first Africans to support Patrice Lumumba's courageous fight against Belgian imperialism.

The PDG built national women's organizations, farmers' unions, and workers' federations. The most influential body, however, was the militant youth organization. La Jeunesse de la Revolution Democratique Africaine (Youth of the African Democratic Revolution, or JDRA) was at the cutting edge of the literacy, health, and economic reforms the PDG had instituted in rural areas.

Another major accomplishment of Toure's revolution was the integration of Guinea's various ethnic groups into the government. Every group was proportionately represented, and Sekou Toure wrote, "Let us accept to become new men; let us kill in us the Malinke man, the Soussou man, the Guerze man, let us accept to be transformed into new men fit to rehabilitate Guinea and Africa, fit to serve the universal cause of man."[16]

In order for Guinea to overcome western subversion and internal sabotage, Toure constantly reminded the PDG and the people that everyone had a role to play. In *Strategies and Tactics of African Revolution*, he wrote:

> There is no individual who does not work. The fellow who refrains from working as he should...is not lazy...dialectically, he is doing something; in reality he is working to ruin the Revolution; he is not a comrade, he is not neutral, he is an enemy of the people...either he refrains from working because he is committed to the ideology of counter-revolution, or he does so because he is unknowingly guided by that ideology.[17]

A country rich in bauxite and minerals but poor in technology and education, Guinea endured extraordinary hardships. Creating a democratic socialism from the stagnation of peasant culture and the shambles of French imperialism was not an easy task. Like Ghana and Zaire (Congo), Guinea was the target of western skulduggery and sabotage. Black Guineans succeeding with an independent African socialism was a grave threat to multinational monopoly capitalism. Western arrogance culminated in Portugal's 1970 invasion of Guinea. Although the invaders were defeated, the West continued clandestine sabotage; aggravating ethnic divisions and withholding aid.

Despite Toure's eloquence and the people's sacrifices, the obstacles to peace and prosperity were almost insurmountable. As Guinea pursued independence and socialism, western countries punished the renegade Toure.

The nation plunged further into poverty, as illiteracy and unemployment persisted. Toure's popularity declined when workers and peasants became impatient with chronic misery. Like Kwame Nkrumah in Ghana, Sekou Toure found himself working to not only improve his country but to fight off the western powers' attempts at subversion. Winning independence proved to be easier than rebuilding through socialism a poor nation surrounded by rich capitalists.

By the late 1970s, Toure was forced to reestablish ties with the West in an attempt to get his sluggish economy moving. When he died in 1984, Sekou Toure never saw the national prosperity he and his people worked so hard to produce. Although he committed forty years to the struggle for Africa's suffering peasants, workers, and students, Sekou Toure could not overcome one hundred years of colonialism and continued western interference. Nevertheless, the victories of Guinean trade unions, Toure's success in bringing ethnic groups together, and the accomplishments of the youth organizations are testaments to the ideology of Sekou Toure and the sacrifices of the Guinean people.

Julius Nyerere and Tanzania

The African nation of Tanganyika was colonized by the British after the victors of the First Imperialist War (also known as World War I) divided among themselves the remains of Germany's African empire. England, however, had no interest in the colony and did little to improve Tanganyika. In the early 1960s, Britain relinquished control and Julius Nyerere and the Tanganyika African National Union (TANU) came to power. Renaming the country Tanzania (after a union with the offshore island of Zanzibar), Nyerere sought to develop his country into an African model of democracy and prosperity.

In February of 1967, Nyerere and TANU unveiled the famous Arusha Declaration, which based Tanzania's reconstruction on a cooperative and democratic socialism. The declaration read:

> Whereas TANU believes...That it is the responsibility of the state to intervene actively in the economic life of the nation so as to ensure the well-being of all citizens and so as to prevent the exploitation of one person by another or one group by another, and so as to prevent the accumulation of wealth to an extent which is inconsistent with the existence of a classless society.[18]

The specific manner in which the Arusha Declaration was to be carried out was discussed by Tanzanians in Dar es Salaam and in the rural areas where the Masai and other groups lived. The people and TANU decided they could build African socialism through

> the decolonization of the education system, with a new emphasis being placed on practical knowledge, and on the social purposes of education, and with disruptive individualism and elitist pretensions being combatted among those being educated; the fostering of a work ethic with emphasis on rural development; the promotion of economic egalitarianism so that a few do not monopolize the national surplus; and the promotion of cultural nationalism by such method as the elevation of Swahili to the status of a national language.[19]

Education for Tanzania's peasants and workers was Nyerere's greatest success. When he came to power in 1964, only 20 percent of the people could read or write. Nineteen years later, 90 percent of the Tanzanian people were literate, educated by the dedicated men, women, and students of the Adult Training Program. African children were not neglected, and all Tanzanian children received primary education which emphasized the values of self-reliance, cooperation, and *ujamaa* (Swahili for "collective work and responsibility"). Without dynamic revolutionary education, Nyerere urged Tanzania's teachers,

> you will produce clerks as the colonialists did. You will not be teaching fighters but a bunch of slaves or semi-slaves. Get your pupils out of the colonial mentality. You have to produce tough people; stubborn youths—who can do something—not hopeless people.[20]

The educational successes were due in large part to Nyerere's insistence that Swahili become Tanzania's language. Diverse ethnic groups were linked by the ability to communicate in one language, and the promotion of Swahili brought about a unity never before experienced by the Tanzanian people. Many see this unification as Nyerere's greatest legacy.

Diseases and malnutrition plagued rural Tanzanian families. While the British neglected African misery, Nyerere and TANU used scarce national resources to create one of the best rural health systems in Africa. "Barefoot doctors," so successful in Mao Zedong's China, fanned out into Tanzania's backcountry to build clinics and hospitals.

Tanzania's progress under Nyerere's socialism was recognized both within the country and around the world. The people revered their president, and often referred to him as *Mwalimu*, Swahili for "teacher." Unlike many of the corrupt neocolonial leaders who came to power in independent African nations, Nyerere continued to live as his people lived. He avoided fancy cars, elaborate villas, and foreign bank accounts, and enforced a code of conduct among the TANU leaders that forbade ownership of rental properties, second incomes, or ownership of private stock.

Nyerere's teachings on socialism and self-reliance were popularized during the upsurge of African revolutions and Afro-American freedom struggles. Both within Tanzania and abroad, Nyerere was seen as a hero of black militancy. His words on self-determination struck a chord among oppressed folk struggling for freedom.

> We have never accepted the argument of 'readiness for independence,' that people are not ready to govern themselves. That is like saying to an individual, 'you are not ready to live.' How do you say to a nation, to a people, 'You are not ready to be human.' It is part of humanness that people should govern themselves. It is incompatible with our being human beings that we be governed against our will.[21]

Dar es Salaam became a center for African liberation activity. Mozambique's FRELIMO and Angola's MPLA both had headquarters-in-exile there, and Guyanese scholar Walter Rodney wrote *How Europe Underdeveloped Africa* in the Tanzanian capital. Nyerere staunchly opposed South African apartheid, and was one of the most vocal African critics of U.S. support for European colonialism.

Economically, however, Tanzania suffered. Nyerere's policy of village socialism entailed resettling Tanzanian farmers onto seventy-five hundred *ujamaa* villages where work, decision-making, and earnings would be collectively shared by the people. Few of these villages produced their quota, and Tanzania's people remained among the poorest on the continent. Like other Third World countries, foreign debt strangled Tanzania, and often almost half the annual export earnings were consumed on back payments on the national debt.

Despite economic woes, Nyerere, TANU, and the Tanzanian people moved forward. A 1987 article in *AfricAsia* notes that Nyerere's legacy includes unstinting support for national liberation movements, twenty years of uninterrupted peace and stability, promotion of basic health and education for all, and the highest life expectancy in Africa. These accomplishments, though tempered by economic lags, attest to the power of the Arusha Declaration's call for socialism and self-reliance.

> We have been oppressed a great deal and we have been disregarded a great deal. It is our weakness that has led to our being oppressed, exploited, degraded. Now we want a revolution—a revolution that brings an end to our weakness, so that we are never again exploited, oppressed, humiliated.[22]

Frantz Fanon

Along with Malcolm X, Algerian revolutionary Frantz Fanon was one of the most influential black radicals of the 1960s. Born on the island of Martinique in 1925, Fanon moved to Algeria in 1951 where he practiced psychiatry. He worked several months in a field hospital during the Algerian war for liberation, and in 1954 he abandoned his practice to join the revolutionaries. The armed liberation war deeply moved Fanon, who believed the Algerian people's struggle foreshadowed later Third World national liberation movements.

Fanon translated the lessons of Algeria's revolution into a global conflict between the haves and the have-nots in his classic work, *The Wretched of the Earth*. Radical movements in Asia, Africa, and Latin America were influenced by his compelling arguments that the oppressed take their destiny into their own hands. Fanon's militant anti-imperialism, his exposure of colonial brutality, and his promotion of violent revolution inspired liberation movements throughout the oppressed Third World. Many were moved by his arguments for armed revolution:

> It is the intuition of the colonized masses that their liberation must, and can only, be achieved by force...for

> the colonized people this violence, because it constitutes their only work, invests their characters with positive and creative qualities.... The armed struggle mobilizes the people; it throws them in one way and in one direction. The mobilization of the masses, when it arises out of the war of liberation, introduces into each man's consciousness the ideas of a common cause, of a national destiny, of a collective history.... At the level of individuals, violence is a cleansing force. It frees the native from his inferiority complex and from his despair and inaction, it makes him fearless and restores his self-respect.[23]

Fanon's words sparked black revolution in Africa, the United States, and the Caribbean. While many moderate leaders called for non-violent protests and restraint, young militants like Huey Newton in America, Maurice Bishop in Grenada, and Amilcar Cabral in Guinea-Bissau saw in Fanon's work the only way to achieve self-determination in the midst of violent suppression. Frantz Fanon was one of those rare people who combined scholarly analysis with active participation in struggles for the people.

George Padmore: Zealot for Black Liberation

Born Malcolm Nurse in Trinidad in 1903, George Padmore came to the United States in 1925 where he met white members of the Communist Party and black members of the Socialist African Blood Brotherhood. In his travels to the West Indies and Harlem, Padmore was moved by the poverty, hopelessness, and despair that gripped his people. His challenge, consequently, became how to assist the descendants of Africa in liberating themselves from the misery and racism of the New World. Impressed with the program of the African Blood Brotherhood and the Communist Party USA, the young Trinidadian joined both the ABB and the CPUSA. In order to protect themselves from the racist anti-Communists running America, many Afro-American

CPUSA members changed their names. Malcolm Nurse was no exception; when he joined the Party in 1927, Nurse changed his name to George Padmore.

Along with Harry Haywood, Cyril Briggs, and Richard Moore, Padmore was one of the leading Afro-American Communists in the 1920s. Intensely dedicated to black people, Padmore selflessly worked in the interest of Afro-American workers, sharecroppers, and unemployed. He spent countless hours writing, agitating, meeting, recruiting, speaking, organizing, teaching, and lecturing on communism as the hope for blacks in the United States and the West Indies. Rising through the ranks of the Communist Party, Padmore became a national organizer of the Trade Union Unity League (TUUL), a federation of left-wing unions with a platform of black and white worker unity.

At the Fifth Congress of Red International Labor Unions (RILU) in Moscow in 1930, the Communist Party leadership created the International Trade Union Committee of Negro Workers. The International Committee was designed to harness the power of black workers in the Caribbean, Africa, and the Unitd States to build a multinational revolutionary trade union movement. Padmore and black labor leaders from Jamaica, Nigeria, French West Africa, South Africa, and Gambia were elected to the executive board. The Committee also published the monthly journal *The Negro Worker*, and employed Padmore as the editor.

Headquartered in Hamburg, Germany, the Committee sent Padmore to Africa and the United States to research the conditions of black workers and organize trade union affiliates of the Committee of Negro Workers. Padmore's exposure to the suffering of Afro-American sharecroppers, Jamaican peasants, and South African miners convinced him that black workers must be reached with communism's message of struggle, organization, and revolution.

As a result of his Committee work, Padmore published *The Life and Struggles of Negro Toilers*, a book that exposes British colonialism as one of the main reasons for

African and Caribbean underdevelopment. Padmore soon became the prime mover of the Committee, and by 1933 he was the foremost black in the Comintern (Third Communist International, composed of those Communist Parties that followed the Russian Bolsheviks).

In 1933, however, Comintern leadership disbanded the International Trade Union Committee of Negro Workers, and Padmore accused the Comintern of deserting the African liberation struggle. This was only the beginning of the rift between Padmore and the Party. In 1935, he learned that Moscow had sent assistance to fascist Italy during Mussolini's Ethiopian invasion and that the Comintern had instructed the French West African Community Party to "go easy" on French colonialism after France and Russia signed a peace pact. These revelations convinced Padmore that African liberation would never come through parties directed from Moscow.

In 1935, Padmore quit the Communist Party and the Comintern. He moved to England and joined C.L.R. James, Paul Robeson, and other blacks in their search for an authentic socialism geared to the needs of black folk. With C.L.R. James, Padmore formed the International African Service Bureau (IASB) as a center for anti-colonial activity.

Padmore's work on behalf of Africa led him to embrace Pan-Africanism. Pan-Africanism held that a unified Africa was more crucial than a unified international working class, and that communism imported from Moscow could not meet the specific needs of Africa's people. His small home in London soon became a forum and clearing-house for the Pan-African movement. On any given evening, one could find Padmore discussing African liberation with Jomo Kenyatta, Kwame Nkrumah, and other future African leaders.

Padmore's zeal for African liberation culminated in the famous 1945 Fifth Pan-African Congress held in Manchester, England. The Manchester Congress was the most significant one up to that time, as it marked the first time African activists were involved in the direction of the congress. W.E.B. Du Bois was the only Afro-American delegate, while the remainder represented African nations suffering under European imperialism and economic domination. After the congress, the Pan-African movement gained momentum and hundreds of African trade union leaders, Socialists, and intellectuals returned home to end foreign rule.

In 1946, Padmore published *How Russia Transformed Her Colonial Empire*, a work which analyzed how Lenin and the Bolsheviks promoted self-determination for those nations previously swallowed up in czarist Russia. Although he was no longer a member of the Communist Party, Padmore still believed Marxism-Leninism contained many revolutionary insights which could not be ignored by those seeking fundamental changes to capitalist exploitation.

After Ghana's independence, Kwame Nkrumah called on Padmore to be one of his closest advisors. It was in Ghana that Padmore published the controversial *Pan-Africanism or Communism*, a work that discusses the history of the Pan-African movement (from Marcus Garvey to Kenya's Mau Mau) and criticizes Communist Party work among Afro-Americans and the African colonies.

Published in 1955, *Pan-Africanism or Communism* contains a harsh critique of Communist Party politics. Padmore's thesis was that Communist Parties working in Africa and the United States were interested in black liberation only to the extent that it served Soviet foreign policy. If black liberation were to run counter to the needs of the Soviet Union, Padmore believed that the Party would abandon its commitment to black people.

According to Padmore, this contradiction was evident when the Communist Party USA did not support A. Philip Randolph's 1941 March on Washington Movement demanding an end to discrimination. Since the Soviet Union was at war with Nazi Germany and America sent arms to the Soviets, the CPUSA believed Afro-Americans should cease militant labor struggles and support America's war machine.

Consequently, Padmore argued that the solution for black folk lay in Pan-Africanism. Pan-Africanism would never compromise black liberation, for it has no loyalty save that of African self-determination. Impressed with the Chinese revolution, Padmore saw Mao Zedong's peasant revolution as Marxism applied to the specific conditions of China. Padmore, therefore, sought an Afro-Asian front against western imperialism where Communist China and Pan-Africanist Africa would be united against the multinational corporations and their stooges.

Pan-Africanism and Communism became the political bible of South Africa's nationalist Pan-African Congress (PAC), and Padmore was revered on the continent as a great teacher and leader. When he died in 1959, thousands of peasants walked miles to Accra, Ghana, to pay tribute to this zealot for black liberation. Afro-American expatriate writer Richard Wright said,

> when George discovered that.... Stalin and his satraps looked upon black men as political pawns in Soviet power politics, to be maneuvered in Russian interests alone, he broke completely with the Kremlin...He continued his work alone, striving to achieve through his own instrumentalities that which he had worked for when he was in the Comintern hierarchy, that is, freedom for black people.[24]

Stokely Carmichael: Kwame Toure

Stokely Carmichael's zeal for black liberation has taken him from his native Trinidad to both the United States and Africa. Carmichael was in America when southern black folk stood up against U.S. apartheid, and he joined the struggle through the militant student Non-Violent Coordinating Committee (SNCC).

In 1961, Stokely Charmichael joined Marion Barry, John Lewis, Ruby Doris-Robinson, Charles Sherrod,

Diane Nash-Bevel, and other black students as a full-time worker for SNCC.

Carmichael became the chairperson of SNCC, which by 1964 was a powerful force in the black liberation movement. Paid a subsistence wage, Carmichael and other SNCC organizers registered southern black voters in Klan-dominated counties in Mississippi, Georgia, and Alabama. SNCC's sit-ins, voter registrations, and mass actions often forced Dr. Martin Luther King into more direct action, and many feel the sacrifices and energy of black students like Carmichael propelled the Civil Rights Movement.

It was Carmichael, during a Mississippi march, who coined the popular chant "Black Power." The slogan galvanized blacks and frightened whites, and Carmichael was viewed by many as one of the most important future black leaders of America. Unlike many of the older black leaders, Carmichael linked Afro-American rebellion with the African revolutions then sweeping the continent.

In 1969, Carmichael moved to Africa and spent several days discussing black survival with Kwame Nkrumah and Sekou Toure. These talks led Carmichael to embrace Pan-Africanism, the ideology that called for the unity of a Socialist Africa. Carmichael took up residence in Guinea, and soon developed into Pan-Africanism's key spokesperson. Carmichael's respect for his two African teachers and his search for a unique African identity led him to change his name to Kwame Toure.

In the 1970s, Toure assumed leadership of the All-African People's Revolutionary Party (AAPRP), which Nkrumah described in *Handbook of Revolutionary Warfare* as the vehicle for implementing Pan-Africanism throughout the continent. As the leader of the AAPRP, Toure claims that traditional Marxist-Leninists do not adequately understand the function of race in the class struggle. In a world stained by racism, the war for African liberation is both a war for black unity and socialism. The AAPRP, therefore, says, "The total liberation and unification of Africa under an All-African socialist government is the prime objective of black revolutionaries all over the world."[25]

Abdul Rahman Mohamed Babu

Abdul Babu was a Zanzibar nationalist who opposed the neocolonial rule of the sheiks left behind by the departing British conquerors. As a leader of the younger radicals on Zanzibar, Babu formed the Umma (masses) Party to help overthrow the corrupt government. After the revolution and union with Tanganyika (which formed the country now named Tanzania), Babu joined the government of Julius Nyerere and became the minister of economic development. Detained for "ultra-leftism," Babu was later released and continues from exile his struggle for a Marxist-Leninist Africa.

A featured author in journals on African affairs, Babu's major contribution to the fight for equality and democracy in Africa is his 1981 book *African Socialism or Socialist Africa*. Written while in detention and sparked from hours of discussions with other detainees, *African Socialism or Socialist Africa* is a compelling indictment of both capitalism and "African socialism."

Babu defines African socialism as the ideology some leaders have adopted which negates class struggle and maintains that Africans are "socialist by nature" and do not require worker revolutions or rigorous planned economies. According to Babu, African socialism is too weak to withstand the intrusions of monopoly capitalism and easily succumbs to western financial interests. Without the rigor of Marxist-Leninist analysis, party-building, and class struggle, Babu condemns African socialism as a dignified neocolonialism.

> It is far better to grant loans to an 'independent' country whose leaders can be trusted to ensure that the working people in a neocolony will be made to labor to pay off the debts with their sweat. Furthermore, such leaders are capable of containing any internal upheavals which may arise as a result of the social contradictions which inevitably intensify as exploitation intensifies. Repression carried out by indigenous leaders is better tolerated internationally than that carried out by a colonial power, although the effects on the worker is the same.[26]

In the chapter, "Discard a False Approach: No Alternative to Socialism," Babu argues that African nationalism is a useless diversion from the task of building socialism.

> Trapped within the imperialist frame of reference, our petty-bourgeois intellectuals strain their imagination, with the help of Western 'Africanists,' in an attempt to produce our own Napoleons, sometimes going as far as to idealize local tyrants and despots as heroes. For socialists the people are the makers of history and their struggle is the expression of that history. Our task as socialists is to carry on the struggle from where our oppressed ancestors left off and carry it through to the end. The ideological and social systems of the past which oppressed them, whether communal or feudal, have their place only in the museum of history.
>
> Most of what took place in the past, apart from the people's struggles, is now obsolete and cannot be applied to the world revolutionary struggle in which Africa is a part.[27]

In that same chapter, Babu passionately argues that socialism cannot be judged by the way it is applied in other countries. Revolutionary African leaders need not look at "models" of other nations, they need to study the concrete conditions of African underdevelopment and poverty and develop their own revolutionary strategy. He writes:

> Socialism has its own culture—the culture of the people, not of the despots and tyrants. Socialism has its own theory—dialectical and historical materialism.... It is not Russian; it is not Chinese. It is not African or Asian or European. It is the only weapon in the hands of the workers and the other oppressed classes. It is the only theory they can use. They do not expect the bourgeois or their class allies to approve of or support socialism, because it is directed against the bourgeois as a class and against its exploitative system.... The Russians, the Chinese and other socialist countries have no monopoly on socialism. They have only applied the theory and

principles of socialism successfully in organizing their respective revolutions.[28]

While criticizing those who have adopted Pan-Africanism or African socialism, Babu still respects their disciplined struggle on behalf of the masses of African workers and peasants. Of Patrice Lumumba, Kwame Nkrumah, Ben Bella, and Sekou Toure, he says,

> All these great and patriotic sons of Africa deserve our respect, not so much for what they have done, which was not much, but for having had a glimpse, only a glimpse, of what could have been a global struggle. Failure was inevitable because they misunderstood the realities which governed all the political and economic aspects of imperialism. Of one thing we can be certain, they were never opportunistic; they erred because of a limited, petty-bourgeois world outlook, but they erred in good faith.[29]

For Babu the future of Africa lies in the hands of African Marxists. Citing past repression, he urges African Marxists to be wary of being isolated and murdered by imperialists and their neocolonial lap dogs. Babu cites the powerful work and tragic ending of African Marxists like Dr. Felix Moumie of the Cameroons, Pio Pinto of Kenya, and Abdulla Kassim Hanga of Tanzania. All three of these men conducted principled struggles within their respective countries, mobilizing African workers and laborers, fighting in united fronts against CIA skulduggery and African treachery, and leading militant African trade unions. Agents of monopoly capital, however, saw their work among the people as a threat. Moumie was poisoned, Pinto gunned down in front of the primary school where he had just dropped off his children, and Hanga was hanged without trial.

In order for a Socialist Africa to become a reality, Babu maintains that African Marxists will have to create clandestine organizations until such time as mass support sustains them against the inevitable counterattacks from the right. He concludes:

Socialism cannot retreat to the past, as the petty-bourgeois idealists would like. It is a forward movement to supercede capitalism's inhuman and unnatural subordination of man, which has resulted in his estrangement... In the final analysis it is the role of the organized working class to take the people of Africa to their historically conditioned destiny. There is no middle way.[30]

Nelson Mandela and the African National Congress

South African apartheid remains the most blatant indictment of the human degradation and misery that result when a heartless capitalism uses racism to profit the few at the expense of the many. In South Africa, racism and class oppression are so aligned that what is perceived as mere race hate is actually a deliberate policy of economic domination. When 40 percent of black South African babies die in Transkei before their first birthday, it is not an accident; it is calculated by the Pretoria government to terrorize blacks into submission and maintain control over their labor force.

The African National Congress (ANC) began its opposition to apartheid in 1912, and much like the Afro-American NAACP, was committed to negotiation and compromise. A few years later, factory worker Walter Sisulu and law students Oliver Tambo and Nelson Mandela formed the more militant ANC Youth League. The young radicals in the Youth League sought to move the ANC moderates to more militant action by demanding equality from the white racists. Each year, more of the Youth League's eloquent revolutionaries were elected to the ANC Board, and soon Congress moderation was replaced with outright defiance.

During this period, Moses Kotane and other black South Africans from the Communist Party (CPSA) served in leadership positions in the ANC. Kotane, at one time general secretary of the CPSA, worked with Mandela, Sisulu, and Tambo to radicalize the ANC, because "the political demands and aims and objects of the ANC and the short-term or immediate goals of the

CPSA were similar."[31]

Nelson Mandela, Oliver Tambo, Walter Sisulu, and the other leaders of the ANC planned a general strike in 1950. The strike failed as security forces murdered eighteen unarmed Africans. Mandela urged a shift in strategy, and the ANC then organized the famous 1952 Defiance Campaign. The Defiance Campaign was a powerful mass movement against the pass laws and the draconian 1950 Suppression of Communism Act (which the South Africans used to jail anyone who believed in equality). Although five thousand Africans were arrested, and many were lashed in public, black South Africans flocked to the ANC. Membership increased from seven thousand to over one hundred thousand as the ANC became the first mass organization in South Africa since the destruction of the Industrial and Commercial Workers' Union (ICU) in the late 1920s.

As the ANC grew, so did South African brutality. Nelson Mandela and Walter Sisulu were declared "statutory Communists," and many ANC members were murdered or jailed. Undaunted, the ANC continued to move forward. In 1955, they formed the Congress Alliance with the South African Congress of Trade Unions, and in 1956 wrote the famous Freedom Charter. Peasants, workers, women, and students were asked, "What would you change about South Africa if you could?" and the result of mass meetings between the ANC and the people was the Freedom Charter:

> The People Shall Govern. All National groups shall have equal rights.
> The people shall share in the country's wealth.
> The land shall be shared among those who work it. There shall be work and security.
> The doors of learning and culture shall be opened.
> There shall be houses and security and comfort.[32]

The Freedom Charter excited the South African masses, and Pretoria was frightened by rising rebellious sentiment. In 1956, one hundred fifty-six Africans were tried in the famous Treason Trial. African resistance continued, and in 1960, South African fascists murdered sixty-seven unarmed Africans at the Sharpeville Massacre. Over half of those murdered were shot in the back.

By 1961, Nelson Mandela had seen enough of black bloodshed. Years of bruises, wounds, cuts, torture, jailings, hangings, and shootings wore down Mandela's patience and he reluctantly embraced violence as the only counter to apartheid. He and other ANC leaders formed the military arm of the ANC, *Umkhonto we Sizwe,* or "Spear of the Nation." After the first bombing of South African facilities, *Umkhonto* leaflets proclaimed:

> We of Umkhonto have always sought—as the liberation movement has sought, to achieve liberation without bloodshed...The time comes in the life of any nation when there remain two choices: submit or fight. That time has come to South Africa. We shall not submit and we have no choice but to hit back by all means within our power in defence of our people, our future, and our freedom. The government has interpreted the peacefulness of the movement as weakness; the people's nonviolent policies have been taken as a green light for government violence...We are striking out along a new road for the liberation of the people of this country.[33]

Mandela soon became a folk hero among the suffering workers, displaced families, and hungry children of South Africa's townships and mining camps. Mandela's courage imbued black South Africans with the belief that they could defeat the well-armed racists and create an equal and just society. When Mandela and Oliver Tambo left their law practice to absorb themselves with the people's struggle, their only aim was to end black suffering. Tambo wrote, "We had arisen to professional status, but in every case in court, every visit to the prisons...reminded us of the humiliation and suffering of our people."

Pretoria could ill-afford to have the charismatic Mandela running loose in South Africa. In 1962, South African police descended on a farm in Rivonia where they arrested Mandela and leaders of the CPSA and *Umkhonto we Sizwe*. Charged with conspiracy to overthrow the government, Mandela and the others were subjected to a two-year trial, during which time South African fascists hanged two Africans every week.

At his trial, Mandela defended himself with a brilliant speech, "I Am The First Accused," in which he outlines the history of the ANC, the aims of the Freedom Charter, the white brutality which led him and others to reluctantly resort to violence as the only road to complete self-determination, and his willingness to die for the creation of a democratic, classless society. During the trial, the people of South Africa demonstrated solidarity with Mandela and the others. On township walls they scrawled, "Mandela, Sisulu, lead us," and word of his defiant speech before the court spread through black South Africa.

In 1964, Nelson Mandela, Walter Sisulu, Raymond Mhlaba, Ahmed Kathrada, Elias Motsoaledi, Andrew Mlangeni, and Dennis Goldberg were given life sentences for plotting to overthrow the government. Nelson Mandela was flown to Robben Island, where this brilliant black South African leader was forced to dig for lime, break rocks, and build roads instead of lead his beloved people to national liberation.

From his greystone 7 x 7 cell, Nelson Mandela continues to embody the revolutionary sentiments of the South African people. Twenty-five years after his life sentence, most black South Africans still view him as the person who will lead the ANC, *Umkhonto we Sizwe*, and the black South African people home to freedom.

When, in 1985, P.W. Botha offered to free Mandela if the latter renounced violence, Mandela thundered from his cell, "Let him renounce the violence of apartheid and I will renounce violence." Under the leadership of Oliver Tambo and the indomitable Winnie Mandela (Nelson's courageous wife, who exemplifies the revolutionary power of African women), the ANC continues its bitter struggle against white economic domination, racist violence, and U.S. support for the fascists of Pretoria.

I have had to separate myself from my dear wife and children, from my mother and my sisters to live as an outlaw in my own land. I have had to close my business, abandon my profession, and live in poverty and misery, as many of my people are doing.

I shall fight the Government side by side with you, inch by inch, and mile by mile, until victory is won. What are you going to do? Will you come along with us, or are you going to co-operate with the Government in its efforts to suppress the claims and aspirations of your own people? Or are you going to remain silent and neutral in a matter of life and death to my people, to our people? For my own part I have made my choice. I will not leave South Africa, nor will I surrender. Only through hardship, sacrifice, and militant action can freedom be won. The struggle is my life, and I will continue fighting until the end of my days.[34]

Nelson Mandela's 1961 press statement "The Struggle Is My Life" issued following his decision to continue political work underground.

Epilogue:
A Luta Continua

In spite of the bombs, jail cells, wire taps and hangman's noose, the black Socialist is not extinct. In the United States, the Caribbean and Africa, their commitment to revolutionary change continues to haunt the rich and powerful. Despite the media proclamations that all is well and the subtle messsages that change is impossible, the black Socialist stands in the shadows and tells us differently.

On the African continent eighteen nations currently follow the path of socialism or Marxism-Leninism. Eleven years of attacks and terrorism by South Africa and the U.S. backed thugs of UNITA has cost Angola and the MPLA $15 billion. Nevertheless, President Jose Eduardo dos Santos and the Angolan peasants and workers continue to follow the arduous path of socialism. Mozambique, Angola's eastern neighbor, survives despite continuing (and, again, U.S. sponsored) attacks by the MNR and South Africa. The 1986 murder of the popular Samora Machel has only increased the resolve of President Joaquim Chissano, FRELIMO and the Mozambican people.

Workers are on the cutting edge of change in South Africa as Amon Msane and the Congress of South African Trade Unions (COSATU) lead thousands of miners, dock workers, and rail workers against apartheid. Despite crushing poverty and foreign meddling, the PAIGC in Cape Verde, TANU in Tanzania, and ZANU in Zimbabwe continue to work toward a society where the wealth is allocated by the workers for health, housing, education and culture.

Despite the 1983 U.S. invasion of Grenada, revolutionary sentiment is not dead in the Caribbean. Don Rojas, Maurice Bishop's press secretary and a member of the New Jewel Movement, urges that we not forget the lessons of the Grenadian Revolution and imperialist aggression. The works and legacy of Walter Rodney and C.L.R. James still imbue West Indian students with an awareness of class struggle and revolutionary change.

Black West Indian Linton Kwesi Johnson has ignited England with powerful political poems and a driving reggae beat. Johnson combines black consciousness and radical analysis to produce music and literature which clearly articulates the struggles of black workers. The songs "All we doin' is defendin' " and "Making History" are typical of Johnson's incessant demand for Freedom Now.

Like Jacques Romain and Aime Cesaire before him, Johnson compliments his cultural work with political organizing. An irrepressible critic of racism and exploitation in England, Johnson helped found the Creation for Liberation and is a member of the Race Today Collective and the Black Parents Movement. Whether through his political work, his books (*Voices of the Living and the Dead, Inglan Is A Bitch*), or his albums (*Dread Beat an' Blood* and *Making History*), Linton Kwesi Johnson delivers the uncompromising message of black liberation and self-determination.

In the United States, politicians, students and artists boldly seek radical transformations in American society. The All-African People's Revolutionary Party as formulated by Sekou Toure and Kwame Nkrumah promotes socialism and Pan-Africanism nationally among black college students. Congressman Ron Dellums (Dellums is the son of C.L. Dellums, a radical leader in the Brotherhood of Sleeping Car Porters) has supported the Democratic Socialists of America and discomforts the House with his stirring calls for equality and justice. No vote for military arms, nuclear buildup, domestic cuts, or U.S. intervention occurs without Dellums promoting peace for the world and justice for the oppressed.

On the cultural front, Amiri Baraka edits the Marxist journal *The Black Nation* and helps guide the League of Revolutionary Struggle. Jayne Cortez uses poetry (the book *Coagulation*) and music (the album *Maintain Control*) to expose the ravages of "free enterprise," racism and nuclear madness. Black scholar Manning

Marable defies academic moderation with his socialist interpretations of history in *From The Grassroots, How Capitalism Underdeveloped Black America*, and *Black American Politics.*

When seen in the context of the brutal murders, bannings, and imprisonments of black Socialists, that any black espouses communism is indeed incredible and a testament to their indestructible spirit of resistance. The struggles of Joaquim Chissano, Linton Johnson, and Amiri Baraka prove that J. Edgar Hoover, CIA treachery and fascist-like apartheid will never squelch black aspirations.

What lessons does the history of black Socialists in the United States, Africa, and the Caribbean provide? Is it simply a futile legacy of lost dreams, wasted martyrs, and unredeemed bloodshed? Are the executioners of Lumumba, Cabral, Rodney, Mondlane, Hampton, Clark, Napier, Hutton, Bishop, Machel, Ndzanga, Gray, Sandy Smith, George Jackson, Jon Jackson, Huggins, Carter, and Khayinga vindicated by our refusal to study and follow the forerunners of black socialism? Are the executioners free to kill again since we so conveniently neglect the reality of class struggle?

Have the car bombs, wiretaps, jail terms, death squads, banning orders, Un-American committees, assassinations, dirty tricks, neocolonial traitors, and lies defeated the people's legitimate demands? *For The People* declares they have not. The sufferings and sacrifices of the MPLA (Popular Movement for the Liberation of Angola), the National Negro Labor Council, and the Sharecroppers' Unions are not in vain. Their successes and failures, their brilliance and their errors, all serve as a beacon for future struggles.

A major legacy of black Socialists is "Black Internationalism." Beginning in 1870 when the Colored National Labor Union opposed restrictions on Chinese immigration (they were the only American labor union to do so), black workers and Socialists have linked their interests and survival with other people of color around the world. Rev. George Washington Woodbey followed in this tradition when in 1903 he mounted the podium at the Socialist Party convention to demand uncompromising support for Chinese railroad workers.

Black internationalism also linked Afro-Americans, West Indians, and Africans in the fight for self-determination. C.L.R. James organized in London, Ethiopia, Trinidad, and Southeast Missouri. Grenadian Maurice Bishop was influenced by America's black power movement and African Liberation Day. Langston Hughes and Richard Wright brought together black writers from Cuba, Haiti and Senegal. African revolutionaries Kwame Nkrumah and Eduardo Mondlane lived in the United States and both learned from and taught their Afro-American brothers and sisters. George Jackson and the Black Panther Party saw themselves within a larger Third World guerrilla army that included Guyanese workers, Vietnamese peasants, and Angolan revolutionaries.

Robeson and Du Bois were the giants of internationalism, reminding Afro-Americans that their freedom was linked to liberation in South Africa, freedom in Haiti, and socialism in China. Amilcar Cabral moved the Congress of Afrikan Peoples toward Marxism though he was three thousand miles away fighting the Portuguese in Guinea-Bissau.

Since 1870, black Socialists and workers have seen themselves not as isolated rabble-rousers but as a conscious part of a radical whole. Black internationalism is a powerful tool that links Afro-American workers with Caribbean laborers and African peasants. Black misery remains so when isolated, but when galvanized by black internationalism it becomes the fuel for revolutionary change. The brilliant Walter Rodney wrote of black internationalism,

> I feel that to the extent that the African struggle advances and that continent is freed from the web of capitalism and imperialism, to that extent the impact on the Caribbean, and particularly, the United States, the black population here is likely to be decisive.... I believe it is an important historical dimension, and, therefore success of the

struggle in Africa is likely to be critical with regard to creating new conditions and new avenues for struggle in what we call the New World.[1]

In *Here I Stand* Paul Robeson wrote,

> The Negro—and I mean American Negroes as well as West Indians and Africans—has a direct and first-hand understanding, which most other people lack, of what imperialism and oppression is. With him, it is no far-off theoretical problem. In his daily life he experiences the same system of job discrimination, segregation and denial of democratic rights whereby the imperialist overlords keep hundreds of people in colonial subjugation throughout the world.[2]

A second legacy of black Socialists is their insistence that workers lead the fight for self-determination and justice. In Africa, Amilcar Cabral embodied the black revolutionaries who believed that workers and peasants were the vanguard of radical change. For Cabral, the struggle against Portuguese fascism was not an idea imported from foreign governments or disgruntled intellectuals; the Guinean revolution was demanded by the workers and the peasants. At a PAIGC seminar Cabral taught Party cadre,

> A basic principle for our struggle is that it is the struggle of our people, and that it is our people who must wage it, and its result is for our people...a people's struggle is effectively theirs if the reason for that struggle is based on the aspirations, the dreams, the desire for justice, and progress of the people themselves and not on the aspirations, dreams or ambitions of a half a dozen persons who are in contradiction with the actual interests of their people...Our struggle is for our people...to lead a decent and worthy life, as all the peoples in the world want, to have peace in order to build progress in their land, to build happiness for their children. We want everything we win in this struggle to belong to our people.[3]

Afro-American Socialists agreed with Cabral on this issue. The two most dramatic examples of revolutionary Afro-American workers are the railroad porters in the Brotherhood of Sleeping Car Porters and the auto workers in the League of Revolutionary Black Workers. When A. Philip Randolph, C.L. Dellums, Milton Webster and others organized the 1941 March on Washington Movement, it marked the first time Afro-American workers led a mass movement for democracy. The 1941 March Movement's significance is clear when we understand it as the direct forerunner to the important 1963 March on Washington.

When in 1969 General Baker, Mike Hamlin, John Watson and others burst from Detroit's sweltering auto plants to form the Marxist-Leninist League of Revolutionary Black Workers, the UAW, Detroit law enforcement agencies, and auto companies shuddered in fear. The League and later the Black Workers' Congress clearly showed both the revolutionary potential of oppressed black laborers and the brutal attempts by American capital to crush such resistance.

In his book *Black American Politics: From the Washington Marches to Jesse Jackson*, Manning Marable weaves a brilliant case for black worker leadership. In the chapter "Black Politicians and Bourgeois Democracy," Marable critiques black protest movements from Reconstruction to the 1980s. He assesses several movements and concludes that Afro-American social reform struggles have not demanded fundamental changes because of black petit bourgeois leadership. Marable argues that the black petit bourgeois is a vacillating class that fights discrimination but retreats from workers' demands for economic justice, broad democracy and working class power.

Black political behavior during Reconstruction supports Marable's thesis. He notes that most of the black Congressmen, state senators, and local leaders were from that elite group of Afro-Americans who possessed land, wealth, and freedom before the Civil War. While Marable concedes these leaders created more of a democracy than the South had ever before witnessed, they nevertheless stopped short of revolutionary change.

The ex-slaves' most insistent demand was for land redistribution. "40 acres and a mule" was not idle chatter, it was the heartfelt aspiration of four millions who worked the land for three centuries without compensation. Marable notes,

> The great failure of the first black political elite was its unwillingness, or inability, to demand land and material compensation for the ex-slaves.... It was increasingly difficult for many black radicals to take the side of the workers and peasantry, given their shifting social class status and material interests.[4]

In addition to their refusal to address land redistribution, many Reconstruction politicians even condemned labor strikes by black workers. Reconstruction leader Richard Cain even wrote, "Let the laws of the country be just; that is all we ask... Place all citizens upon one broad platform; and if the Negro is not qualified to hoe his own in this contest of life, then let him go down.[5] (The black Socialist does not follow this traitorous logic; "the Negro" and other workers create the wealth and the state is obligated to ensure they benefit from this wealth. And if any group suffers, the black Socialist does not say, "let him suffer," the black Socialist demands that the entire society change to end such suffering.)

Manning Marable, like the black Socialists before him, believes that the movement must be led by Afro-American workers. Since workers suffer most from America's racist "free market," they will not vacillate like the petit bourgeois and the clergy. They have nothing to lose and no interest to protect, and consequently will fight until society is completely changed. Marable writes,

> Miltant, uncompromising leaders from the oppressed social classes emerge only when the masses themselves, conscious of their capacity for altering their relationships with dominant structures, seek to create new history. Ideologically, too, this requires that such women and

men see themselves both as the products of past struggles and as the bearers of that radical tradition.[6]

If black workers are not in the vanguard of struggle, the black movement will slip sadly into accommodationism with a ferocious monopoly capitalist system that fails to provide self-determination or progress to people of color. Black capitalism, while it may alleviate temporarily the suffering of a few blacks, will taken to its extreme create blacks so wedded to America's "goodies" that we will gladly invade Grenada, bomb Libya, support South African fascists, and murder Nicaraguan children. (Some black republican lap dogs now avidly claim South Africa's growing economy is the only solution to oppression of the black majority there.) We may become so immersed in overseas investments, so captivated by U.S. economic dominance, and so afraid of Third World struggles that we lose the sense of justice that has distinguished Afro-Americans since slavery.

This tragic scenario of oppressed Afro-Americans supporting U.S. imperialism will never happen if workers lead the black liberation movement. Black song writer and Southern Tenant Farmers's Union leader John Hancock wrote the song "Mean Things Happenin' In This Land." For black workers, mean things are still happening in this land, and workers therefore do not vacilate, quiver, or flip-flop on the question of Afro-American survival.

A third lesson is the urgent need to build a radical black movement. From Camp Hill to the Transvaal, from Oakland to Cabo Delgado, capitalism's atrocities against outnumbered black Socialists is horrifyingly brutal. (See "In Memoriam" below.) Until the black left links with other workers and progressive international movements, our best leaders will be hunted and murdered like dogs. Amiri Baraka writes in the journal *The Black Nation*,

> The murders of Rodney, Mikey Smith, and Bishop speak directly to our lack of strong...organization among black revolutionaries....Unless we are willing to organize ourselves as revolutionary fighters, in command

of the historical legacy of working class political analysis and led by the masses of people themselves, carrying our various national liberation and independence struggles through to the end, that is, to socialism, we will always be tortured and weakened by the murders of our most brilliant brothers and sisters by our enemies.[7]

The history of black socialism teaches that revolutionary movements are built very simply. Black Socialists imbued with Marxist-Leninist theories of class struggle, the vanguard party, and national liberation, spread their message among oppressed Afro-American workers whose experience verifies the need for profound social change. Richard Wright, Angelo Herndon, Hosea Hudson, Rev. George Slater, Sala N'tonton (Guinea-Bissau), Joaquim Machival (Mozambique) and others became communists because they believed black suffering required radical solutions and because socialism alone equipped them to take charge of their destiny. Joaquim Machival wrote,

> In 1964 I joined FRELIMO because our people were exploited. I still did not know properly what to do about it. We had heard our neighbors in Malawi had been liberated and would come to liberate us, but we soon learnt that we would have to liberate ourselves. The party told us that we and no one else are responsible for ourselves.[8]

A fourth lesson is the need for more study. The struggles, victories, failures, and weaknesses of the black left are seriously neglected. Future black radical movements will be crippled by ignorance of past struggles. So many questions need to be answered. What is really happening with the MPLA in Angola? What are the real gains of socialism in Robert Mugabe's Zimbabwe? What are the lessons of Ujamaaa in Tanzania? Can FRELIMO survive South Africa and famine to build a productive Mozambique? What's happening in Ghana since Nkrumah? Guinea since Toure? Guinea-Bissau since Cabral?

And what about the Caribbean? How has life changed for the Grenadian people since the invasion of 1983? Is their any legacy of the struggle begun by Walter Rodney and the Working Peoples' Alliance? Is there a black left presence on Jamaica? Trinidad? Haiti?

In America where is the detailed history of the Black Panther Party, the African Blood Brotherhood, and the Congress of Afrikan Peoples? How could Afro-American writers, actors and prisoners survive in the 1980s and 1990s if they espoused the radicalism of Langston Hughes, Paul Robeson, and George Jackson? What were the concrete gains of the Communist Party's Sharecroppers' Unions and Unemployment Councils during the Depression? Will conditions ever produce another National Negro Labor Council, League of Revolutionary Black Workers, or National Negro Congress?

A fifth lesson from the history of Afro-American, Caribbean, and African radicals is that they were devoted to socialism only to the extent that socialism could result in black liberation. Blacks were loyal to socialism because it was a means by which their people could be freed from exploitation and poverty.

If socialism or communism strayed from black liberation, then the black radical abandoned the party to struggle through other means. When in 1929 the Socialist Party wavered on the question of justice for black workers, Dr. W.E.B. Du Bois thundered,

> The sooner the Socialist Party braves the artificially encouraged race prejudice of white laborers in the South and comes out in speech and platform for democracy despite color, for economic justice despite race prejudice, the sooner will the Socialist Party begin to grow on solid foundations... Everybody is in favor of justice so long as it costs them no effort. If American socialism cannot stand for the American Negro, the American Negro will not stand for socialism.[9]

Du Bois's sentiment was echoed by other militants when Socialist organizations betrayed black self-determination. When Moscow liquidated the International Trade Union Committee of Negro Workers in 1933, Communist Party leader George Padmore felt Stalin abandoned African and Afro-American workers at the time of their greatest need. Angered by this move, George Padmore left the Party to seek black liberation through Pan-Africanism.

When in 1957 the CPUSA abandoned the political objective of Self-determination for the Black Belt South, Harry Haywood left despite thirty years of leadership and struggle in the Party. When the French Communist Party supported their country's colonial war against the Algerian revolutionaries, Aime Cesaire of Martinique left the French CP in 1956. He warned, "What I demand of Marxism and Communism is that they serve the black peoples, not that the black peoples serve Marxism and Communism."[10]

Just as blacks left communism when it betrayed their hopes, they also remained in those organizations that placed black liberation at the top of their political program. When the Communist Party USA, the Sharecroppers' Unions, the Black Panther Party, the Front for the Liberation of Mozambique (FRELIMO), the African Blood Brotherhood, the Southern Tenant Farmers' Union, the New Jewel Movement, the African National Congress and other groups committed themselves wholly to black self-determination, black Socialists gave those organizations their undying devotion.

The sixth and greatest legacy of the black Socialist is the revolutionary optimism which holds that through organization, work, and sacrifice we can create a better world for all people. It is this legacy that will hopefully fuel future movements for radical change and transform America from rampant militarism, nuclear madness, and overseas adventurism to a nation truly dedicated to the welfare of its children, its elderly, its workers, its women, and its people of color. In a 1975 issue of *The Black Scholar* Baraka boldly affirms his task as a black Communist,

> What do we mean to liberate ourselves? We mean the right of self-determination, to use our lives in ways we can understand are most beneficial, to make full use of those lives and to make use of the world. By liberation we mean also, the other side of self-determination, free access to our democratic rights. To receive whatever is of value in the society we choose to live in, and to benefit completely in any way that any other citizen has benefited; to develop ourselves and our families as completely as any citizen of the society has developed. In other words, to live full open creative lives as respected resourceful human beings.[11]

The goal of the black Socialist, then, is to build a world where racism, war, and poverty, become the historical relics of a bygone era and humans, yes, even black humans can develop into all they are capable of becoming.

Society's move toward socialism must be brought about by individuals who themselves mirror the values of the new society. The lofty aims of economic justice, peoples' democracy, and cultural fulfillment must be matched by the dedication of those committed to making those goals a reality. New societies do not evolve or come into being by magic, they are built by hard work, sacrifice and struggle. The martyred Samora Machel of Mozambique left us this challenge:

> It so happens that we are all born into an exploitative society and have been imbued with its ideology and culture. This is why the internal fight against what we believe to constitute our moral framework is difficult and may sometimes seem impossible.
>
> Divesting ourselves of the exploitative ideology and adopting and living, in each detail of everyday life, the ideology required for the revolution is the essence of the fight to create the new man (and woman).
>
> It is not the personal fight of one man (or woman) wrapped up in himself (herself). It is a mass struggle in which we must accept criticism and do self-criticism, purifying ourselves in their fire, which makes us conscious of the path to be followed and fills us with hatred of the negative values of the old society.[12]

In Memoriam: Roll Call

Samora Machel, murdered in South Africa
Caleb Mayekiso, murdered in South Africa
Wilson Khayinga, murdered in South Africa
Zinakile Mkaba, murdered in South Africa
Looksmart Ngudle, murdered in South Africa
Elijah Loza, murdered in South Africa
Lawrence Ndzanga, murdered in South Africa
Vuysile Mini, murdered in South Africa
Pio Pinto, murdered in Kenya
Dedam Kimathi, murdered in Kenya
Patrice Lumumba, murdered in Zaire
Dr. Felix Moumie, murdered in the Cameroons
Abdulla Kassim Hanga, murdered in Tanzania
Amilcar Cabral, murdered in Guinea-Bissau
Eduardo Mondlane, murdered in Dar es Salaam
Hoji Ya Henda, murdered in Angola
Edward Dublin, murdered in Guyana
Ohene Koama, murdered in Guyana
Walter Rodney, murdered in Guyana
Michael Smith, murdered in Jamaica
Maurice Bishop, murdered in Grenada
Unison Whiteman, murdered in Grenada
Jacqueline Creft, murdered in Grenada
Fitzroy Bain, murdered in Grenada
Vincent Noel, murdered in Grenada
George Jackson, murdered in San Quentin
Jonathan Jackson, murdered in San Rafael
Fred Hampton, murdered in Chicago
Mark Clark, murdered in Chicago
Sam Napier, murdered in New York
Cleveland Edwards, murdered in Soledad
Jon Huggins, murdered in Los Angeles
Bunch Carter, murdered in Los Angeles
Walter Pope, murdered in Los Angeles
Bobby Hutton, murdered in Oakland
Sandy Smith, murdered in South Carolina
George Cox, murdered in Louisiana
Henry Cox, murdered in Louisiana
Ralph Gray, murdered in Alabama

An oppressed class that does not strive to use arms, to acquire arms, only deserves to be treated like slaves. We cannot forget, unless we become bourgeois pacifists or opportunists, that we are living in a class society, that there is no way out of this society, and there can be none, except by means of class struggle. In every class society, whether it is based on slavery, serfdom, or....wage labor, the oppressing class is armed.[13]

V.I. Lenin

The Funeral of Samora Machel

A LUTA CONTINUA!

NOTES

FOOTNOTES - UNDER THE HAMMER

1 Christopher Hill, <u>Lenin and the Russian Revolution</u>. New York: Penguin Books 1971, p. 157
2 Walter Rodney, <u>How Europe Underdeveloped Africa</u>. Washington, D.C.: Howard Univ. Press 1981, p. 77
3 Mary Frances Berry & John W. Blassingame, <u>Long Memory: The Black Experience in America</u>. New York: Oxford Univ. Press 1982, p. 196
4 Philip S. Foner, <u>Organized Labor & the Black Worker: 1619-1981</u>. New York: International Publishers 1981, p. 111
5 ibid., p. 115
6 ibid., p. 117
7 ibid., p. 232
8 ibid., p. 285
9 ibid., p. 297
10 Freedomways Editors, ed. <u>Paul Robeson: The Great Forerunner</u>. New York: International Publishers 1985, p. 223
11 Philip Foner, <u>Organized Labor & the Black Worker</u>, p. 311
12 ibid., p. 390
13 ibid., p. 287
14 Berry & Blassingame, <u>Long Memory: The Black Experience in America</u>, p. 222
15 Manning Marable, <u>From The Grassroots</u>. Boston: South End Press 1980, p. 69
16 Manning Marable, <u>From The Grassroots</u>, p. 60
17 Harry Haywood, <u>Black Bolshevik: Autobiography of an Afro-American Communist</u> Chicago: Liberator Press 1978, p. 459
18 Philip Foner, <u>Organized Labor & The Black Worker</u>. p. 241
19 Nell Irvin Painter, <u>The Narrative of Hosea Hudson: His Life as a Negro Communist in the South</u>. Cambridge: Harvard 1979, p. 87

20 ibid., pp. 87
21 ibid., p. 101
22 ibid., p. 352
23 ibid., p. 253
24 ibid., p. 21
25 ibid., p. 22
26 ibid., p. 38
27 ibid., p. 18
28 ibid., p. 385
29 Hosea Hudson, Black Worker in the Deep South. New York: International Publishers 1972, p. 130
30 Philip Foner, Organized Labor & The Black Worker, p. 410
31 James Geschwender, Class, Race & Worker Insurgency. Cambridge: Cambridge University Press 1977, p. 127
32 Philip Foner, Organized Labor & The Black Worker, p. 422
33 James Geschwender, Class, Race & Worker Insurgency, p. 144, 145
34 Charles Denby, Indignant Heart: A Black Workers Journal Boston: South End Press 1978, p. 291
35 ibid., p. 294
36 James Boggs, "Black Revolutionary Power" Ebony. August 1970, pp 152-153
37 ibid., p. 153
38 ibid., p. 154
39 Ken Luckhardt & Brenda Wall, Organize...or Starve! The History of the South African Congress of Trade Unions. New York: International 1980, p. 94
40 ibid., p. 137
41 ibid., p. 323
42 Mae Ngai, "South Africa Labor Calls For Divestment" Unity. January 17, 1986, p. 9

OTHER SOURCES - UNDER THE HAMMER

Anderson, Jervis A. Philip Randolph: A

Biographical Portrait. New York, 1972
Foster, William Z. The Negro People in American History. New York: International 1954
Franklin, John Hope From Slavery To Freedom. New York: Alfred A. Knopf 1947
Green, James ed. Workers' Struggles, Past & Present. Philadelphia: Temple Univ. 1983
Green, Pippa "The Battle Against Influx Control is Far From Over" In These Times. May 6 - 12, 1987
Harris, William Keeping the Faith: A. Philip Randolph, Milton Webster, & The Brotherhood of Sleeping Car Porters. Urbana: University of Illinois 1977
Harris, William H. The Harder We Run: Black Workers Since the Civil War. New York: Oxford Univ. Press 1982
Harsch, Ernest South Africa: White Rule Black Revolt. New York: Monad 1980
Mannix, Daniel & Cowley, Malcolm Black Cargoes: A History of the Atlantic Slave Trade 1518-1865. New York: The Viking Press 1962
Marable, Manning How Capitalism Underdeveloped Black America. Boston: South End 1983
Ngai, Mae "Unity interviews Amon Masane, South African Trade Union leader" Unity. July 25, 1986
Wilhelm, Sidney Who Needs the Negro. New York: Doubleday & Co 1971
Yette, Samuel F. The Choice: The Issue of Black Survival in America. NY: Berkley Pub 1971

FOOTNOTES - SISTERS IN STRUGGLE

1 V.I. Lenin, The Emancipation of Women. New York: International 1934, pp. 74,75
2 Angela Davis, With My Mind On Freedom. New York: Random House 1974, p. 109
3 ibid., p. 110
4 ibid., pp. 110-111
5 ibid., pp. 186,188
6 Angela Davis, et al., If They Come In The

Morning. New York: Signet 1971, p. 185
7 Angela Davis, With My Mind On Freedom p. 250
8 ibid., p. 255
9 ibid., p. 266
10 ibid., p. 160
11 Angela Davis, Women Race & Class. New York: Vintage Books 1983, p. 154
12 ibid., 157
13 ibid., 158
14 Harry Haywood, Black Bolshevik: Autobiography of an Afro-American Communist. Chicago: Liberator Press 1978, p. 551
15 Mark Naison, Communists In Harlem During the Depression. New York: Grove 1983 p. 169
16 Angela Davis, If They Come In The Morning p. 125
17 ibid., p. 111
18 ibid., p. 115,116
19 ibid., p. 119,120
20 Donald Freed, Agony In New Haven: The Trial of Bobby Seale, Ericka Huggins and The Black Panther Party. New York: Simon & Schuster 1973, p. 63
21 Mary Frances Berry & John W. Blassingame, Long Memory: The Black Experience in America. New York: Oxford University Press 1982, pp. 252, 253
22 Slyvia Hill, "Facing Social Reconstruction In Zimbabwe" Black Scholar. May/June 1980, p. 42
23 Alexandra Johnson, "Zimbabwe: Change is Slow, But Coming" AfricAsia. November 1986, p. 30

OTHER SOURCES - SISTERS IN STRUGGLE

Aptheker, Bettina The Morning Breaks: The Trial of Angela Davis. New York: Intern'tl 1975
Batezat, Eleanor "Towards Equality for Zimbabwe's Women" AfricAsia. August 1986
Berry, Faith Langston Hughes: Before and Beyond Harlem. Westport: Lawrence Hill, 1983
Johnson, Nelson & Thompson, Phil "Which Way

Forward For The Black Liberation Movement" The Black Scholar. March/April 1980

Lewis, David When Harlem Was In Vogue. New York: Random House, 1982

Sundiata, Sekou "On The Whereabouts of Assata Shakur" The Black Nation. Summer/Fall 1983

FOOTNOTES - IN THE VANGUARD

1 James Forman,Self-Determination and the Afro-American People. Seattle: Open Hand Publishing 1984, p. 39
2 Mark Naison,Communists in Harlem During the Depression. New York: Grove 1983, p. 36
3 Amiri Baraka, "The Congress of Afrikan People: A Position Paper" The Black Scholar. Jan-Feb 1975, p. 8
4 ibid., p. 11
5 Second Congress of the U.S. League of Revolutionary Struggle, Peace, Justice, Equality and Socialism. Oakland: GT Publications 1984, p. 62
6 Bruce Marcus & Michael Taber ed. Maurice Bishop Speaks: The Grenada Revolution 1979-83. New York: Pathfinder Press 1983, p. 25
7 Hugh O´Shaughnessy, Grenada. New York: Dodd, Mead & Co. 1984, p. 81
8 Marcus & Taber, Maurice Bishop Speaks, pp. 29-30
9 ibid., p. 42
10 ibid., p. 272
11 ibid., p. 83, 84
12 Steve Wattenmaker, "Grenada: What Went Wrong? An Interview with New Jewel Movement Leader Don Rojas" The Black Nation. Summer/Fall 1984, p. 24
13 Huey Newton,Revolutionary Suicide. New York: Harcourt Brace Jovanovich 1973, p. 41
14 ibid., p. 69
15 Reginald Major,A Panther Is A Black Cat. New York: William Morrow & Co. 1971, p. 285
16 Huey Newton,To Die For The People. New York:

Random House 1972, p. 67
17 Huey Newton, "The Black Panthers" _Ebony_. August 1969, p. 109
18 ibid., p. 110
19 ibid., p. 110
20 Huey Newton, _To Die For The People_, p. 189
21 Manning Marable, _Black American Politics: From The Washington Marches To Jesse Jackson_. London: Verso 1985, p. 185
22 ibid., p. 185
23 Angela Davis, et al, _If They Come In the Morning_. New York: Signet 1971, p. 124
24 Manning Marable, _Black American Politics_, p. 185
25 Julian Bond et al, _The "Trial" of Bobby Seale_. New York: Grove Press 1970, p. 29
26 Reginald Major, _A Panther Is A Black Cat_ p. 193
27 ibid., p. 123
28 ibid., p. 146
29 Donald Freed, _Agony In New Haven: The Trial of Bobby Seale, Ericka Huggins and the Black Panther Party_. New York: Simon & Schuster 1973, pp. 193-196
30 Sue Gegner, "Former Black Panther Leader Seeks Freedom" _Unity_. March 16, 1987, p. 6

OTHER SOURCES - IN THE VANGUARD

Barry, Tom et al _The Other Side of Paradise: Foreign Control in the Caribbean_. New York: Grove Press, 1984.
Blair, Tom _Retreat to the Ghetto_. New York: Hill & Wang, 1977.
Haywood, Harry _Black Bolshevik: Autobiography of Afro-American Communist_. Chicago: Liberator Press, 1978
Lynch, Charles "Education and the New Grenada" _The Black Scholar_. July/August 1981
Moore, Dhoruba "Strategies of Repression Against the Black Movement" _The Black Scholar_. May/June 1981

Seale, Bobby *Seize the Time*. New York: Random House, 1968.
Seale, Bobby *A Lonely Rage:The Autobiography of Bobby Seale*. New York: Times Books, 1978.
"The Revolutionary Communist League (M-L-M) and the League of Revolutionary Struggle (M-L) Unite!" *Forward*. January 1980

FOOTNOTES - PARTY OF THE NEGRO PEOPLE

1 William Foster,*The Negro People in American History* New York: International 1954, p. 456
2 Mark Naison, *Communists In Harlem During The Depression*. New York: Grove Press 1983, p. 258
3 ibid., p. 78
4 Harry Haywood, *Black Bolshevik: Autobiography of an Afro-American Communist*. Chicago: Liberator Press 1978, p. 347
5 William Harris, *The Harder We Run: Black Workers Since The Civil War*. New York: Oxford Univ. 1982, p. 112
6 Mark Naison, *Communists In Harlem*, p. 259
7 ibid., p. 259
8 Jessica Mitford, *A Fine Old Conflict*. New York: Knopf Publishers 1977, p. 186
9 Mark Naison, *Communists In Harlem*, p. 277
10 James Jackson, *Revolutionary Tracings in World Politics and Black Liberation*. New York: International 1974, p. 149
11 Harry Haywood, *Black Bolshevik*, p. 32, 33
12 ibid., p. 33
13 ibid., p. 55
14 ibid., p. 4
15 ibid., p. 114
16 ibid., p. 117
17 ibid., p. 131
18 ibid., p. 234
19 Harry Haywood, *Negro Liberation*. New York: International 1948, p. 22
20 ibid., p. 162

21 Harry Haywood, Black Bolshevik, p. 640
22 Angelo Herndon, Let Me Live. New York: Arno Press 1969, p. 35
23 ibid., p. 41
24 ibid., p. 42
25 ibid., p. 55
26 ibid., p. 55
27 ibid., p. 73
28 ibid., p. 77, 78
29 ibid., p. 78
30 ibid., p. 89
31 ibid., p. 103
32 Harry Haywood, Black Bolshevik, p. 381
33 Angelo Herndon Let Me Live, p. 202
34 ibid., p. 228
35 ibid., p. 238
36 Howard Zinn, A Peoples´ History of the United States. New York: Harper & Row 1980 p. 439
37 Herbert Aptheker, ed. A Documentary History of the Negro People in the United States, Vol Three. Secaucus: Citadel 1974, pp. 7, 8
38 Mary Frances Berry and John Blassingame, Long Memory: The Black Experience in America. New York: Oxford Univ. Press 1982, p. 225
39 Nikolai Mostovets, Henry Winston: Profile of a U.S. Communist. Moscow: Progress Publishers 1983, p. 41
40 ibid., p. 67

OTHER SOURCES - PARTY OF THE NEGRO PEOPLE

Foner, Philip Organized Labor and the Black Worker, 1619-1981. New York: International, 1981.
Forman, James, Self-Determination and the African-American People. Seattle: Open Hand Publishing, 1981.
Lightfoot, Claude Human Rights U.S. Style. New York: International Publishers, 1977.
Winston, Henry Class, Race and Black Liberation. New York: International, 1977.

FOOTNOTES - INCARCERATED REVOLUTIONARIES

1 George Jackson, Soledad Brother: The Prison Letters of George Jackson. New York: Bantam 1970, p. 21
2 ibid., p. 96
3 George Jackson, Blood In My Eye. New York: Bantam 1972, p. 90
4 Angela Davis et al, If They Come In The Morning. New York: Signet 1971, p. 131
5 ibid., p. 153
6 George Jackson, Soledad Brother, p. 75
7 Angela Davis, If They Come In The Morning, p. 131
8 ibid., p. 153
9 George Jackson, Blood In My Eye, p. 6
10 George Jackson, Soledad Brother, p. 252
11 George Jackson, Blood In My Eye, p. 150
12 George Jackson, Soledad Brother pp. 96, 132, 176
13 George Jackson, Blood In My Eye, p. 61
14 ibid., p. 25
15 ibid., p. 65
16 ibid., p. 62
17 ibid., p. 94
18 George Jackson Soledad Brother, p. 31
19 ibid., p. 238
20 George Jackson Blood In My Eye, p. xviii
21 ibid., p. 106
22 George Jackson, Soledad Brother, p. 101
23 ibid., p. 204
24 George Jackson, Blood In My Eye, p. 21
25 ibid., p. 22
26 ibid., p. 62
27 George Jackson, Soledad Brother, p. 250
28 Angela Davis, With My Mind On Freedom. New York: Bantam 1974, p. 279
29 Angela Davis et al, If They Come In the Morning, p. 176

OTHER SOURCES - INCARCERATED REVOLUTIONARIES

Aptheker, Bettina *The Morning Breaks: The Trial of Angela Davis*, New York: International 1975.

FOOTNOTES - REVOLUTIONARY GIANTS

1 Philip Foner, ed., *Paul Robeson Speaks*. Secaucus: Citadel Press 1978, p. 91
2 Freedomways Editors, *Paul Robeson: The Great Forerunner*. New York, International 1985, p. 200
3 Philip Foner, ed., *Paul Robeson Speaks*, p. 15
4 ibid., p. 19
5 ibid., pp. 124, 125
6 ibid., pp. 118, 119
7 ibid., p. 14
8 ibid., p. 10
9 Freedomways, *Paul Robeson: The Great Forerunner*, p. 133
10 Philip Foner, ed., *Paul Robeson Speaks*, pp. 202, 203
11 ibid., pp. 202, 203
12 ibid., p. 12, 13
13 Freedomways, *Paul Robeson: The Great Forerunner*, p. 65, 66
14 ibid., pp. 399, 400
15 ibid., pp. 223, 224
16 Philip Foner ed., *Paul Robeson Speaks*, p. 18
17 ibid., p. 18
18 ibid., p. 427
19 ibid., p. 440
20 Paul Robeson, *Here I Stand*. Boston: Beacon Press 1958, p. 39
21 Philip Foner, *W.E.B. Du Bois Speaks: 1920-1963*. New York: Pathfinder 1970, p. 190
22 ibid., pp. 44, 45
23 Paul Robeson *Here I Stand*, p. 3

24 W.E.B. Du Bois, Black Reconstruction In America: 1860-1880. New York: Antheneum 1985, pp. 15, 16
25 ibid., p. 638
26 ibid., p. 586
27 ibid., p. 727
28 Philip Foner, W.E.B. Du Bois Speaks, pp. 224 - 225
29 W.E.B. Du Bois The Autobiography of W.E.B. Du Bois. New York: Internat'l 1968, p. 376
30 ibid., pp. 393, 370
31 ibid., p. 390
32 Philip Foner, W.E.B. Du Bois Speaks, pp. 316, 317
33 W.E.B. Du Bois The Autobiography of W.E.B. Du Bois, p. 57
34 Philip Foner, W.E.B. Du Bois Speaks, p. 18

OTHER SOURCES - REVOLUTIONARY GIANTS

Du Bois, W.E.B. The World And Africa. New York: International, 1980.
Du Bois, W.E.B. Writings: The Suppression of the African Slave Trade, The Souls of Black Folk, Dusk of Dawn, Essays. New York: The Library of America, 1986.
Du Bois, W.E.B. The Souls of Black Folk. Greenwich: Fawcett, 1961.
Du Bois, W.E.B. John Brown. New York: International, 1974.
Foner, Philip W.E.B. DuBois Speaks: 1890 - 1919 New York: Pathfinder, 1970.
Horne, Gerald Black & Red: W.E.B. Du Bois and the Afro-American Response to the Cold War, 1944 - 1963. Albany: SUNY Press, 1986.

FOOTNOTES – ARMED REVOLUTIONS IN AFRICA

1 Amilcar Cabral, *Unity And Struggle: The Speeches And Writings of Amilcar Cabral*. New York: Monthly Review 1979, p. xxv
2 ibid., p. xxvii
3 Basil Davidson, *No Fist Is Big Enough To Hide The Sky: The Liberation of Guinea-Bissau and Cape Verde*. London: Zed Books 1984, p. 96
4 ibid., pp. 18, 19
5 ibid., p. 30
6 Amilcar Cabral, *Unity And Struggle*, p. 174
7 ibid., p. 173
8 Barry Munslow, ed. *Samora Machel: An African Revolutionary*. Totowa: Zed 1985, p. 169
9 Africa Information Service, ed. *Return To The Source: Selected Speeches of Amilcar Cabral*. New York: Monthly Review 1973, pp. 88, 89
10 Cabral *Unity And Struggle*, p. 46
11 Davidson *No Fist Is Big Enough To Hide The Sky*, p. 27, 28
12 Cabral *Unity And Struggle*, p. 141
13 ibid., p. 290, 297
14 Cabral *Return To The Source*, p. 25
15 Eduardo Mondlane, *The Struggle For Mozambique* London: Zed 1969, p. 33
16 ibid., pp. 44, 45
17 ibid., p. 85
18 Barry Munslow, *Samora Machel: An African Revolutionary*, p. xii
19 Mondlane *The Struggle For Mozambique*, p. 117
20 ibid., p. 127
21 ibid., p. 126
22 ibid., p. 13
23 ibid., p. 138
24 Munslow *Samora Machel: An African Revolutionary*, p. 196
25 Mondlane *The Struggle For Mozambique*, p. 147
26 ibid., p. 149
27 ibid., p. x

28 ibid., p. xxviii
29 ibid., p. 225
30 Munslow *Samora Machel: An African Revolutionary*, p. xix
31 ibid., p. xxi
32 Mohamed El-Khawas, "Problems of Nation-Building in Mozambique" *Black Scholar*. May/June 1980, p. 25
33 Munslow *Samora Machel: An African Revolutionary*, p. 43
34 Augusta Conchiglia "Africa's Tragic Loss" *AfricAsia*. Nov. 1986, p. 11
35 Munslow *Samora Machel*, p. 94
36 ibid., p. 130
37 John Saul, *A Difficult Road: The Transition to Socialism in Mozambique*. New York: Monthly Review Press 1985, p. 414
38 "In Memoriam: Agostinho Neto" *The Black Scholar*. May/June 1980, p. 69
39 Michael Wolfers and Jane Bergerol *Angola: In The Front Line*. London: Zed Books 1985, p. 110
40 Margaret Novicki, "Maria Eugenia Neto" *Africa Report*. Jan - Feb 1987, pp. 32, 33
41 Aquino de Braganca and Immanuel Wallerstein ed. *The African Liberation Reader: Volume 3, The Strategy of Liberation*. London: Zed Books 1982, p. 210 - 219
42 R.A. Ulyanovsky, *Fighters For National Liberation*. Moscow: Progress Publishers 1983, p. 118
43 Andrew Meldrum, "The Struggle For Independence: A People's War" *AfricAsia*. August 1986, p. 34

OTHER SOURCES - ARMED REVOLUTIONS IN AFRICA

Braganca and Wallerstein, ed. *The African Liberation Reader: Vol 1, The Anatomy of Colonialism*. London: Zed Books, 1982.

Braganca and Wallerstein, ed. The African Liberation Reader: Vol 2, The National Liberation Movements. London: Zed 1982.

Fogel, D. Africa In Struggle. Seattle: Ism Press, 1982.

Munslow, Barry ed., Africa: Problems in the Transition to Socialism. London: Zed, 1986

Stravrianos, L.S. Global Rift: The Third World Comes of Age. New York: William Morrow & Co., 1981.

FOOTNOTES – WRITERS AND REVOLUTION

1 Faith Berry, Langston Hughes: Before and Beyond Harlem. Westport: Lawrence Hill 1983, pp. 29 - 30
2 Faith Berry, ed., Good Morning Revolution: Uncollected Social Protest Writings by Langston Hughes. Westport: Lawrence Hill 1973, p. 26
3 "A Play By Langston Hughes: Scottsboro Limited" The Black Nation. Fall/Winter, pp. 23 - 27
4 ibid., p. 28
5 Berry Langston Hughes: Before and Beyond Harlem, p. 161
6 Berry Good Morning Revolution, pp. 77, 78
7 ibid., pp. 89, 90
8 ibid., pp. 3, 4
9 ibid., p. 9
10 ibid., pp. 36, 37
11 Berry Langston Hughes, p. 207
12 ibid., p. 193
13 Berry, Good Morning, Revolution pp. 118 - 119
14 ibid., p. 120
15 ibid., p. 117
16 ibid., p. 143
17 Michael Fabre, The Unfinished Quest of Richard Wright. New York: William Morrow & Co., 1973, p. 89
18 Richard Wright, American Hunger. New York: Harper & Row 1944, pp. 62, 63

19 Herbert Aptheker, ed. Documentary History of the Negro People in the United States: 1933 - 1945. Secaucus: Citadel 1974, pp. 60, 61
20 Michael Fabre, The Unfinished Quest of Richard Wright, p. 98
21 Richard Wright, Black Boy. New York: Harper & Row 1966, pp. 42, 43
22 Michael Fabre, The Unfinished Quest of Richard Wright, p. 186
23 Cedric Robinson, Black Marxism: The Making of The Black Radical Tradition London: Zed Press 1983, p. 422
24 Mark Naison, Communist In Harlem During The Depression. New York: Grove Press 1983, pp. 210, 211
25 Fabre, The Unfinished Quest of Richard Wright p. 434
26 Addison Gayle, Richard Wright: Ordeal of a Native Son. Garden City: Doubleday 1980 p. 1
27 Fabre, The Unfinished Quest of Richard Wright p. 209
28 Gayle, Richard Wright, p. 28
29 Amiri Baraka, "The Congress of Afrikan People: A Position Paper" The Black Scholar. Jan/Feb 1975, pp. 8, 9
30 Amiri Baraka, "Countries Want Independence, Nations Want Liberation, and the People, the People Want Revolution" Forward. Jan. 1980, p. 9
31 Amiri Baraka, Daggers and Javelins. New York: Quill 1984, pp. 49, 50
32 ibid., p. 47
33 ibid., p. 197
34 Robinson, Black Marxism, p. 260
35 Aime Cesaire, Discourse on Colonialism. New York: Monthly Review Press 1972, p. 21
36 Faith Berry Langston Hughes, pp. 209, 210
37 ibid., p. 210
38 Ngugi wa Thiong'o Detained: A Writer's Prison Diary. London: Heinemann 1981, p. 69

39 Ngugi wa Thiong'o <u>Writers In Politics</u>. London: Heinemann 1981, p. 47
40 Ngugi <u>Detained</u>, pp. 12, 13
41 ibid., p. 79
42 Ngugi wa Thiong'o <u>Homecoming: Essays on African and Caribbean Literature Culture and Politics</u>. Westport: Lawrence Hill 1983, p. 49, 50
43 Ngugi <u>Writers In Politics</u>, pp. 78 - 80
44 Ngugi wa Thiong'o <u>Barrel Of A Pen: Resistance to Repression in Neo-colonial Kenya</u>. Trenton: Africa World Press 1983, pp. 37, 38
45 ibid., p. 6
46 Mao Tse-Tung, <u>Talks at the Yenan Forum on Literature and Art</u>. Peking: Foreign Languages Press 1967, p. 11.

OTHER SOURCES - WRITERS AND REVOLUTION

Hughes, Langston <u>The Panther and The Lash</u>. New York: Alfred Knopf, 1980.
Hughes, Langston <u>Selected Poems</u>. New York: Vintage, 1974.
Jones, Leroi <u>Blues People: Negro Music in White America</u>. New York: Quill, 1963.
Jones, Leroi <u>Black Music</u>. New York: Quill, 1967
Lewis, David Levering <u>When Harlem Was In Vogue</u>. New York: Vintage, 1982.
Lomax, Alan and Adbul, Raoul ed., <u>3000 Years of Black Poetry</u>. New York: Dodd, Meade, 1970.
Ngugi wa Thiong'o <u>Decolonising The Mind: The Politics of Language in African Literature</u> Portsmouth: Heinemann, 1986.
Wright, Richard <u>Uncle Tom's Children</u>. New York: Harper & Row, 1965.
Wright, Richard <u>Black Boy</u>. New York: Harper & Row, 1966.
Wright, Richard <u>Native Son</u>. New York: Harper & Row, 1966.

FOOTNOTES - SCHOLARS IN SERVICE TO THE MASSES

1 Edward Alpers and Pierre-Michel Fontaine, ed. Walter Rodney, Revolutionary And Scholar: A Tribute, Los Angeles: UCLA Center for Afro-American Studies 1982, p. 61
2 ibid., 69
3 ibid., 68
4 Walter Rodney, How Europe Underdeveloped Africa. Washington D.C.: Howard University Press 1981, pp. 27, 28
5 ibid., pp. 131, 132
6 ibid., p. 199
7 ibid., p. 255
8 ibid., p. xviii
9 Alpers and Fontaine Walter Rodney, p. 124
10 Rodney, How Europe Underdeveloped Africa, p. xix
11 Alpers and Fontaine Walter Rodney, p. 152, 60
12 ibid., p. 162
13 ibid., p. 161
14 ibid., p. 3
15 ibid., p. 84
16 ibid., p. 151
17 ibid., p. 161
18 Alpers and Fontaine, Walter Rodney, p. 30
19 Cedric Robinson, Black Marxism: The Making of The Black Radical Tradition. London: Zed Press 1983, pp. 374, 375
20 ibid., p. 382
21 ibid., pp. 384, 385
22 ibid., p. 388
23 C.L.R. James, The Future In The Present. Westport: Lawrence Hill 1980, p. 117
24 ibid., pp. 120, 121
25 ibid., p. 124
26 ibid., p. 127
27 C.L.R. James, Modern Politics. Detroit: Bewick 1973, p. 115
28 ibid., p. 115
29 ibid., p. 154, 155

OTHER SOURCES - SCHOLARS

Baraka, Amiri "Bloody Colonialism or the murders of Mikey Smith, Walter Rodney and Maurice Bishop" The Black Nation. Summer/Fall 1984

James, C.L.R. Spheres of Existence. Westport: Lawrence Hill, 1980.

James, C.L.R. The Black Jacobins: Toussaint L'Overture and the San Domingo Revolution. New York: Vintage, 1963.

James, C.L.R. A History of Pan-African Revolt. Washington DC: Drum and Spear Press, 1969

Rodney, Walter A History of the Guyanese Working People: 1881-1905 Baltimore: Johns Hopkins University Press, 1981.

FOOTNOTES - BLACK SOCIALIST PREACHERS

1 Philip Foner, Black Socialist Preacher. San Fransisco: Synthesis 1983, p. 9
2 ibid., p. 29
3 ibid., p. 35
4 ibid., p. 243
5 ibid., p. 10
6 ibid., p. 46
7 ibid., p. 58
8 ibid., p. 86
9 ibid., p. 161
10 ibid., p. 165
11 ibid., p. 25
12 ibid., p. 25
13 ibid., p. 252
14 ibid., pp. 297, 298
15 ibid., p. 316
16 ibid., p. 306
17 ibid., pp. 332, 333
18 ibid., p. 279
19 ibid., p. 284
20 ibid., p. 289
21 ibid., p. 285

FOOTNOTES - AFRICAN SOCIALISM

1 Kwame Nkrumah, Revolutionary Path. New York: International 1973, p. 13
2 Kwame Nkurmah, Ghana: The Autobiography of Kwame Nkrumah. New York: International 1971 pp. 46, 47
3 ibid., p. 53
4 ibid., p. 303
5 ibid., p. 104
6 Juluis Nyerere, "Unity For A New Order" The Black Scholar. May/June 1980, p. 63
7 R.A. Ulyanovsky, Fighters for National Liberation. Moscow: Progress 1983, p. 140
8 Robin McKown, Patrice Lumumba. Garden City: Doubleday 1969, pp. 101 - 103
9 An Interim Report of the Select Committee to Study Governmental Operations with Respect to Intelligence Activities. Washington: Government Printing Office 1975, p. 15
10 Robin McKown, Patrice Lumumba, pp. 176 - 177
11 Chinweizu, The West And The Rest Of Us. London: NOK 1978, p. 148
12 Ronald Segal, ed. African Profiles. Baltimore: Penquin Books 1962, p. 264
13 Ladipo Adamolekun, Sekou Toure's Guinea. London: Methuen 1976, p. 1
14 ibid., p. v
15 ibid., p. 119
16 ibid., p. 129
17 Sekou Toure, Strategies and Tactics of The African Revolution. Conakry: National Printing Press 1977, pp. 280 - 281
18 Julius Nyerere, Ujammaa: Essays On Socialism London: Oxford Univ. 1968, p. 14
19 Chinweizu, The West And The Rest Of Us, p. 246
20 Ngugi wa Thiong'o Homecoming: Essays on African and Caribbean Literature Culture and Politics. Westport: Lawrence Hill 1983 p. 19

21 William Edgett Smith, We Must Run While They Walk. New York: Random House 1971, p. 83
22 Nyerere Essays On Socialism, p. 18
23 Mary Frances Berry and John Blassingame, Long Memory: The Black Experience In America. New York: Oxford 1982, p. 418
24 George Padmore, Pan-Africanism or Communism. Garden City: Doubleday 1972, pp. xxiii - xxiv
25 Stokely Carmichael, "Marxism-Leninism and Nkrumahism" The Black Scholar. Feb. 1973 p. 43
26 A. M. Babu African Socialism or Socialist Africa. London: Zed Press 1982, pp. 48, 49
27 ibid., p. 53
28 ibid., pp. 70, 71
29 ibid., 112
30 ibid., pp. 137, 138
31 "Interview with Moses Kotane, Treasurer of the ANC" Sechaba ANC. August 1968, p. 8
32 Mandela, Nelson The Struggle Is My Life. London: Internt´l Fund 1978, p. 50
33 ibid., pp. 153, 154
34 ibid., p. 115

OTHER SOURCES - AFRICAN SOCIALISM

Benson, Mary Nelson Mandela: The Man and The Movement. New York: W.W. Norton, 1986.

Esedebe, P. Olisanwuche Pan-Africanism: The Idea and Movement, 1776-1963. Washington D.C.: Howard University Press, 1982

Harsch, Ernest South Africa: White Rule, Black Revolt. New York: Monad Press, 1980.

Irvine, Keith The Rise of The Colored Races. New York: W.W. Norton, 1970.

Mandela, Nelson No Easy Walk To Freedom. London: Heinemann, 1965.

Murphy, E. Jefferson History of African Civilization. New York: Delta, 1972.

Nkrumah, Kwame Africa Must Unite. New York: International, 1963.

Nkrumah, Kwame *Neo-Colonialism: The Last Stage of Imperialism*. New York: Internat'l 1965.
Nyerere, Juluis *Man and Development*. London, Oxford Univ. Press, 1974
Thomas, Tim "Hold High The Lessons of SNCC" *Unity*. April 20, 1987.

Order Form

To order, tear carefully from the book and send to:

Asante Publications
Post Office Box 1085
San Diego, Ca. 92112

Please send me _ copies of **For The People** by Daryl Grigsby at $9.00 each.

Name: _____

Address: _____
_____ ZIP _____

Californians: Please add 6% Sales Tax (.54) per book

For Shipping, please add $1.00 for the first book and .25 for each additional book.

Thank You